Unsettled Account

THE PRINCETON ECONOMIC HISTORY OF
THE WESTERN WORLD

Joel Mokyr, Series Editor

Unsettled Account

THE EVOLUTION OF BANKING
IN THE INDUSTRIALIZED WORLD
SINCE 1800

Richard S. Grossman

PRINCETON UNIVERSITY PRESS

PRINCETON AND OXFORD

Copyright © 2010 by Princeton University Press

Published by Princeton University Press, 41 William Street, Princeton, New Jersey 08540
In the United Kingdom: Princeton University Press, 6 Oxford Street, Woodstock,
Oxfordshire OX20 1TW
press.princeton.edu

Library of Congress Cataloging-in-Publication Data
Grossman, Richard S.
Unsettled account : the evolution of banking in the industrialized world since 1800 /
Richard S. Grossman.
    p.   cm. — (The Princeton economic history of the western world)
Includes bibliographical references and index.
ISBN 978-0-691-13905-0 (cloth : alk. paper)
1. Banks and banking—History. 2. Banks and banking—Government policy.
3. Bank failures. 4. Financial crises.   I. Title.
HG1551.G76 2010
332.109—dc22   2010004675

British Library Cataloging-in-Publication Data is available

This book has been composed in Sabon

Printed on acid-free paper. ∞

Printed in the United States of America

10   9   8   7   6   5   4   3   2   1

For my parents, Bette and Bernard Grossman, ז״ל
because they were always so proud.

It suddenly struck me that every move in chess
was old and had already been played by someone.
Perhaps our history has already been played too,
and we shift our figures with the same moves to the
same checks as in time long past.

　—Karel Čapek, *War with the Newts*

Contents

Illustrations

Tables

Preface

I have perhaps gone a little more into details than is customary
on these occasions, but the times have been unusually
interesting . . .

> —Governor H. L. Holland,
> Speech to Proprietors of the Bank of England
> (shortly after the Overend, Gurney crisis),
> September 13, 1866

THE WORLDWIDE FINANCIAL CRISIS that erupted during the second half
of 2008 is among the worst the industrialized world has ever known. Previously solid financial institutions collapsed, securities markets crashed,
and even countries went to the brink of bankruptcy—and beyond. At the
time of this writing, commentators continue to speculate on how long
the crisis will last, when the accompanying recession—or is it something
worse?—will end, and what the financial system will look like when the
dust has settled. At the same time, politicians struggle to devise rescue
plans and to reformulate regulations with the three-fold goal of mitigating the current crisis, preventing a recurrence, and satisfying their con-
stituents.

According to Mark Twain, "History doesn't repeat itself, but it does
rhyme." This certainly holds true with respect to recent financial events.
The causes of the current crisis bear more than a passing resemblance
to those responsible for innumerable crises during the past two centuries. The fallout from the crisis is, in many ways, similar to that of its
predecessors. And the dilemmas facing today's policy makers are very
much like those encountered by earlier generations of policy makers in
the aftermath of financial crises. Differences abound, of course, but the
parallels make seeking out the rhymes especially tempting.

This book focuses on the history of one part of the financial system,
banks, with a particular emphasis on incorporated commercial banks,
institutions that make loans financed by the issue of demand deposits or
currency. The commercial bank, in its earliest form, was one of the first
types of financial institutions to develop and is, in its present form, the
one with which consumers are the most familiar. Commercial banks have
taken a leading role in financing commerce and industry from the beginnings of industrialization until the present day.

The novelty of this book lies in the fact that it considers the development of this one type of financial institution over a long time period and across a large number of countries. The approach is thematic, rather than geographic or chronological, focusing on four major elements that have contributed to banking evolution: crises, bailouts, merger movements, and regulation. Alternative approaches have their advantages. Focusing on the history of just one country allows more in-depth coverage of a national experience, encompassing securities markets and a wider variety of financial institutions, but loses the comparative angle. A number of excellent volumes on comparative banking history (Journal of Commerce and Commercial Bulletin 1896; Willis and Beckhart 1929; Beckhart 1954; Cameron 1967, 1972) consist of chapters by different authors, each focusing on one particular country, sometimes even with a common framework in mind; however, the comparative element in these studies, if it exists at all, is typically relegated to a concluding essay.

Although the approach adopted here has many advantages, it is not costless. I cannot claim to be an expert on the history—banking or otherwise—of all the countries covered, nor to have a reading knowledge of all the languages of all the countries involved. I freely admit to reading neither Finnish nor Japanese (and maybe one or two others), but have the *chutzpah* to write about the intricacies of the banking systems of countries in which the laws and history are written in these languages anyway. In short, the comparative nature of the book comes at a cost, but I am convinced that the price is worth paying.

Bankers and those who write about them are well acquainted with debts, and I have incurred many in the writing of this book. I owe profound thanks to my friend and teacher Barry Eichengreen for his wise counsel and support. If not for him, I would surely be in a different line of work. Jeff Williamson has been a source of boundless enthusiasm: when he writes "Go get 'em, Tiger!" on a draft, it's hard not to, well, go get 'em. I am also grateful to Jeff for an invitation to spend a sabbatical in the Economics Department at Harvard a number of years ago, where I began work on this book. I thank Michael Bordo for his enthusiastic and consistent support of this project . . . even before it was a project.

I am grateful to a number of people who read and commented on the manuscript, in whole or in part, including Asher Blass, Howard Bodenhorn, Michael Bordo, Forrest Capie, Jerry Caprio, Michael Collins, Barry Eichengreen, Jeff Frieden, Per Hanson, Masami Imai, Harold James, Joost Jonker, Lars Jonung, Michael Lovell, Joel Mokyr, Anders Ögren, Ronnie Phillips, Carlos Ramirez, Anna Schwartz, Richard Sylla, David Wheelock, Eugene White, and Jeff Williamson. I am particularly indebted to Tim Guinnane, both for his penetrating—but gently put—comments, as well as for his advice and friendship. I have learned from and drawn on joint work with coauthors Asher Blass, Lawrence Broz, and Masami Imai.

Many people answered my questions ranging from those on specific historical episodes, to those on points of law, to those seeking data sources. For helpful correspondence and conversations, I would like to thank Pierluigi Ciocca, Giulio Gallarotti, Robert Glauber, Jeff Grossman, Robert Grossman, Lars Jonung, Stan Lebergott, Håkan Lobell, Herbert Matis, Michelangelo Van Meerten, Angela Redish, Norio Tamaki, Gianni Toniolo, Claus Vastrup, and Herman van der Wee. I am grateful to Anne Mintz for copyediting the manuscript, to Richard Comfort for compiling the index, and to production editor Jill Harris and those with whom she works at Princeton University Press for their care in producing the final product.

I acknowledge the permission of the following publishers to reprint copyrighted material: Cambridge University Press for Grossman (1994) in chapter 3, Grossman (2001b) in chapter 6, and Grossman (1999) in chapter 7; Elsevier for Grossman (1993) in chapters 3 and 9 and for Broz and Grossman (2004) in chapter 7; MIT Press for Grossman (2007b) in chapter 6; and Ashgate publishers for Grossman (2010) in chapter 6. I thank Leslie Bricusse for permission to use the quote from *The Roar of the Greasepaint, the Smell of the Crowd* at the beginning of chapter 2.

I acknowledge the Governor and Company of the Bank of England for permission to cite from materials in the bank's archives. I thank Lloyds TSB Group Archives for permission to cite from materials in their archives and HSBC for permission to cite from the HSBC Group archives. I am grateful to Harvard's Institute of Quantitative Social Science for its hospitality, to the IQSS Political Economy Group for tolerating a lowly economist, and especially to Jeff Frieden for his advice, encouragement, and friendship.

I thank the German Marshall Fund of the United States for two research fellowships which helped me advance this work and the National Science Foundation (Grants SBR 9408619 and SES 0418352) for generous financial support that allowed me to hire many talented research assistants who entered data, often in languages that they didn't understand, with patience and diligence. I am particularly grateful to John Dolfin, Eleni Lionaki, and Aaron Siskind, both for their exceptional research assistance and for the good judgment they brought to their tasks.

Our children, Dina, Joshua, Yonatan, and Yael, are a constant source of delight, amazement, and pure joy. I sometimes worried that the job of author was taking time away from the far more important job of fatherhood, but was consoled by the fact that our home office is equipped with neither a lock nor soundproofing.

My greatest debt is to my wife, Ruth. Ruth read and commented on the manuscript, helped with translations, patiently listened to—and talked me through—many organizational snags, and learned more about banking history than any neurolinguist should have to. Most importantly, when I was convinced that I would never finish, she assured me with complete confidence that I would. She was, as usual, right. In the words of Reinhard Mey: "Ich liebe sie . . . immer mehr!"

Newton Centre, Massachusetts
July 2009

Unsettled Account

CHAPTER 1

Introduction

> "The distinctive function of the banker,"—says Ricardo,
> "begins as soon as he uses the money of *others*"; as long as he
> uses his own money he is only a capitalist.
>
> —Walter Bagehot (1924: 21)

THE CHALLENGE OF INTERMEDIATION

A fundamental challenge faced by economies for centuries has been to efficiently channel—"intermediate" in economic terminology—society's aggregate savings toward productive enterprise. Ancient and modern economies alike have devised facilities for intermediating between savers and investors. In ancient Babylon, palace and temple officials loaned their own funds and, in time, deposits that were entrusted to them. In medieval Italy and Spain, institutions were established for the purpose of funneling private savings toward public use, in particular to fund the government's debt. The roughly contemporaneous development of financial instruments, such as the bill of exchange, helped to channel savings toward the finance of both domestic and international trade. In modern industrial economies, intermediation falls primarily to securities markets and financial institutions.

Perhaps the best way to appreciate the importance of financial intermediators is to consider what the world would look like without them. In their absence, firms seeking finance and savers looking for investment opportunities would have to find each other and negotiate detailed contracts. Will funds be loaned or will they purchase a share of the enterprise? If loaned, for how long, at what interest rate, and against what collateral? If the funds purchase an ownership share, to what fraction of profits and seats on the board of directors will investors be entitled and, if the enterprise fails, how much liability will they bear? A system without financial intermediators would be, to put it mildly, inefficient. The transaction costs involved in seeking out investors and reaching agreements would be prohibitive, and firm managers, in all likelihood, would be forced to rely on retained earnings (i.e., funds generated by the firm but not distributed to owners) and the fortunes of friends and family to finance expansion. Economic growth, as typified by the modern industrialized—or industrializing—economy would seem impossible.

This book focuses on one type of financial intermediator: banks. More specifically, it analyzes the forces that have been responsible for the evolution—sometimes slow, sometimes dramatically rapid—of banking, particularly commercial banking, in the industrialized world during the past two centuries. This should be of interest for at least four reasons.

First, banks are among the oldest extant forms of financial intermediator. They are also among the most familiar. And, despite the growth of alternative intermediaries, particularly securities markets, banks remain an integral part of the financial system. In short, the answer to the question posed by Boyd and Gertler (1994), "Are Banks Dead?" is "no."

Second, if banking is an essential determinant of economic growth, its evolution may affect long-term economic performance and therefore help to account for countries' differing historical and prospective growth trajectories. A substantial academic literature considers the merits of many aspects of banking systems, including the extent of concentration and branching, the relative sizes of the banking industry, securities markets, and other financial intermediaries, and the costs and benefits of different regulatory restrictions on banks. This literature tends to assume—incorrectly—that the key characteristics of the banking system were predetermined at some distant historical date, rather than as the product of a longer-term evolution, potentially biasing its results.

Third, banking stability may have important short-run economic and political consequences. Banking crises have been a common feature of the world economy for the past two centuries and can generate economic fluctuations or exacerbate those already under way. Since certain types of banking systems may be more resistant to crisis than others, understanding the forces that govern the evolution of banking may help to explain differences—both across countries and through time—in the severity of cyclical fluctuations and their political fallout.

Finally, banking systems across the industrialized world have undergone revolutionary changes since the early 1970s. Banking crises and subsequent government rescues, consolidation among banks and between banks and other types of financial institutions, and changes in national, international, and supranational regulatory efforts have dramatically altered the financial landscape in recent years and, given recent financial turmoil, will continue to do so for the foreseeable future. Identifying the forces that historically have been responsible for banking evolution may provide some insight into understanding those at work today.

This book focuses on four types of events that have been both characteristic features of the life cycle of commercial banking systems and have brought about important structural changes in banking: crises, rescues, merger movements, and regulation. The detailed studies of these events through time and across countries presented in subsequent chapters reveals that they are the result of multiple, and frequently idiosyncratic, causes. Nonetheless, several commonalities emerge.

Banking crises have been a prominent feature of the financial landscape from the earliest days of commercial banking, of which the subprime mortgage crisis is merely the most recent example. Banking crises have three primary causes: (1) "boom-bust" (or macroeconomic) fluctuations; (2) shocks to confidence; and (3) structural weakness. Boom-bust fluctuations have long been a feature of the modern industrialized economy. If banking growth is especially vigorous during a period of robust macroeconomic expansion, the subsequent contraction may strain the banking system to the point of crisis. Shocks to confidence arising from, for example, concerns about the continued convertibility of the currency—raising the specter that deposits may only be redeemable in devalued currency—or the anticipation of an impending war or other event that reduces confidence in the stability of the banking system, may generate panic withdrawals and precipitate a crisis. Finally, the likelihood of crises can be affected by the structure of the banking system. A banking system composed of many small banks or governed by one set of regulations may be more prone to crisis, no matter what the source of disturbance, than one characterized by fewer, larger institutions or governed by a different regulatory framework.

Because crises are costly and may spread if not controlled, private and public actors have incentives to engage in rescue operations. Rescues may be confined to bailing out one troubled institution or may extend to the banking system more generally through lender of last resort operations; they may be of limited scope or may consist of relatively extreme measures, such as wholesale bank nationalization. The consequences of the type of rescue undertaken can have long-lasting effects on the banking system. If a rescue entails sustaining weaker banks, it may encourage other banks to undertake riskier activities secure in the knowledge that they too will be rescued in case of distress, a phenomenon known as "moral hazard." Thus, rescues may contribute to yet another boom-bust cycle marked by overexpansion and ending in crisis.

Crises typically leave a number of devastated banks in their wake. One consequence of this may be an increase in bank merger activity, as healthy banks absorb troubled institutions. Yet merger movements are not solely the creatures of economic downturns: economic expansion can also stimulate mergers if increased financing requirements are better met by larger financial institutions. The wealth effects of rising equity prices during an economic boom may also increase the willingness of potential acquirers to initiate mergers while rising share prices may make potential targets more willing to be acquired.

Another, usually not quite so immediate, consequence of crises is a change in banking regulations. Government regulation shapes many aspects of banking, ranging from rules governing entry, to those setting capital requirements, reserve requirements, and a variety of balance sheet ratios. Regulations govern whether banks can maintain branches, engage in securities market transactions, and the extent to which shareholders are liable for the losses of the bank. Although promoting banking soundness and stability—and indeed the public interest more generally—is frequently cited as the prime motive for government regulation, the private interests of different sectors of finance, industry, and government also influence the process generating new regulations.

Efforts at stability-promoting reform typically take one of two paths. Stricter regulation, including measures that strengthen safety and soundness requirements, curtail bank powers, and increase the reach and authority of regulators, constrains banks and makes it more difficult for them to get into trouble. An alternative regulatory approach takes a seemingly opposite course: expanding the powers of existing institutions—possibly combined with competition-reducing measures—in an effort to strengthen banks and render them less vulnerable to shocks.

These paths have very different consequences for the banking system and will find support among different private interest groups. Reforms aimed at restricting competition can lead to an excessively constrained banking system, although such reforms may be supported by financial incumbents protecting their private interests (Rajan and Zingales 2003b). Such constraints may eventually render the banking system less able to contribute to economic growth and lead to calls for deregulation. Reforms that allow an expansion of banking powers will have different consequences and will have different advocates. If such regulations are anticompetitive, they may lead to increased—perhaps to an uncomfortably high level—banking concentration. By granting wide-ranging powers, such reforms allow banks to increase risk-taking and may thus lead to greater instability.

In addition to the interplay between public and private interests, regulation will evolve as a result of unintended consequences. For example, regulations aimed at making banking safer by establishing more stringent standards may be so strict that they drive potential bankers to seek ways of avoiding the newly enacted regulations altogether: rather than acquire a government-issued charter, potential bankers might decide to operate as private partnerships or as off-shore enterprises, if doing so allows them to escape the stringent regulation. Bank efforts to avoid regulation lead legislators and regulators to devise new regulations which, in turn, encourage banks to find even newer ways of avoiding them.

BANKING AND ECONOMIC GROWTH

An important motive for studying banking evolution is its potential influence on economic growth. The theoretical literature on the interaction between the financial system, particularly banking, and economic growth is long and has a good pedigree. In his classic work, *The Wealth of Nations*, Adam Smith (1776 [1994]: 349) highlights the importance of banks in mobilizing capital:

> It is not by augmenting the capital of the country, but by rendering a greater part of that capital active and productive than would otherwise be so, that the most judicious operations of banking can increase the industry of a country. That part of capital which a dealer is obliged to keep by him unemployed, and in ready money, for answering occasional demands, is so much dead stock, which, so long as it remains in this situation, produces nothing either to him or his country. The judicious operations of banking enable him to convert this dead stock into active and productive stock; into materials to work upon, into tools to work with, and into provisions and subsistence to work for; into stock which produces something both to himself and to his country.

Henry Thornton (1802 [1939]: 176) quibbles with Smith's characterization, suggesting that banks are important not only because they *mobilize* credit, but because, in the course of supplying paper money, they also *create* credit: "Whether the introduction of the use of paper is spoken of as turning dead and unproductive stock into stock which is active and productive, or as *adding* to the stock of the country is much the same thing."

The proper role of banks in creating credit by increasing issues of money was frequently debated in nineteenth-century Britain. Two instances stand out: the Bullionist controversy following Britain's suspension of the gold standard in 1797, and the clash between the Currency School and the Banking School, which arose around the time of the reorganization and recharter of the Bank of England in 1844. The crux of these arguments was the proper regulation of note issue. According to the Bullionists and the Currency School, in order to prevent an inflationary over-issue of currency, the note issue should vary "exactly as it would have done were it wholly metallic."[1] The Anti-Bullionists and the Banking School argued that as long as issuers maintained sufficient metallic reserves to insure convertibility, the note issue ought to vary with the needs of trade. If notes were issued only against the security of actual commercial transactions—the "real bills doctrine," which became a pillar of nineteenth-century banking orthodoxy in Britain and elsewhere—an

---

[1]Morgan (1943: 130). See also Andréadès (1966) and Fetter (1965) on these debates.

inflationary over-issue would not be possible. An implication of the Anti-Bullionist/Banking School view is that the inability to issue notes and create credit in response to an increased demand for real commercial transactions would retard economic growth.

Joseph Schumpeter (1934: 74) argues that bankers play a key role in economic growth, explicitly highlighting their role in credit creation:

> The banker, therefore, is not so much primarily a middleman in the commodity of "purchasing power" as a *producer* of this commodity. However, since all reserve funds and savings to-day usually flow to him, and the total demand for free purchasing power, whether existing or to be created, concentrates on him, he has either replaced private capitalists or become their agent; he has himself become the capitalist par excellence. He stands between those who wish to form new combinations and the possessors of productive means. He is essentially a phenomenon of development, though only when no central authority directs the social process. He makes possible the carrying out of new combinations, authorizes people, in the name of society as it were, to form them. He is the ephor of the exchange economy.

John Hicks (1969: 78, 94–97) juxtaposes the above approaches by describing three stages through which banking develops. In the first stage, banks operate solely as trusted middlemen: borrowing, re-lending, and profiting on the spread between borrowing and lending rates. In the second stage, the banker begins to accept deposits that can be withdrawn on demand. At this point, the banker becomes a principal in the transaction, accepting the risk of a bank run if liquid assets are not sufficient to redeem demand liabilities. In the third stage, deposits subject to withdrawal become transferable, either by check or note. According to Hicks, "... it is at this point that the bank becomes able to create what is in effect money."

A related strand of literature focuses not directly on the credit-creating powers of banks, but on banks more generally in the realm of firm finance. Gurley and Shaw (1955) characterize earlier forms of firm finance as "self-finance," in which firms finance investment projects from undistributed profits, and "direct finance," in which firms borrow directly from savers. The next stage of financial development, termed "indirect finance," occurs when banks issue their own debt and use the proceeds to finance investment projects. Gurley and Shaw argue that failure to develop this type of indirect finance through financial intermediators can retard economic development.[2]

---

[2]Nonetheless Gurley's (1967: 953) review of Cameron (1967) argues that: "... recent experience strongly suggests that banking systems as intermediaries are not highly essential to the growth process."

Alexander Gerschenkron (1962) also takes up the idea of investment finance, arguing that the importance of financial intermediators rose with the level of economic "backwardness." He asserts that in Britain, the most developed economy of the eighteenth and nineteenth centuries, industrialization was financed primarily with the retained earnings of industrialists. In moderately backwards economies, exemplified by Germany, banks played a crucial role in mobilizing savings during industrialization—a role that had not been necessary in economically developed Britain. In the most backwards of countries, exemplified by Russia, he argues that financing industrialization was too great a task for banks to accomplish, and so the leading role had to be undertaken by the state.

Yet not all economic theorists have viewed finance as quite the lynchpin that these others seem to think it is. Joan Robinson (1952: 86) argues that:

> ... [t]here is a general tendency for the supply of finance to move with the demand for it. It is true, of course, that at any moment there are many excellent ideas which cannot be implemented because those that conceive them cannot back them up with finance. But, by and large, it seems to be the case that where enterprise leads finance follows.

And, according to Robert Lucas (1988: 6), economists "badly overstress" the role of financial factors in economic growth. Further, Ross Levine (1997: 688) argues that economists who study the developing world express their skepticism about the role of the financial system in promoting growth "by ignoring it."

Empirically, there is no doubt that finance and economic development move together. However, the question remains: does causality run primarily from finance to development or vice versa? Certainly, during financial crises, disintegration of the financial sector leads to a short-term deterioration in economic performance. Does the reverse hold? And does it hold in the longer run?

Raymond Goldsmith (1969) provides the first systematic empirical attempt to discern the relationship between financial system development and economic growth. This work provides detailed data on the financial systems of thirty-five countries at twenty-year intervals from as early as 1860. Goldsmith calculates the ratio of financial claims to national wealth, what he terms "the financial inter-relations ratio" (FIR), in order to determine the importance of the financial superstructure in economic growth. Goldsmith (1969: 390–91) states the task in the following way:

> One of the most important problems in the field of finance, if not the single most important one, almost everyone would agree, is the effect that financial structure and development have on economic growth.

Does it make a measurable difference in the speed or character of economic growth how large a country's financial superstructure is compared to its national wealth and product; how rapidly and regularly the financial superstructure expands in nominal and real terms; how much of a country's investment is financed externally through the issuance of financial instruments rather than internally out of investors' own saving or through involuntary transfer like taxation; what types of financial instruments exist; what are their relative importance and penetration throughout the economy; what are the character, the methods of operation, the degree of specialization and concentration, the geographic distribution of financial institutions; and whether financial institutions are owned or operated privately, cooperatively, or by the government?

He then elaborates on the difficulty in finding an answer:

These questions and many others directed toward the nature of the financial superstructure and of changes in it are easy to pose, but most questioners are unaware how difficult and precarious answers are, both methodologically and factually. . . .

To assess the role of financial development and structure in economic growth we may turn, depending on our philosophical predilections, to economic theory or to economic history. We shall unfortunately find that in the present state of the theory of economic growth and with the present lack of sufficiently intensive historical studies of financial development we cannot get definite answers from either discipline. The reader who is looking for simple, unambiguous, and enduring solutions may as well, therefore, stop here.

Goldsmith finds that the FIR increased—up to a certain point—with the level of development. He also argues that, given the wide range of experiences across countries and the relatively low frequency of the data, it is impossible to definitively establish causality.

Around the same time, Rondo Cameron and coauthors (1967, 1972) undertook case studies on the role played by banks in the economic development of about a dozen countries. The results of these studies are mixed: in some countries (Belgium, Japan, Scotland, and the United States) the authors find that banking systems contributed to growth; in others (France, Italy, Russia, and Spain) the banking systems are found either to have responded passively to economic development or, where government intervention was misguided, to have hindered development by misallocating funds.

Starting in the 1990s, economists began to bring more sophisticated statistical techniques to bear on the relationship between finance and economic growth (Demirgüç-Kunt and Levine 2001). The data sets analyzed typically include both greater numbers of countries and higher frequency data than previous efforts. King and Levine (1993) examine the relationship between economic growth and various measures of financial development across eighty countries during 1960–89 and find financial development to be a good predictor of economic growth over the subsequent ten to thirty years. De Gregorio and Guidotti (1995), Levine, Loayza, and Beck (2000), and Levine and Zervos (1998) reach similar findings for financial intermediator development—both banks and stock markets—and economic growth during various subperiods from the 1960s through the 1990s. Rajan and Zingales (1998) find that industrial sectors that were more highly dependent on external finance benefited more from greater financial sector development and Beck, Demirgüç-Kunt, Laeven, and Levine (2008) find that small firms benefited disproportionately from financial sector development.

Rousseau and Wachtel (1998) take a slightly different approach, analyzing data from fewer countries (Canada, Norway, Sweden, the United Kingdom, and the United States) over a longer period (1870–1929). They conclude that in most cases causality runs from financial sector development to real economic activity, although their findings are stronger for some countries than for others. Rousseau and Sylla (2003) examine a sample seventeen countries during 1850–1997 and find a robust correlation between financial factors and economic growth ". . . consistent with a leading role for finance." Other empirical studies of periods of a century or more for Sweden (Hansson and Jonung 1997) and Canada (Wilson 2001) suggest that, for at least several subperiods and possibly for different stages of economic development, the direction of causality between financial sector development and economic growth is more ambiguous.

The literature on the causal relationship between financial sector development in general—and banking in particular—and economic development is inconclusive. Modern studies focusing on three decades of annual data on large panels of countries of varying levels of economic development suggest that financial sector development leads to economic growth. Despite the sweeping geographic scope of these studies, they consider relatively short periods of time: if the relationship between finance and growth changes over time or with the level of development—or if the development path of countries differs—studies with limited time horizons may not detect a relationship.

Although this book will touch on the relationship between banking and economic growth, its main goal is to discover the forces that drive the evolution of banking systems. If finance leads economic growth, as a number of studies suggest, then banking may well have an important effect on long-run economic growth. Even if no causal connection to long-run growth is found, if banking structure and economic stability are causally connected, the shape of the banking system may have important consequences for short-term economic fluctuations.

SECURITIES MARKETS, BANKS, AND OTHER INTERMEDIATORS

Although the focus of this book is on commercial banks, it will be useful to place them in the context of the broader financial system. Economists ascribe a variety of functions to the financial system that are important in economic development (Levine 1997). These include facilitating trade in goods and services, providing liquidity services, mobilizing savings, allocating resources, facilitating the trading of risk, collecting and communicating information, and providing a means for monitoring managers and exerting corporate control.

Among the most basic services provided by the financial system are those that enable trade. As the use of coins spread from Lydia and Ionia throughout the ancient Mediterranean world, one of the earliest banking functions to develop was money changing, that is, the trading of moneys of different realms, or what we would today call the foreign exchange business.[3] Another early banking function involved facilitating the transfer of funds from one individual to another—possibly separated by some distance—via book transfers and bills of exchange.

The economic impact of the development of money changing and remitting facilities was considerable, permitting the expansion of interregional and international commerce, which in turn promoted regional specialization in production. Specialization contributed to greater technological progress and increased consumption possibilities. In the words of Adam Smith (1776 [1994]: 18):

> Among men . . . the most dissimilar geniuses are of use to one another; the different produces of their respective talents, by the general disposition to truck, barter, and exchange, being brought, as it were, into a common stock, where every man may purchase whatever part of the produce of other men's talents he has occasion for.

A second function of the financial system is the provision of liquidity services. Liquidity is "the ease and speed with which agents can convert assets into purchasing power at agreed prices" (Levine 1997: 692). By

---

[3]Davies (1994: 60ff.). Strictly speaking, money changing is distinct from banking, although money changers often subsequently became bankers. The development of money, which we do not discuss in detail here, is a crucial prerequisite for economic exchange. Without some form of money, all trade must take place through barter.

issuing banknotes and demand deposits, banks *create* liquidity. Hicks (1969) asserts that the provision of liquidity services was vital to industrial development, since industrialization requires large sums of fixed capital for extended periods of time. Enabling firm owners to sell a portion of their equity via securities markets, or to borrow on the security of these holdings from banks, reduces the liquidity risk to investors of tying up a large fraction of their wealth in one project and allows more investment projects to be funded.

A further function of the financial system is to accumulate the aggregate savings of an economy and channel it to areas where it can be put to productive use. This is particularly important if large quantities of capital are required, as is generally the case in industrialized and industrializing economies. The point is brought home by Postan (1935: 2), who argues that:

> By the beginning of the eighteenth century there were enough rich people in the country to finance an economic effort far in excess of the modest activity of the leaders of the Industrial Revolution. It can, indeed, be doubted whether there had ever been a period in English history when the accumulated wealth of landlords and merchants, of religious and educational institutions would have been inadequate for that purpose.

The financial system also provides a mechanism for the trading and pooling of risk. For example, the owner of a company who sells shares on the stock exchange is effectively selling some of the accompanying risk to investors. Since individual investors can each purchase a small proportion of the shares offered, they are able to diversify their portfolios by purchasing a variety of assets with different risk characteristics. Similarly, banks pool risk by lending accumulated depositor funds to a variety of projects, hence reducing the risk to depositors from the failure of any one project.

Financial intermediaries also provide information services and a mechanism for monitoring managers and exerting corporate control. Banks acquire information on the credit-worthiness of borrowers, the soundness of the collateral, and the likelihood of success of proposed projects prior to making loans. They may also be able to exercise oversight as to how the money is spent. This benefits depositors, since they do not have to gather information—either before or after the loan is made—on those to whom their money is lent. Securities markets gather and channel information. The up- or downwards movement of securities prices reflect the flow of information about the prospects for a given private or public debt or equity issuer. Further, because shares may be publicly traded, the opportunity exists for investors to buy a large enough share of a company to effect a change in the management—this prospect may be higher if the share price has fallen due to poor management or some other factor (Mørck, Shleifer, and Vishny 1988, 1989).

We have, until now, spoken mostly about intermediation and the financial system in broad non-specific terms, noting the presence of both financial institutions and securities markets, but not dwelling excessively on their different characteristics. Although they perform many of the same functions, it is necessary to distinguish the two.

Securities markets, in their most basic form, are markets for debt (IOUs) and equity (ownership shares). Because of the generally poor quality of information, the earliest securities markets were primarily debt markets: traded debt consisted almost entirely of government debt, presumably with a good reputation for repayment,[4] or by debt backed by inventories of goods (i.e., trade credit), which could be seized if the borrower did not pay off the debt.[5] The number and types of securities markets have proliferated, and today include markets for types of debt, equity, and derivative securities that were not contemplated even a few years ago.

In a theoretical economic sense, securities markets provide the optimal form of intermediation: those who need funds for investment projects can offer their wares in the financial marketplace and savers can shop for the financial product with the attributes (e.g., maturity, risk, return, collateral) that suit their preferences (Rajan and Zingales 2003a,c). If the market is active, transaction costs are low, and all parties have sufficient information, buyers and sellers will get the best price possible. Market prices will continuously adjust to reflect changes in supply and demand for securities which, in turn, reflect new information about the underlying investments. If circumstances warrant, adjustments can take place through the market: firms and other demanders of funds can purchase their own debt or equity if the funds are no longer needed; savers can sell securities at any time and gain access to their funds.

These desirable qualities of securities markets are highlighted in Walter Bagehot's (1924: 12–13) classic description of the London money market: "English capital runs as surely and instantly where it is most

[4]Sovereign borrowers were not always credit-worthy, although they were likely more reliable than private borrowers. England's Charles II unilaterally stopped all payment of principal to his creditors in 1672, during the so-called "Stop of the Exchequer." North and Weingast (1989) argued that by placing national finances under Parliamentary control, the Glorious Revolution of 1689 increased the credibility and creditworthiness—hence lowering borrowing costs—of the British government. See, however, Sussman and Yafeh (2004).

[5]The ability of the lender to seize collateral depends crucially upon a variety of institutional details, including property rights and enforcement mechanisms. LaPorta et al. (1997) spawned a substantial literature that focuses on the rights of creditors under Anglo-Saxon and continental legal systems.

wanted, and where there is most to be made of it, as water runs to find its level."

Despite the many theoretical advantages of securities markets, the conditions necessary to secure those advantages—an active market with many buyers and sellers, low transaction costs, and ample information—have historically been rare. Even with today's deep and liquid securities markets, the transaction and information costs (e.g., securing a bond rating, complying with government and exchange requirements) for small firms or firms in less developed countries may render access to securities markets impractical. Historically, the obstacles were much higher: active securities markets were few and far between, high transaction costs limited market access to only the largest and most credit-worthy borrowers, and information flows were poor by contemporary standards. Without solutions to the information problem, capital may not flow in sufficient quantities to where it is most wanted, but to where high transaction costs and imperfect information direct (Stiglitz and Weiss 1981).

Although both securities markets and banks are vulnerable to imperfect information and high transaction costs, banks may be superior to securities markets in coping with these defects, particularly in the early stages of development (Sylla 1998: 84). As lenders, banks can screen individual loan applicants and evaluate the credit-worthiness of proposed projects, thus making funds available to borrowers that are neither very large nor particularly well-known. Banks can also monitor the progress of projects, assess the need for additional funding, and evaluate the behavior of the managers, sometimes through a seat on the board of directors (DeLong 1991). In the course of these operations banks may develop expertise in evaluating firms in a particular industry or geographic region, lowering both transaction and information costs.

As borrowers, banks may also offer some transaction and information cost advantages over securities markets. Banks can mobilize substantial sums relatively cheaply by collecting deposits from large and small savers alike. By contrast, high minimum share prices, such as the £100 set by England's 1844 Joint Stock Banking Act, discouraged the participation of less well-heeled investors. Additionally, a bank's capital—committed to depositors in case of failure—and reputation may ameliorate the information asymmetry between banks and their depositors, which might otherwise discourage individuals from entrusting a bank with their savings.

THE SCOPE OF THIS BOOK

In some ways, the scope of this book is narrow; in others it is quite broad. It is narrow in that it focuses on financial institutions and largely ignores securities markets, the other major component of modern financial systems. This narrowing is not as complete as one might think, however: many types of financial institutions exist, including commercial banks, savings banks, investment banks, life insurance companies, and credit cooperatives, among others. In 1963 the United States and most western European countries had between sixteen and twenty-four different types of financial institutions; Japan had as many as thirty-three. These numbers are not entirely the result of twentieth-century developments: as early as 1900, Belgium, Canada, Germany, Britain, Italy, Japan, the Netherlands, Norway, Sweden, and the United States each had more than ten different types of financial institutions (Goldsmith 1969: 354).

This book focuses on banks, with a particular emphasis on shareholder-owned incorporated banks that make loans financed by the issue of liquid liabilities, such as demand deposits and currency, which the bank must be prepared to redeem at short notice. Depending on the country, these institutions may be known as commercial banks, joint stock banks, chartered banks, credit banks, trading banks, national banks, or ordinary banks.

This narrow focus is warranted for several reasons. First, commercial banks have typically been among the largest and most influential of intermediaries, and in many countries have taken the lead in financing trade and industry, crucial factors in economic growth and development. Second, commercial banks have relied to a large extent on demand liabilities, highlighting their role both in overcoming the information asymmetries that may retard early economic growth and as providers of a large proportion of the means of payment.[6] This reliance on liquid liabilities to fund less liquid loans has subjected commercial banks to greater risk of panic-induced withdrawals, in turn leading to financial crises, than other financial institutions (Diamond and Dybvig 1983). Finally, narrowing the scope makes the analysis far more tractable: because each type of financial institution has its own legal and economic origins, it is impossible to make an in-depth comparison of all types of financial institutions across multiple countries.

Commercial banks were not the only institutions to make loans financed by the issuance of money-like instruments: government banks and private banks frequently undertook these tasks long before commercial banks emerged. Government banks, however, were a special case of commercial bank: although frequently created as ordinary commercial banks, they typically had a special relationship with the state—both in terms of rights and responsibilities—that distinguished them from other commercial banks. The quasi-public role of these banks increased

---

[6]Savings banks, credit cooperatives, and other thrift institutions have also relied heavily on deposits; however, primarily on less liquid savings deposits.

during the late nineteenth and early twentieth centuries as they evolved into modern central banks. Although private bankers were sometimes important members of the financial system (e.g., the Rothschilds), most were typically smaller than commercial banks. As incorporated commercial banking progressed, private banks became, in aggregate, much less important.

An additional practical hindrance to a systematic study of private banks is the lack of data. Commercial banks were typically brought into existence with government sanction in the form of a charter and were required to provide periodic accounts to government authorities. Private banks were generally under no such obligation, and our knowledge of them is much more limited, coming primarily from company histories which rely on archival sources.[7]

The narrow focus on commercial banks comes at a cost, however. Guinnane's (2002) analysis of the nineteenth-century German financial system demonstrates that restricting such an analysis to commercial banks omits several crucial intermediators, including savings banks, mortgage banks, and credit cooperatives. Savings banks, both government-sponsored and private, have long been important parts of the financial system, particularly in Germany and the Scandinavian countries, in some cases exceeding the aggregate size of the commercial banking sector. Although these institutions were often important intermediators, their role was usually quite different from that of commercial banks. Savings banks typically collected funds from small depositors and made long-term loans to households, often for housing finance, or purchased long-term government securities, the proceeds of which were loaned by government-sponsored institutions. Although savings banks have played an important role in many countries' financial systems, because they have not been a major source of funds for trade and industry they will not take center stage here.

Geographically and chronologically, the scope of this book is quite broad, covering western Europe, Australia, Canada, Japan, and the United States from the beginnings of industrialization. These countries were both among the first to develop modern commercial banking systems and the first to industrialize, typically accomplishing both before the end of the nineteenth century. Hence, they all have relatively long continuous histories of both banking and industrial development. The broad coverage is warranted on two counts. First, since banking systems typically evolve slowly, determining the forces generating such evolution

---

[7]See, however, Pressnell (1956) on English country banks in the eighteenth and nineteenth centuries and Jonker (1996a) on a variety of private Dutch financial institutions in the first half of the nineteenth century. See also Joslin (1954) and Temin and Voth (2008).

can only be discerned by analyzing a long time period. Consider, for example, banking regulation. Limiting the study to the last quarter of the twentieth century constrains its focus to *de*regulation. Since the historical experience has included—and, given the recent turbulence in the financial system, the future certainly will include—both periods of increased regulation, as well as deregulation, a complete picture of the forces driving regulatory changes can only be discerned by examining a longer time period. Furthermore, because the cause-and-effect relationship between banking regulation and other economic and political events is complicated, examining a longer time series will make it easier to disentangle the channels of causality. Second, since the path of regulation and deregulation across countries has been highly idiosyncratic, a systematic assessment can be made only by examining the experiences of a large number of countries.

Given the above argument in favor of breadth, it would seem logical to expand the study to include a longer time period and more countries. Doing so would be problematic for two reasons. First, commercial banking only emerged in force in the industrialized world in the nineteenth century. Banking in the seventeenth and eighteenth centuries consisted primarily of government banks and largely undocumented private banks. Second, given the close relationship between banking and industry, it is reasonable to conclude that banking evolution differed systematically between the industrialized and the non-industrialized worlds.

The approach of the book is thematic and comparative, focusing on the forces generating important structural changes in banking across countries. The book is by no means exhaustive or encyclopedic: even the three chapters on individual countries do not present comprehensive banking histories. Rather, the book considers the major forces—crises, bailouts, merger movements, and regulation—that have shaped banking systems in a comparative framework. The bulk of the book is focused on the period from the beginnings of industrialization through the Great Depression of the 1930s. A final chapter assesses developments from the Depression through the turn of the twenty-first century.

THE ARGUMENT

A main thesis—and organizing principle—of this book is that the four types of structure-altering events discussed above (crises, bailouts, merger movements, and regulation) combined to generate an archetypical life cycle in the commercial banking systems of the industrialized world from their earliest days through the first third of the twentieth century. A stylized view of that life cycle is presented in figure 1.1. Although the pat-

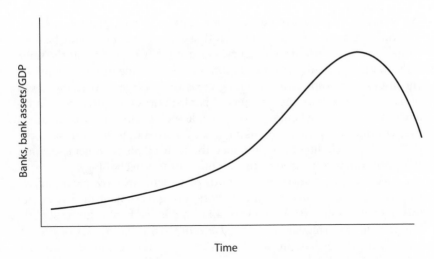

Figure 1.1. A stylized view of the life cycle of banking systems.

tern presented shows a smooth rise and fall in the number of banks, in fact, national experiences differed substantially and the pattern outlined below was rarely smooth. Nonetheless, a broadly similar pattern holds across countries: a period of expanding bank population, followed by a peak, followed by a more or less rapid decline. A theoretical and empirical literature on product life cycles posits a similar pattern in competitive industries.[8] Although the life cycle posited by this literature is similar to the banking pattern presented here, there are a number of important differences, which are highlighted in the description that follows.

The introduction of commercial banking, as with any successful industrial innovation, leads to rapid growth at first. The speed and strength of this early growth depends positively on the demand for banking services, derived from the current and expected future financing needs of commerce and industry, and negatively on the severity of the regulatory constraints placed on banks and competition from other intermediators. Commercial banking growth may be strengthened if it takes over some of the functions of preexisting financial intermediators (Lindgren 2002). This early growth is susceptible to a variety of economic and regulatory shocks and, as noted above, will not be in any sense smooth or constant. Although figure 1.1 implies that paths of both the numbers and assets of banks move together, this need not be the case.

[8]Gort and Klepper (1982), Klepper and Graddy (1990), Klepper (1996, 2002), Klepper and Simons (2005), and Jovanovic and MacDonald (1994).

The general upward trend continues until a turning point is reached. The turning points in the number and assets of banks may not be contemporaneous in any given country, nor need they take place at the same stage in any particular country's economic development, but usually occur in close proximity to a banking crisis or a merger movement. Both of these events reduce the numbers of banks: crises typically lead to a reduction in aggregate banking assets, while mergers may be accompanied by a continued increase in banking assets. This stands in contrast to the product life cycle literature, in which the turning point coincides with a shakeout, often connected to the adoption of new technology.

Crises generate two reactions, both of which can have profound effects on banking structure. In the short run, government or private actors may attempt to rescue some or all of the failed banks. In the slightly longer run, governments may impose more stringent regulations in an attempt to bolster banking stability. Mergers, if they result in a substantial increase in banking concentration, may also encourage regulators to intervene in order to reduce the likelihood of a monopolized banking sector. Government efforts to rein in banks via regulation—whether due to crises or heightened merger activity—will be met with increasingly inventive means of circumventing such regulation, which itself may lead to yet further regulation. Edward Kane (1977) aptly refers to these cycles of moves and counter-moves as the "regulatory dialectic."

Figures 1.2 through 1.10 present country-specific data on the number and assets of commercial banks from the nineteenth and early twentieth centuries. Before discussing the figures in detail, several warnings are in order. First, the data vary widely in quality: some series come from official sources, others from the financial press; some were compiled contemporaneously, others were assembled retrospectively. Second, they vary in coverage: some series contain gaps, others consist of two or more distinct series spliced together, and still others include more than one type of financial institution. Finally, for some countries comprehensive data are not available at all. Although future researchers will, no doubt, compile superior data, the current series are sufficient to illustrate the argument: banking systems experience a period of expanding population, followed by a peak, followed by a more or less rapid decline. In considering this pattern, I divide the life cycle into three phases: early expansion, later expansion and peak, and contraction.

Although the relationship between economic growth and financial development is not precisely understood, the data suggest that banking and economic development move together in the early phase of the banking life cycle. As noted above, the initial growth in banking depends positively on the demand for increased banking services brought about by economic growth, the rapidity with which commercial banking takes

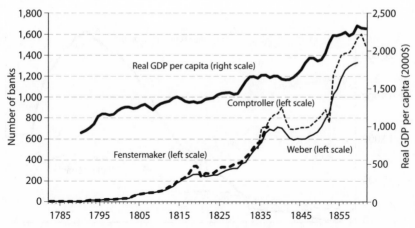

Figure 1.2a. Number of banks and real GDP per capita in the United States, 1782–1861. *Sources*: Number of banks: Fenstermaker (1965: 111), U.S. Comptroller of the Currency (1876: 94), and Weber (2005); real GDP per capita: Johnston and Williamson (2008).

over the functions of preexisting financial institutions, and negatively on the restraining hand of regulation and the presence of competing intermediators that retard the development of commercial banking.

Figure 1.2a presents data on the numbers of banks in the United States from the early expansion phase of U.S. commercial banking, 1782 to 1861, as well as data on the level of real gross domestic product per capita (i.e., total economic output per person) from 1790 to 1861. Banking data from 1862–1939 are presented in figure 1.2b. The data presented in figure 1.2a are suggestive: declines in the number of banks in the late 1810s, early and late 1840s, and around 1860 coincide with or are preceded by declines in real GDP per capita; rapid banking growth during the 1830s and 1850s coincide with strong economic growth. Although this correlation is notable, it does not answer the question of whether banking expanded to meet the needs—contemporary or anticipated—of commerce and industry, or if real economic activity expanded because of the increase in the numbers and activities of banks.

Similar patterns can be seen in the growth of Australian and Canadian banking during the first half of the nineteenth century (figure 1.3). Banking expansion was particularly strong during boom periods (e.g., the Australian gold rush of the early 1850s); declines occurred during severe economic downturns (e.g., Canada 1837, Australia 1841–43). The first half-century or so of Nordic banking also demonstrates the positive relationship between economic growth and banking development (figure 1.4). Denmark and Sweden, the most prosperous and rapidly growing of

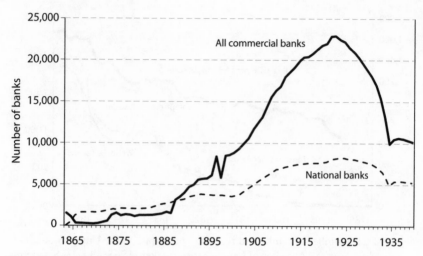

Figure 1.2b. Number of banks in the United States, 1862–1939. *Source*: U.S. Department of Commerce (1989).

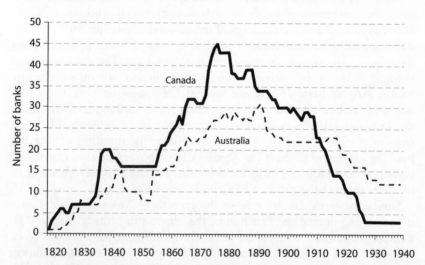

Figure 1.3. Number of banks in Australia and Canada, 1817–1939. *Sources*: Australia: Butlin, Hall, and White (1971) and Butlin (1986); Canada: Breckenridge (1910), *Canada Year Book* (various), Curtis, Taylor, and Michell (1931: 3–4), and League of Nations (1938).

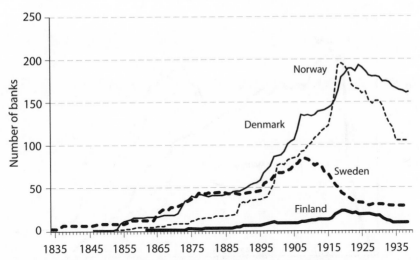

Figure 1.4. Number of banks in the Nordic countries, 1834–1939. *Sources*: Denmark: Danmarks Statistik (1969) and Johansen (1985); Finland: *Suomen Tilastollinen Vuosikirja* (various); Norway: Norges Offisielle Statistikk (1948); Sweden: Sveriges Riksbank (1931) and League of Nations (1938).

the Nordic countries, experienced more rapid growth in banking than relatively less developed Norway. Finland, which was the least economically developed of the four, saw the slowest and latest banking growth.

Economic growth—or lack thereof—was not the only factor limiting banking expansion during this early phase. Government restrictions sometimes retarded banking growth. The most obvious example is England,[9] where legislation prevented the establishment of incorporated banks other than the Bank of England for more than a century prior to 1826, despite accelerating economic growth during the preceding several decades (figure 1.5).[10] The removal of this restriction had dramatic results: more than one hundred such banks were established between 1826 and 1836.

---

[9]The terms "England" and "England and Wales" are used interchangeably throughout this book. Banks in England and Wales were governed by the same laws during the period under study and contemporaries generally did not distinguish between them (e.g., *Economist* Banking Supplement). The banking data employed are for England and Wales; crisis data (appendix 3.1 and 3.2) are labeled as England, even though other parts of the United Kingdom were frequently also affected; other data employed (e.g., GDP, population) are for Great Britain or the United Kingdom, as available. The words "Britain" and "British" are also used in a variety of circumstances (e.g., Parliament).

[10]Crafts (1983) and Harley (1982) note that economic growth during this period was slower than scholars had previously estimated. Nonetheless, they both acknowledge at least a gradual acceleration in the rate of economic growth starting in the last two decades of the eighteenth century.

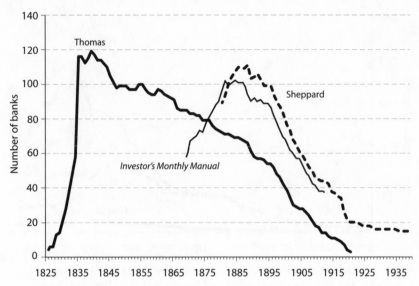

Figure 1.5. Number of banks in England, 1826–1939. *Sources*: *Investor's Monthly Manual* (various), Sheppard (1972), and Thomas (1934: appendix M).

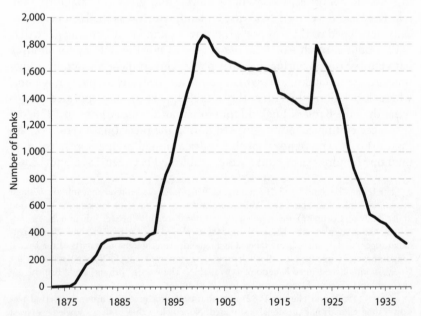

Figure 1.6. Number of banks in Japan, 1873–1939. *Source*: Bank of Japan (1966a).

Similarly, in Japan, regulations constrained growth during the early phase of commercial banking (figure 1.6). Under the 1872 National Banking Regulations (patterned on the U.S. National Banking Acts of 1863–64), commercial ("national") banks were empowered to issue banknotes—redeemable in specie (i.e., gold or silver)—against the security of government bonds. Regulations promulgated in 1876 removed the requirement to redeem national banknotes in specie and, not surprisingly, the number of national banks and the size of the national banknote issue expanded dramatically. As a result of the over-issue, in 1879 the government prohibited the chartering of new banks, halting bank expansion for the next twenty years, and in 1883 it restricted the note issue to the Bank of Japan. Once new banks were again allowed to be chartered, under the Ordinary Banking Regulations, which took effect in 1893, the number of banks rose from 400 to more than 1,800 in less than a decade.

The number of institutions provides a good measure of the spread of banking during the early phase of commercial banking development, since most of the increase results from the entry of new firms. As banking becomes more established, however, a larger proportion of the growth comes through the growth of existing institutions, rather than from new entrants. Hence, in considering the later expansion, it will be useful to also consider measures of the size, as well as the number, of banks. Unfortunately, information on aggregate bank assets is even more fragmentary than data on bank population.

Banking growth during the later expansion phase occurs primarily through the expansion of existing banks rather than from the entry of new banks. In Canada, for example, the peak number of banks was reached in 1875; however, bank assets as a fraction of total economic output continued to rise until 1927 (figure 1.7). Similarly, the number of banks in Sweden peaked in 1907, although bank assets as a share of total output did not reach a peak until 1922 (figure 1.8). And in England the number of commercial banks peaked around 1890, while bank assets continued to grow until the 1930s (figure 1.7). In each of these countries, aggregate banking assets grew despite a decline in the number of banks, indicating that the continued growth resulted in part from an increase in bank merger activity. Heightened merger activity also led to the growth of branch networks, as newly acquired banks became part of the branch networks of the banks that purchased them.

In other countries, such as Denmark, Finland, and Norway (figure 1.8), where both the number and assets of commercial banks reached peaks shortly after World War I and prior to postwar slumps, and in Japan and the United States (figure 1.9), where peaks occurred prior to the depths of the Great Depression, the turning points in numbers and

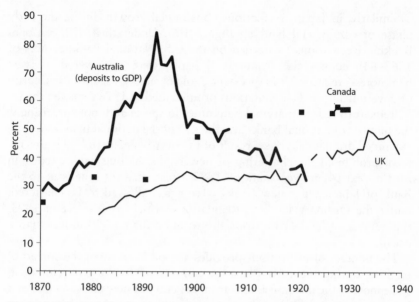

Figure 1.7. Ratio of bank assets to GDP: Australia, Canada, and England and Wales, 1870–1939. *Sources*: See figures 1.3 and 1.5 and Urquhart and Buckley (1965). *Note*: The ratio for England and Wales consists of assets of bank in England and Wales divided by GDP for the entire United Kingdom.

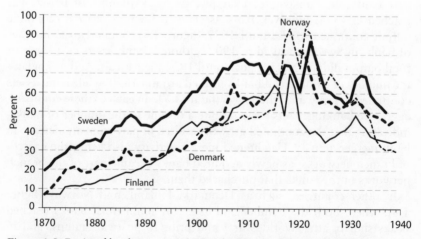

Figure 1.8. Ratio of bank assets to GDP: The Nordic countries, 1870–1939. *Sources*: Bank assets: see figure 1.4; GDP: Mitchell (1978) and Hjerppe (1989).

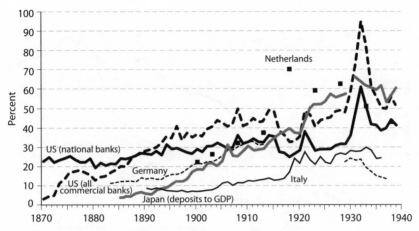

Figure 1.9. Ratio of bank assets to GDP: Germany, Italy, Japan, the Netherlands, and the United States, 1870–1939. *Sources*: Bank assets: Deutsche Bundesbank (1976), Cotula et al. (1996), Bank of Japan (1966a), Nederlandsche Bank (1986), and U.S. Department of Commerce (1989); GDP: Mitchell (1989, 1995) and Balke and Gordon (1986).

assets were chronologically close. In these countries, the peak typically coincided with the onset of a banking crisis.

The later expansion is followed by a decline—either rapid or not so rapid—in the banking population. This decline generally occurs as the result of a banking crisis or a merger movement, and can be augmented by the growth in popularity of alternative intermediators, such as savings banks. Banking crises lead to a reduction in both the number and the aggregate assets of the banking sector; mergers thin the ranks of banking institutions, but they need not lead to a reduction in aggregate bank assets. Banking crises may also lead to bank mergers, as failing banks are absorbed by healthier institutions, and so increases in mergers and bank failures may occur at the same time.

More fragmentary bank population data, starting with the later expansion phase, are presented for Belgium, Germany, Italy, and the Netherlands in figure 1.10. Each of these countries follows the general life cycle outlined above. Germany's banking population reached a peak in 1908, amidst a gathering bank and industrial merger movement.[11] The banking populations of Belgium, Italy, and the Netherlands reached peaks in the

---

[11]Riesser (1911: 602ff.) ascribes the merger movement to a variety of factors, including an industrial merger movement, the growth of "communities of interest" in banking, as well as measures which hindered firm access to the stock exchange and hastened the need for even larger banks.

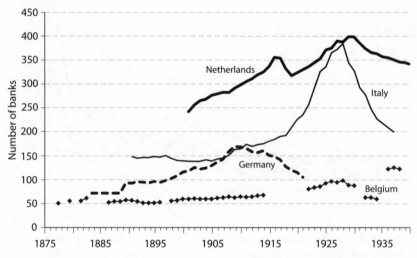

Figure 1.10. Number of banks in Belgium, Germany, Italy, and the Netherlands, 1877–1939. *Sources: Moniteur des Intérêts Matériels* (various), Deutsche Bundesbank (1976), Cotula et al. (1996), and Nederlandsche Bank (1986).

later 1920s, just prior to the onset of the Great Depression.[12] The relatively late—and dramatic—rise in the number of Dutch banks resulted from the fact that banks in the Netherlands had faced tough competition during much of the later nineteenth century from an alternative funding source: the well-developed money market. The decline of this market, especially during World War I, spurred a rapid growth in banking.

No matter where countries were within the life cycle described above, the Great Depression and World War II halted the process. The enormity of the financial devastation caused by both of these events led countries to impose rules and regulations that severely constrained banks. It was hoped that this financial lockdown would usher in a period of greater banking stability. And, in fact, these constraints, combined with the healthy economic environment of the post–World War II period, led to nearly three decades of uninterrupted banking stability. This stability, however, came at a cost. Even though banking grew and prospered, the strict constraints under which it operated ensured that there would be no substantial innovations in the business of banking. When market interest rates rose in the late 1960s and early 1970s, the post–World War II constraints, which had been a relatively minor inconvenience until that

[12]The increase in the number of banks in Belgium in 1935 resulted from a law that forced commercial banks to divest themselves of their investment banking enterprises and spin them off into new entities.

point, made it impossible for the banking system to adapt to the new environment. This initiated a process of deregulation in the 1970s which continued, for the most part uninterrupted, until the early twenty-first century. The last quarter of the twentieth century and early years of the twenty-first have seen a resurgence of crises, bailouts, merger movements, and regulatory reform.

CHAPTER OUTLINE

The life cycle of banks described above provides the roadmap for this book. The next chapter describes the rise of commercial banking. Starting in antiquity, it discusses the evolution of the different elements that allowed for the emergence of commercial banking in the eighteenth and nineteenth centuries: private banking, bills of exchange, public debt, and government banks.

Chapters 3 to 6 take a comparative approach to the evolution of banking structure, comparing the forces leading to banking crises, bailouts, merger movements, and regulatory reforms across the industrialized world. Broadly speaking, this is what economists call cross-section analysis: comparing similar phenomena across geographic and other categories. The strength of this approach is that the same phenomena can be compared in different settings, making it possible to isolate the common factors behind them. Its weakness is that it ignores an important time-series element and thus may miss some of the interactions between these phenomena over time. For example, if crises lead to regulatory reforms, which lead banks to engage in new practices in order to avoid these reforms, which then lead to further reforms, comparing crises or regulatory evolution across countries may not catch this dynamic. In order to capture the interplay between the different factors that affect banking structure, the subsequent three chapters each focus on one country with a long banking history: England, Sweden, and the United States.

The final chapter concentrates on the last two-thirds of the twentieth century and the beginnings of the twenty-first, starting with the regulations imposed in the aftermath of the Great Depression and World War II that essentially ended the life cycle pattern outlined above. It considers the forces behind the trend toward deregulation beginning in the 1970s, and continues with a discussion of the crises, bailouts, mergers, and regulatory reforms that have followed. The great variety of developments during this period truly demands a book of its own: this is clearly not that volume. Nonetheless, given the possibility that the longer historical record may shed some light on more recent events, this book concludes with an abbreviated look at contemporary history.

CHAPTER 2

The Origins of Banking

> LE BEAU: I will tell you the beginning; and, if it please your lady-
> ships, you may see the end; for the best is yet to do; and here,
> where you are, they are coming to perform it.
> CELIA: Well, the beginning, that is dead and buried.
>
> —*As You Like It* (I, ii)
>
> SIR: If we hadn't written everything down as we went along,
> we wouldn't know where we are now. And if we don't write ev-
> erything down now, we won't know where we are in the future.
> And if we don't know where we are in the future, we'll never be
> able to look back and say, "Well . . . at least we knew where we
> were in the past!"
>
> —Leslie Bricusse and Anthony Newley,
> *The Roar of the Greasepaint, the Smell of the Crowd*

THE MODERN COMMERCIAL BANK dates from the late eighteenth and early
nineteenth centuries. Early examples include the Bank of New South
Wales (Australia, 1817), Société Générale (Belgium, 1822), the Bank of
Montreal (Canada, 1820), Fyens Discontokasse (Denmark, 1846), A.
Schaaffhausen'scher Bankverein (Germany, 1848), Christiana Bank og
Kreditkasse (Norway, 1848), and the Bank of North America (United
States, 1782). In England, joint stock banks other than the Bank of En-
gland were first established in 1826; in Sweden, commercial banks were
first chartered in 1830.[1]

Although these institutions and their successors differed in many ways
from each other, they were united—and distinguished from their fore-
bears—in two important characteristics. First, these were wholly private
institutions. Predecessor institutions of the seventeenth century had been
either founded or managed by, or established primarily for the benefit of,
the state or municipality. The giro (exchange) banks established in Amsterdam (Wisselbank, 1609), Venice (Banco del Giro, 1619), Hamburg

---

[1] Several Scottish commercial banks were chartered before 1826, including the Bank
of Scotland (1695), the Royal Bank of Scotland (1727), and the British Linen Company
(1746). In Sweden, two short-lived quasi-private discount companies were chartered in the
late eighteenth century.

(Die Hamburger Bank, 1619), and elsewhere, were typically founded—and managed—by the municipality, and granted wide-ranging privileges, including monopolies on certain kinds of transactions.[2] Of the two government banks founded later in the seventeenth century, the Swedish Riksbank (1668) was owned and managed by the Diet (Parliament), and the Bank of England (1694), although privately owned, had been established primarily for the purpose of providing government finance. The extent of government involvement in later commercial banks was less than in the giro and government banks: aside from granting a charter or otherwise specifying the terms under which the bank would operate, these institutions were relatively free from government interference in their day-to-day activities.

Second, these banks had a corporate form of organization. Although a variety of forms of business organization were known in the ancient and medieval worlds, financial institutions were not commonly organized as corporations.[3] Earlier Italian financial institutions, such as the Medici Bank and those of the Venetian Republic, were primarily partnerships, frequently organized among members of a family (Lane 1944, De Roover 1948b: 5ff.). The incorporation of banks had several important effects. First, unlike partnerships, which might be dissolved or require reorganization upon the death of one of the partners, corporations could exist, in theory, indefinitely. Second, the corporate form of organization made it easier for banks to amass funds from a large pool of shareholders, enabling corporations to command more resources than partnerships.

Although these early commercial banks had a relatively modern form of corporate organization, they did not typically operate with limited liability, a common feature of modern corporations. Under limited liability, if a firm fails, shareholder losses are limited to the sums already invested in the company. By contrast, the failure of an unlimited liability firm exposes partners to liability in excess—possibly considerably in excess—of moneys invested in the firm. Because of the danger that they might issue notes in excess of their ability to redeem them, note-issuing banks were almost always subject to unlimited liability.

In England, joint stock banks were required to operate under unlimited liability until 1858 when non-note-issuing banks were allowed, like other non-banking companies, to incorporate with limited liability. By this time, the process of consolidating the note issue within the Bank of England was more than a decade old and note-issuing banks were less common. In

[2] Van Dillen (1934), Gillard (2004), Dunbar (1892), Soetbeer (1866), and Sieveking (1934).

[3] See, however, Fratianni (2006) on the Casa di San Giorgio. Ferrarini (2002) and Kohn (2003) discuss the evolution corporation law in the medieval period. Guinnane et al. (2007) discuss the advantages of various corporate forms.

Sweden, a royal decree of 1824 allowed the creation of note-issuing un-limited liability incorporated banks; four decades later non-note-issuing limited liability banks were permitted. In countries where the note issue was already monopolized by the central bank (e.g., Belgium, Denmark, France, Norway), banks were typically free to incorporate with limited liability in the same manner as any non-financial company.

A curious exception to the above examples is Australia, where the first note-issuing commercial bank enjoyed limited liability, at least temporarily. Hoping to help the Bank of New South Wales become established, Governor General Lachlan Macquarie granted the new institution a seven-year charter with limited liability. When Macquarie's superiors in London learned of this, they informed him that limited liability could only be conferred by a royal charter or by an act of Parliament. Macquarie delayed the implementation of this directive by writing "a masterful dispatch" to his superiors in London, requesting clarification and effectively extending his de facto grant of limited liability by several months (Butlin 1953: 112ff.).

Although the modern commercial bank is only about two centuries old, it has numerous antecedents. The remainder of this chapter will trace the origins of the modern commercial bank by examining predecessor institutions and developments that led to its creation, stretching back from the ancient world through the end of the eighteenth century.

EARLY BANKING FUNCTIONS

Banking is hardly a novel endeavor. Tasks which we recognize as those of bankers—taking deposits and making loans—have been undertaken by human society for at least four millennia, although banking firms *per se*, did not emerge until about 2,600 years ago in Mesopotamia and Greece.[4] The oldest known banking firm in the world outside China, the House of Egibi, conducted business in Babylon from the seventh to the fifth century BCE (Heichelheim 1964: 72, Van Driel 1985–86, Wunsch 1999). Greek banking firms, called *trapezitae* after the tables or benches (*trapeza*) where they conducted business—just as the English word *bank* derives from the Latin *bancus*—also emerged at about this time. Similar institutions first appeared in the Forum in Rome between 318 and 310 BCE (Andreau 1999: 30). Well before the emergence of the ancient precursor of the modern banking firm, however, the elements of banking were already well established.

[4]Heichelheim (1958: 134), Orsingher (1967: vii–ix, 1–5), Lopez (1979), and Bromberg (1942).

The earliest loans among the Indo-Germanic, Semito-Hamitic, Ural-Altaic, and Sumerian nations date from 5000 BCE, if not earlier (Heichelheim 1958, Bromberg 1942). These first interest-bearing loans were of food, such as dates, olives, figs, nuts, or seeds, with a portion of the resulting harvest paid as interest, or animals, with interest set as a fixed percentage of the animals born subsequently. Heichelheim (1958: 105) notes that the Sumerian word for interest and calves was identical, and that the Egyptian word for interest derived from the verb *to give birth*. The development of towns in the fourth millennium BCE led to increased use of inorganic moneys—especially metals—and interest-bearing loans in these newer materials. Lending was both secured and unsecured, and interest rates varied with business conditions. By the time of the Hammurabi dynasty in the first half of the second millennium BCE, more sophisticated forms of lending, denominated in goods and metal, were known. Orsingher (1967: viii) notes that the Code of Hammurabi, ". . . contains about 150 paragraphs which deal with nearly all cases arising from loans, interest, pledges, guarantees, the presence or absence of evidence, natural accidents, loss, theft, etc."

The ancient world was also familiar with deposit-taking. An early form of deposit was the "closed deposit," which resembled a safe deposit box more than a modern bank deposit. In classical Greece, these deposits, which may have included documents in addition to money, were frequently left in sealed containers in temples. Depositors paid a fee at the time of the deposit, and their containers were labeled with a record of the contents and instructions as to how to recognize, by means of a symbol, a legitimate claimant to the contents (Westermann 1930: 34–36, Heichelheim 1964: 76). A so-called "irregular deposit," the proceeds of which could be loaned out by the banker, consisted of money placed on deposit with a person or institution. In redeeming such a deposit, the banker needed only to return an equivalent amount of money—not the identical coins—as had been placed on deposit (Orsingher 1967: 3, Calhoun 1930).

Thus, the principal functions of modern banking predate the emergence of banking institutions by more than two thousand years. In addition to loans and deposits, the ancient world saw the development of money changing, coin assaying, accounting, a system whereby agents took in and paid out money on behalf of clients, and a mechanism for banks to accomplish book transfers of funds between customers without the need for a physical transfer of money.[5]

---

[5]Heichelheim (1964: 77) argues that such cashless transfers (giro) did not take place before the fourth century BCE because of the cumbersome nature of the written contract that governed irregular deposits, although he admits that this is disputed in the historical literature.

Banking in ancient Greece evolved out of money changing. In fact, the Greek word trapezite designated both a banker and a money changer. Bogaert (1968: 305ff.) cites Usher (1943: 3), who asserts that during the Middle Ages, "[i]t is difficult to distinguish trade in coin and bullion from deposit banking in the strict sense of the word." The large number of city-states and variety of weights and fineness of coins in circulation in the Greek world made money changing and assaying an important function. The first coins are believed to have been minted in Lydia, located in what is now Turkey, during the seventh century BCE, and the first trapezitae appeared within a century or so. Money changers soon began to attract deposits in the course of their exchange business and, in time, used these funds to extend credit.

By the time they were established in Rome, banks had existed in the Greek world for more than a century. It is therefore unlikely that Roman bankers evolved out of money changers, but rather emulated the existing Greek model.[6] Roman banks developed even more specialized functions, including professional money-receiver (coactor) and money-receiver/ deposit banker (coactor argentarius). Bankers also attended auctions, providing credit to buyers.

The evolution of banking from the fall of Rome until the emergence of joint stock banking more than one thousand years later was by no means direct or continuous and contains many substantial gaps in both time and space. In the spirit of that meandering development, this chapter also takes a nonlinear path, considering, in rough chronological order, the development of some of the main elements that comprise modern joint stock banking.

CREDIT CREATION

Although taking deposits and making loans constitute the key occupations of bankers, economists have long argued that the essential function of banking involves the creation and transfer of credit. Credit creation consists of issuing notes or creating deposits beyond the amount

---

[6]Despite the fact that the first Roman bankers were known as *argentarii*, Andreau (1999: 30ff.) argues that they did not originate as silversmiths. Silversmiths were known as *fabri argentarii* or *vascularii argentarii*, but never simply *argentarii*. He also notes that the variety of moneys in circulation was far more limited in the Roman world, further reducing the centrality of the money-changing function of bankers. *Nummularii*, or money changers/ assayers, did not become involved in deposit banking until the first half of the second century CE. See also Orsingher (1967: 5–10).

of money on deposit (Schumpeter 1934, Usher 1943, and Hicks 1969). Money changing—simply exchanging one currency for another, a common activity of early bankers—does not constitute banking under this definition. Put succinctly by Schumpeter (1934: 73), "It is always a question, not of transforming purchasing power which already exists in someone's possession, but of the creation of purchasing power out of nothing . . ."

For example, consider a simplified economy in which the only recognized money is gold. Barter may take place on a small scale, but the principal medium of exchange is gold of a certain defined weight and fineness. If banks merely provide depositors with safekeeping, holding gold on behalf of customers, they do not create credit. Similarly, banks do not create credit if they operate as money changers, exchanging coins of one jurisdiction for those of another. Finally, if banks take in a quantity of gold on deposit and lend out the same amount, they again do not create credit since the quantity of credit remains limited to the total amount of gold held on deposit.

Consider, however, an alternative situation familiar to readers of introductory economics texts. Suppose again that gold is the only widely used money. The very wealthy might be able to afford a castle or at least to hire armed guards to protect their treasure. Those with not quite so much gold might be prepared to pay a reputable third party with good security to keep their gold for them. Goldsmiths, since they dealt in large quantities of precious metals, would have had a safe or other means to secure their own gold. Thus, for a fee, individuals deposited gold with a goldsmith for safekeeping, and in return received a receipt indicating exactly how much gold was held on deposit. Initially, depositors went to the goldsmith every time they wanted to make a transaction, the goldsmith returned as much of the depositor's gold as requested, and altered the receipt accordingly. With the passage of time, instead of making trips to the goldsmith in order to make a withdrawal, receipts were passed from hand to hand as currency. The receipts retained value since they represented a quantity of gold that could be withdrawn at any time.

Because a substantial portion of receipts remained in circulation, goldsmiths eventually came to realize that they could issue more receipts than they had gold in the vault (what we know today as "fractional reserve banking"), and could create and lend excess receipts at interest. This is the beginning of credit creation or, in the words of Schumpeter, "creating new purchasing power out of nothing." Credit-creating loans (i.e., loans over and beyond the amount of gold reserves held) need not be extended in receipts, but could take the form of deposits, as long as those deposits are somehow spendable, either via written order to a third party or via

TABLE 2.1
Balance Sheet of Child's Bank, London (mid-1680s)

Assets		Liabilities	
Cash	£57,622	Deposits (receipts)	£100,000
Loans	£29,620		
Diamonds, rings, etc.	£12,758		
Total	£100,000	Total	£100,000

Source: Joslin (1954: 168). Figures approximate.

a transfer on the books of a banker.[7] Kindleberger (1984: 35) calls this "usual textbook story" about the beginnings of banking "well told, but inaccurate," since goldsmiths only evolved into bankers in England in the middle of the seventeenth century. Bogaert (1968) argues that banks did, in fact, evolve from coin dealers and assayers. True or not, the story is instructive.

Table 2.1 presents an approximation of the balance sheet of Francis Child, a prominent London goldsmith banker in the mid-1680s. Assets, what the bank owns or is owed, consist of vault cash, outstanding loans, and the precious metals and stones that constituted the goldsmith's working capital. Liabilities, or what the bank owes, consist of the receipts that circulate or, equivalently, of the evidence of deposits at the bank. The amount by which receipts exceed the vault cash, or just over £42,000, is the extent of credit creation. In other words, for each £1 of bank liability, Child held nearly £0.58 in cash. Over the next two centuries, as the business of banking became more established, bankers needed even less cash to secure their deposits: by 1885 the joint stock banks of England and Wales held approximately 12 percent of their deposits in cash (Sheppard 1971: 118).

Credit-creating, fractional reserve banking presents the banker with conflicting goals. On the one hand, by lending as many receipts as possible, the banker can earn a greater return. On the other hand, by issuing too many notes the banker runs the risk that depositors with claims representing greater sums than the banker has in the vault will request payment. When this occurs, unless the banker is able to call in or sell loans, or borrow money elsewhere, the bank will be forced to close.

[7]This is why the transfer of funds is essential to the business of banking. Usher (1934: 400) notes the distinction in a 1421 Venice ordinance between *contadi di banco*, bank money, and *denari contadi*, or cash.

MEDIEVAL BEGINNINGS, MODERN PREREQUISITES

The barbarian invasions that led to the fall of the Roman Empire in the west in 476 CE put a stop to further innovations in banking, and indeed to banking itself, for many years (Orsingher 1967: 10). Money changing, small scale moneylending, and pawn-broking were all that remained of banking for the next six centuries. Scholars date the emergence of primitive banks of deposit to the close of the twelfth century, although documentary evidence of credit-creating banks is scarce until the thirteenth century.[8] The development of a credit-creating banking system rested on the evolution of a variety of legal, accounting, and financing techniques which took place gradually over a period stretching back to antiquity and, consequently, are difficult to date precisely (Usher 1943: 95). These include enforceable contracts, written orders of payment, negotiability, and book transfers, some of which date from Roman times, some of which developed much later (Lopez 1971: 73–79, Usher 1943: 28ff.).

Among the most important of these prerequisites was the development of written orders of payment, which made it practical to transmit large sums of money over substantial distances. In the absence of such orders or financial institutions with widely dispersed branches or agencies, transactions would have to take place by the physical transfer of metallic money, which was risky: Spufford (1988: 255n) cites the example of Pope John XXII's shipment of 60,000 florins to pay his army in Lombardy, which, despite the presence of an armed guard of 150 cavalrymen, was ambushed and robbed of half of the money.

Prior to the emergence of the bill of exchange, the vast majority of financial contracts were oral, taking place with the assistance of witnesses and, from later Roman times, public notaries who kept written records of the contract. They were frequently concluded by the transfer of purchasing power from one depositor to another on the books of their mutual banker, or of their two bankers who could make book transfers between them. Among the earliest medieval written orders of payment was the *cambium*, or exchange contract. Popular from the thirteenth to the early fourteenth century, the cambium was "a solemn and verbose promise," executed by a notary. The *cambium nauticum*, or sea exchange contract, was similar, although the payment of the debt in this case was contingent on the safe arrival of the ship. The main feature of these exchange contracts was the receipt of money with a promise to repay at a specified

[8]Hotchkiss (1888: 13) asserts definitively that, "[t]he first chartered bank on this planet was established at Venice in the year 1171." Usher (1934: 404) notes the presence of the word "bankers" in notarial documents from Genoa spanning the years 1155 to 1164 and in records from Sienna in 1156; however, he suggests that these references may have been to merchants who extended credit to their customers, rather than to full-fledged deposit bankers.

time and place in a foreign currency. Cambia frequently contained clauses allowing both parties to specify that agents could conduct the transaction on their behalf, although this did not transform it into a negotiable instrument since the transaction still had to be concluded by the contracting parties (De Roover 1948a: 51).

Medieval fairs constituted an important stage in the development of credit-creating banking. Unlike local markets, which took place in countless towns across Europe and processed primarily local transactions (the settlement of which typically occurred in metallic money, book transfers, or local loans), fairs existed primarily to deal in wholesale interregional trade. Fairs took place in a variety of places, including Bruges and Antwerp in the Low Countries; Besançon, Champagne, and Lyons in France; Geneva in Switzerland; Medina del Campo in Spain; and around Genoa in Italy. Among the most important of these were the fairs of Champagne where, among other things, silks and spices that had made their way to Italy from the east and Flemish cloth were traded.[9]

It is difficult to date the beginning of the fairs with any precision, or to determine when banking became an important part of the business conducted. Usher (1943: 115ff.) notes references to fairs in Champagne in the late Roman period and in the ninth century, although he says that there is no evidence that the fairs existed continuously during the entire period and dates the beginning of large scale trading as occurring in the twelfth century. What is known is that any particular fair occurred at regular intervals, typically every three or six months, for set periods of time. The fairs, which lasted anywhere from two weeks to fifty-one days had periods designated for the trading of particular items. For example, for the fair of St. Ayoul at Provins, which lasted from September 14 through November 1, nine days were set aside for trade in cloth, eleven days for leather, and two weeks for *avoirdupois* (spices, drugs, and other goods sold by weight). At the settlement period, during the last of the three trading sessions, officials of the fair would validate claims in merchants' books, canceling out credits and debits in order to minimize the need to exchange money. Payment would then be effected with coins, cambia, bills of exchange, or new bills drawn to carry the claim over to the next fair.

The cambium became less popular during the fourteenth century, roughly contemporary with, and perhaps a result of, the decline of the fairs at Champagne—where much long distance trade took place face to face and, conveniently, in the presence of notaries—as well as the establishment of correspondent banking networks, and was largely replaced

---

[9]Ehrenberg (1928), Usher (1943), Kindleberger (1984), Verlinden (1963), and De Roover (1963: 42–43).

by the bill of exchange. Scholars date the introduction of the modern bill of exchange as early as the thirteenth century, although evidence exists of a similar instrument in the Roman Empire. The bill of exchange, which emerged during a period of relatively rapid economic growth and increasing international trade, facilitated the development of new ways of doing business and new types of commerce (Bernard 1976: 174). For example, the bill of exchange allowed a greater amount of interregional trade without quite so much travel on the part of the principals and their money and made it easier to transfer funds for commercial and non-commercial purposes.

Unlike the cambium, which involved only two parties, the bill of exchange typically involved four: two principals (e.g., importer and exporter) and two corresponding merchants who effected payment. A bill of exchange consisted of a brief letter from one merchant to the other, requesting that funds on behalf of the importer be paid to the exporter in a distant city (in the distant city's local currency) at a particular future date. A bill of exchange could have arisen as a consequence of a commercial transaction or, alternatively, could have been used to pay off a debt or transfer money.

The bill of exchange was composed of two different transactions. First, the bill was a foreign exchange transaction, since the exporter was typically paid in a currency other than that of the importer. Second, the bill was a loan, since the funds were not paid until sometime in the future. Because of the Catholic Church's prohibition against usury, the interest component of these transactions during the Middle Ages was usually disguised within the exchange component (Le Goff 1979). According to Hicks (1969: 78):

> It was sinful to lend at interest (the sort of sin one confessed on one's deathbed), but it was a sin that was very generally committed. It was better for the interest element to be concealed . . . the combination of a loan with an exchange transaction was the commonest way of concealing it. But it is not to be supposed that the merchants themselves, or the lawyers who were concerned with mercantile transactions, were taken in by such devices. They were becoming very tolerant. There is evidence that by such people, in fourteenth-century Florence, only rates of interest in excess of 20 percent were regarded as usurious; 15–20 percent has been described as a 'grey zone.'[10]

In the Middle Ages, parties held bills of exchange until maturity and collected the funds due. Starting in the sixteenth century, bills of exchange

---

[10]A. Sapori, 'L'interesse del denaro,' in his *Studi di storia economica medievale*, Florence (1947: 111).

gradually became negotiable: if the payee wanted to receive funds prior to the maturity date of a bill, the bill could be "discounted," that is, ownership could be transferred to another party by means of an endorsement in return for the amount inscribed on the bill minus interest.[11] When a bill was endorsed in this way, the endorser, in addition to the issuer, acquired responsibility for the bill's eventual payment. As bills were serially endorsed, they acquired more and more guarantors and thus became more secure.

The development of negotiability further enhanced the role of bills of exchange in both commercial and strictly financial transactions. Negotiability allowed the evolution of written orders of payment from a simple means of transferring funds into a financial instrument which could be priced, traded, and used to move funds for non-commercial purposes. The development of the bill of exchange both facilitated long-range commerce by reducing the need for metallic money in transactions, and contributed to credit creation.

The fairs of Champagne began to decline after 1300. By this time, Italian merchants had set up permanent offices to act as correspondents in Bruges and elsewhere in Flanders, reducing the need for fairs. Soon after arriving, merchants from different regions (e.g., Genoa, Venice, Lucca, Florence, Milan) established settlements ("colonies"), and sought official diplomatic recognition of their incorporation and to obtain commercial privileges from the local authorities. By the second half of the fifteenth century, trade in Antwerp—which had taken over from Bruges—became a permanent, year-round feature and, in 1531, an exchange was built. The exchange, patterned on the one in Place de la Bourse in Bruges, was called the bourse, from which the word for stock market derives in many languages (De Roover 1942: 54). With the siege of Antwerp by the Spanish and the Dutch in the late sixteenth century, the principal market moved to Amsterdam, which dominated trade and finance for the next 150 years (Kindleberger 1984: 36, De Roover 1948a: 13, 1963: 43).

GOVERNMENT DEBT AND THE BEGINNINGS OF GOVERNMENT BANKS

The late Middle Ages and early Renaissance saw the rise of nation-states and, increasingly, wars between them. In order to finance these wars, as

[11]Usher (1943: 98) asserts that negotiability came to be accepted between 1527 and 1728. De Roover (1948a: 54) dates the earliest negotiable bills in Italy to 1611. Neal (1990: 7) suggests that negotiability was known in Antwerp prior to 1585. See also Van der Wee (1963: 340).

well as to provide public goods, states began to borrow. From the point of view of banking, the development of public debt led to two important innovations. First, public debt was among the first examples of long-term debt. Commercial loans had, for the most part, been of short duration, usually no more than several months, in order to fund a specific commercial venture.[12] Second, these debts led some governments to found public banks to manage their obligations.

When the Venetian Treasury was exhausted in 1156, the Doge Vital Michel proposed levying a forced loan on Venice's wealthiest citizens, assuring them a 4 percent return: Des Essars (1896: 153) claims this to be the first example of public debt. Within several years, the debts were consolidated into a *monte*, ". . . or fund of indebtedness, in which loans . . . lost their individuality and became claims, sometimes to the repayment of principal but always to payment of interest."[13] In Venice, the monte came to be known as the Monte Vecchio, or "Old Loan Fund," so-called after the subsequent establishment of two loan funds, the Monte Nuovo, or "New Loan Fund," in 1482, and the Monte Nuovissimo, or "Newest Loan Fund," in 1509 (Lane 1937: 198, Mueller 1997: 453). Shares in the monti could be transferred on the books of the institution, and hence were marketable. The markets for these claims were frequently quite active.[14]

Although Des Essars (1896: 154) argues that the remains of the monti ". . . served for the construction of the Bank of Venice," Dunbar (1892) makes it clear that the first public bank in Venice, the Banco della Piazza di Rialto, which was authorized by an act of the Venetian Senate in 1584 and opened in 1587, was neither an outgrowth of the monti nor related to the Bank of Venice, which was created in 1619. The Banco della Piazza di Rialto was modeled on the Bank of Barcelona (1401),[15] Bank of Valencia

---

[12]In the same way that private borrowers might have secured loans by pledging the rents from a specific property or transaction to the lender (Usher 1943: 135), public debts were sometimes guaranteed by revenues from specific sources. For example, in 1164 twelve men lent 1,150 marks of silver to Venice in return for a claim on the revenues of the state-owned Rialto market. In Verona, ". . . citizens who had lent some 27,000 ducats during the war against the coalition of Venice and Florence (1337–39) formed themselves into a consortium, the *Universitas Civium*, which established control over the large parts of the public domain which had been pledged as surety." Mueller (1997: 456, 459).

[13]The description is of the debts of Venice, Genoa, and Florence. Mueller (1997: 456).

[14]The Bank of Saint George (*Casa di San Georgio*), established in Genoa in 1407, was similarly an amalgamation of creditors of the state which had claims on certain public revenues. It began to take deposits in 1586.

[15]The Bank of Barcelona was created as a department of the city government in order to provide credit to the city. Deposits in the bank were guaranteed by the city. Usher (1943).

(1408), and other institutions in Spain, and had three main functions: (1) to accept and repay deposits; (2) to make transfers between accounts; and (3) credit bills of exchange payable to clients. This innovation spread with the establishment of government-sponsored public banks of deposit and transfer in Milan (Banco di San Ambrogio, 1593) and Rome (Banco del Spirito Santo, 1605) (Parker 1974: 549).

In Amsterdam, as in Barcelona, the city took an active role in the promotion of a bank. Unlike the Italian banks mentioned above, which were founded in order to finance state debt, the government bank in Amsterdam was introduced to help bring order to a confused monetary system by establishing a standard monetary unit, economizing on the use of coin, and rationalizing the payments system.

After the decline of Antwerp in the late sixteenth century, Amsterdam grew in importance as a commercial and financial center. Because of this growth, the volume and variety of financial transactions rose substantially, leading to an increase in the circulation of many types of written orders of payment and different intermediators. Among the most important of these intermediators were "cashiers" or "cash-keepers" (*kassiers*). Cashiers were merchants' agents who were authorized to pay their creditors and collect debts owed. This class of intermediator grew rapidly, as did the wide circulation of their written orders of payment, which were endorsable (Van der Borght 1896: 196–200, 't Hart, Jonker, and Van Zanden 1997: 42ff.).

Simultaneously, the currency situation in the Netherlands had become quite disorganized. The Revolt in the Netherlands in 1572 resulted in a decentralized monetary system, including the establishment of fourteen official mints. As a result, many different types of coins—foreign and domestic—came into circulation. By the end of the sixteenth century, nearly 800 foreign coins were officially permitted in the Dutch Republic while the coins of one province were not necessarily permitted to circulate in another. It was not until 1638 that Amsterdam and 1659 that the States General introduced a standardized silver guilder.

The combination of the disorganized monetary situation and the multiplicity of money dealers led the city of Amsterdam to establish the Amsterdam Wisselbank (Exchange Bank) in 1609 (Quinn and Roberds 2006). Simultaneously the city temporarily outlawed cashiers, guaranteeing the bank a central place in the financial system. Modeled in part on the Banco della Piazza di Rialto and a similar institution in Seville, the bank was to receive deposits—which were to be guaranteed by the city—and effect transfers between customers through a clearing system based on accounts held at the bank in standard guilders (Van Dillen 1934: 79–80). The Wisselbank did not extend credit, but all substantial bills of exchange (600 guilders or above, 300 guilders from 1643) were required to be deposited, at least initially, into the bank.[16] The bank earned fees because all major merchants had to have accounts in order to redeem bills of exchange on which they were the payee. The system was copied in other Dutch cities and elsewhere in northern Europe.

The emergence of government debt, and banks to manage that debt and to relieve monetary confusion, marked the beginning of a new phase in banking. This stage saw the beginning of long-term lending, a distinct departure from banking practices of earlier times. The development of government banks, either for rationalizing the payments system, as in the case of the Wisselbank, or for managing the public debt, as in Venice, was also a radical departure from previous practice. The establishment of the Wisselbank, in particular, and its focus on effecting transfers among depositors, was an especially important advance because it both established deposit banking in Amsterdam and made it an indispensable element of the economy.

GOVERNMENT BANKS

The model of the Wisselbank was very much on the mind of the Swedish king and his advisors when, in 1656, he granted a charter to Johan Palmstruch to open Stockholms Banco (Bank of Stockholm). The government had wanted to establish a bank, but had been unsuccessful: various proposals had been raised during the preceding fifty years and, in fact, a charter had been issued ten years earlier, although the bank never commenced operation. Thus, Palmstruch's petition to create a bank that would "deal in exchange and grant loans for the advantage of commercial enterprise" came at an opportune time (Flux 1910: 13). The motivation for granting a charter was to provide both a source of credit and exchange facilities. Palmstruch's plan was to create a bank with two departments: an Exchange Bank (Wexelbank, a literal translation of the Dutch Wisselbank), to take deposits and make transfers, and a Lending Bank (Länebank, from Amsterdam's Huys van Leening), to make loans for a term of one year and six weeks.

Although the bank's charter did not grant it the right to issue banknotes, as early as 1661 it had begun to do so, making it the first bank of issue in Europe. Before long, however, the over-issue of notes led to financial difficulties and the revocation of the charter in 1668. Despite the failure of Palmstruch's bank, it was thought that the institution had been useful,

---

[16]The city of Amsterdam established the Huys van Leening (Bank of Lending) in 1614, which did extend credit. Heckscher (1934: 162), 't Hart, Jonker, and Van Zanden (1997: 44ff.).

so the Parliament, the Diet of the Four Estates, took it over and reconstituted the bank with a new charter as the Riksens Ständers Bank (Estates of the Realm Bank), renamed the Riksbank in the nineteenth century. The new charter prohibited the institution from issuing banknotes, although by 1701 it was doing just that (Capie et al. 1994: 123–24). The notes were innovative in that they were printed according to a form (with only some parts filled out by hand) and denominated in round numbers. The widespread acceptance of paper money was no doubt enhanced by Sweden's copper currency, which featured coins weighing as much as 19.7 kilograms, or about forty-three pounds (Heckscher 1934: 170–71).

The widespread acceptance of notes was an important milestone in the development of credit-creating banking for two reasons. First, it allowed banks to create credit in the form of banknotes, without which the only effective means for a bank to extend credit was via deposit creation. Deposit creation could only have been effective if the use of deposit accounts, written orders of payment, and book transfers was widespread. The use of notes allowed credit creation even where deposit banking was not well developed. Second, unlike bills of exchange, banknotes had no maturity date, and hence could circulate indefinitely. The longer a given quantity of notes circulated outside of the issuing institution, the more notes the institution could put in circulation and the greater the net credit creation.

In England, the motive for founding a government bank was overwhelmingly fiscal. Founded in 1694, the Bank of England was established to help the government raise money for war against France.[17] The bank's capital of £1,200,000 was accumulated through stock subscriptions which were loaned to the government in return for an annual payment of £100,000 per year. The bank was expressly given the power to issue notes which were to be redeemable in silver and which competed with the notes issued by the government and private banks. The bank was also permitted to trade bills of exchange and bullion, but was not allowed to deal in goods. Customers could maintain deposit accounts with the bank, which were transferable to other parties via written orders of payment (Richards 1929, Clapham 1945, I: 15ff., Capie et al. 1994: 127). Thus, the bank was an issuer of both notes and transferable written orders of payment.

Neither the Riksbank nor the Bank of England were central banks at the time of their founding, although they—and many government banks founded later—did evolve into central banks. Modern central banks act

---

[17] In addition to the need to raise money, ". . . the view had become current that a bank was needed to stabilize financial activity in London, which had been subject to periodic fluctuations in the availability of currency and credit." Capie et al. (1994: 126).

as a country's monetary authority, regulating domestic credit conditions and, depending on the exchange rate regime, intervening in the foreign exchange market. In its role as regulator of domestic credit, the central bank typically serves as the bankers' bank, and, in time of crisis, as the banking system's lender of last resort. Central banks may also serve as the government's fiscal agent and, increasingly in recent years, have been designated as the principal banking supervisor. Prior to the nineteenth century, however, there was no accepted concept of a central bank. Although the modern notion of a central bank can be traced as far back as Baring (1797 [1993]) and Thornton (1802 [1939]), it was only with the 1873 publication of Bagehot's classic, *Lombard Street*, that the modern concept of central bank began to gain widespread acceptance.

In most cases, the government banks that would evolve into central banks were merely the first government-chartered banking institutions in the country.[18] The government banks of Sweden (1668), England (1694), Finland (1811), Norway (1816), Austria (1816), and Denmark (1818) were, at the time of their founding, the first and only chartered banks in these countries, although those of Austria and Denmark had defunct predecessors. In some cases, they remained the only bank for a considerable period of time, often because the demand for banking services was low. Following the initial charter of the Riksbank, for example, no other bank was chartered in Sweden for more than a century; in Finland and Denmark, additional chartered banks were not established for several decades after the founding of the government bank. Appendix table 2.1 describes the circumstances surrounding the creation of a number of government, subsequently central, banks.

Frequently, government banks were chartered with a public purpose in mind: clearing up monetary disarray (e.g., Denmark, Norway), raising funds for the government (e.g., England), or facilitating trade by extending banking services (e.g., the Netherlands). The new institutions also frequently acted as the government's fiscal agent. Despite these public purposes, sometimes combined with provisions granting the government the right to appoint some of the bank's management, the first government banks were typically private profit-maximizing institutions, albeit with special privileges and/or responsibilities.[19]

A key motivation for the establishment of many government banks was to clear up monetary disarray. For example, shortly after Finland

---

[18]Exceptions include Japan, where commercial banking predated the establishment of a central bank by a decade, and Australia and Canada, which did not establish central banks until about a century after the foundation of their first commercial banks.

[19]Exceptions include Sweden's Riksbank and the Royal Giro and Loan Bank of Berlin (Konigliche Giro- und Lehn- bank zu Berlin), which were publicly owned. The reconstituted Prussian Bank, however, was not wholly government-owned.

was annexed to Russia, the Bank of Finland was established in order to drive Swedish currency out of circulation in favor of Russian. The Austrian National Bank was established with a monopoly on banknote issue following several decades that had been characterized by an over-issue of government currency. And the establishment of government banks in Norway (1816) and Denmark (1818) followed a period of monetary confusion, which culminated in the *Statsbankerot* (state bankruptcy) in Denmark. Both of these banks were given a monopoly on note-issuing at the time of their founding. Later in the nineteenth century, following national unification, the German Reichsbank (1876)[20] and the Banca d'Italia (1893)[21] were positioned to consolidate several preexisting note-issuing institutions.

In addition to any role government banks may have been given in sorting out monetary confusion, they frequently played a large role in providing government finance. The classic case is the Bank of England, which was granted a charter in return for a loan of £1.2 million. Napoleon's creation of the Bank of France in 1800 was intended both to provide war finance and to establish monetary order following the collapse of the Revolution's inflationary *assignat* regime. A selling point advanced by partisans of both the First (1791–1811) and Second (1816–36) Banks of the United States was that they would enhance the government's ability to raise funds, as well as promote credit creation and monetary stability.

Other government banks were created to provide credit to the economy and to stimulate commerce. The Netherlands Bank was established during a period of slack economic activity, in part to replace the Wisselbanken of Amsterdam and other cities which had begun to decline in the 1790s. The National Bank of Belgium was similarly founded to contribute to domestic commerce following the revolutions and monetary disturbances of 1848 as well as to issue notes and handle public moneys.

The functions that we associate today with central banks were largely absent during the early years of most of these government banks. Although a number of the early government banks were founded in order to clear up monetary disarray, only a minority were, in fact, given a monopoly of domestic note issue at the time of their establishment, although all had some monetary role. The development of the government bank as a banker's bank and keeper of the reserves of the banking

---

[20]Shortly after its establishment, seventeen of thirty-three note-issuing banks in Germany ceded their note issue privileges to the Reichsbank. The Reichsbank traces its ancestry back to the Royal Giro and Loan Bank, which was founded by Frederick the Great of Prussia in 1765 to provide credit and monetary stability following the Seven Years' War. This was liquidated and reconstituted as the Prussian Bank in 1846.

[21]The Banca d'Italia replaced four banks of issue (Banca Nazionale del Regno, Banca Nazionale Toscana, Banca Toscana di Credito, and Banca Romana, which was liquidated in 1892). The Bank of Naples and Bank of Sicily continued to issue notes until 1926.

system was also a later development. And these banks did not adopt the role of lender of last resort until well after their founding.

The role of banking supervisor was assuredly not on the minds of the founders of government banks. First, these banks were often the first chartered commercial bank of any sort, and frequently the only such bank for many years. It is therefore extremely unlikely that the founders would have been foresighted enough to envision a situation in which there would be a banking "system" to regulate and supervise. Any preexisting private banks, typically partnerships which operated without explicit government sanction or charter, would have been well outside the purview of any regulators. Second, as noted above, these banks were private, profit-maximizing institutions. Hence, it is unlikely that governments would have put them in charge of supervising their competitors.

The establishment of government banks was an important step along the road to incorporated commercial banking. These banks were frequently a country's first chartered commercial bank. In some countries, they were the first chartered bank for decades and therefore, in some way, may have served as a model for the banks that were to follow. The creation of government banks was frequently connected to the establishment of a stable monetary unit and uniform currency, which created a common unit of account. Importantly, government banks frequently established discounting facilities, further enhancing the marketability and usefulness of debt instruments and, therefore, enhancing credit creation.

PRIVATE BANKS

The charters of the government banks discussed above granted the bank a corporate identity and spelled out, sometimes in great detail, what sorts of business the bank could—and could not—conduct. Usually, government banks were authorized to make loans, take deposits, discount bills of exchange, and deal in gold, silver, and other monies; they were typically prohibited from dealing in goods and real estate beyond what was needed for banking premises.[22] Some government banks were explicitly permitted to issue notes, although others took on this role without specific authorization. They were frequently required to report to the government or some government-appointed body on their condition, hence, many modern central banks have some statistical records of their earliest years. And although government banks were frequently assigned specific responsibilities toward the government that granted the charter, they were by and large private, profit-maximizing institutions.

[22]The Riksbank was expressly permitted to operate its paper mills and printing works.

Although government banks were typically the first chartered banks in most countries, they were not usually the first banks of any sort: that distinction was generally held by private banks. Private bank, in this case, refers to an entity that operated as a partnership (i.e., unincorporated) and without the explicit sanction of the government in the form of a charter. A private bank was an association of individuals that were governed by the terms of their partnership agreement and were not bound by laws beyond those that applied to individuals.

Because private banks were unchartered, they were not restricted to specific fields of endeavor and hence could engage in a variety of banking and non-banking activities. These included money changing, pawnbroking, cash-keeping, and, most importantly, providing domestic and international trade credit. In discussing private banking in the Rhineland during the first half of the nineteenth century, Tilly (1966: 47) writes:

> [T]here is great uncertainty as to when a man was a banker and when he was not. Many persons provided banking services—either as a sideline or on a small scale—long before they called themselves bankers. . . . At the same time, the title 'banker' was sometimes given to a businessman whose resources were employed mainly in non-banking lines.

Frequently, private banks started out as purely commercial—and often family-based—firms and, because of the need to extend credit for trade finance, evolved into institutions where banking soon overshadowed the non-financial side of the business.

Private bankers had already been in existence in London for at least a half a century when the Bank of England was founded in 1694: there were reportedly twenty-nine in 1754, fifty-one in 1776, and fifty-two in 1786, although these figures likely understate the true number (Cameron 1967: 20–22, Joslin 1954: 173). These included goldsmith bankers and others that, prior to the establishment of the Bank of England, had issued notes. Private banknote issues were soon driven out of circulation by the banknotes issued by the much larger Bank of England, which had been granted in its charter the privilege of "exclusive banking" (i.e., the only joint stock bank) in England and Wales. The London private bankers compensated for the eclipse of their banknote issues by developing other aspects of the private banking business: taking deposits subject to check, issuing and dealing in bills of exchange, and serving as correspondents for their provincial clients.

Country banks (i.e., banks outside of London), which numbered about a dozen in 1750, grew to more than 600 around the turn of the nineteenth century. A total of 783 institutions were licensed to issue banknotes in 1810, although this figure is probably understated (Cameron 1967: 23–24, Pressnell 1956). These institutions arranged remittances to and from

London for both tax and commercial purposes, graded and sold bills of exchange, and issued currency.

Private banking predated the emergence of joint stock banking elsewhere as well. Despite the fact that French bankers kept a low profile during the Revolution, as many as sixty private banks and four joint stock banks were in operation before the Bank of France was founded in 1800 (Des Essars 1896: 8, Cameron 1967: 111). These private bankers engaged in a variety of activities, including discounting paper and loaning funds to business enterprises, although their main occupation was lending money to the government. In addition, French notaries took on some of the functions of private bankers (Hoffman, Postel-Vinay, and Rosenthal 2000). In the German Rhineland, private bankers invariably started out as wholesale merchants who loaned their capital and extended credit as a sideline to their main business. Once established in banking, they began to take deposits and engage in credit creation. These institutions did not issue currency, which remained largely the province of the Bank of Prussia, but did issue and deal in bills of exchange.

The emergence of private banks preceded that of incorporated commercial banks in other countries as well. There were eighty-four private bankers in Belgium in 1833, at which time the only chartered bank was the Société Générale, which undertook a range of activities, although deposit taking does not seem to have been an important one (Cameron 1967: 131ff.). In Austria, private bankers included large private houses that made loans to the government and nobility and were the primary customers of the government bank (Rudolph 1976: 68, 91). In the Netherlands most towns had a cashier or two, who changed money, made short-term—and occasionally long-term—loans, and retailed securities, although they rarely took deposits ('t Hart, Jonker, and Van Zanden 1997: 98, Jonker 1996a: 233–48). And in Switzerland private banks, with origins in trade, emerged in Basel, Geneva, Berne, and Zurich in the late eighteenth century (Schwartzenback 1929: 1076).

In Australia, private banking began shortly after settlement. According to Butlin (1953: 13) the equipment of the First Fleet did not include money, since it was expected that the colony would be populated primarily by convicts, who would work as directed, and by their guards, who would be paid by the government. The circulation of tokens and notes ("currency") and the issuing of notes ("petty banking") within a very few years of settlement became widespread enough to catch the attention of the governor, William Bligh, who attempted to do away with currency by a widely ignored order of 1807. Bligh's successor, Lachlan Macquarie, who arrived in 1809, planned to do away with the business of petty banking by supporting the establishment a chartered bank, the Bank of New South Wales. His plans were thwarted until 1817.

It is impossible to precisely date the beginnings of private banking. Whereas government banks typically came into existence with a birth certificate in the form of an act of the legislature or a charter granted by the sovereign, private banks emerged gradually, and without any official paperwork. Frequently, they began their existence as non-financial firms and only entered banking some years later. The lack of enabling legislation and rules and regulations that inevitably accompanied the beginnings of government banks, and the multiplicity of names and forms under which they conducted business, makes it much harder to trace the development of private banking. Yet private banks are important predecessors of the modern commercial bank. They were the first note issuers in many countries, and were among first non-governmental providers of trade, industrial, and government finance. In time, the leading role in these areas was taken over by incorporated commercial banks.

COMMERCIAL BANKS

Why did incorporated commercial banking emerge? After all, government banks and private banks were already performing the functions that would later be adopted by commercial banks: taking deposits and providing credit for commercial transactions, the purchase of raw materials to be processed into finished goods, and the provision of fixed capital, among other things. Why didn't these banks remain the dominant financial institutions, instead of the commercial banks that would later supplant them? Demand side factors figure prominently in the answer. Starting in the eighteenth century, the growth and increasing complexity of economic activity raised the demand for financial services. The sources of the increased demand included the growth and commercialization of agriculture, greater urbanization, industrialization, and a substantial increase in the quantity of trade and commerce.[23] This increased demand for financing was met in part by the growth of debt and equity markets and in part by an increase in the facilities provided by banks.

Why was the increased demand for banking facilities not met with more or larger private banks? Even if private banks could have formed lending syndicates, it would have been less costly for the financing to be provided by fewer large firms than by many small ones. Why then, was this increase in demand for large-scale finance not met by ever-larger private banks? Private banks were frequently family-run concerns, with

---

[23]Deane (1979) discusses the various economic developments that immediately preceded British industrialization. See Pollard (1990) on industrialization more generally. Findlay and O'Rourke (2003) provide statistics on the growth of trade during 1500–2000.

resources limited to those of the family. Of course, such firms included those of the Rothschild family as well as other firms that commanded substantial resources, but more often than not were considerably smaller. In addition, because private banks were partnerships and were not chartered, they were not able to incorporate or to operate under limited liability. The absence of the corporate form, which enables individuals to more easily buy and sell shares of the firm, and of limited liability, which protects investors' personal assets in case the firm fails, made it difficult for private banks to raise sufficient funds to grow large enough to meet the needs generated by a growing economy.

Although strong demand was necessary for the emergence of incorporated commercial banking, purely economic factors alone were not sufficient. The timing of the process was crucially affected by political-economic factors, such as interest group pressure, ideology, and legal evolution. Appendix table 2.2 presents dates of establishment of the first private (i.e., non-government) incorporated commercial banks. The mere establishment of such a bank may not be the best measure of the vitality of commercial banking in a given place at a certain time: both the Netherlands and France, for example, had early experiences with joint stock banking, although Dutch and French incorporated commercial banks did not become common until much later. Nonetheless, examining at the earliest instances of these banks will help to identify the forces responsible for the transition from private to commercial banking.

The data suggest a positive relationship between demand factors and the emergence of commercial banking. Belgium and the Netherlands were the first countries in Europe to experiment with this type of banking and, in both cases, the sources of demand are apparent. Belgium, with its ample supplies of iron ore and coal, was the first country on the continent to develop capital-intensive heavy industry, increasing the demands for banking services.[24] The Netherlands had long been a leader in international trade and finance and had the highest GDP per capita in Europe during the first half of the nineteenth century, and so had both expertise with and demand for large-scale financing. Despite this demand, the first Dutch experiment with commercial banking was short-lived. The Associatie Cassa, established in Amsterdam in 1806, was a cashier-like institution which was chartered and took on commercial banking functions. This firm soon retreated from commercial banking, which would not reassert itself in the Netherlands until the second half of the nineteenth

[24]Pollard (1990: 23–26), Dhondt and Bruwier (1975), and Chlepner (1943). By contrast, Switzerland, also early to industrialize, did not develop incorporated commercial banking until somewhat later. This may have been because Swiss industrialization was based on less capital-intensive industries. Biucchi (1975).

century (Jonker 1996a: 239). One reason for this delay is that the sophisticated Dutch money market already served the needs of trade quite well and reduced the demand for commercial banking ('t Hart, Jonker, and Van Zanden 1997).

Demand factors appear to explain several intercountry differences in the timing of the emergence of commercial banking. Sweden, for example, industrialized relatively early vis-à-vis its Nordic neighbors, and was also the earliest of the four to develop commercial banking. The slowest of the four to develop economically, Finland, was the last to develop commercial banking. Similarly, the United States, which was more economically advanced than Canada, developed commercial banking forty years before its neighbor to the north. If demand was the only factor responsible for the transition from private to commercial banking, it would be fairly easy to predict the date—or at least the order—in which countries made that transition: commercial and industrial leaders would be in the vanguard; less sophisticated economies would lag. It is clear, however, that political-economic factors also affected banking development in a number of countries.

England was the first country to undergo an industrial revolution, generally reckoned to have occurred sometime during the eighteenth century, and was one of the world's most economically advanced countries of the time. Yet England did not charter its first private joint stock bank until 1826.[25] The delay in the establishment of joint stock banking can be attributed to two factors. First, the collapse of the South Sea Bubble in 1720 and the subsequent Bubble Act limited the use of joint stock corporations—including banks—until well into the nineteenth century. Second, and more importantly, the Bank of England used its leverage as the government's creditor to pressure it into maintaining the Bank of England's position as England's only incorporated commercial bank for more than 125 years. Political-economic factors also delayed the emergence of commercial banking in France. The disastrous effects of the first attempt at incorporated commercial banking, John Law's Banque Générale and Banque Royale, also around 1720, discouraged the French from founding anything with the word "bank" in the title until 1859. A second attempt, the Caisse d'Escompte, was established in 1766, but was suppressed by the Revolution in 1793. The Revolution, Napoleon's well-known mistrust of finance, and speculation further postponed the emer-

---

[25]Scottish banking development and law was quite distinct from that of England and Wales and is briefly discussed in chapter 7. For the most part, the discussion of banking in Britain focuses on England and Wales. Some data presented (e.g., GDP), are only available for Great Britain or the entire United Kingdom and are labeled as such.

gence of commercial banking in France, so that for most of the eighteenth and much of the nineteenth centuries, notaries and other private functionaries conducted most French banking functions (Des Essars 1896, Hoffman, Postel-Vinay, and Rosenthal 2000).

Legal evolution also played a role in the emergence of commercial banking, particularly with the nineteenth-century spread of general incorporation laws that allowed firms, often including banks, to incorporate more easily. In France, the corporation law of 1867 replaced charters granted by a central authority with simple registration, and applied to banks as well as to other type of firms. The French change can be traced, in part, to a desire to keep up with the liberal company law passed in Britain some years earlier (Freedeman 1979). In Germany, attempts to enact banking laws were forestalled by clauses in the constitution and a prevailing ideology supporting a laissez-faire economic environment (Honold 1956).

Interestingly, commercial banks emerged in a number of British colonies and ex-colonies prior to the mother country: the United States in 1780, Australia in 1817, and Canada in 1820. In the United States, the first and simplest reason for early banking development is "because they could." Independence from Britain nullified Parliament's 1740 declaration that the Bubble Act was to apply to the colonies. As a result, political or economic forces in favor of commercial banking would not be constrained by preexisting law or the influence of an existing government-sponsored bank. Second, the military expenditures brought about by the War of Independence put the government under fiscal stress. Robert Morris's plan that evolved into the Bank of North America was inspired in large part on the Bank of England's by then century-old ability to raise funds on behalf of the Crown. Finally, the founding and early success of the First Bank of the United States encouraged the establishment of more banks. In Australia, Lachlan Macquarie's single-handed chartering, with limited liability, of the Bank of New South Wales in 1817 has been discussed above. The first durable Australian bank charter was not approved by London until 1834.

Canada's first attempt at a commercial bank was the short-lived Canada Banking Company, established in 1792, about which little is known except that it did issue notes (Breckenridge 1910: 3). In 1817, nine Montreal merchants signed articles of association to form the Bank of Montreal (Shortt 1897a, McIvor 1958: 25). This bank operated without statutory authority, but soon petitioned the Legislature of Lower Canada for a charter. Although the request was initially turned down, it was approved the following year. Final approval of the charter, in the form of the Royal Assent, was not given until 1822. Among the reasons given for the early need for banking services were the confusing variety of currency and promissory notes in circulation, the general shortage of currency and capital, and the success of the First Bank of the United States.

Incorporated commercial banking emerged as the culmination of several centuries—even millennia—of development. Starting with the first moneylenders and deposit takers in the ancient world, banking evolved through the development of money, trade credit, medieval fairs, and— with the beginnings of the nation-state—through the evolution of government banks, and finally private banks. The eighteenth and nineteenth centuries saw the evolution of incorporated commercial banks. Although similar to their predecessors in many of the functions they undertook, the adoption of the corporate form and limited liability allowed commercial banks to become larger, more active players in the growing economies of the eighteenth and nineteenth centuries.

There is a clear correlation between economic development and the emergence of commercial banking. Although the association is clear, it need not imply causality: the correlation could be merely coincidental, although there are good reasons to believe that it is not. Each stage of banking development was accompanied by some important advance in political and economic development: public banks and the growth of the nation state, exchange banks, like the Wisselbank, and the growth of domestic trade, and private banks and the growth of interregional and international trade. Nonetheless, determining definitively the existence of a causal relationship, and the direction of causation, is a difficult task, and one beyond the scope of this work.

The pattern of banking evolution illustrates the potency of market forces. These forces, particularly the growth of trade and commerce, spurred the development of the bill of exchange and, later, both private and commercial banking. The historical experience also illustrates the difficulty of standing in the way of market forces for an extended period of time. For example, the Catholic Church's prohibition on payment of interest was evaded by combining exchange transactions with loan transactions. And although the British government opposed the emergence of joint stock banking in England and in the colonies, its opposition was ultimately ineffective. At home, the banking difficulties of the early 1820s made it clear to policymakers that the absence of joint stock banking was not in the public interest. The constraints that held back the mother country from developing joint stock banking did not exist in the colonies, allowing them to develop it earlier. In Australia this was accomplished by a determined and independent-minded colonial governor, in Canada by the local legislature, and in the United States by a revolution.

CHAPTER 3

Banking Crises

> It is astonishing how money grows when it is in the way of growing—when it has the genuine impulse and rolls every kindred atom near it, according to some occult law of attraction, into itself. But just as wonderfully as money grows does it melt away when the other—the contrary process—has begun.
> —Margaret Oliphant, *Hester*

> But, after all, there is no education like adversity.
> —Benjamin Disraeli, *Endymion*

> [A]nd the *Jules Flambeau* sank 5 minutes after the commander, the last one to go, left with the memorable words: "It can't be helped."
> —Karel Čapek, *War with the Newts*

ACCORDING TO CHARLES KINDLEBERGER (1996: 1), "There is hardly a more conventional subject in economic literature than financial crises." This is not surprising, given his catalogue of thirty-four financial crises during 1618–1990, or about one every eleven years. For the period 1800–1990, Kindleberger catalogues twenty-six crises, or about one every seven years. Despite the fact that the majority (seventeen out of twenty-six) of these crises took place before 1900, financial crises cannot be classified as relics of the nineteenth century: the Great Depression of the 1930s was, at least until 2009, widely considered to be by far the developed world's most severe financial crisis of all time.

Still, if modern financial crises were confined to the pre–World War II period, it might be reasonable to assert that they were no longer of importance. However, crises seem not to have gone out of style during the closing decades of the twentieth century, with severe episodes erupting in Asia, Latin America, Scandinavia, and elsewhere. Lindgren, Garcia, and Saal (1996: 20–35) find that 133—or nearly three-quarters—of the International Monetary Fund's 181 member countries experienced significant banking sector problems between 1980 and the spring of 1996. Of these, they classify forty-one instances in thirty-six countries, or nearly one-fifth of IMF membership, as crises. Bordo et al. (2001: 53) declare: "The crisis problem was one of the dominant features of the 1990s."

Nor did the crisis problem end with the twentieth century. The world-wide financial crisis that erupted in 2008, touched off by the collapse of the U.S. subprime mortgage market, was severe enough to prompt meaningful comparisons with the Great Depression. Further, Eichengreen and O'Rourke (2009) argue that the decline in worldwide economic activity one year into that crisis was comparable to that of the first year of the Great Depression. Thus, financial crises remain very much a feature of the modern economy.

In addition to their persistence, crises have been notable for their serious and wide-ranging consequences. Banking crises can lead to disruptions in foreign exchange and securities markets, and can spread regionally and internationally. They can have adverse fiscal consequences for governments and taxpayers (Honohan and Klingebiel 2003), and can have severe effects on aggregate economic activity: estimates place the cumulative loss in aggregate economic activity due to a banking crisis as high as 20 percent of aggregate economic output (Grossman 1993, Bordo et al. 2001a). Finally, crises can have substantial effects on the structure of the banking system. These include a decrease in the number and assets of financial institutions, a corresponding increase in banking concentration, a greater scope for direct government involvement in banking, and substantial changes in the regulatory environment.

FINANCIAL CRISES AND BANKING CRISES

Surprisingly, for a phenomenon that has been the focus of much attention by academics, journalists, and policy makers for more than two centuries, there is no consensus definition of a financial crisis. Hyman Minsky (1982b: 13) asserts that a definition is unnecessary, since the major episodes can be identified by pointing. Kindleberger (1978: 21–22) argues that ". . . the genus 'crises' should be divided into species labeled commercial, industrial, monetary, banking, fiscal, financial (in the sense of financial markets), and so on, or into groups called local, regional, national, and international." Eichengreen and Portes (1987: 10), like Kindleberger, recognize the multifaceted nature of financial crisis, yet devise a unified definition of crisis as ". . . a disturbance to financial markets, associated typically with falling asset prices and insolvency among debtors and intermediaries, which ramifies through the financial system, disrupting the market's capacity to allocate capital . . ." This contrasts with Friedman and Schwartz's (1963) focus on liquidity shortage as the hallmark of financial crises and Schwartz's (1986) classification of asset price declines and other financial disturbances in the absence of such a shortage as "pseudo-crises."

TABLE 3.1
Simplified Bank Balance Sheet

Assets	Liabilities
Liquid assets	Demand liabilities
Cash	Demand deposits
Deposits with the central bank	Currency
Earning assets	Time (savings) deposits
Securities	Other liabilities
Loans	
Other assets	Capital (net worth)
Total	Total

Although "banking crisis" is a narrower category than "financial crisis," it is not possible to completely disentangle banking crises from the other types of associated financial disturbances (Jonker and van Zanden 1995). For example, a currency crisis caused by panic selling in the belief that depreciation is imminent might lead to a banking crisis if it entails large-scale withdrawals from banks in order to sell the suspect currency. Conversely, a banking sector collapse could raise doubts about the sustainability of an exchange rate and lead to a currency crisis. Similarly, a stock market crash might translate into a banking crisis, or vice versa.

A useful starting point for a discussion of banking crises is a bank balance sheet; a simplified example is presented in table 3.1. By convention, bank capital (net worth)—the excess of assets over liabilities—is listed on the liabilities side of the balance sheet. Cash and deposits at the central bank are the bank's safest assets. These pose little risk of loss, since they are unlikely to decline in value, and are liquid, meaning that they can be quickly and cheaply employed to meet depositor withdrawals. Securities typically consist of debt (i.e., IOUs); however, where not prevented by law or tradition, they may also include equity (i.e., stocks). Securities typically earn a greater return than cash and deposits at the central bank, but are accompanied by two types of risk. First, unlike cash, the price of debt and equity will rise and fall with the fortunes of the issuing entity, as well as with overall market conditions. Second, securities are not as liquid as cash or cash-like assets. Although organized secondary markets exist for many types of securities, allowing them to be converted into cash, the costs involved in doing so can be quite high.

The third major class of assets is loans. Loans may have longer or shorter maturities; they may charge higher or lower interest rates; they may be business, personal, or mortgage loans; and they may be secured by collateral, which the bank will have a claim to if the borrower is unable to repay the loan; or they may be unsecured. Loans, on average, earn greater returns, but are less liquid than securities: because they differ on so many dimensions, such as maturity, interest rate, collateral quality, and borrower quality, there are relatively few markets in which loans can be bought and sold. Although today many types of loans are "securitized," meaning that pools of these assets can be traded on secondary markets, a bank's loan portfolio is likely less liquid than its securities portfolio.

The largest category on the liabilities side of the balance sheet is demand liabilities. Demand liabilities consist primarily of demand deposits, such as checking accounts, which have to be redeemed by the bank when requested by the depositor. When banks issued their own notes, this circulating currency was also a demand liability, redeemable in metallic money, notes of the central bank, or some other spendable asset (i.e., cash) at 100 percent of its value upon demand. Because a substantial portion of bank liabilities are payable on demand, while most of their assets cannot immediately be converted to cash, banks are subject to "runs," substantial withdrawals of deposits or requests for note redemption that may exceed the bank's ability to satisfy these requests.

Although the likelihood of a run depends on both the asset and liability sides of the bank balance sheet, ultimately a bank's closure is precipitated by an inability to meet withdrawals of demand liabilities. Before discussing the factors that might lead to a surge in withdrawals of demand liabilities, it is worth discussing the asset side of the balance sheet and distinguishing between two types of asset impairment that can contribute to banking difficulties. When bank assets are of such poor or deteriorating quality that they are insufficient to redeem liabilities under any circumstances the bank is "insolvent." Alternatively, when a bank's assets are of better quality but, because of turbulence in securities markets, cannot be sold, it is characterized as "illiquid." The difference between insolvency and illiquidity has implications for appropriate policy responses, which are discussed in the next chapter.

One practice that might eliminate the possibility of bank runs would be to keep a very high proportion of demand liabilities in cash—at the limit, 100 percent—as prescribed by Fisher (1935), Friedman (1959), and others. Although in theory possible, this is not practical: banks that keep 100 percent of their demand liabilities in cash cannot engage in credit creation and, hence, would not be banks as we know them. Realistically, under most circumstances, the fraction of deposits banks must hold in reserves is less than 100 percent. The actual proportion of demand liabilities held in liquid assets may be solely a matter of bank policy or may be constrained by government regulation. Hence, the level of reserves ultimately held will depend on a variety of factors, including custom, regulation, predictability of deposit inflows and outflows, and the risk-aversion of the management (Collins and Baker 2003).

Before discussing specific events that might lead to a bank run, it is important to note the mechanics and information quality of such a run. Because bank runs are driven by the threat that the bank will not have enough cash to redeem demand liabilities, depositors have an incentive to be at the front of the line should a generalized panic materialize (Diamond and Dybvig 1983). Thus, even if the bad news discussed below is not sufficient to convince depositors that their bank is likely to fail, it may still be rational for them to nonetheless withdraw funds as a precautionary measure. As more depositors reach the same conclusion, panic withdrawals may spread through what Friedman and Schwartz (1963) characterize as a "contagion of fear."

Depositors and note holders might panic if an important asset or class of assets on the bank's balance sheet were discovered to be of questionable value. For example, a bank that had made a large fraction of its loans to, or owned a large quantity of bonds of, a company that failed, or to an industry that suffered a severe downturn, could face a run. Similarly, a bank with substantial funds on deposit with a failing bank could be subject to a run. The discovery of large-scale losses due to fraud that was serious enough to erode a bank's ability to redeem deposits could also lead to a run. Because banks have not always made their balance sheets and income statements public in a timely fashion, it is possible that depositors would not know of these developments until the problems were so advanced that a run was likely, further encouraging them to withdraw their deposits at the slightest hint of trouble.

Bank runs can be precipitated by events having little to do with the condition of the bank itself. For example, the failure of a neighboring bank or the bankruptcy of a local but otherwise unrelated company might lead depositors to conclude that trouble is likely to spread to their bank and that their deposits are not safe. Since economic downturns are often accompanied by bank and business failures, these too could precipitate bank runs. And even if depositors were not worried about the safety of their deposits, they might worry about the value of those deposits. For example, concerns that a devaluation (or a substantial depreciation of a floating exchange rate) was imminent might lead depositors to make large withdrawals in order to convert their holdings into another—more stable—currency.

Bank runs are characterized by rapid deposit withdrawals, culminating in the bank's inability to meet its demand liabilities. A bank has several options to forestall a run. First, it can pay off depositors using liquid reserves, since failure to pay would force the bank to close immediately. If the bank is able to pay out substantial sums for a prolonged period without flinching, depositors may be convinced of the bank's solvency and the tide of withdrawals may subside. Second, the bank can raise more cash by selling assets. Because they are more liquid than loans, banks would probably first sell securities. If generalized pressure led to panic selling of securities by banks and others, however, securities prices would fall and reduce the funds that could be raised by such sales. Third, banks can try to sell loans or borrow against them. Since loans are not as liquid as securities, this is likely to be less successful unless a lender is willing to accept a portion of the bank's loan portfolio as collateral or to extend an unsecured loan. If these means are not sufficient, the bank will fail.

At what point do individual bank failures become a banking crisis? Lindgren, Garcia, and Saal (1996: 9) define a *sound* banking system as one in which:

> . . . most banks (those accounting for most of the system's assets and liabilities) are solvent and likely to remain so. Solvency is reflected in the positive net worth of a bank, as measured by the difference between assets and liabilities . . .

In contrast, Bordo et al. (2001: 55), relying on Caprio and Klingebiel (1996, 1999), assert that a banking *crisis* occurs when financial distress leads to ". . . the erosion of most or all of aggregate banking system capital." Although the gap between sound ("most banks solvent") and unsound ("most bank capital eroded") banking systems under the above definitions is wide, it is clear from both that an isolated bank failure does not constitute a banking crisis.

Both of the above definitions rely on measures of bank capital, which is unfortunate for two reasons. First, although soundness is straightforward to define in terms of the ratio of capital to total assets, in practice it is quite difficult to measure, since loans—the largest component of bank assets—and capital are notoriously difficult to value at any given time.[1] Second, although low capital-to-asset ratios are often symptomatic of an ailing bank or banking system and the erosion of most (a vague standard) or all banking capital would certainly constitute a crisis, some banks and banking systems have survived with low levels of capital, and other seemingly well-capitalized banking systems have plunged into crisis.

Friedman and Schwartz (1963), in their classic volume on American monetary history, assert that banking crises should be defined by changes in the currency-to-deposit ratio. As deposits are withdrawn from banks

---

[1]Traditionally, bank balance sheets have valued both loans and capital at book (historical) value rather than being "marked-to-market," or stated at market value.

in favor of currency, this ratio rises. When the banking system's aggregate currency-to-deposit ratio exceeds a certain (unspecified) amount, the banking system is in crisis. Bernanke and James (1991) offer not so much a detailed definition of banking crises, but a catalogue of countries where they believe crises occurred during the troubled years of the early 1930s. They are skeptical of defining banking crises in terms of some precise numerical indicator, since such measures frequently lead to classifications that are at odds with generally accepted financial history.

Like Bernanke and James, and in the "narrative approach" of Romer and Romer (1989), I rely on a reading of the historical literature, rather than strict numerical indicators, in order to determine where and when banking crises occurred. Although banking crises have differed in character and severity across countries and time, I conclude that they typically included one of the following three elements: (1) a high proportion of banks failed (e.g., the United States during the Great Depression, Austria following 1873); (2) an especially large or important bank failed (e.g., France's Union Générale in 1881, Scotland's City of Glasgow Bank in 1878, Austria's Credit Anstalt in 1931); or (3) failures of the type described in (1) or (2) were prevented only by extraordinary and direct intervention by the government or some other actor, through the declaration of a bank holiday, or a reorganization or nationalization of the banking sector (e.g., Italy's banking reorganization following the crisis of 1931, the rescue of Baring Brothers in England in 1890). The advantage of such a definition is that it is flexible enough to take into account episodes that the historical literature considers to be crises, but may not meet a quantitative definition of crisis. The drawback is its lack of precision. The appendix to this chapter presents a catalogue of crises, along with a justification as to why some episodes are included and others excluded.

THE CONSEQUENCES OF BANKING CRISES

The costs of banking crises fall first on shareholders, depositors, and those holding banknotes of affected banks. Since most banks today operate with limited liability, the main consequence for the typical shareholder would be to see the value of those shares decline, possibly to zero. In earlier periods, in which shareholder liability was not always limited, the costs to shareholders could be greater. In the United States during the late nineteenth and early twentieth centuries, banks chartered by the federal government and those chartered by a number of states operated with double liability, under which shareholders of failed banks, in addition to seeing the value of their shares decline to zero, could be called on to pay an amount equal to their initial investment in order to satisfy creditors. Elsewhere, unlimited liability was the rule, meaning that shareholders' personal wealth could be called on to pay off the bank's debts. Following the failure of the City of Glasgow Bank in 1878, owners of each £100 share were called on to pay in a total of £2,750 to settle the bank's outstanding debts, leading to the insolvency of more than 85 percent of the shareholders, including one bank that had inadvertently acquired four shares (Checkland 1975: 471).

Holders of demand liabilities are also among the first to suffer when banks fail. Because depositors and note holders have a higher priority claim to a failed bank's assets than other creditors and shareholders, they should fare better in a bankruptcy than other claimants. Depositors in U.S. banks lost $1.3 billion during the Great Depression; this exceeded shareholder losses of $0.9 billion but as a percentage of total deposits was a far smaller loss than that experienced by shareholders (Friedman and Schwartz 1963: 351). Note holders of the City of Glasgow Bank were paid in full. Even if depositors and note holders were eventually able to get their funds following liquidation or takeover, the fact that they may have been without access to their money for a considerable period of time could have forced them to default on obligations of their own.

Governments, quasi-government agencies, and the taxpayers who support them frequently bear some of the costs of banking crises via assistance to failing or failed banks. This assistance can take at least three forms. First, the government can close the affected institutions, sell off the assets, and pay off depositors. If a crisis leads to panic selling of assets, the amount realized from their sale will decline and the net cost to the taxpayer will rise. Second, the government may pay another, presumably healthier institution to take over the liabilities of a failed bank. The eventual cost of such an operation depends on the deal struck by the government and the purchasing bank and any subsequent change in the market value of the assets acquired. Third, the government may act more directly by contributing capital (with or without taking a management role), making deposits, or nationalizing the bank. In a survey of banking distress during the last two decades of the twentieth century, Caprio and Klingebiel (1999, revised 2003) estimate the fiscal costs of bank recapitalizations as 8 percent of GDP in Norway (1987–93), 11.2 percent in Finland (1991–94), and 24 percent in Japan (1990–2003); Blass and Grossman (2001) estimate the fiscal cost of the Israeli bank shares crisis of the 1980s at about 20 percent of GDP.

Banking crises can have disruptive effects on securities and currency markets, as well as macroeconomic costs. Doubts about the solvency of a country's banking system can lead investors to pull their money out of the country. Such "capital flight" can lead to substantial volatility in exchange markets. Similarly, widespread fears about the stability of the banking system can lead to a disruption in securities markets, both because of the decline in bank share prices and because of distress selling by banks of their securities portfolios. The accumulated effects described above, combined with the increased cost of credit intermediation (Bernanke 1983), can lead to macroeconomic costs as high as 20 percent of GDP (Grossman 1993).

Crises can have substantial effects on the structure of the banking system as well. These include a decrease in the number and aggregate assets of financial institutions, along with a corresponding increase in concentration. Crises can also lead to a greater role for the government in the management of affected institutions. Finally, crises often lead policy makers to make changes to banking regulations. Following crises, reforms aimed at making the banking system more resistant to crises are politically popular; at the same time, interest groups take advantage of the sentiment in favor of reform to advance their own agendas. And even when crises do not lead to changes in the rules and regulations, they can often lead to changes in accepted practices as bankers seek to reassure depositors and shareholders in a post-crisis environment.

The Causes of Banking Crises: Hypotheses

Banking crises are both common and costly, and it is important to understand why they occur. A simple—if not particularly helpful—answer is that a bank failure occurs when depositors attempt to withdraw more funds than the bank has in liquid reserves, and a banking crisis occurs when the pattern is widespread. Identifying features that are correlated systematically with the incidence of banking crises across countries and time is a difficult exercise. Bordo et al. (2001: 64) assert that:

> . . . attempts to statistically relate crises to fundamentals are unlikely to have a high explanatory power because fundamentals are only part of the explanation. Models of self-fulfilling 'bank runs' and multiple equilibria in foreign exchange markets (so-called second generation models of speculative attacks) suggest that there is unlikely to be a simple mapping from fundamentals to crisis incidence.

Nonetheless, I identify three broad categories of causes of banking crises: boom-bust fluctuations, shocks to confidence, and structural weakness.

Boom-bust or macroeconomic fluctuations can contribute to the onset of a banking crisis through at least two channels. First, macroeconomic downturns typically lead to increases in business failures and, as a result, loan defaults. Second, downturns often coincide with declines in the prices of financial and "real" assets (e.g., real estate, commodities), which may follow the bursting of a pre-crisis speculative bubble and can have serious implications for bank portfolios. The causal link running from macroeconomic downturns to banking crises may be difficult to establish statistically, however, since banking crises themselves can generate or exacerbate an economic downturn.

Macroeconomic boom-bust fluctuations play a central role in models of financial crises dating back at least as far as Irving Fisher (1932, 1933).[2] Fisher, one of the first modern economists to take an analytical approach to financial crises, argues that crises result from the cyclical nature of real economic activity. Economic expansion leads to a growth in the number and size of bank loans, as well as to an increase in the relative indebtedness of non-bank firms. As economic expansion proceeds and bankers seek more profitable investments, less worthwhile investment projects receive funding. Fisher (1932: 43) laments the excessive buildup of debt during cyclical upswings: "If only the (upward) movement would stop at equilibrium!" When the expansion ends, these marginal firms are unable to meet their debt service obligations. This leads to loan defaults and declines in the prices of outputs and securities, further exacerbating the distress. The debt-deflation spiral feeds on itself: loan defaults lead to bank failures, exacerbating the macroeconomic downturn already under way.

A second explanation of banking crises centers on shocks to confidence. Friedman and Schwartz (1963) argue that shocks to confidence in the United States during the half-century or so following the Civil War emanated from suspicions that the United States would abandon the gold standard, thus devaluing the dollar. If it had done so, dollar-denominated deposits would have been worth less in terms of gold and other currencies, so the anticipated abandonment would have led to substantial deposit withdrawals. Worries about a potential devaluation and devaluation-induced deposit outflows were spread via a "contagion of fear" (Friedman and Schwartz 1963: 308). The existence of a gold standard is not necessary for such a scenario: lack of confidence in the sustainability of any fixed exchange rate—or even in the continued stability of a floating exchange rate—could lead to substantial withdrawals.

Shocks to confidence need not be directly related to concerns about the sustainability of the exchange rate. For example, the threat of war could shake confidence in the ability of the government to continue servicing its debt and have serious consequences for securities markets. Such a

---

[2]Sprague (1910), Evans (1859 [1969]: 1). Kindleberger (1996: 12) argues that Minsky's (1975, 1982a) model of financial crises is a lineal descendant of those of John Stuart Mill, Alfred Marshall, and Knut Wicksell.

threat might also spark inflation if the government resorts to monetary expansion to pay for war expenses; this too could encourage individuals to withdraw their bank deposits in favor of hard assets that might retain their value better during an inflationary period. Severe inflation would put downward pressure on the value of the currency, further encouraging the switch to hard assets. Similarly, confidence could be shaken by threats to the political status quo, if the end result was likely to be a takeover of the government by parties with an agenda detrimental to banks.

A third category of explanation for banking crises is structural weakness. Such weakness might emanate from the size, number, and distribution of banking firms, or from a poorly designed financial architecture. Unlike boom-bust downturns and shocks to confidence, structural weakness is unlikely to trigger a banking crisis on its own. It could, however, render the banking system vulnerable to the point where a relatively minor macroeconomic downturn or shock to confidence could lead to a full-scale banking crisis.

Banking systems composed of fewer, larger, more extensively branched banks might be more resistant to crises because of their superior ability to diversify, rendering them less susceptible to downturns in any one region or industrial sector. Conversely, if such banks achieved their greater size by expanding more rapidly than was prudent, they might be more likely to collapse during a crisis. Large institutions might be more stable because they are better positioned to lend to larger, more credit-worthy borrowers than smaller banks,[3] and may also be able to devote more resources to professional management and internal control systems than smaller banks. Banks that make many and large loans may be able to economize on transaction, information, and monitoring costs per loan, that is, they may benefit from what economists call economies of scale. Entry restrictions may create fewer, larger, more crisis-resistant banks. If barriers prevent the entry of competitors, existing banks should be more profitable and better able to protect themselves during economic downturns, although lack of competition might render them less efficient and, therefore possibly more susceptible to crisis. A smaller group of large financial institutions might find it easier to formulate a coordinated response to a financial emergency, including pressuring public institutions for assistance; however, in a system composed of only a few large banks, the failure of one of these would be more likely to trigger a full-fledged

---

[3]Sykes (1926: 187). Chlepner (1943) attributes the emergence of commercial banking in Belgium to the country's early development of heavy industry and the accompanying increased demand for capital. A similar argument about the merits of large banks was made in Britain before the 1917 Treasury Committee on Bank Amalgamations that ultimately decided to slow the process of amalgamation in British banking.

crisis. Thus, although it is unclear if there is an "optimal" banking structure, it is clear that structural factors can alter a banking system's resistance to crisis.

Aside from the size, number, and distribution of banks, structural weakness might also arise from a poorly designed financial architecture, such as the absence of a lender of last resort or an inadequate regulatory structure. Lenders of last resort, which will be discussed in greater detail in the following chapter, provide funds to the banking system by making otherwise illiquid assets (e.g., loans, securities for which the market has dried up) liquid via secured lending. Although the absence of a lender of last resort seems unlikely to pose an existential threat to banking stability when the macroeconomic environment is placid and there are no threats to confidence, a well-functioning lender of last resort may reduce the risk of a banking crisis when circumstances are more treacherous. Poorly designed regulations and institutions may also lead to instability. For example, a deposit insurance system that does not charge higher premia for institutions engaging in risky practices may, in fact, encourage excessive risk-taking.

The categories boom-bust fluctuations, shocks to confidence, and structural weakness are neither exhaustive, nor mutually exclusive. "Boom-bust" fluctuations conducive to a banking crisis might not actually result in a crisis in the absence of a shock to confidence. Further, a macroeconomic downturn might only lead to a crisis in the presence of certain structural factors. Systematic identification of the main culprits behind banking crises can only be determined by considering the historical record.

EVIDENCE FROM BEFORE 1870

Any assessment of the causes of banking crises prior to 1870 is hampered by a lack of data. Banking data from this period are scarce and of poor quality in comparison with those from later periods, when the quality and quantity of data gathered by government regulators and supervisors, newspapers, and financial institutions themselves improved markedly. Economic data with which to formally test the hypotheses are not available either: annual historical GDP data, for example, are not available for many countries prior to 1850. A further complication is that incorporated commercial banking was not well established in many countries prior to 1870. Consequently, episodes of financial distress centered on private banks, other financial institutions, or financial markets will not be included. For example, the German banking crisis of 1847–48 can hardly constitute a commercial banking crisis, since Germany's first incorporated commercial bank was only established in 1848. The same can be said of the closure of almost all of the *caisses* in France in 1848 and the forced closure of nine of the ten Japanese exchange companies (predecessors of commercial banks) in 1871. Additionally, although the failure of one of only a handful of extant banks, which might occur early in a banking system's development (e.g., Australia in 1826), certainly meets the definition of a banking crisis outlined above, such a crisis is clearly of a different character from one that occurs in a more mature banking system. Nevertheless, despite these drawbacks, a number of notable banking crises did occur in the years leading up to 1870.

Many of the banking crises in the pre-1870 period occurred during boom-bust fluctuations. The common pattern of financial crises was not lost on contemporary observers. Evans (1859 [1969]: 1) opens his history of the crises of the late 1850s, noting:

> Within the last sixty years, at comparatively short intervals, the commercial world has been disturbed by a succession of those terrible convulsions that are now but too familiar to every ear by the expressive name 'panic.' Each separate panic has its own distinctive features, but all have resembled each other in occurring immediately after a period of apparent prosperity, the hollowness of which it has exposed. So uniform is this sequence, that whenever we find ourselves under circumstances that enable the acquisition of rapid fortunes, otherwise than by the road of plodding industry, we may almost be justified in arguing that the time for panic is at hand.

To reiterate, macroeconomic expansion encourages firms to undertake more investment projects. This leads to a growth in the number and size of loans made by banks—and quite possibly also to an increase in the number of banks themselves—as well as an increase in the indebtedness of nonbank firms. As the cyclical upswing progresses and high-quality investment projects are exhausted, banks provide funds to more marginal endeavors. When the expansion ends, the lower-quality projects are unable to generate enough revenue to meet their debt service obligations. This leads to loan defaults and a decline in securities and commodities prices, which hurts both banks and non-financial firms. The downward spiral feeds on itself: loan defaults lead to bank failures, which reduce credit availability, which exacerbates the macroeconomic downturn already under way.

The above scenario aptly describes many pre-1870 crises. For example, England suffered crises in 1825, 1836–39, 1847, 1857, and 1866. Each of these was preceded by several years of rapid economic growth, frequently fuelled by abundant harvests, and accompanied by increased speculation. The object of speculation varied from crisis to crisis and included at different times Latin American investments, limited liability companies, joint stock banks, railroads, and grain. A similar scenario can explain the 1837 crises in the United States and Canada, as well as the 1857 crises, which started in the United States and spread to Austria, Denmark, and Germany. Similarly, the Australian crisis of 1843 came at the end of a long period of pastoral expansion and speculative boom in land and grain.

Although macroeconomic boom-bust fluctuations played an important part in many of the banking crises of the pre-1870 period, in others it played a minor role. For example, although macroeconomic factors contributed to the banking crisis in Belgium in 1838–39, they were not the only contributing factor. This crisis was precipitated by the breakdown of diplomacy between Belgium and the Netherlands and the accompanying fear that a war might break out between the two. A decade later, the Paris Revolution of 1848 inspired a similar crisis of confidence that touched off another Belgian banking crisis and contributed to the subsequent demise of the French caisses. The Belgian crisis of 1838–39 was further exacerbated by a structural issue, namely, conflict between the country's two principal banks. The older of these banks, the Société Générale, had been established in 1822 by William I of the Netherlands, also the principal shareholder at the time of its founding, eight years prior to Belgian independence. Its main competitor, the Banque de Belgique, had been established in 1835 by a Belgian politician, Charles de Broukère, with French financial backing. Animosity between the two institutions was not long in appearing: during one week in December 1838, Société Générale presented banknotes worth 1.4 million Belgian francs to the Banque de Belgique, demanding payment and forcing it to shut its doors. Parliament—and later the government—extended loans of five million francs to the Banque de Belgique, allowing it to open three weeks later (Chlepner 1943: 11–21). A similar bank war, between the established Bank of New South Wales and the new Bank of Australia, combined with macroeconomic factors, contributed to a banking crisis in Australia in 1826.

Evidence from 1870 to World War I

By 1870, commercial banking was well established throughout the industrialized world. Earlier in the century, incorporated commercial banks were relatively rare and the process of chartering new ones was cumbersome. In many countries, the earliest banks were established by charters granted by the legislature or at the pleasure of the sovereign. As the century progressed, national authorities regularized the process of bank entry by introducing banking codes or by allowing banks to be formed under general incorporation law.

Another important change in the economic environment was the dramatic increase in the international movement of goods, labor, and money during what has since become termed the "first era of globalization" (O'Rourke and Williamson 1999). The process of globalization was helped along by declines in tariff rates and by widespread adoption of the gold standard. Aside from Britain, which had been on gold from 1821, and Australia and Canada, which had adopted it in 1852–53, most industrialized countries did not adopt the gold standard until the 1870s: Germany (1872); Denmark, Norway, and Sweden (1873); the Netherlands (1875); Finland (1877); Belgium, France, and Switzerland (1878); and the United States (1879).[4]

Because of its requirement that central banks be prepared to redeem the domestic currency in gold, the gold standard limited monetary expansion and imparted a deflationary bias to its adopters: on average, prices in the industrialized countries declined by nearly 1.5 percent per year during 1873–93. Falling prices increased the debt burden on borrowers and, in line with the emphasis placed on debt-deflation by Fisher (1933), may have contributed to the high incidence of crises during this period. The spread of the gold standard and the rise of globalization also increased the synchronization of cyclical fluctuations—including the boom-bust cycles and the ensuing banking crises—between countries. Although the transmission of financial panics from one region to another was a common feature of the pre-1870 period (Kindleberger 1996: 116), it became even more pronounced during the first era of globalization.

"Boom-bust" fluctuations were at the heart of most of the banking crises during 1870–1913, the most notable of which occurred during 1873–78, 1893, and 1907–8. The crises of the 1870s to a large extent had their origins in boom-bust cycles following wars, including the U.S. Civil War (1861–65), the Austro-Prussian War (1866), and the Franco-Prussian War (1870). Following their victory in 1870, Germany imposed substantial reparations payments upon France—approximately 5 billion francs, or about one quarter of France's annual GDP (White 2001: 351, Baltzer 2006: 5). These payments allowed the newly formed German Reich to substantially pay down its national debt and enabled Germans to seek alternative investment vehicles, such as equities. This process led to an economic boom and substantial increases in German and Austrian stock markets. The boom came to an abrupt halt in May of 1873 with banking crises in Austria and Germany, which subsequently spread to Italy.[5] The

[4]The law authorizing the resumption of the gold standard in the U.S. as of 1879 was enacted in 1875. Italy adopted the gold standard in 1884 and Japan in 1897. See Oppers (1996) and Meissner (2005) on the spread of the gold standard.

[5]Kindleberger (1996: 121) cites McCartney (1935) as stating that the 1873 financial crisis was the first truly international crisis: ". . . it erupted in Austria and Germany in May,

United States experienced a substantial bubble in land and railroads following the end of the Civil War, which burst in September 1873, leading to a severe banking crisis. As the ensuing recession deepened, more or less severe banking crises struck Belgium (1876), Denmark (1877–78), Sweden (1877–78), Finland (1878), and Canada (1879).

According to Conant (1915: 668), ". . . the financial crisis of 1893 was in large measure an afterclap of the Baring failure in 1890." The rise and fall of Baring Brothers, an old established London merchant bank which collapsed when economic and political events undermined its substantial portfolio of Latin American—in particular, Argentinean—securities, is discussed at greater length in the next chapter. The failure of Baring and subsequent mistrust of Latin American securities, combined with the low rates of return available on British securities, encouraged investors to look elsewhere for profitable returns on their funds. Popular destinations for investment were Australia, where agricultural land was a favored target, and the United States, where the investment boom was aided by monetary expansion brought about by the Sherman Silver Purchase Act of 1890. The end of the boom in these investments led to severe banking crises in Australia and the United States and, subsequently, to banking disruptions in Germany and Italy.

A third series of boom-bust banking crises erupted in 1907. The recession associated with the 1893 crisis, which lasted into the second half of the decade, was followed by a pronounced increase in economic activity, including substantially increased investment in both public infrastructure and private manufacturing. The surge in investment was fuelled by an increasing money supply due to substantial gold discoveries in Australia, Canada, and South Africa. The boom came to an end when the Spanish-American War (1898), Boer War (1899–1902), and Russo-Japanese War (1904–5), and earthquakes in Valparaíso and San Francisco (1906), led to greater demands for funds, a tightening of credit conditions, and, eventually, banking crises that were most serious in the United States, Italy, Denmark, and Sweden.

Table 3.2 presents data on the average annual growth rate of real gross domestic product and the number and assets of commercial banks, along with average levels of interest and inflation rates, during business-cycle expansions during 1883–1913. In addition, two annual averages are presented: one for cyclical expansions that were followed by banking crises and one for cyclical expansions that were not followed by crises. The data presented are not without their limitations. First, with the exception of the

---

spread to Italy, Holland, and Belgium, leapt the Atlantic in September, and crossed back again to involve England, France, and Russia." Durviaux (1947: 75), however, asserts that the Belgian banking crisis occurred later.

TABLE 3.2
Macroeconomic and Banking Conditions during Crisis and Non-Crisis Cyclical Expansions, 1883–1913

	Change in real GDP (percent)				Change in number of commercial banks (percent)		
	Crisis	Non-crisis	Crisis minus non-crisis		Crisis	Non-crisis	Crisis minus non-crisis
Australia	5.53	3.26	2.27	Australia	0.022	−0.009	0.031
Canada	7.53	5.09	2.44	Canada	0.000	−0.048	0.048
Denmark	3.28	2.94	0.34	Denmark	0.061	0.037	0.024
Finland	5.93	3.63	2.30	England	−0.011	−0.040	0.029
France	1.39	1.59	−0.20	Finland	0.042	0.033	0.009
Germany	3.42	2.90	0.52	Germany	0.020	−0.007	0.027
Italy	2.27	5.83	−3.56	Italy	0.005	−0.011	0.016
Japan	0.87	2.60	−1.73	Japan	−0.029	0.057	−0.086
Norway	2.11	2.71	−0.60	Norway	0.112	0.094	0.018
United Kingdom	3.16	2.26	0.90	United States	0.076	0.060	0.016
United States	3.42	4.19	−0.77				
				All cycles	0.033	0.023	
All cycles	3.43	2.93					

	Inflation (percent)				Change in commercial bank assets (percent)		
	Crisis	Non-crisis	Crisis minus non-crisis		Crisis	Non-crisis	Crisis minus non-crisis
Canada	1.15	1.63	−0.48	Canada	0.113	0.069	0.044
Denmark	0.02	0.56	−0.54	Denmark	0.129	0.050	0.079
Finland	−4.18	−0.99	−3.19	England	0.042	0.033	0.009
France	−4.32	0.07	−4.39	Finland	0.163	0.061	0.102
Germany	1.14	0.41	0.73	Italy	0.067	0.106	−0.039
Italy	1.52	−0.08	1.60	Norway	0.064	0.064	0.000
Norway	1.75	1.67	0.08	United States	0.063	0.064	−0.001
United Kingdom	0.21	0.12	0.09				
United States	0.31	−0.48	0.79	All cycles	0.082	0.059	
All cycles	0.49	0.24					

	Change in short-term interest rate (percentage points)		
	Crisis	Non-crisis	Crisis minus non-crisis
France	0.11	−0.01	0.12
Germany	0.04	0.01	0.03
United Kingdom	0.30	0.17	0.13
United States	0.19	−0.42	0.61
All cycles	0.14	−0.14	

Sources: Countries that had crises: appendix to chapter 3; banking data: figures 1.2–1.10; real GDP: Maddison (2001); business-cycle dating: Bordo et al. (2001), Burns and Mitchell (1946: 78), and Friedman and Schwartz (1982: 77). Interest rate data provided by Michael Bordo.

Note: Calculations weight all cycles equally.

United Kingdom and the United States, business-cycle dating was determined by a mechanically applied statistical technique.[6] Second, because business-cycle turning points need not correspond with the end of the calendar year, although the economic data do, the results may be slightly muddled. Finally, because the number of observations is quite small, the differences observed are not statistically significant at standard levels.

Despite these drawbacks, the data tell a remarkably consistent story. Inflation and growth of real GDP were typically higher during cyclical expansions that were followed by banking crises than during those that were not. Additionally, short term interest rates rose more during expansions that preceded crises than during those that did not, suggesting that banking crises were preceded by stronger than average cyclical expansions. The banking data present an even more unambiguous picture: in almost all cases the number and assets of banks expanded more rapidly during business cycles that culminated with banking crises than during those that did not.

The above analysis can be replicated with data from the United States, for which we have both higher frequency data (i.e., quarterly and, in some cases, monthly) and more precise dating of business cycles than for most countries. Data on the average business cycle pattern of real GDP relative to trend, inflation, and interest rates in the United States during 1879–1912 are presented in figures 3.1–3.3. Banking crises were preceded by expansions characterized by more rapid growth in real economic output, higher inflation, and tighter credit conditions than in expansions that did not precede crises. This evidence is consistent with the notion that the boom-bust macroeconomic fluctuations that characterized the 1870–1913 period contributed to banking crises in the United States.

It is much more difficult to make a systematic assessment of the impact of shocks to confidence on banking stability for the simple reason that reliable indicators of confidence do not exist.[7] Despite this difficulty, several examples of banking crises from the 1870–World War I period stand out as having been caused by shocks to confidence. The onset of war and the panic-driven demand for liquidity triggered crises on at least two occasions: the Franco-Prussian War led to banking crises in France and Switzerland, while the outbreak of World War I led to banking crises in Belgium, Italy, and Switzerland, and would also have led to a crisis in

---

[6]Bordo et al. (2001b: 3–4). The NBER's dating of business cycles in the United Kingdom and the United States takes into account more series and uses a more nuanced approach.

[7]Indices of consumer sentiment are a relatively recent phenomenon. One could make a case for constructing a confidence index from financial market price and volatility data, however, since financial market fluctuations reflect many disparate influences, it would be difficult to isolate the effects of shocks to confidence.

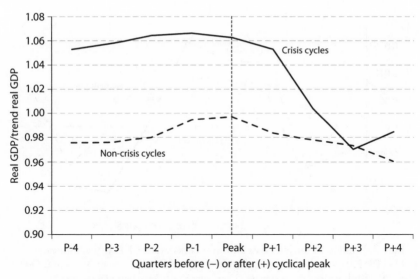

Figure 3.1. Real GDP during crisis and non-crisis cycles: The United States, 1879–1912. *Sources*: Real GDP and trend real GDP from Balke and Gordon (1986); business-cycle dating from Burns and Mitchell (1946: 78).

the United Kingdom without the extraordinary intervention by the Bank of England (see chapter 4).

Another type of shock to confidence that might lead to a banking crisis is one that raises doubts about the continued value of the domestic currency. Worries about inflation or an anticipated fall in the value of the currency could lead to panic-inducing withdrawals from banks, as depositors seek to exchange their domestic currency-denominated deposits for commodities or foreign currency-denominated assets. Such a potential threat may have been partly responsible for the Bank of England's decision to intervene in the Baring Brothers crisis of 1890. Unlike earlier British crises, which were essentially domestic in character, Baring was a prominent international firm and its failure would have led to substantial outflows of gold from the United Kingdom which could have threatened Britain's ability to maintain the gold standard.

Friedman and Schwartz (1963) ascribe the crisis of 1893 in the United States in some measure to doubts about the continued convertibility of the dollar into gold. They argue that these doubts were aroused by passage of the Sherman Silver Purchase Act in 1890, which roughly doubled the Treasury's monthly purchases of silver and led to a correspondingly substantial increase in the currency supply. Continued agitation by western silver producers, and Senate passage of a free silver coinage measure—which never became law, they argue—convinced the anxious both

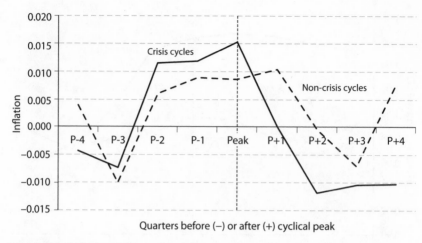

Figure 3.2. Inflation during crisis and non-crisis cycles: The United States, 1879–1912. *Sources*: Inflation calculated from GDP deflator in Balke and Gordon (1986); business-cycle dating from Burns and Mitchell (1946: 78).

at home and abroad that an inflationary silver regime would replace the gold standard.

Structural issues are also difficult to assess systematically for at least two reasons. First, there are a variety of structural factors, many of which are hard to quantify. Second, because many of these changed over time, disentangling the effects of structural factors from boom-bust fluctuations and shocks to confidence is complicated. Despite these difficulties, we can make some tentative observations. Countries that did not experience banking crises during the decades of the 1870s, 1890s, and 1900s entered the decade with larger banks, as measured by the ratio of aggregate bank capital or assets to gross domestic product, relative to those that did experience crises during those decades. Similarly, countries that did not experience crises during the 1870s and 1900s began those decades with more concentrated banking systems, imperfectly measured by average population-per-bank, than those that did suffer crises, a result that does not hold for the crises of the 1890s.

In statistical analysis of the bank structure data over the entire 1870–World War I period, I find a weak negative relationship between population-per-bank and banking stability, as well as a similarly negative relationship between the presence of branch banking and banking stability. That is, banking systems characterized by fewer, larger, and more extensively branched banks had a lower incidence of banking crisis, although the statistical relationship is tenuous at best and does not control for the pos-

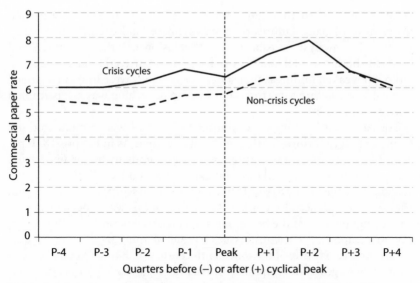

Figure 3.3. Interest rates during crisis and non-crisis cycles: The United States, 1879–1912. *Sources*: Commercial paper rate from Balke and Gordon (1986); business-cycle dating from Burns and Mitchell (1946: 78).

sible influence of macroeconomic effects or shocks to confidence. The outstanding example of the relationship between banking structure and stability is the United States, which was characterized by many small, unbranched banks as well as by frequent banking crises.

The above results are, in addition to being statistically weak, problematic for other reasons. First, the measure of banking instability used is crude: countries are categorized as either having had or not had a banking crisis at a particular point in time. Second, because of the many differences in financial structure, including regulatory differences and the presence of different types of intermediators, the data on banking structure may not be comparable across countries. An alternative empirical strategy is to use data on bank structure and banking stability from the different states of the United States. These data offer two important advantages over cross-country data. First, the U.S. data allow the calculation of a much more subtle measure of banking instability: the percentage of banks (or of bank assets) that failed within a state. Second, because federally chartered national banks operated under identical rules in each state, they provide a good basis for cross-state comparisons. A disadvantage of using U.S. data is that since the majority of U.S. banks were small unit (i.e., unbranched) banks, the results of this analysis might not be applicable to countries where the banking system consisted of fewer, larger banks. I find that states where banks were relatively large had lower rates of bank failures than states where banks were, on average, smaller. The analysis is robust to the inclusion of other variables, and holds for both national banks as well as state-chartered banks. A second, although weaker, finding is that states where banks were branched tended to have lower failure rates than states where branching was not permitted (Grossman 2007b).

The causes of banking crises during 1870–1914 were similar to those from the first two-thirds of the nineteenth century. As in the pre-1870 period, macroeconomic fluctuations were the dominant factor underlying crises, which were clustered around the boom-bust cyclical downturns centered on the mid-1870s, 1893, and 1907. As in the earlier period, shocks to confidence also contributed to crises: this was especially apparent during the wars at the beginning and end of the period. It is difficult to say how important structural issues were in shaping banking crises during the first two thirds of the nineteenth century. Banking systems were in their early stages of development and neither legal frameworks nor banking conventions were well established. And the notion of a lender of last resort was not yet current. As banking systems matured, those consisting of fewer, larger banks tended to be more resistant to crises than those composed of many small banks.

EVIDENCE FROM THE INTERWAR PERIOD

Banking crises, both large and small, were relatively common in the late nineteenth and early twentieth centuries. The interwar period, however, stands out for both the frequency and severity of its banking crises. For example, in the United States approximately 11,000 banks suspended in 1933 alone; although many of these banks reopened relatively quickly, the total number of commercial banks fell by more than 40 percent between 1929 and 1933. In Italy, the crisis of the 1930s led to widespread bank nationalization. And in Austria, Belgium, Germany, and Norway, one or more of the largest banks in the country collapsed, along with many smaller ones.

Whatever other factors may have been at work generating the banking crises of the interwar period, macroeconomic fluctuations were by far the most important source of banking instability. This is straightforward to demonstrate: the interwar period was subject to a series of two sharp "boom-bust" cycles, each of which led to banking crises. The first began with the end of World War I and the subsequent rebuilding boom. The collapse of this boom around 1921 led to banking crises in Belgium, Denmark, Italy, the Netherlands, Norway, and Sweden.

The second wave of boom-bust banking crises came with the onset of the Great Depression in 1929–30. The causes and extraordinary severity of the Great Depression and the role of banking crises in its propagation are the subjects of a voluminous literature.[8] Although the answers provided by this literature are far from definitive, it is clear that the banking crises of the Great Depression were driven in large part by cyclical factors: the expansion of real economic activity in countries that subsequently endured banking crises was about 1 percent per year greater in the decade between the end of World War I and the beginning of the Great Depression than among those countries that did not experience banking crises. Figure 3.4 illustrates the performance of real GDP in a sample of twenty-five countries, thirteen of which experienced banking crises. Although banking crises themselves no doubt exacerbated the initial macroeconomic downturn, there is ample evidence to suggest that macroeconomic conditions were paramount in bringing about the crises.

Because of the obvious importance of macroeconomic factors, the interwar period provides a useful laboratory in which to examine the relative importance of structural factors and shocks to confidence. Although harder to quantify, shocks to confidence were important in several crises during the interwar period. Friedman and Schwartz (1963: 308) note that several bank failures in October 1930 led to a contagion of fear among depositors and produced the first wave of bank failures in the United States. The crisis of confidence following the failure of the Austrian Credit Anstalt in 1931 led to bank runs in Hungary and Yugoslavia. And the failure of the Norddeutsche Wollkämmerei und Kammgarnspinnerei (Nordwolle) German textile firm in 1931 led to a run on, and the collapse of, the Darmstädter und Nationalbank (Danat-Bank). Both Austria and Germany had large outstanding short-term foreign debts, and doubts about the continued convertibility of their currencies led to capital flight which exacerbated the banking crises.

The evidence suggests that banking structure also played a role in crises during the interwar period. That is, although all countries were hit by a severe macroeconomic downturn, some banking structures were more resistant to banking crises than others (Grossman 1994).

The interwar era witnessed two periods of heightened banking instability, the early 1920s and the early to mid-1930s. Countries that experienced banking crises in the 1920s were less likely to experience crises in the 1930s. For example, Denmark, the Netherlands, and Sweden all experienced crises in the early 1920s but had relatively stable banking systems during the 1930s. By contrast, several countries that experienced

---

[8]Important works include Friedman and Schwartz (1963), Temin (1976, 1989), and Eichengreen (1992).

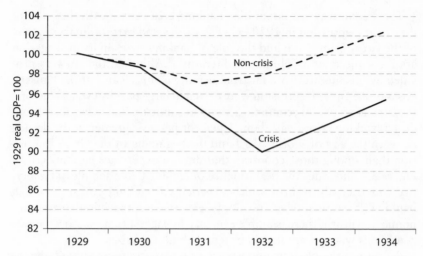

Figure 3.4. Real GDP in crisis and non-crisis countries, 1929–34. *Source*: Maddison (2001), appendix table 3.2.

banking crises in the 1930s (e.g., Belgium, Switzerland) had been spared the worst of the post–World War I boom-bust banking crises. This may be accounted for by the fact that structurally weak banking systems in 1920 suffered crises during the post–World War I boom-bust episode, but the exit of many poorly performing banks left the surviving banking system more resistant to crises. Banking systems that had been more structurally sound at the end of World War I did not endure banking crises in the early 1920s and the accompanying shakeout of the banking system. It may be that a banking system that was sound enough to survive a post–World War I–sized shock was not necessarily resilient enough to survive a Great Depression–sized shock. Alternatively, it may be that in countries that did not experience a post–World War I banking crisis, there was not a sufficient check to banking growth in the subsequent decade.

Table 3.3 presents data on bank branching across countries during the Great Depression. Banks in non-crisis countries had, on average, substantially more branches per bank than their counterparts in crisis countries. Banks in England (613 branches per bank) and Canada (370) were by far the most extensively branched in the sample, although those in the non-crisis countries of Sweden (34), Czechoslovakia (27), and the Netherlands (24) also had more branches per bank than all but one of the crisis country banking systems (Finland, with 36 branches per bank). Australia (not included for data reasons) also had upwards of 200 branches per bank around this time, bolstering support for the stability-promoting powers of branching; however, if the non-major banks in France, Germany,

TABLE 3.3
Bank Branching and Concentration, 1930

Countries	Branches per bank	Population per bank (thousands)
Crisis countries		
Belgium	14.16	92.6
Estonia	1.70	27.9
Finland	35.94	198.2
France	9.46*	160.9
Germany	3.06*	176.1
Hungary	1.00	16.3
Italy	1.91*	104.8
Latvia	6.05	95.0
Norway	1.87	25.0
Poland	4.71	487.9
Romania	1.00	16.0
Switzerland	3.50	19.2
United States	1.14	16.2
Yugoslavia	1.00	21.1
Non-crisis countries		
Bulgaria	1.43	43.1
Canada	369.91	896.4
Czechoslovakia	27.32	666.2
Denmark	3.06	19.6
England	613.44	2,481.3
Greece	7.43	180.3
Japan	6.14	82.4
Lithuania	7.22	260.0
Netherlands	24.00	1,305.5
Portugal	3.26	252.6
Spain	5.08	105.9
Sweden	33.83	204.0
Crisis average	6.18	104.1
Non-crisis average	91.84	541.4
Statistical significance of difference between crisis and non-crisis averages (p-value of one-tail test)	7.7%	3.1%

Sources: Number of banks: League of Nations (1934, 1938) and the *Banker's Almanac* (1930); population: League of Nations, *Statistical Year-Book* (various).
*Includes only branches of major banks; other banks assumed to have no branches.

and Italy were not assumed to be unit (i.e., unbranched) banks, support would be weaker. Overall, the evidence does support the stabilizing effects of branching, although the support is not overwhelming.

The Canadian experience, especially as compared with that of the United States, lends support to the argument that branch banking contributed to stability.[9] Macroeconomic performance during the Depression was dismal in both the United States and Canada, although the extensively branched Canadian banking system survived intact while approximately 5,000 U.S. banks, primarily unit banks, failed. Although the United States–Canada comparison is suggestive, numerous counterexamples cast doubt on the ability of branching to assure stability.

Although the vast majority of American bank failures in the 1930s were unit banks, prominent exceptions included Caldwell and Company, which had over one hundred branches and affiliates in several southern states, and the Bank of United States, which had fifty-nine branches at the time of its failure (Wicker 1980, Friedman and Schwartz 1963: 309–11, Temin 1976: 90–94). Austria's largest and most extensively branched bank, the Credit Anstalt, failed in May 1931. In Germany, the Danat-Bank, third among Berlin's great banks with 207 branches, failed weeks later. In France, the country's fourth largest bank, the Banque National de Crédit, failed following two runs. And the Italian banking system, which was dominated by four extensively branched institutions, also experienced a crisis. Still, the branching argument is difficult to dismiss: neither the Caldwell group nor the Bank of United States had a nationwide system of branches. And in Austria, France, Germany, and Italy a few large banks with nationwide branch systems coexisted with as many as several hundred less well-branched banks.

The evidence suggests that branching contributed to banking stability during the Great Depression, although the evidence comes with several caveats. The presence of extensively branched banks within a system that also included many less well-branched banks seems to lessen the stabilizing effects of branching. There are enough exceptions, moreover, to indicate that branching alone was not enough to guarantee stability. Banks in Belgium and France, for example, were extensively branched and did suffer crises, while the unit bank system of Bulgaria did not. This suggests that branching may have been but one factor contributing to banking stability.

---

[9]See Bordo, Rockoff, and Redish (1994, 1996) on the Canada–United States comparison. Kryzanowski and Roberts (1993, 1999) argue that Canadian stability depended upon capital forbearance. Carr, Mathewson, and Quigley (1995) argue that nationwide branching, management prudence, and shareholder and regulator monitoring bolstered the Canadian banking system.

Table 3.3 presents data on concentration in 1930, admittedly imperfectly measured by population-per-bank. Banks in countries that did not subsequently endure crises had concentration levels that were, on average, more than five times those of crisis countries, and the difference is statistically significant at standard levels. England (with a population of nearly 2.5 million per bank) was easily the most concentrated, while the Netherlands (1.3 million), Canada (896,400), and Czechoslovakia (666,200) also had highly concentrated banking systems. The most concentrated crisis country was Poland (487,900); no other crisis country had levels greater than 200,000. Not surprisingly, concentration was quite low in the unit-bank dominated United States (16,200).

Banking systems characterized by more highly concentrated banks may have been more stable because coordinated action—as well as coordinated pressure on official institutions—is easier in times of crisis. For example, the effort to rescue Baring Brothers in 1890 involved a coordinated effort by the City of London's largest firms. In Canada, the takeovers of the Bank of Ontario (1906) and Sovereign Bank (1908) were also cooperative efforts, while the May 1931 absorption of Weyburn Security Bank was accomplished by the Imperial Bank acting alone (Johnson 1910: 104–27). And in Britain, Williams Deacon's Bank was taken over by the Royal Bank of Scotland in 1929–30 with the assistance of the Bank of England.

Table 3.4 presents cross-country data on average bank size, as measured by capital and reserves, assets, and deposits, in 1930. By all three indicators, banks in non-crisis countries were substantially larger than those in countries that suffered banking crises. This is consistent with the notion advanced above that banking systems characterized by larger, more concentrated, more extensively branched banks are more resistant to economic shocks. The average bank in non-crisis countries was larger, more extensively branched, and part of a more highly concentrated banking system—although not more highly capitalized—than the average bank in crisis countries, although the statistical evidence is not completely unambiguous. The mechanism through which these structural issues may have enhanced banking stability is not entirely clear: since bank branching, size, and concentration are correlated, it is difficult to disentangle their effects. It could be that larger, branched banks were better able to achieve diversification across geographic areas and industries, or that more concentrated banks were more profitable—because there were fewer of them—or better able to cooperate in times of financial stringency.

Banking crises during the interwar period—especially during the Great Depression—were more severe and more widespread than they had ever been before. Although the Great Depression ushered in the worst banking

TABLE 3.4
Bank Size and Capitalization, 1930

Countries	Average capital + reserves ($)	Average assets ($)	Average deposits ($)	Capital-to-assets ratio
Crisis countries				
Belgium	2.62	12.53	9.66	0.118
Estonia	0.07	0.93	0.46	0.062
Finland	2.54	15.63	11.41	0.106
Germany	1.30	13.09	8.27	0.099
Hungary	0.20	1.53	0.98	0.083
Italy	0.62	5.25	1.45	0.118
Latvia	0.33	1.78	0.61	0.165
Norway	0.65	4.09	2.57	0.117
Poland	0.60	5.35	2.10	0.087
Romania	0.09	0.45	0.29	0.128
Switzerland	2.24	18.36	13.52	0.094
United States	0.47	3.86	2.63	0.060
Yugoslavia	0.10	0.50	0.39	0.163
Non-crisis countries				
Bulgaria	0.07	0.40	0.31	0.146
Canada	27.87	285.23	225.67	0.046
Czechoslovakia	4.42	43.03	26.76	0.058
Denmark	0.63	4.52	3.14	0.093
England	43.92	686.09	601.26	0.035
Japan	1.20	7.61	5.57	0.109
Lithuania	0.30	1.47	0.93	0.192
Netherlands	26.69	137.69	98.70	0.128
Portugal	0.55	2.73	1.72	0.141
Spain	0.77	6.69	3.72	0.081
Sweden	7.46	50.98	32.44	0.090
Crisis average	0.91	6.41	4.18	0.11
Non-crisis average	10.35	111.49	90.93	0.10
Statistical significance of difference between crisis and non-crisis averages (p-value of one-tail test)	3.3%	6.4%	7.3%	36.3%

Sources: League of Nations (1934, 1938).

instability of the period, the end of the World War I boom also led to severe and widespread banking difficulties. The dominant causal factor in banking instability during this period was, as in earlier periods, the boom-bust conditions that existed both during the post–World War I period and even more strongly during the Great Depression. Despite the overwhelming importance of boom-bust fluctuations, shocks to confidence and bank structure were also important in determining where and when crises did—and did not—occur.

A DURABLE PATTERN

Despite the substantial changes in banking, and the economic environment more generally, the causes of banking crises have remained remarkably consistent during the past two centuries. Macroeconomic boom-bust cycles stand out as the most common cause of the banking crises catalogued in appendix 3.1; it has also been the driving force behind the crisis that emerged in 2008–9. The subprime crisis originated with a speculative boom in U.S. real estate, fueled by expansionary fiscal and monetary policies, which burst in 2008 when real estate prices collapsed. The boom-bust cycle was exacerbated by a variety of structural and other factors, including government promotion of home ownership—and increased indebtedness—by those least economically able to afford it, the easing of rules on loan-to-value ratios (i.e., those on minimum down payments), and weak regulatory oversight. The unfettered use of instruments designed to facilitate the diversification of risk to undertake increased risk further magnified problems. Finally, the increasing globalization of finance and improvements in communication increased the popularity of unwise practices, the speed with which the crisis travelled, and the area within which it spread.

Although macroeconomic causes have been paramount, shocks to confidence and structural weakness have played an important role. Because the collapse of boom-bust cycles and banking crises frequently coincide with shocks to confidence, it is not always straightforward to identify the effect of these shocks on financial instability. Despite these difficulties, there were a number of instances before World War I in which war— or the fear of war—was clearly exogenous to the business cycle and a crucial factor in generating crises. Structural issues have often played a more preventive, rather than causative, role. During the Great Depression, when almost all countries were hit by a severe macroeconomic shock, banking systems composed of larger, more concentrated, more extensively branched banks—in short, banking systems that in non-crisis periods might be considered problematic because of their uncompetitive nature—demonstrated themselves to be more crisis-resistant.

Although this chapter has concentrated on the causes of banking crises, it is also the case that crises themselves have consequences for bank structure beyond those discussed here. Additional consequences of banking crises include rescue operations, heightened merger activity, and efforts by regulators and policy makers to change the rules under which banks operate so as to reduce the likelihood of failure in the future. The next three chapters address these issues.

CHAPTER 4

Rescuing the Banking System: Bailouts, Lenders of Last Resort, and More Extreme Measures

> [I]f, after Barings' accounts have been examined, you can as-
> sure me that in the Bank's opinion the firm, if time were given,
> would be fully solvent, I want you to do all you can to save
> them, and I will give you all the support in my power. If you
> cannot give me this assurance I must leave the Bank to act as
> they see proper. Whatever the consequences, I will not interfere
> on behalf of an insolvent House.
> —Chancellor of the Exchequer George Goschen, 1890[1]

> I have never seen, in visits to central banks, a door marked
> "lender-of-last resort department," nor met a vice president in
> charge of such an activity.
> —Federal Reserve Governor Henry Wallich (1977: 91)

CRISES CAN HAVE PROFOUND EFFECTS on the structure of the banking system. First, crises typically lead to an immediate—and sometimes substantial—reduction in the number of banking institutions, as failed banks exit the system. Second, crises may lead to mergers, as banks that survive crises in a weakened state are absorbed by stronger firms. Third, crises frequently encourage governments to intervene in the banking sector by enacting stability-enhancing rules and regulations. Mergers and regulatory changes typically take place in the weeks, months, and years, following a crisis. Merger movements in Germany (1901–13) and Finland (1929–35), for example, occurred over a prolonged period of time following major banking disruptions in those countries. Governments frequently respond to banking crises by appointing committees (e.g., Denmark's Parliamentary Committee (1910), the U.S.'s National Monetary Commission (1910), and Japan's Financial System Investigative Council (1926)) to consider their causes and suggest reforms. Whether or not formal investigative committees are appointed, substantial regulatory changes typically follow in the wake of a crisis.

Other reactions take place in the hours and days following the onset of crises. In fact, sometimes the most successful of these interventions take

---

[1]Bank of England Archives, G15/191.

place even before news of the crisis has reached the general public. For the time being, I will refer to these interventions as "rescues." Modern examples of rescues of banking and other financial institutions are plentiful and well-known. Sprague (1986) presents an insider's account of the U.S. experience during the 1970s and 1980s. Other well-known episodes include those of Britain's Johnson Matthey Bankers in 1984 and the U.S.'s Long Term Capital Management in 1998. Rescues were widespread during the Asian crisis that started in 1997: no domestic bank in Korea, Taiwan, Thailand, or Malaysia was allowed to fail and close (Dekle and Kletzer 2002). The subprime crisis that erupted in 2008 has led to a surge in both the number and size of rescues undertaken worldwide—and in the debate over what types of rescues, if any, are warranted. I define a rescue as an intervention by a party not directly involved in a crisis to extend some sort of crisis-averting or crisis-ameliorating assistance to those that are directly involved. If that definition is vague, it is because rescues can take many forms: the rescuer can be a government agency or a private actor; the rescue can consist of more or less substantial assistance offered with a variety of conditions; and can be offered to one firm, several firms, or the entire market.

Why rescue a bank that is on the point of failure? Simply put, a rescue is desirable for all the reasons that crises are undesirable. First, it may save owners of rescued institutions from losing some or all of their equity. Second, banking crises can be contagious: one bank's collapse may have a domino effect, bringing down its creditors as well. Further, rescuing troubled institutions may help to avoid the spread of crisis through a contagion of fear. Because bankers know more about the condition of their own institution than their customers do, a situation economists call "asymmetric information," the failure of one bank might lead those with deposits in perfectly sound banks to question the security of their deposits. These doubts could easily translate into substantial deposit withdrawals from sound institutions, weakening those institutions to the point of failure (Diamond and Dybvig 1983, Mishkin 1991). Third, in the absence of a rescue troubled institutions may undertake panic-sales of assets in an attempt to raise cash, leading to a collapse in securities prices and panic in securities markets. Finally, banking crises can contribute to a slowdown in aggregate economic activity.

The distribution of the costs of crises described above suggests what constituencies will be most supportive of rescues. First and foremost, shareholders and depositors of institutions to be saved will favor rescues. If affected institutions constitute only a small portion of the banking market, political pressure in favor of such an operation will not be great. If there is concern that the crisis might spread to seemingly healthy institutions, however, support for a rescue may extend to a broader segment of the financial community and the population at large. If the crisis is seen as likely to affect asset market prices and overall economic activity, popular sentiment in favor of a rescue may be widespread. In each case, support for a rescue will depend on which segment of the population bears the cost of a rescue.

Despite the benefits listed above, there are circumstances under which a rescue would be unwise and, depending on who bears the cost of the rescue, unpopular. It could be argued that banking crises are most hazardous to inefficient institutions and therefore rescuing such institutions involves a misallocation of societal resources. The delay in closing troubled banks in Japan during the crisis-ridden 1990s has been blamed for the substantial cost of that crisis (Hoshi and Kashyap 2001: 272). The argument in favor of letting banks fail rests crucially on the difference between "bank failures" and "banking crises." Individual bank failures may well provide a net benefit to the system as a whole by eliminating weak, inefficient banks; however, the domino and contagion effects of those failures may nonetheless be costly.

Another potential cost of engaging in a rescue is moral hazard. The term "moral hazard" is borrowed from the insurance literature and describes the tendency of the insured to engage in riskier behavior than otherwise identical, but uninsured, counterparts (Grubel 1971). If bank managers believe that some agent will stand ready to rescue them in case of a crisis, they may be more inclined to take risks and therefore be more likely to put themselves in a situation in which they require a rescue.[2] Thus, a commitment *not* to rescue may well reduce the likelihood of the very crisis that a rescue is meant to alleviate.

In the classic case of moral hazard, the insurer and the insured are clearly defined and the contract between them is explicit: an insurer can attempt to mitigate moral hazard by making certain standards of performance a condition of the insurance, such as smoke detectors for fire insurance. Historically, in the case of banking rescues, it has often been the case that neither the parties nor the relationship between them have been clearly defined. Freixas (1999) contends that "constructive ambiguity," in which a rescue is by no means certain, can help alleviate moral hazard. Such ambiguity was alluded to by a special commission in Belgium following the bailout of 1838 and by former British Prime Minister Sir Robert Peel following the Bank of England's lender of last resort

---

[2]The incentive to avoid failure falls both upon the bank's shareholders, who could find their shares worth less—possibly nothing—in the case of failure, and managers, who could lose their jobs and suffer damage to their reputations. It is possible that managers and shareholders do not have identical preferences, leading to what economists call the "principal-agent" problem. Glassman and Rhoades (1980).

operations during the crisis of 1847 (Chlepner 1926: 173–84, Andréadès 1966: 329). In recent years, rescuers have typically come from the ranks of governments, government-supported agencies, central banks, and international financial institutions, with taxpayers ultimately footing the bill for the rescue. This was certainly the case in the U.S. savings and loan crisis in the 1980s and the Asian and Nordic crises of the 1990s. Historically, however, rescues were often undertaken by non-government actors in addition to governments. Additionally, aside from explicit guarantee arrangements such as deposit insurance, the decision of whether to engage in a rescue was typically taken on a case-by-case basis, so the certainty of rescues may have been very much in doubt.

Before proceeding, it will be useful to discuss the basic mechanics of a rescue. Recall the bank balance sheet presented in the previous chapter. The main components of bank assets include liquid reserves (e.g., cash, including gold, deposits at the central bank), and less liquid earning assets (e.g., securities, loans). Liabilities consist mainly of demand liabilities: demand deposits or, in an earlier time, banknotes. Bank failures, the essential element of a banking crisis, occur when liquid reserves are insufficient to meet withdrawals of demand liabilities. This highlights the distinction between illiquidity, in which banks have sufficient—but not liquid enough—assets to cover demand liabilities, and insolvent banks, where assets are, even under good conditions, insufficient.

Crises can be alleviated in several ways. First, the bank can acquire more capital, as investors put up cash in return for an equity stake in the institution. Second, the bank can solicit loans of liquid reserves, which can be either unsecured or secured by some of its earning assets. Alternatively, instead of trying to borrow against its earning assets, the bank can try to sell them. If there is a widespread sale of such assets, then their value—to sell or as collateral—will fall, reducing their ability to alleviate the liquidity shortage. Assistance can also take the form of a variety of measures to stem the outflow of demand liabilities, including restricting deposit withdrawals or providing a guarantee to depositors.

The subsequent sections of this chapter consider three main types of rescues: rescues of individual firms, which I term "bailouts"; assistance to the market, or "lender of last resort operations"; and direct government intervention in the banking system, or "more extreme measures."

BAILOUTS

The most straightforward type of rescue is a bailout, in which the rescuing institution offers assistance directly to one or more ailing firms. The assistance can be via loans or a purchase of shares of the troubled institution (Okazaki and Sawada 2007). The assistance is targeted at a limited number of banks, not necessarily any and all troubled institutions. Bailouts raise two immediate questions. First, under what circumstances should a rescue be undertaken? Put more simply, given that bailing out a firm is an option, how should the "to bail, or not to bail" question be answered? Second, who is responsible for undertaking such a rescue?

Given that failures of large, important banks are more likely to spread to other institutions through domino and contagion effects, it is not surprising that these banks have the highest likelihood of being bailed out. The U.S. Comptroller of the Currency enunciated this policy in Congressional testimony in 1984, stating that the eleven largest banks in the country were "too big to fail" (O'Hara and Shaw 1990, Black et al. 1997). In addition, banks that have influence among politicians, regulators, and other potential rescuers will be more likely to receive assistance. Finally, depending on the identity and resources of the institution that is doing the bailing out, the decision to offer assistance may be based on the perceived condition of the institution to be rescued. That is, if it seems improbable that the bank in question will return to profitability, and therefore will be unable to repay loans or maintain (or increase) the market value of capital injected, a bailout may be less likely.

The identity of the rescuer has changed over time. In the earliest episodes, governments typically financed and managed bailouts. This may have been the case because of the government's superior command of resources and because in an environment with only a few banking firms, private institutions may have felt disinclined to assist their competitors. By the middle of the nineteenth century, the identity of rescuer migrated away from governments to quasi-private central banks and wholly private financial institutions. This may have resulted from a philosophical aversion to government interference in the workings of the banking system or of the private economy more generally. It is not until the twentieth century, specifically after World War II, that bailouts came again to be the prerogative of the national governments and central banks (Redish 2001).

Bailout was the means chosen in three of the earliest bank rescues on record: the Bank of New South Wales in Australia during the spring and summer of 1826, the Banque de Belgique in 1838, and the Schaaffhausen Bank of Cologne in 1848. The Bank of New South Wales, established in 1817, was the first bank founded in Australia. And although it was, in fact, a private institution, it had had some official help in its founding. The Governor of Australia, Lachlan Macquarie, granted the bank's initial seven-year charter with the promise of limited liability, even though he did not have the authority to grant a royal charter or to substitute for an act of Parliament in London. Macquarie supported the bank because he believed that it would lead to the elimination of petty banking, that is, the practice of small-scale note-issuing and lending by shopkeepers and other traders.

The Bank of New South Wales remained the only bank of importance in New South Wales for a decade.[3] The booming conditions of the early to middle 1820s combined with an absence of competitors made the bank extremely profitable, and able to pay dividends at a rate of 53.5 percent in January 1826. It soon began to over-issue notes. In 1826, the bank's prosperity attracted new competition in the form of the Bank of Australia, which held its first meeting of prospective shareholders in February and opened for business in July. The new competition forced the Bank of New South Wales to cut its lending rates. Furthermore, the new entry led to a substantial drain of cash as deposits were withdrawn to pay for shares in the new bank. This situation was compounded by a currency crisis in April.[4] During the period April 3 to May 10, the bank's reserves of dollars had fallen from $122,933 to just $4,739 and rumors that the bank would soon stop payment had spread.

The pressure on the bank led it to apply to the Government for a loan of £20,000. The Governor, Ralph Darling, appointed a Board of Inquiry to inspect the bank's records. The board found that the ratio of cash to notes and deposits had fallen to less than 6 percent from over 27 percent the previous December (Butlin 1953: 195ff., 586, 589). The Government approved the loan, but several conditions were attached. First, the government would appoint three of the bank's directors. Second, the bank would reduce its discounts (i.e., loans) by one quarter over the following nine months. Third, the bank would call up all its unpaid capital.[5] Fourth, the bank would change to sterling accounting. At first the loan

---

[3]Waterloo Company, which had its origins in a flour milling company, Hutchinson, Terry, and Company, began to issue notes in 1822, although it did not conduct an extensive banking business. The other Australian banks in existence at the time were the Bank of Van Diemen's Land (1824) and Tasmanian Bank (1826); however, these were located in Tasmania, not New South Wales.

[4]A surge in imports in the preceding years had led to large outflows of currency. The colonial administration at that time had determined to move the colony to a sterling standard, which further led to an outflow of the Spanish dollar currency which had made up a large portion of the domestic money stock. Butlin (1953: ch. 6) and Fitz-Gibbon and Gizycki (2001: 11).

[5]Banks and other corporations in the nineteenth century frequently had a "nominal" (sometimes called "subscribed" or "authorized") capital, that is, the amount of share capital permitted to be issued under the terms of its incorporation or deed of settlement. Of this amount, frequently only a portion would be "paid in" or "paid up" at the time of the company's formation. Thus, a £20 share in an institution may have had £12 paid-in capital and another £8 unpaid capital, meaning that the if the firm needed additional capital, either because of business difficulties or for expansion purposes, shareholders could be called upon to pay in up to an additional £8 per share.

was not needed, since the guarantee calmed the panic. But eventually, the bank borrowed £15,000 on the security of bills and mortgage deeds, which it repaid by January 1827.

A similar situation unfolded in Belgium in late 1838 and early 1839, when the Banque de Belgique suspended payments and appeared to be about to close permanently. The bank had been founded in 1833, shortly after the Belgian Revolution of 1830, as a counterweight to the Société Générale pour favoriser l'Industrie nationale, which had been established by the Dutch King William of Orange-Nassau in 1822 (Lemoine 1929a: 176). The Dutch did not recognize the new kingdom and, by the end of 1838, it appeared that hostilities might erupt between the two countries. The breakdown of diplomacy led to panic among investors in the Banque de Belgique and the price of its shares fell dramatically on the Paris Stock Exchange. On December 10, the Société Générale presented 1.2 million francs of the Banque de Belgique's notes for redemption, more than one-third of what its total note issue had been in 1837. Five days later, the Société Générale presented another 300,000 francs; the Banque de Belgique could not redeem the notes and, on December 17, announced that it was suspending payments (Chlepner 1926: 78, 164, Chlepner 1943: 20).

Prior to the suspension, the Banque de Belgique had asked the government for assistance which was refused. The bank's suspension soon began to affect commerce and industry: companies were not able to obtain funds to meet payrolls and other current expenses, and pressure began to mount for politicians to do something about the crisis. By December 22, the Minister of Finance brought a proposal to Parliament to assist the bank (Chlepner 1943: 21). The explanation of the government's motivation was particularly brief, occupying less than twenty lines in the official gazette, and emphasized that although the bank was a private institution with no special relationship to the Treasury, the suspension had had serious effects on commerce and industry that should be contained (Chlepner 1926: 172–73). The government extended the bank a credit of 4 million francs, at an interest rate of 5 percent; it subsequently authorized a credit of an additional million francs. In reporting back to Parliament, the commission of inquiry appointed by the government acknowledged that moral hazard might be engendered by such a precedent, but that the danger of not dealing with the threat was even more dangerous.[6]

The similarities between these bailouts are striking. Both banks were large and, for the place and time, well established. The Bank of New

---

[6]"Personne dans votre commission ne s'est dissimulé, disait-il (Devaux), ce que l'intervention de l'Etat dans des affaires privées avait d'extraordinare et de dangereux en thèse générale; mais nous avons tous pensé que la situation, momentanément extraordinaire aussi, de la Belgique, légitimait suffisamment cette intervention, et lui ôtait *le danger d'un precedent*." Chlepner (1926: 173–74), italics added.

South Wales was the first bank in Australia and, aside from the relatively less important Waterloo Company and the proposed but not yet operational Bank of Australia, the only bank in Sydney. The Banque de Belgique was the second largest and second oldest bank in the country, the first founded in an independent Belgium, and after Société Générale, the most important bank in the country. The potentially devastating consequences of its suspension for commerce and industry were important motives for the bailout. Thus, in both cases, the institutions were both important enough to warrant saving; in other words, they were too big to fail.

In both the Australian and Belgian cases, the government alone had sufficient resources to undertake the bailouts. The rest of the financial system was relatively primitive and there were no other civic institutions with enough resources to intervene. Similarly, both governments were concerned about the ability of the rescued banks to repay the loans, as well as about the precedent that the bailouts would set, and so appointed special commissions to investigate the solvency of the banks. Both institutions were helped with loans, not grants or infusions of capital, although the conditions on the Bank of New South Wales bailout did entail the government appointment of three directors to the bank's board. The Belgian commission of inquiry touched on the issue of the dangerous precedent set by the arrangement, recognized the potential for moral hazard, and concluded that the effects of the crisis on the economy outweighed any potential moral hazard consequences.

Another early bailout was that of the A. Schaaffhausen Company of Cologne in 1848, which had been the largest private bank in the Rhineland. During the financial crisis of 1848, the bank became illiquid, and on March 29, suspended payments. In fact, the bank's balance sheet showed that the value of its assets exceeded the value of its liabilities, although the assets could not be turned into cash quickly enough to satisfy the demands of their creditors (Tilly 1966: 112, Born 1977: 101). The bailout of Schaaffhausen differed from those of the Bank of New South Wales and the Banque de Belgique. The Prussian government converted Schaaffhausen into an incorporated commercial bank, Schaaffhausen'scher Bankverein, and its creditors into shareholders. Half of the new shares were guaranteed to pay an annual dividend of 4.5 percent, plus back payments of 10 percent per year until 1858. The other shares were not guaranteed, and were to pay no more than 4 percent. The shares remaining to the original owners were not to pay more than 2 percent through 1858. In addition, the Prussian trade minister was entitled to choose one of the bank's three directors.

The Schaaffhausen bailout had two things in common with those of the Bank of New South Wales and Banque de Belgique. First, it was a large and important financial institution, the failure of which would have had severe implications for an economy that was already reeling from a financial crisis. Second, the government combined its assistance with the appointment of a director. And, in terms of safeguarding the bank's ability to repay its debtors, the dividends on a substantial portion of the new shares were limited under the terms of the bailout.

The Schaaffhausen bailout did introduce some novel elements. First, it resulted in the first private commercial bank incorporation in Germany. The incorporation did not signal a change in the legal basis of German banking: it would be five years before another bank, the Darmstädter, was incorporated. This form of bailout may have been adopted so as not to signal that the reorganization indicated a new willingness by the Prussian government to bail out troubled institutions and thereby to ameliorate any moral hazard fallout from the bailout. Second, the bailout converted the bank's creditors into shareholders or, perhaps given the conditions on the dividends, preferred shareholders or even bondholders. Third, the bailout limited the direct fiscal contribution of the Prussian government to guaranteeing dividend payments, but otherwise insulated the Prussian Treasury from any fallout from the rescue: the fiscal impact of bailouts remains a contentious political issue today.

As the nineteenth century progressed, bailouts became more and more the province of central banks and private financial institutions, albeit with the consent—and even support—of governments. This pattern was adopted in the bailouts of the Comptoir d'Escompte of Paris in 1889 and of Baring Brothers in London in 1890. The Comptoir d'Escompte was established by a decree of March 8, 1848.[7] One-third of the Comptoir's capital had been supplied by the shareholders, with the remainder being provided by the state and the city of Paris, although its profits were to accrue to the shareholders only. The institution's original purpose had been to provide discounting facilities (i.e., access to credit) to the tradesmen of Paris in order to foster commerce. The Comptoir grew rapidly and its capital was doubled in 1853 and again in 1860. The additional funds were entirely private—the ownership shares of the government and city of Paris were gradually bought back. At the same time, restrictions on the Comptoir's activities were relaxed and it engaged in lending as well as discounting and other banking transactions (Des Essars 1896: 101–5).

During the 1880s, the Comptoir made substantial loans to the Société des Métaux, a metals company. In the later part of the decade, the Société attempted to corner the market on copper by acquiring control over the

---

[7]An earlier, temporary institution in Paris, the Comptoir d'Escompt, which had been established with government funds, had operated between 1830 and 1832. Des Essars (1896: 63).

output of a large number of producers. Unfortunately for the Société and, as it turned out, the Comptoir, the production of firms that were not in the copper syndicate continued to grow throughout 1888 and the price of copper fell. In early March 1889, the decline in copper prices led to a panic and a run on the Comptoir, which had advanced a large sum to support copper prices.

The crisis broke on March 5, coinciding with the suicide of Comptoir's chief, Eugène Denfert-Rochereau. According to Des Essars (1896: 105), Denfert-Rochereau had made several commitments on the Comptoir's behalf without the knowledge of the administrative council. In a display of "damage control," officials at the Comptoir insisted that his death, which occurred as soon as the institution's plight became public, had not been suicide. According to the *New York Times* (March 6, 1889), officials at the Comptoir said that he had, ". . . a fainting fit while driving from the Comptoir d'Escompte to the Banque de Pays Bas. He recovered and was taken home, where he died an hour afterward." The next day the *Times*, quoting a Paris newspaper, noted that he had taken his own life with a revolver.

Within days, the Banque de France had agreed to lend 100 million francs (withdrawals from the Comptoir totaled 37.5 million francs on March 6) and the Minister of Finance (Rouvier) encouraged the larger bankers to guarantee the loan. According to the *New York Times* on March 9:

> A meeting of bankers, presided over by M. Rouvier, sat at the Ministry of Finance from 10 P.M. yesterday until 3 A.M. to-day. Several speeches were made. Finally M. Rouvier, losing patience, protested against the unwillingness of the bankers to guarantee the loan, and their own refusal to recognize their own private fortunes and public prosperity in question, and he threatened to announce to Parliament that the Government alone was ready to do its duty. The speech produced a great impression, and a syndicate including Rothschild, Malet, Andre, and Girod, Heine, Hottinguer, the Crédit Foncier, and the Banque d'Escompte was formed to guarantee the loan. The Crédit Lyonnais and the Société Générale did not join the syndicate because they require funds themselves in view of the crisis. The panic is now practically ended, the sums withdrawn being redeposited in other banks.

The government's role, then, was to encourage, and, if necessary, threaten the bankers to subscribe to the guarantee for the Comptoir's debts.

The bailout of the Comptoir d'Escompte was not dissimilar to that of Baring Brothers, which took place the following year in London. Baring had been founded in 1763 as the John and Francis Baring Company, which was renamed Baring Brothers in 1806 (Hidy 1949, Ziegler 1988). The firm began as import and export agents, but soon expanded into merchant banking activities (i.e., trade finance) and underwriting public and private securities, as well as insurance. Its prominence was such that the Duc de Richelieu had referred to the firm as the "sixth (great) power" in Europe, after Great Britain, France, Russia, Austria, and Prussia.

Baring Brothers was especially active in providing finance to South American countries, having made its first loan to Argentina in 1824. During the next sixty-five years, the firm became increasingly committed to issuing and underwriting loans on behalf of South American governments and public works projects. Low domestic interest rates during the last quarter of the century, combined with higher returns offered by investments in Latin America and elsewhere, provided further incentive for British overseas investment, which peaked in 1890 (Edelstein 1982: 313–14). By this time, loans to the rapidly expanding Argentinean and Uruguayan economies accounted for about three-quarters of Baring's portfolio. The booming conditions in Argentina that had prevailed during the 1880s led to a rapid increase in land prices, as well as the buildup of a substantial external debt. By 1890, the large external debt discouraged European investors from taking more Argentinean securities, and the value of the country's inconvertible paper currency fell. In 1890 Argentina experienced civil disturbances, a collapse of the land boom (in which land prices fell by 50 percent), a run on the banking system, and an abortive attempt to arrange a moratorium on withdrawing bank deposits (Batchelor 1986: 49–54, Hawtrey 1938: 105–10). By Saturday, November 8, the directors of Baring were aware that they might be forced to suspend.[8]

The Governor of the Bank of England, William Lidderdale, arranged for a detailed examination of Baring's accounts, as well as for separate meetings with the directors of Baring and the Chancellor of the Exchequer, George Goschen, on Monday, November 10. Goschen was a former director of the Bank of England, who, unlike many of his predecessors, was on good terms with the bank. Having been convinced that Baring was solvent, but illiquid, the bank began to lend money against the security of Baring-issued acceptances (i.e., securities). As the week progressed, the bank found itself in possession of a large and growing amount of Baring's paper and the Governor approached the Prime Minister (Lord Salisbury) and Chancellor of the Exchequer, telling them that unless the Government agreed to bear some of the risk of the loss on the securities

---

[8]The following description of the bailout comes from the account of William Lidderdale, the Governor of the Bank of England. Bank of England Archives G15/192.

he would, ". . . return (to the bank) at once and throw out all further acceptances of the firm."

With the Government's assurance that it would indeed bear some of the risk, Lidderdale began assembling subscriptions to a guarantee fund. The subscribers would not need to advance any money and would only be called on to pay if the bank-supervised liquidation of Baring's assets was not sufficient to meet its liabilities. Lidderdale placed the Bank of England's name at the top of the list of subscribers to the guarantee fund for £1 million and set about coaxing, cajoling, and, in some cases, even threatening potential subscribers.[9] By 5:30 pm, he had commitments of £3.25 million; by 11:00 am the next morning, £6.5 million; and by 4:00 pm, he had commitments of nearly £10 million, "thus . . . securing the Public from the calamity of a failure of Messrs. Baring Brothers" (Bank of England Archives, G4/113). Baring was liquidated, along with the personal fortunes of a number of its directors, in an orderly manner and the company was reestablished as a limited liability company, which continued to conduct business in the City of London—until it failed again in 1995 due to fraud.

Like the Comptoir d'Escompte, Baring Brothers was a large and well-established firm, whose owners and directors were well connected to the political and financial elites: members of the Baring firm had been directors of the Bank of England continuously since 1840 and seventeen members of the extended Baring family sat in Parliament between 1812 and 1918 (Lisle-Williams 1984). Like the bailout of the Comptoir d'Escompte, the bailout of Baring was orchestrated by the central bank with the support of the government. In both cases, the financial community was dragooned into participating in the bailouts. The bailouts themselves did not require a large immediate outlay of funds, but did involve the acceptance of a substantial contingent liability.

The early part of this section considered several nineteenth-century bailouts. The institutions involved and terms of these rescues have been described in some detail. The first question raised in this section—to bail or not to bail?—cannot be addressed fully without considering instances in which bailouts could have occurred but, for one reason or another, did

---

[9] In a letter to Robert Davidson, Lidderdale, a fellow Scot, complained about the small subscriptions undertaken by his countrymen. He pointed out that the Scottish were dependent upon the Bank of England, "for the prompt return of the large sums employed in this market, and for the safety of a considerable part of the security you hold against that money." He further asked: "Are you wise to be so shabby? The presence of your agencies in London is not so favorably regarded in England, and the next time your privileges reconsidered . . . it will little help you to have it on record that the Scotch Banks did so little in November 1890 for the common good." Letter dated November 18, 1890. Bank of England Archives, G23/85.

not. I briefly consider examples from Britain and France of banks that were arguably good candidates for a bailout but were not rescued.

Just seven years before the bailout of the Comptoir d'Escompte in Paris, another substantial French banking institution, the Banque de l'Union Générale, failed. The Union Générale had been founded in 1878 by Eugène Bontoux.[10] It had strong ties to the Catholic Church, having been formed with official church sanction and with numerous Catholic dignitaries on its board of directors as well as among its depositors. It had established a number of branches and had aggressively courted deposits. The bank grew rapidly, increasing its capital substantially and riding a boom in railroad investments, both in France and southeastern Europe, especially the Balkans. The collapse of the railroad boom toward the end of 1881 hit the Union Générale hard: its shares fell by two-thirds during January 4–19, 1882, and despite receiving loans of 18.1 million francs between January 19 and January 25, the bank was forced to suspend by the end of the month.

Why didn't the Ministry of Finance, Banque de France, and the financial community bail out the Union Générale? Bontoux blamed the downfall of the Union Générale on a cabal of Jewish-owned private financial houses, the primarily Jewish- and Protestant-owned *haute banque*; however, Bouvier (1960) finds no evidence of this (Cameron 1953: 462). One possible explanation is that the bank's affairs were such that it was viewed as not salvageable: the Union Générale had falsified some of its bookkeeping and Bontoux was subsequently arrested. Inaction by the government may also have been a function of timing: the bank collapsed on January 30—shortly after the fall of the Gambetta Ministry on January 25, but prior to the installation of the Freycinet Ministry on January 31. Bouvier (1960) expresses no such concern, noting that the affair was managed after discussions between the haute banque and the outgoing (Allain-Targé) and incoming (Say) finance ministers (White 2007). Kindleberger (1996: 152) suggests that the French financial establishment was not inclined to engage in bailouts at all, which explains why it did not bail out the Union Générale and, earlier, the Crédit Mobilier in 1868. He further argues that the Comptoir d'Escompte was bailed out because it was thought that a second large bank failure in the span of seven years might have destroyed the credibility of the French financial system.[11]

---

[10]For details of the rise and fall of the Union Générale see Bouvier (1960), Bonin (1992: 141), Saint Marc (1983: 171–72), Des Essars (1896: 71–72), and Liesse (1910: 173–77). The story of the Union Générale is told, in fictionalized form, in the 1891 novel *Argent* (*Money*), by Émile Zola.

[11]In contrast to the Union Générale, Kindleberger (1996: 151) argues that the Péreire Brothers' Crédit Mobilier was allowed to fail because it had presented a challenge to the

Britain presents two analogous cases of bailouts being refused in the period leading up to the Baring bailout, those of Overend, Gurney in 1866 and the City of Glasgow Bank in 1878. The firm that eventually became Overend, Gurney, and Company originated with the Gurney family of Norwich. Long established as wool merchants, and later as country bankers, they merged with a firm of London bill brokers, Richardson, Overend, and Company, in 1807. The firm grew to such status, according to the *Times* of London (May 11, 1866), that it could, ". . . rightly claim to be the greatest instrument of credit in the Kingdom." When questioned about the extent of his firm's business before a House of Lords committee in 1848, Samuel Gurney conceded that it was about equal to all of their competitors combined (King 1936: 117). A new generation of ownership at Overend came into open conflict with the Bank of England following the crisis of 1857. The Bank of England decided to curtail the credit it was prepared to offer the bill brokers, because they borrowed heavily when they were short of funds and left little on deposit when funds were plentiful. Overend protested this new policy in 1860 when it engineered substantial withdrawals from the Bank of England, leading that bank's reserve to decline by £2 million out of a total of £7 million, or by nearly 29 percent. The action had apparently been undertaken by Overend, Gurney in concert with other Quaker businessmen: the Bank of England received an anonymous letter saying that Overend and its friends were capable of further withdrawals. Unfortunately for Overend, the Bank of England had a long memory. When, six years later, the value of Overend, Gurney's portfolio collapsed, the Bank of England refused its request for assistance, saying that the security offered was insufficient.

The City of Glasgow Bank, established in 1839, had been forced to suspend during the crisis of 1857, although it later reopened (Checkland 1975: 469ff.). Like the Union Générale, it pursued aggressively expansionary policies, lending against large amounts of questionable foreign securities as well as financing highly speculative investments in New Zealand. The bank's loans were concentrated to an unusual degree: three firms accounted for 45 percent of its loan portfolio. Following several years of fraudulent accounting, it was only a matter of time before the bank ran into difficulties, which finally came in 1878. Although it is not clear whether the City of Glasgow Bank approached the Bank of England, it did request assistance from the committee of Scottish banks, which was promptly denied on the grounds that the bank's affairs were in a terrible state. The directors were subsequently tried for falsifying bank statements, found guilty, and sentenced to prison (Wallace 1905).

---

established Rothschilds. In the Crédit Mobilier's final days, the Bank of France refused to accept its securities as collateral for loans.

Consider the two questions that were raised at the outset. First, which firms get bailed out? Based on the limited number of cases examined here, it appears that the decision to bail out a firm depends on at least three things. First, the perceived seriousness of the fallout from the failure: each of the rescued firms mentioned were large and important—in some cases the only bank in the country, in other cases, one of the largest. Clearly, fallout was not the only factor, since several large and important firms (e.g., Union Générale and Overend, Gurney) were allowed to fail, leading to extraordinary crises. The Overend and Baring crises are further distinguished by the orientation of these firms: Overend's business was primarily domestic and its failure led to an increased demand for domestic withdrawals from the Bank of England, which it was able to address by issuing notes; Baring was internationally oriented and its collapse might have led to foreign withdrawals, threatening the Bank of England's gold reserves. Hence, it could be argued that the fallout of a failure of Barings would have been more difficult to combat with the weapons in the Bank of England's arsenal. Second, the decision depended on the fundamental soundness of the institution to be rescued: neither governments, nor central banks, nor private firms were anxious to bail out an institution that would not be able to repay the debt. Therefore, the institution coordinating the rescue typically undertook some sort of examination to assess whether the firm could be salvaged. Banks that were manifestly not in that category, such as the City of Glasgow Bank, were denied funds. In addition to the potential financial burden, rescuers were concerned about perceived moral hazard consequences, which would have been greater if manifestly unsound institutions were routinely bailed out. Third, connections did matter. The Bank of New South Wales, the Banque de Belgique, and Baring Brothers had important political backers. Overend, Gurney was a known opponent of the Bank of England, the institution that would have had an important role in any bailout.

The second question posed was: who undertakes the rescue? The earliest bailouts were made by state institutions: the government in the case of the Bank of New South Wales and Banque de Belgique. Quite simply, there was no other institution with the resources to preserve financial stability. In time, the responsibility for the bailout was passed to quasi-private central banks and private financial institutions, such as J. P. Morgan during the U.S. crises of 1890 and 1907 (Wicker 2000: 50, 88ff.). Schaaffhausen marks an early case where the capital for the rescue was put up, at government insistence, by the creditors themselves. Although the state stood ready to provide additional funds, in fact, the funds that were required were dragooned from the creditors. Later in the period, the responsibility passed to the private sector and central banks. Despite this trend, however, governments remained important players, encouraging these institutions to support bailouts, if not actually providing the support themselves.

LENDERS OF LAST RESORT

In contrast to the bailouts described above, where assistance—typically in the form of secured or unsecured lending or a guarantee—is directed to one or more specific firms, consider a situation in which less targeted assistance is rendered. This type of rescue comes in the form of secured loans which are available to any and all banks with sufficient collateral, and is known as lender of last resort, the name given to it by a long and distinguished intellectual lineage, including Henry Thornton and Walter Bagehot. Both Thornton and Bagehot specifically excluded bailouts of individual firms from their prescription of how lender of last resort operations were to work and specifically included the notion of collateral.

Capie (2002: 310) provides a nice description of how the lender of last resort function should work in practice, which illustrates in stark detail how it differs from a bailout.

> The mechanism can be thought of as the central bank with a discount window that is of frosted glass and is raised just a few inches. Representatives of institutions could therefore appear at the window and push through the paper they wanted discounted. The central bankers would return the appropriate amount of cash, reflecting the going interest rate. The central banker does not know, nor does he care, who is on the other side of the window. He simply discounts good quality paper or lends on the basis of good collateral.

The identity, creditworthiness, and importance of the borrower are completely irrelevant to the process—the lender of last resort merely lends against sound collateral.

Such an operation might be necessary for several reasons. If, for whatever reason, enough depositors panicked and sought to withdraw their deposits, banks under pressure would find themselves short of cash necessary to satisfy these demands. The lender of last resort provides a mechanism for transforming earning assets (i.e., securities), which are illiquid relative to reserves, into cash to meet increased demands from depositors. In the absence of such a lender, banks would have insufficient liquidity to meet withdrawal demands and would have to close. Further, to the extent that a market for such collateral existed, attempts to sell the securities in large amounts would lead to sharp decline in securities prices, which might contribute to, rather than calm, the panic.

The central bank has one particular feature that makes it uniquely qualified for the role of lender of last resort: it is the ultimate source of domestic liquidity. That is, since the central bank creates money by printing notes and creating deposits, it is well positioned to create liquidity in quantities sufficient for domestic lender of last resort purposes. Central banks' ability to undertake the role of lender of last resort, at least in the later nineteenth century, was hampered by a commitment to the gold standard by many countries. Under the gold standard, central banks were required to redeem their notes for gold at a fixed rate of exchange. The requirement to maintain this rate of exchange limited the ability to expand liquidity in order to meet a crisis, since a monetary expansion caused by lender of last resort operations might lead to a depreciation of the exchange rate. Furthermore, a run on the domestic currency, which might accompany or precipitate a banking crisis, presents the central bank with a stark policy choice: maintain the gold standard by undertaking monetary tightening (i.e., restriction of credit, higher interest rates) at the cost of slowing the economy, or abandon the gold standard and undertake expansionary lending policies to ameliorate the banking crisis. Expansionary monetary policy presents less of a problem for a country that is not on the gold standard and instead has a floating exchange rate; however, it could still lead to inflation and exchange rate depreciation.

Although the central bank is the most likely candidate to act as lender of last resort, governments have also taken on that role. The U.S. Treasury acted as lender of last resort from the earliest days of the Republic (Taus 1943, Sylla, Wright, and Cowan 2009). The federal government in Canada was empowered to act as lender of last resort—and did so—under the terms of the Finance Act of 1914 (McIvor 1958). Nongovernment entities with sufficient resources to provide the requisite liquidity, such as the regional clearinghouses in the United States discussed below, have also acted in that role.

The lender of last resort function has a long intellectual history (Humphrey 1975, Bordo 1990). The first to explicitly discuss it was Sir Francis Baring, writing in the wake of the crisis of 1793. Baring (1797 [1993]: 20–21) described the general shortage of money caused by the crisis, as well as the Bank of England's tentative response:

In this predicament the country at large could have no other resource but London; and, after having exhausted the Bankers, that resource finally terminated in the Bank of England. In the mean while, the alarm in the country continued to increase; confidence in their Banks vanished; every creditor was clamorous for payment, which he insisted should be made in gold, and which was complied with, until the Bankers in London were exhausted. At first the Bank accommodated themselves to the circumstances, and furnished large supplies; but unfortunately the Directors caught the panic; their nerves could not support the daily and constant demand for guineas (i.e., gold); and for the purpose of checking that demand, they curtailed their discounts to a point never before experienced, and which placed every part of the commerce of the country in a considerable degree of danger.

Baring went on to say that: "In such cases the Bank are not an intermediate body, or power; there is no resource on their refusal, for they are the *dernier resort.*" Baring used the French legal term indicating the court of last appeal quite deliberately: as the ultimate holder of banking reserves in the country, the Bank of England was the only institution in the country that could lend in times of distress. If it did not, no one else would.

Henry Thornton refined the concept in speeches in Parliament, evidence given before Parliamentary committee in 1797, and in a subsequently published volume. Thornton argued that in normal times the Bank of England ought to regulate the money stock so that it grew at roughly the same rate as output. He also argued that the bank ought to undertake restrictive monetary policy in response to an external drain of gold, such as might occur due to a balance of payments deficit. Restrictive policy would raise interest rates and attract gold flows from overseas. In considering situations in which the lender of last resort might be useful, he argued that the bank ought to temporarily expand its loans and note issues in response to an internal drain, when domestic residents had heightened demands for liquidity. In discussing the crisis of 1793, Thornton (1802 [1939]: 127) noted: "If there has been any fault in the conduct of the Bank of England, the fault, as I conceive, has rather been . . . on the side of too much restricting its notes in the late seasons of alarm, than on that of too much enlarging them."

The concept of the lender of last resort is most often associated with Walter Bagehot (1848, 1924), who developed it in a series of articles, as well as in his classic 1873 volume *Lombard Street.* Bagehot recognized that internal and external drains could take place simultaneously and, in fact, believed that a persistent external drain would lead to an internal drain due to doubts over the stability of the currency. Bagehot recommended that the Bank of England "lend freely at a penalty rate," that is, provide ample liquidity, but do so at a high rate of interest to prevent a run on the currency and discourage non-emergency borrowing. Bagehot's innovations were both his policy prescription and his insistence that the bank should publicly commit to this policy before it was actually needed.

Both Thornton and Bagehot strongly opposed the notion of bailouts (Humphrey 1975: 6). Thornton (1802 [1939]: 188) explicitly recognized the moral hazard that such bailouts might engender:

It is by no means intended to imply, that it would become the Bank of England to relieve every distress which the rashness of country banks may bring upon them: the bank, by doing this, might encourage their improvidence. There seems to be a medium at which a public bank should aim in granting aid to inferior establishments, and which it must often find very difficult to be observed. The relief should be neither so prompt and liberal as to exempt those who misconduct their business from all natural causes of their fault, nor so scanty and slow as deeply to involve the general interests.

Both argued that the role of the lender of last resort was not to prevent crises from occurring, but to provide relief to the general market after crises and to prevent their spread. In discussing the causes that might generate a crisis, Bagehot (1924: 118) mentioned, "a bad harvest, an apprehension of a foreign invasion, a sudden failure of a great firm which everybody trusted." Or (p. 251), the failure of a large bank: "Now, no cause is more capable of producing a panic, perhaps none is so capable, as the failure of a first-rate joint stock bank in London." His remedy (p. 51), in terms of extending loans was that the Bank of England ". . . must lend to merchants, to minor bankers, to 'this man and that man,' whenever the security is good." He makes no mention of lending to a failing institution in order to prevent a crisis, since the job of the lender of last resort is to contain the crisis once it occurs, not to prevent it by a bailout.

The Bank of England was the first institution to develop into a consistent lender of last resort. The evolution was neither direct nor quick.[12] The bank had been granted a charter as England's only joint stock bank in 1694 in return for a loan to the Crown and its monopoly privileges continued until the nineteenth century. Despite its quasi-public character, beyond its fiscal relationship with the government, the Bank of England was regarded both by the government and by itself as an essentially private institution with limited responsibility to the banking and financial communities. In time, the bank—and government—came to see it as playing a broader public role in maintaining banking and financial stability.

In other times and places, the evolution of central banks into lenders of last resort was much quicker. For example, the Bank of Japan intervened to provide additional liquidity during the stock market crisis of 1890, just eight years after its founding. Had it not done so, a substantial banking crisis would likely have developed (Tamaki 1995: 66–67). Lenders of last resort were quickly established in northern Europe during the

---

[12]Lovell (1957) dates the beginnings of the Bank of England as lender of last resort to the eighteenth century.

worldwide crisis of 1857. Although many major commercial centers were hard hit, the crisis was especially severe in Hamburg. As an important *entrepôt* in trade between Scandinavia, northern Germany, Britain, and the Americas, the expansion in the issue of Hamburg bills of exchange in the years leading up to the crisis left it particularly vulnerable (Wirth 1874: 373ff.). The government of Hamburg, after arguing over whether to increase the note issue, which could have depreciated the silver-backed currency, created a new bank to discount mercantile trade bills. The new bank was funded with securities deposited by the Treasury, as well as government-borrowed silver. The Bank of Prussia, caught up in the crisis itself, refused to lend the required silver. Austria, however, which was on an inconvertible paper standard, loaned 10 million marks banco against the collateral of 5 million mark's worth of securities. The arrival of the train carrying the silver (*Silberzug*) is said to have calmed the crisis almost immediately (Flandreau 1997: 750, Kindleberger 1996, Ahrens 1986). Thus, the crisis led to the establishment of a new institution. Elsewhere in northern Europe, governments and central banks acted as lender of last resort. The Danmarks Nationalbank unilaterally extended the maturity on all Hamburg bills it held by three months and the legal limit on the quantity of notes it could issue was abolished. Sweden and Norway contracted large state loans to tide the markets over the crisis (Jensen 1896: 380, *Times* of London, December 7, 1857).

The Bank of England evolved into a lender of last resort during the nineteenth century. This evolution took place over the course of a number of crises, each of which was followed by long and detailed examination by policy makers of how the bank ought to act in times of crisis. The evolution was essentially complete by the time of the publication of *Lombard Street*. On the other hand, in Japan (1890) and Hamburg (1857), where institutions capable of acting as lenders of last resort either did not exist, or had not acted in that capacity, they emerged more quickly. A third type of lender of last resort institution developed in the nineteenth century in the United States. Unlike the quasi-official Bank of England, and state-owned and/or funded institutions in Japan and Hamburg, the institutions that arose in the United States, clearinghouses, were entirely private.

Bank clearinghouses emerged in the United States in the nineteenth century. The New York clearinghouse was officially formed in 1853 (although clearinghouses may have existed as early as 1831), and was soon followed by those in Boston (1856) and Philadelphia (1858). Clearinghouses were established not only in large banking centers, but also in smaller banking markets including Topeka, Kansas and St, Joseph, Missouri (Cannon 1900, 1910). The main purpose of a clearinghouse is to provide a central location where bank representatives can meet and cancel out claims against one another, thus reducing the time, effort, and cash necessary to do so. For example, if Bank A owes Bank B $10 and Bank B owes Bank C $10, the debts can be settled with one payment from Bank A to Bank C, rather than two payments (A to B and B to C). If A owes B $10, B owes C $10, and C owes A $10, the accounts can be settled with no payment whatsoever, rather than three individual payments of $10. Clearinghouses settled a variety of claims, including banknotes, checks, drafts, and bills of exchange. They also set rules for the behavior of member banks, including limiting deposit rates and setting prices on claims to be traded.

Clearinghouses took on special importance during crises (Gorton 1985: 280–81, Cannon 1900, 1910, Timberlake 1984). In the event of a panic, the clearinghouse would authorize the issuance of clearinghouse loan certificates. A bank facing a shortfall of cash could apply to the clearinghouse loan committee for certificates, against which the bank would submit a portion of its securities portfolio as collateral. Certificates were issued with maturities of from one to three months, carried an interest charge, and were issued in large denominations. They could then be used in place of cash in the clearing, allowing banks to have more cash on hand to satisfy depositors' demands.

American clearinghouses worked, in some ways, like the Bank of England had during nineteenth-century crises, creating liquidity in the form of loan certificates during emergencies. The loan certificates were the joint obligations of the members of the clearinghouse, so that if the security posted as collateral was not sufficient to redeem the loan, the responsibility fell on the surviving members. Like the Bank of England, the clearinghouses issued additional liquidity on the security of collateral, and discounted the collateral as warranted.

The operations of the clearinghouses differed from the Bank of England in a number of important respects, however. Because the clearinghouses were private institutions and were not subject to government supervision or regulation, they did not require legislative approval to increase the supply of money or reserves beyond some government-imposed limit. Second, at least in earlier crises, the clearinghouse created liquidity only in the form of large-denomination clearinghouse loan certificates, which were used solely for interbank clearing, unlike Bank of England notes which were useful both as reserves and as circulating currency. During the crises of 1893 and 1907, American clearinghouses began to issue small denomination loan certificates directly to the public. In 1893 these issues amounted to approximately $100 million, or 2.5 percent of the total outstanding money stock, and in 1907 they increased to $500 million, or about 4.5 percent of the money stock (Gorton 1985: 282). The private issuance of currency was soon brought to the attention of the government. The Aldrich-Vreeland Act (1908), passed in the aftermath of the 1907 crisis, brought the authority for the issue of emergency currency under the Secretary of the Treasury.

Finally, clearinghouses differed markedly from the Bank of England in their willingness and ability to micro-manage banking affairs during crises. Gorton (1985) notes that the clearinghouse directed loans from healthy banks to ailing banks, and that banks that were in poor condition were generally not allowed to fail during crises, but were expelled for failing to repay loans after the panic had ended. Thus, although clearinghouses fulfilled the classical role of the lender of last resort, they also appear to have instituted elements of a bailout, by directing credit to ailing institutions, and those of a regulator, with the authority to discipline poorly behaving banks. The implicit guarantee offered by membership in the clearinghouse during panics suggests more extreme types of intervention.

MORE EXTREME MEASURES

Both bailouts and lender of last resort–style rescues provide an infusion of cash, so that demands by depositors can be met in a timely manner and banks need not close. In the case of bailouts, liquid assets are loaned—collateralized or uncollateralized—after the lending institution makes some effort to determine whether the borrowing institution will be able to repay the loan. In the case of lender of last resort operations, the lender does not concern itself with the overall solvency of any particular borrower since it merely transforms less liquid collateral into cash.

Since a crisis occurs when depositor demands exceed the ability of institutions to pay out their depositors, another possible rescue scenario is for an institution with sufficient resources to guarantee that bank deposits will be paid under any circumstances. This could be through public or private deposit insurance that had been established prior to any financial stress; alternatively, a deposit guarantee could be instituted once a crisis has erupted. If the guarantee is credible, it might halt a panic, reassuring depositors that their funds will be available under any circumstances. If the guarantee is not credible, but the guaranteeing institution has sufficient funds to meet all withdrawals, the panic should be quelled by the payoff of all depositors who insist on immediate payment. Because this type of rescue does not involve keeping banks open, but somehow closing, guaranteeing, or taking them over, these responses are qualitatively different from bailouts and lender of last resort operations.

Deposit insurance has had a long history in the United States, where the first plan was adopted by the state of New York in 1829 (Calomiris 1989, 1990, Bodenhorn 2003: 155ff.). All banks applying for a new charter or a charter renewal were required to contribute to the newly created

Safety Fund; since charters were of limited duration, by 1837 more than 90 percent of the state's banks were participants in the system. Bankers were required to pay an annual assessment of 0.5 percent of the paid-in capital stock, until the total amount paid equaled 3 percent of the capital stock. Special assessments could be made if the fund fell below a minimum required level. The Safety Fund was to compensate the creditors of failed banks if the liquidation of failed banks was insufficient to do so. Given the possibility of moral hazard, the Safety Fund's commissioners were given authority to examine the condition of banks fully, "... in short a degree of supervision almost unthinkable at the time" (Golembe 1960: 183). Similar laws were soon passed in Vermont (1831) and Michigan (1836); slightly different insurance plans were adopted in Indiana (1834), Ohio (1845), and Iowa (1858). Of these systems, Michigan's collapsed under the weight of the crisis of 1837, the New York system became bankrupt in 1841 and had to be reformulated and refunded, and the Vermont system was unable to pay all claimants, although it, like the others, lasted until 1865–66.

Although additional measures for state and federal deposit insurance were debated, the next set of deposit insurance laws was not passed until after the crisis of 1907. During that decade, eight states established deposit insurance systems: Oklahoma, Kansas, Nebraska, Texas (1909); Mississippi (1914); South Dakota (1915); North Dakota and Washington (1917) (Blocker 1929, American Bankers Association 1933). These systems were established with a variety of features: some were compulsory, others voluntary; each had different levels of assessments, both regular and special; each entailed different levels of regulation and had different organizational structures, although they were all state- and not bank-run. Each ran into difficulty with the decline in agricultural prices in the 1920s, and either collapsed or became inoperative. The guarantee of bank deposits became more firmly established during the Great Depression. In the United States, federal deposit insurance was created under the Banking Act of 1933. In Norway, the government placed a moratorium on withdrawing old deposits and a government guarantee on new deposits.

Another extreme form of rescue is for banks to be prevented from paying out to depositors, even if they might wish to do so. If banks' demand liabilities are somehow rendered less demandable, then the threat of closure may also be reduced. Under this strategy, deposits can be frozen, guaranteed, or their obligation can be transferred to a third party. The simplest of these measures is for the government to declare a bank holiday, relieving banks of the obligation to pay off panicking depositors. California resorted to this method in the wake of the San Francisco earthquake and fire of 1906, and it was used around the country during the crisis of 1907 (Andrew 1908). In 1907, runs on banks and trust companies in New York City began around October 21–23, and by October 26, the New York clearinghouse began issuing clearinghouse loan certificates. On October 24, the governor of Nevada declared a bank holiday until November 4; on October 28, the governor of Oregon declared a bank holiday, which was extended by subsequent proclamations until December 14; and in California, a bank holiday was declared on October 31 and was subsequently extended until December 21. Friedman and Schwartz (1963: 161n) note that banks were, in fact, still open during these bank holidays, paying out cash substitutes (i.e., scrip), but that the holiday closed the courts, thereby preventing them from ordering banks to pay out cash. According to Andrew (1908: 498):

> This method of relieving business involved great inconvenience in unexpected ways. The whole judicial system was thereby brought to a standstill, the courts being restrained from trying criminal cases. The governor of California very soon felt obliged to call a special session of the state legislature, and so secured the authority to declare "special holidays" during which only civil actions based on express or implied contracts for the payment of money would be excluded.

The United Kingdom followed this example prior to the outbreak of World War I. It became clear on Saturday, August 1 that the country would be involved in the hostilities, although war on Germany was not declared until August 5. Monday, August 3, was a regularly scheduled "bank holiday," and the government extended the holiday two more days in order to avoid a panic. In addition, an emergency supply of one pound notes was issued to meet any increased demand due to the outbreak of war, much like the issue of additional clearinghouse currency in the United States. Further, the Bank of England agreed to discount (i.e., lend against the collateral of) German bills of exchange, which had no chance of being paid off during hostilities, and hold them in "cold storage" until after the war. The British response to the outbreak of war was thus multi-faceted, including elements of lender of last resort as well as more extreme measures. And in Italy during the 1921–22 crisis, the government reinstated portions of a repealed 1903 law that allowed the Banca di Sconto to apply for a moratorium (Sraffa 1922).

The banking crises of the early 1930s led to the imposition of bank holidays and moratoria, both in Europe and the United States. In 1931, bank holidays and moratoria on deposit withdrawals were instituted in Germany, Hungary, Norway, Latvia, and Romania, for varying periods of time and as part of broader packages. In the United States, bank holidays were declared by Oregon (October 1932), Nevada (November 1932), several cities in Illinois (January 1933), Michigan, Maryland, and cities in Ohio and Indiana (February 1933), as well as several states in March prior to the declaration of a national banking holiday on March 6.

Perhaps the most extreme form of rescue involves a direct state take-over of one or more troubled financial institutions. It could be argued that a government takeover (i.e., nationalization) does not differ much from a bailout or lender of last resort operation—instead of making a loan or buying collateral, the government injects capital into the troubled institution. However, such rescues are different for at least two reasons. First, by obtaining an equity stake, the government can only claim a share of the bank's assets after depositors, bondholders, and certain other creditors' claims have been satisfied, increasing the likelihood that the operation will be costly to taxpayers. Second, by acquiring an ownership stake the government is more likely to take an active role in management, which may be costly (Blass and Grossman 2001). A management role would not be undertaken by the rescuer in the case of a lender of last resort operation, although it might be the case in a bailout.

Nationalizations were not common before the twentieth century. During the banking crises associated with the Great Depression, however, such intervention became more commonplace. In Austria, for example, the government contributed substantial amounts to the failed Credit Anstalt and, along with foreign creditors, became the bank's joint owner (League of Nations 1934: 44–45). The government also contributed to the reorganization of other large Vienna banks. In Germany, the government contributed 400 million rentenmarks to the institutions amalgamating into the Dresdner Bank in order to enable them to write off bad assets, in return for which they received equity with a nominal value of RM152 million. Other substantial capital infusions were made to the Commerz- und Privat-Bank and Deutsche Bank. As a result, by 1934 the Reich held over 70 percent of all the capital of German banks with share capitals exceeding RM10 million. Only one of the large Berlin banks remained completely privately held. In Italy, the government established the Istituto per la Ricostruzione Industriale (IRI) which took over ownership of the country's three largest banks as well as a variety of industrial enterprises. Other state ownership came about after the 1931 financial crises in Romania, Switzerland, and Sweden. In the United States, the Reconstruction Finance Corporation (RFC) made substantial loans to banks in 1932 and 1933. By the last quarter of 1933, the RFC authorized the purchase of preferred shares in institutions (Butkiewicz 1995).

Making the Cure Less Costly than the Disease

Banking rescues of one sort or another have been a common feature of the financial landscape since the earliest banking crises. It is not difficult to understand the incentives to rescue troubled banks: in the absence of a rescue, a domino effect or contagion of fear may lead to the failure of otherwise healthy institutions, disruptions in securities markets, and a slowdown in aggregate economic activity. Thus, there are important reasons—both economic and political—to initiate a rescue. Rescues can have substantial costs, however. In addition to the resources spent on the rescue itself, such actions run the risk of rescuing perennially weak firms that survive only because of successive bailouts and may be a case of throwing good money after bad. Further, such rescues may introduce moral hazard, encouraging greater risk-taking behavior on the part of other firms that may become convinced that, in case of trouble, they too will be rescued.

In considering whether to engage in bailouts, governments and bankers have long been aware of their fiscal costs and of the problem of moral hazard. In the earliest bailouts, those providing the assistance were careful to assess the financial strength of the bank to be rescued, offering assistance only when there was a good chance to recoup the funds. In lender of last resort operations, moral hazard can be reduced by lending against sound collateral and by charging an appropriately high rate of interest in order to discourage frivolous borrowing. The success of lender of last resort operations depends on the ability of the lender to create, or provide from its own resources, liquidity. Central banks are well positioned to undertake this task, although governments and commercial banks themselves, through the clearinghouses, have done so historically. In the United States prior to 1990, policy makers attempted to check moral hazard solely via bank examination, rather than by charging higher deposit insurance premia to riskier institutions. The failure of examinations to contain moral hazard engendered by flat-rate deposit insurance premia, which contributed to the United States' savings and loan crisis of the 1980s, highlights the superiority of market-based incentives to reduce risk-taking and demonstrates the limits of regulation to do so on its own. Bank holidays, deposit moratoria, and nationalizations were so rare and only occurred in such extreme crises, that policy makers were less concerned about their potential to generate moral hazard.

Fiscally speaking, bailouts could be quite costly, since they usually involved an outlay of funds on the part of the rescuer which would only be paid back if the rescued institution recovered. Similarly, any procedure involving recapitalization and reorganization could involve substantial expense on the part of taxpayers. Unlike bailouts and the more extreme measures discussed here, lender of last resort operations were less fiscally demanding: because lenders required credit-worthy collateral, the worst they could suffer was fluctuations in the value of that collateral.

The identity of the rescuer evolved during the course of the nineteenth and early twentieth centuries. The first bailouts were generally undertaken by governments: at the early stages of commercial banking development, governments were the only entities with sufficient resources to provide for the bailout. In time, central banks and the private financial sector, with or without encouragement from the government, took on the leading role in bailouts as well as in lender of last resort operations. In the United States, the evolving role of private clearinghouses illustrates the potential importance of non-governmental actors in undertaking rescues.

More extreme measures, such as deposit moratoria, bank holidays, and nationalization, were first employed on a large scale during the Great Depression and made something of a comeback in the aftermath of the worldwide financial crisis that erupted in 2008. That crisis left financial institutions with large amounts of mortgage-related securities of questionable value (i.e., "toxic assets") on their balance sheets. In order for a rescue to be successful, these assets must be taken off the hands of banks, or counterbalanced with capital injections or extensive loans from the private or public sector. When employing extreme measures, rescuers must also instill confidence in depositors so that they do not exacerbate the crisis through massive deposit withdrawals. Among the industrialized countries, governments met this challenge by raising deposit insurance limits, extending guarantees to deposits that were previously uninsured, providing extraordinary financing facilities, injecting capital, and, in some cases, nationalizing banks.[13] As in the Great Depression, the 2008–9 crisis was so severe that governments correctly viewed the moral hazard consequences of rescue operations as small compared to the cost of not intervening.

[13]For a detailed chronology of responses to the financial crisis of 2008–9 see http://www.ny.frb.org/research/global_economy/Crisis_Timeline.pdf and http://www.ny.frb.org/research/global_economy/IRCTimelinePublic.pdf.

CHAPTER 5

Merger Movements

> [The merger] movement appears to have by no means reached
> its limits, and it is neither safe nor easy to predict with any
> confidence the eventual outcome of a movement of which the
> development is incomplete. Whether or not . . . in the course
> of a few more years all banking business in this country will be
> monopolised by some half dozen powerful institutions, there
> seems little reason to doubt that many of the old inducements
> to amalgamation still operate, and that the closing years of the
> century will witness a further reduction in the number of exist-
> ing banks. In any event, conjecture as to the ultimate outcome
> of the tendency must be mainly based on past experience, and in
> light of that experience the question of whether the movement
> is likely on the whole to be a beneficial one must be discussed.
> —Steele (1897: 112)

> There are two incentives to Private Bankers to form combina-
> tions among themselves, or to become absorbed with large
> undertakings. Either they are too rich or they are too poor.
> —Salt (1891: 611)

FEW TRENDS IN MODERN banking have been more pronounced than that
toward consolidation. Steele's observation was as appropriate in 1997 as
it had been in 1897. According to the Bank for International Settlements
(1996: 86), during 1980–95, the numbers of depository institutions in
fifteen advanced industrialized countries fell from their peak numbers
by amounts ranging from 8 to 81 percent. Although some of this reduction in bank population was the result of failures, the majority was due
to merger activity: the United States lost more than four times as many
banks to mergers as it did to failures during 1980–95, a period of unusually high bank failures. During the subsequent decade the ratio of
unassisted mergers to failures in the United States was nearly 100:1. Bank
merger activity among industrialized countries remained strong in the
decade following 1995, and analysts speculate that merger activity will
pick up following the subprime mortgage crisis.[1]

---

[1]Bank merger data and analysis from European Commission (2005), Hosono, Sakai,
and Tsuru (2007), and the Federal Deposit Insurance Corporation's "Historical Statistics

The merger trend is by no means new. Virtually every industrialized country underwent at least one bank merger wave prior to the Great Depression, and some countries experienced several. England registered ten or more bank mergers in at least one year of the decades of the 1830s, 1860s, 1870s, 1880s, 1890s, 1900s, and the 1910s. Australia experienced a relatively high incidence of mergers in the 1840s, 1880s–90s, and in the post–World War I decade. Similar examples from elsewhere in the industrialized world abound.

CONSEQUENCES OF MERGERS

Mergers, in the absence of contemporaneous entries into banking, result in greater concentration, in other words, a smaller number of, on average, larger banking firms. The possible benefits of concentration, previously discussed, include: (1) greater geographic and sectoral diversification, which may increase stability; (2) greater economies of scale, through ability to service larger borrowers and develop more professional management and control systems; and (3) fewer institutions, leading to greater profitability and greater scope for coordination in times of crisis.

The benefits of increased consolidation have been touted in modern mergers, with managers of acquiring banks arguing that the mergers allow them to close duplicate branches and operations centers. Such cost-savings benefits are not always evident, however: British bankers argued before the 1917 Treasury Committee on Bank Amalgamations that the larger networks of branches acquired during the course of nineteenth-century mergers were costly to own and operate. And, as late as 1996, the *Financial Times* noted that despite reductions in staff and domestic branches, Britain's National Westminster Bank still suffered from a bloated branch network, the legacy of the quarter-century-old merger between the National Provincial Bank and the Westminster Bank.[2] Recent research, summarized by Amel et al. (2004) and Berger, Demsetz, and Strahan (1999), finds that economies of scale exist in banking, but the extent of these economies depends on the countries and time periods analyzed. Perhaps not surprisingly, managers typically do not trumpet the benefits of greater cooperation arising from a smaller number of institutions. Nonetheless, the operation of clearinghouses during crises in the United States prior to the founding of the Federal Reserve and the

---

on Banking." On the potential for increased mergers, see Rob Cox and Dwight Cass, "Tests May Spur Bank Mergers," *New York Times*, May 7, 2009.

[2] John Gapper, "Investors Begin to Listen to NatWest's Alternative Message," *Financial Times*, July 29, 1996, p. 17.

success of the coordinated rescues of Baring Brothers and the Comptoir d'Escompte suggest this as a potential benefit.

Although banking consolidation may lead to economies of scale and have some stability-enhancing benefits, high concentration may prove problematic in other ways. The failure of large banks may be more likely to lead to a contagion of fear and banking crisis than that of smaller banks. Thus, the Depression-era failures of the Credit Anstalt in Austria, the Danat-Bank in Germany, the Bank of United States, and France's Banque nationale pour le Commerce et l'Industrie each proved more dangerous for financial stability than the contemporary failures of smaller institutions.

A banking system composed of a smaller number of banks may also prove to be inefficient because it is less competitive: banks that face less competition have an incentive to limit the quantity and raise the price of loans they offer, charge higher fees, and pay lower interest rates on deposits than they would in a more competitive banking environment. If there are no legal or other barriers to the formation of new banks, the higher profitability brought about by mergers might encourage the entry of new banks and reduce these competition-stifling effects. Bordo, Rockoff, and Redish (1994, 1996) find that the more concentrated Canadian banking system was more stable and no less efficient than that of the United States during much of the twentieth century. Grossman (1999), on the contrary, argues that the concentration that resulted from the bank merger movement in England during the half-century prior to World War I rendered it less efficient than it would otherwise have been. The literature considering the consequences of increased concentration on the banking system of the United States in the last two decades of the twentieth century is decidedly mixed (Berger, Demsetz, and Strahan 1999).

The Urge to Merge

To discover the motives for bank mergers, we need look no further than their consequences, discussed in the previous section, which can be grouped under two broad headings: efficiency and market power.[3] Although these motives are presumably ever-present, the periodic emergence of merger waves suggests that they wax and wane. Because mergers involve both buyers and sellers, I consider the motives of each, starting with acquirers.

[3]This categorization ignores several objectives other than maximizing firm profits, such as empire-building or pay maximization on the part of managers. Hughes et al. (2003), Group of Ten (2001: 66ff.).

One motive facing potential acquirers is economies of scale and scope. Large banks may have efficiency advantages over smaller banks. First, by conducting more business, they may be able to do so at a lower average cost (i.e., economies of scale), giving them a competitive advantage over smaller rivals. Second, merely by having more resources at their disposal, they may be better able to service the borrowing needs of larger firms. Third, larger banks may be better able to diversify, both geographically (through branch networks) and functionally (across product lines), than smaller banks.

Economies of scale may be more important at some times and places than others. Economic growth, in particular the kind that accompanies industrialization, and that often involves an increase in average firm size, may increase the returns to economies of scale. Larger firms usually have greater financing requirements than smaller ones, since they involve higher concentrations of capital. Thus, industrialization—or any other development that leads to an increase in average firm size, such as mergers among industrial firms—could encourage combinations among banks (Lamoreaux 1991, Sykes 1926: 187, White 1985). Another potential factor encouraging mergers is a change in the geographic distribution of the population and therefore the demand for financial services. As new areas become settled, banks in more established areas might have reason to expand into these areas by acquiring local banks as a cheaper alternative to establishing new branches. Finally, as an economy develops it demands more sophisticated banking services, such as trade credit, short-term business finance, and securities underwriting, and therefore the variety of services demanded of banks may grow as well. Greater functional and geographic diversification also can be attained through internal growth and the establishment of new branches and new products. It is, of course, quicker to achieve these ends through mergers, although it is not obvious where the cost advantage lies.

We can think of banks as having a preferred or "optimal" size (Krasa and Villamil 1992). The optimal size need not be the same for all banks: banks with a small geographic or functional niche will have a relatively small optimal size; banks serving larger firms, a more geographically far-flung or diverse client base will have a larger optimal size. The growth of the size, sophistication, financing needs, and geographic spread of borrowers will increase the *average* optimal bank size and therefore, on average, the incentive for mergers (figure 5.1). The decision to undertake acquisitions can be thought of in terms of a threshold model: when the optimal size of banks exceeds the actual bank size (i.e., when the actual bank size is below the diagonal line), the urge to merge is high; the larger the gap, the greater the incentive to merge.

Despite the incentives described above, the urge to merge may be checked by a variety of factors. Legal and regulatory impediments may

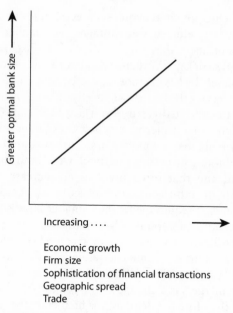

Figure 5.1. Optimal bank size.

provide one obstacle to mergers. Failure to develop limited liability company law and to apply that law to banks could limit bank size: unlimited liability would discourage banks from growing too large since failure could mean personal ruin for the partners. Strict regulation of entry, merger, and branching could also impair bank efforts to achieve optimal size through mergers, as could tax and antitrust policies. Aspects of the financial infrastructure could also present obstacles to mergers. For example, the absence of liquid and deep capital markets would make it more difficult to amass the required capital to carry out acquisitions. On the other hand, the existence of effective alternative intermediators—either institutions or securities markets—might reduce the incentive for commercial bank mergers. Finally, mergers might be infeasible for technological reasons: lack of the necessary communication and transportation infrastructure may make the creation of large or geographically far-flung organizations impossible. In each of the above cases loosening the constraint through legal changes, regulatory easing, or technological improvement could lead to a sudden increase in merger activity.

A second motive for bank mergers is the desire for market power. More concentrated banks should yield their owners greater influence over market conditions, such as interest rates and fees paid by borrowers and interest rates paid and services provided to depositors. The desire for market power could be predatory in nature, in the sense that bank managers try to increase their presence in a market in order to extract monopoly profits. On the other hand, such market share-induced mergers could be a defensive reaction to other mergers and an effort not to lose market share to a growing competitor. Finally, such actions could be opportunistic. If a bank is weakened, either due to poor management or to circumstances beyond the management's control, it might become an attractive takeover target.

On the seller's side, there are several reasons to favor being acquired. First, banks facing an increasingly competitive environment or an economic slowdown might be more inclined to merge out of fear that they are not large enough to survive the changes on their own. Hence, sellers might wish to merge for purely defensive reasons. An extreme version of this scenario would be a bank on the point of failure that is prepared to be acquired rather than to fail.

Another reason for mergers, frequently cited in connection with those in non-financial sectors, includes the growth of and fluctuations in capital markets (White 1985). The development of equities markets enables firm owners to realize profits more easily through the sale of some or all of their shares. Thus, the evolution of equities markets should increase the likelihood of bank owners cashing in by selling their equity. In addition to the evolution of the markets themselves, fluctuations in those markets will affect the willingness of sellers and potential buyers to engage in a merger transaction. Rising share values should increase the willingness of bank owners who are considering selling to sell. Increases in share values of potential buyers may make them more willing and able to acquire new enterprises, either for cash or for appreciated shares. Declines in market interest rates reduce the cost of borrowing and, to the extent that purchases are made with borrowed funds, will increase the willingness of potential buyers to engage in a merger. Finally, the development of new types of instruments (e.g., options, different classes of shares) and the entry of new types of investors (e.g., foreign, institutional) may make more money available for—and stimulate—merger activity.

EVIDENCE

Before discussing where and when bank merger movements took place, it is critical to clarify the term *merger movements*. This is far from a straightforward exercise for at least two reasons. First, there is no commonly accepted definition of what constitutes a merger movement—in banking or in any other industry—although the general description, mergers leading to greater concentration, is clear enough. Yet, there is

TABLE 5.1
Varieties of Financial Institutions in Operation, 1860–1963

Country	1860	1880	1900	1910	1929	1938	1948	1963
Argentina			5	7	7	8	10	10
Australia			7	7	9	11	13	15
Belgium		10	11	12	15	18	18	20
Canada		11	11	11	13	16	17	17
Denmark		7	9	9	12	12	12	16
France	9	9	11	11	13	14	19	20
Germany	12	12	15	18	20	21	22	23
Great Britain	13	14	16	17	23	23	23	23
Greece				4	7	7	8	8
Italy		11	12	14	14	15	17	17
Japan		5	10	10	13	15	19	33
Mexico			4	4	9	16	20	20
Netherlands		10	11	11	16	17	18	18
New Zealand		8	8	11	11	12	14	14
Norway		6	10	12	12	12	16	16
South Africa				8	10	10	13	16
Spain			6	6	10	11	12	14
Sweden		8	12	15	18	18	20	22
Switzerland	7	7	7	11	15	15	18	17
United States	7	9	10	12	19	19	19	20
Venezuela				3	3	3	6	14

Source: Goldsmith (1969: 345).

no commonly accepted standard number of mergers or percent of institutions affected or increase in concentration that constitute a merger movement in industrial organization texts. Moreover, it would be important, in making such a definition, to distinguish between individual bank mergers—which might take place for a variety of idiosyncratic reasons—and merger *movements*.

Second, given that even modern banking data are notoriously difficult to compare across countries, institutional differences make cross-country comparisons of historical data problematic. Contemporary merger data from the Bank for International Settlements (1996: 86) discussed earlier contain almost as many explanatory notes as there are countries in the sample. Modern data are made more problematic by the increasing numbers of mergers that take place between banks based in different countries and between banks and other types of financial firms (e.g., insurance companies). Data difficulties are not restricted to modern data. Table 5.1 illustrates the numbers of different types of financial institutions in

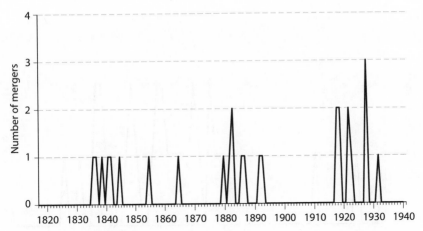

Figure 5.2. Bank mergers in Australia, 1817–1940. *Source*: Butlin, Hall, and White (1971).

twenty-one countries from 1860 to 1963, suggesting that aggregate comparisons of one of the types of financial institutions might not adequately capture merger movements.

Data on the numbers and, in some cases, assets of various national bank populations are presented in figures 5.2 through 5.8. These constitute the best and most reliable time series on banking populations available. Unfortunately, in the absence of detailed data on failures and voluntary

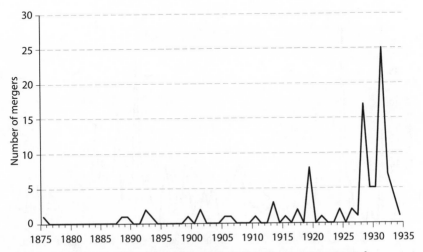

Figure 5.3. Bank mergers in Belgium, 1875–1934. *Sources*: *Moniteur des Intérêts Matériels* (various) and Banque nationale de Belgique (1934).

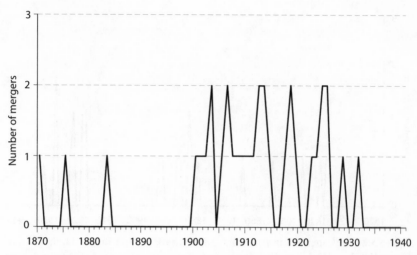

Figure 5.4. Bank mergers in Canada, 1870–1940. *Sources*: Breckenridge (1910) and Curtis, Taylor, and Michell (1931).

liquidations, changes in the bank population cannot be ascribed solely to mergers. Merger data are much more fragmentary and of lower quality: the majority come from retrospective studies rather than contemporary accounts. Figures 5.2–5.8 present the available data, covering different time periods, on bank mergers for Australia, Belgium, Canada, England and Wales, the Netherlands, Sweden, and the United States. For the most

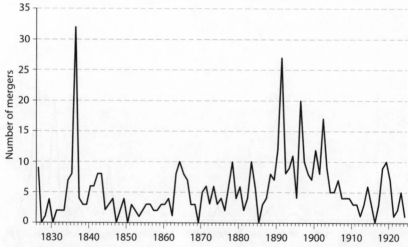

Figure 5.5. Bank mergers in England and Wales, 1826–1924. *Source*: Sykes (1926: appendix I).

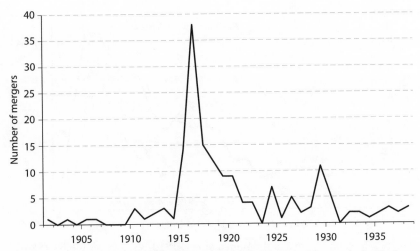

Figure 5.6. Bank mergers in the Netherlands, 1901–38. *Source*: Nederlandsche Bank (1986).

part, these graphs merely present the number of mergers, rather than the assets of the newly merged banks, although figure 5.8 presents data on both the numbers and assets of merged banks in the United States which suggest that the two series are correlated.

Australian data (figure 5.2) show a cluster of bank mergers around 1840, another in the 1880s, and another starting in the 1910s and extending into the 1920s. The Belgian data (figure 5.3) illustrate a substantial grouping of mergers in the late 1920s, although this probably

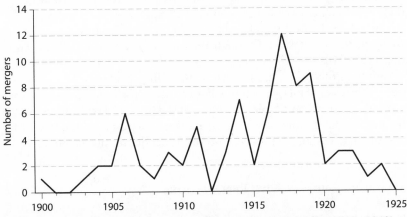

Figure 5.7. Bank mergers in Sweden, 1900–1926. *Source*: Melin (1929: 1049).

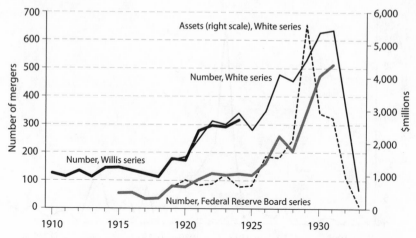

Figure 5.8. Bank mergers in the United States, 1910–33. *Source*: White (1985).

understates the merger activity reflected in the growth of the Banque de Bruxelles affiliate system from four banks 1913, to ten in 1920, and twenty-one in 1925 (Lemoine 1929a: 237). The Canadian data (figure 5.4) show a persistent trend toward mergers over a three-decade period starting around the turn of the twentieth century.

The English data (figure 5.5) show several peaks in merger activity: one in the 1830s, one in the 1860s, and one beginning in the 1880s and persisting through the 1890s. In fact, because the number of banks was much smaller by the turn of the century, the English merger wave that started in the 1880s can be said to have continued until after World War I. Both the Dutch (figure 5.6) and the Swedish (figure 5.7) data show elevated levels of merger activity during and shortly after World War I, although the Swedish data show heightened merger activity in the pre–World War I period as well. And the U.S. data (figure 5.8) show a pronounced upswing in the late 1920s, although the numbers were not trivial even in the early 1910s.

Although these data are imperfect, they do provide a general illustration of the level of merger activity. For countries for which precise quantitative data are not available, a reading of the historical record can inform the discussion. A summary of merger events, based on both quantitative and qualitative data, is presented in the appendix to this chapter.

MATCHING EVIDENCE WITH EXPLANATIONS

How well do the motives discussed above explain the admittedly fragmentary evidence on merger movements presented in the appendix? A simple one-to-one correspondence between each merger wave and a motivating factor is unlikely for several reasons. First, merger waves may occur—or not occur—for multiple reasons. Economic growth that leads to an increase in optimal bank size may not lead to mergers if the regulatory environment restricts banking combinations. A regulatory easing on mergers may not lead to an increase in merger activity if average bank size equals or exceeds optimal bank size. Second, the causes of merger movements may be correlated. Because macroeconomic and securities market fluctuations often go hand in hand, it is difficult to determine whether economic growth or rising equity values were responsible for a particular merger movement. Despite these difficulties, I try to isolate the principal causes of the merger waves listed in the appendix.

One hypothesis advanced above is that bank merger movements might result from an increase in optimal bank size which might occur if the average non-bank firm increased in size, geographic spread, or demand for more complex banking services. Although comprehensive data on average industrial firm size across countries in the late nineteenth and early twentieth centuries is hard to come by, a variety of indicators might serve as proxies for the growth of large-scale enterprise. One obvious indicator of industrial firm size growth is the presence of a merger movement among non-financial firms, since such a movement would undoubtedly lead to larger industrial firms.

Economic growth and industrialization, and with them increasing economies of scale in banking, contributed to bank mergers in a number of instances. The German bank merger movement of the 1890s coincided with an industrial concentration movement that resulted in the formation of a number of industrial cartels (Webb 1980). Data on pig iron production, as an indicator of industrial growth, and GDP growth confirm that the period was one of increasing industrial output for the country as a whole. This episode coincided with the formation of banking groups (called "communities of interest"), which increased not only their size, but also their geographic spread.

The Dutch bank merger movement following 1894—which represented a seven-fold increase in the number of mergers seen during the preceding twenty years—appears also to have had its origins in industrial growth. Heavy industry, although present in the Netherlands before the 1890s, grew at a more rapid rate starting around the middle of the decade (van Zanden, Luiten, and Van Riel 2004: 304ff.). Industrialization led to greater demands for credit by firms which increased the incentive for banks to grow rapidly. The closing of the stock exchange during World War I further increased the demand for bank financing. Sweden also experienced a surge in industrialization beginning in the mid-1890s. Sweden's industrialization accelerated during World War I, when—as a neutral country—its industries experienced strong export demand from the combatants. In addition, Swedish industry became more geographically dispersed during this time. Concomitant with the mergers of the 1910s, the number of bank branches in Sweden rose while the number of banks decreased. This trend suggests that bank mergers were, at least in part, a means for banks to increase their branch networks.

Industrialization and the spur that World War I gave to it led to an increase in optimal bank size elsewhere as well. The post-1900 Japanese bank merger movement, which accelerated during 1911–23, was supported in part by the war. The fighting did not extend to Japan itself, although the Japanese benefited by acquiring Germany's Pacific colonies and territorial concessions in China, as well as supplanting—at least for a time—other industrial suppliers of Asia. This boost to Japan's industrial sector raised optimal bank size and encouraged mergers.

The Australian bank mergers of the 1840s and 1880s were also driven by increases in optimal bank size. In the 1840s, small, local banks were absorbed by larger, primarily London-based banks. Although this could demonstrate a desire among large banks to establish monopoly power, it is more likely that during this period of pastoral expansion, small domestically based banks were unable to muster the resources to serve their client base, and relied on capital inflows from large foreign-owned banks. The later merger movement centered on Australian-owned banks and was characterized by the establishment, in part through mergers, of national networks of branches.

Although increasing growth, economic sophistication, and geographic spread all contributed to merger movements, these and other episodes were also fed by important legal and regulatory changes. Mergers had been rare in Sweden during the nineteenth century. An 1897 law declared that the note-issuing privileges of unlimited liability *enskilda* banks would expire in 1903, by which time the Riksbank would have a monopoly on note issue. The removal of note-issuing privileges encouraged enskilda banks to merge as part of a general reorganization. Swedish legislation of 1909 and 1911 raised minimum capital requirements for banks, allowed banks to issue shares, and made it easier for banks to acquire limited liability. Each of these encouraged the growth of larger banks, which took place largely through mergers. Similarly, in Switzerland the establishment of, and concentration of note issue in, the Swiss National Bank in 1907 led to the elimination, through absorption or merger, of many small note-issuing banks.

Japan's merger movements in the late nineteenth and early twentieth centuries can be ascribed to a combination of regulatory changes and increasing optimal bank size, as already discussed. The merger wave of the 1890s resulted from a major overhaul of the Japanese banking law, in which the National Banking regulations were replaced with the Ordinary Banking regulations: prior to the expiration of the final 153 national bank charters in the late 1890s, sixteen were merged before becoming ordinary banks. The Japanese merger wave of the early twentieth century was also stimulated by government policy promoting consolidation. As early as 1900, government officials expressed an interest in promoting consolidation among banks, hoping to emulate the stability of the extensively branched UK system. The Bank Act of 1927 set high minimum capital requirements: ¥1 million for most banks, ¥2 million for those headquartered in Tokyo or Osaka, and ¥500,000 for those headquartered in a town or village of less than 10,000 people. By 1928, over half of all banks did not meet the requirements and were under pressure to merge. Under the terms of the law, banks that did not meet the new requirements by the end of 1928 were required to be liquidated or merged with qualifying bank, consequently, the number of mergers surged in the later part of 1928 (Tamaki 1995, Sawada and Okazaki 2004, Grossman and Imai 2008). Also in 1927, Belgium increased the incentive for mergers by temporarily reducing fees associated with them (Durviaux 1947: 108).

Although banking had a long history in England, restrictive legislation of the seventeenth and eighteenth centuries had prevented the formation of joint stock banks. These restrictions were eliminated by legislation of 1826, which allowed the formation of joint stock banks outside a sixty-five-mile radius from London, and legislation of 1833, which allowed the formation of non-note-issuing joint stock banks within the sixty-five-mile limit. Easing restrictions on the formation of joint stock banks encouraged both their establishment and their absorption of private banks: the dominant type of merger during this period was between joint stock banks and private banks. Other legislative changes were associated with the bank merger wave of the 1860s. Banks could be incorporated with limited liability as early as 1858, although an 1862 change to the law made doing so more practical. Around the same time, laws that had restricted the formation of limited liability companies were also eased, and many new corporations were formed. The combination of the growth of large non-financial corporations, plus newfound limited liability in banking led to an increase in bank mergers in the 1860s.

In the United States, two pieces of banking legislation played a key role in the bank merger movement of the 1920s. First, a law passed in 1918 established a procedure for the merger of two national banks. Prior to its enactment, such a merger would have required one bank to be liquidated and the other to purchase its assets and assume its liabilities. The law increased flexibility by allowing banks to consolidate under either bank's charter, subject to regulatory approval. Second, the McFadden Act of 1927 provided a similar mechanism for the merger of state-chartered and national banks (White 1985: 288).

Weakness could also encourage banks to seek a buyer and therefore contribute to merger activity, if banks on the verge of failure view being acquired as preferable to failure. Such absorptions have been common. Consolidation in Germany accelerated following the stock market collapse of 1873 and the crisis of 1901, as it did in Austria following the crises in 1857 and 1873. In England, the widespread failures of the 1830s led to a spike in the number of mergers, as did the financial turbulence surrounding the Baring crisis in 1890.[4] On a less dramatic note, Beckhart (1929) notes that the elevated level of mergers in Canada during the first three decades of the twentieth century were primarily the result of healthy banks taking over those that would soon have become insolvent.

The post–World War I recession and the financial crises of the Great Depression also led to widespread mergers. The Netherlands and Sweden, each of which prospered during the post–World War I boom, experienced sharp recessions in the early 1920s which led to merger waves. In contrast to the pre-1920s mergers in Sweden, the mergers of the early 1920s led to a decrease in both the number of banks and branches, suggesting that the 1920s mergers were defensive. In Austria, the dismemberment of the Austro-Hungarian Empire—and with it, some empire-wide banks—after World War I led to an increase in mergers. Finland and Italy experienced heightened levels of mergers resulting from the downturn associated with the Great Depression.

It is more difficult to assess the importance of the market power hypothesis. We know that one of the consequences of merger movements can be reduced competition. It is not clear, however, why there is a greater inducement to merger movements at some times rather than at others. According to Britain's Treasury Committee on Bank Amalgamations (the Colwyn Committee), appointed in 1917, one of the consequences of bank mergers leading to a relatively consolidated banking market was competitive pressure on banks to merge. Their report stated: "Experience shows that, in order to preserve an approximate equality of resources and of competitive power, the larger English banks consider it necessary to meet each important amalgamation, sooner or later, by another" (Sykes 1926: 226).

Heightened merger activity in England during the late nineteenth and early twentieth centuries was associated with increased banking profitability (Grossman 1999). In several instances bankers spoke explicitly of merging in order to improve their competitive position by stifling compe-

---

[4]Sykes (1926: 4, 47–48) notes that the 1890s were a period of low interest rates, which encouraged bankers to look to bank acquisitions as a way of employing their funds. The period around the turn of the century saw an increase in British industrial mergers, which may also have contributed to the bank merger movement. Utton (1991).

tition. In 1889, Lloyds Bank—itself a Birmingham-based bank—acquired the Birmingham Joint Stock, "our powerful opponent and competitor," according to general manager Howard Lloyd. Although the acquisition was expensive for Lloyds, which paid a premium of 5 to 10 percent on the purchase, Howard Lloyd viewed long-term benefits—perhaps implicitly calculating the value of future monopoly profits—as substantial:

> Of the terms on which this amalgamation was effected perhaps the less said the better, so manifestly was the advantage on the side of the Joint Stock Bank's shareholders. But in giving a consideration beyond the actual value of the Joint Stock Bank in actual assets or profits our Directors saw they were both giving a real impetus and addition to the Bank's prestige and growth, and at the same time extinguishing a powerful and trying competitor in the Midland banking district. And the judgment that determined upon this policy—which certainly looked like giving 21/- or 22/- at least for a sovereign—has been well vindicated by the history of subsequent years. Strict monetary valuation is not the only consideration in a transaction of importance . . .[5]

More forthrightly, Edward Holden, then managing director of Midland Bank, noted following a private discussion with an official of the Yorkshire Banking Company in 1900:

> He enquired whether I seriously considered that an amalgamation would be for the benefit of both institutions. I replied that it was the policy of the day to form large institutions; our bank combined with his would command the best business and destroy active competition.[6]

The increasing concentration in British banking did not go unnoticed. The Colwyn Committee, appointed to consider the effects of mergers reported:

> While we believe that there is at present no idea of a Money Trust, it appears to us not altogether impossible that circumstances might produce something approaching to it at a comparatively early date.[7]

It seems likely that many merger waves were aided and abetted by the desire for increased market power; however, it is difficult to find evidence of merger waves that were inaugurated primarily by the desire for market power. In the highly concentrated British banking system, competitive

[5]Howard Lloyd, "Notes and Reminiscences of Lloyds Bank, 1862–92" manuscript in Lloyds TSB Group Archives, HO/GM/How/4 (pp. 53–54).

[6]Diary entry of Sir Edward Holden, February 22, 1900. HSBC Group Archives 0026/002.

[7]Report of the Treasury Committee on Bank Amalgamations (Colwyn Committee), March 11, 1918, reprinted in Sykes (1926: appendix III).

considerations provided powerful inducements to merger. Fully half of the dozen mergers that took place in Australia during the 1917–31 period involved banks with nationwide business on one or both sides of the transaction, while two mergers included regional banks from the same region. This suggests a desire for greater market share rather than an attempt to gain a branch network.

Many of the episodes of increasing optimal bank size discussed took place during periods of rising equity prices, suggesting that stock market booms encouraged merger waves. Because of the absence of quantitative data on both mergers and stock prices for many countries at this time, it is difficult to statistically test the relationship between equity values and mergers. Using data for the United States during 1921–33, Eugene White (1985) finds a strong positive statistical relationship between quarterly merger activity and stock prices. The 1890s merger wave in England and Wales was preceded by a surge in equity prices during 1888–89, which was itself fueled in part by an 1888 debt conversion operation which lowered interest rates on £600 million of outstanding British government debt (Grossman 2002).

In attempting to explain where merger movements took place, it may also be useful to consider where they *did not* take place. France experienced considerable growth in its bank branch networks during the late nineteenth and early twentieth centuries; however, this growth was accomplished primarily via the creation of new bank branches, rather than through acquisitions. The absence of a merger movement may be explained by the fact that France's large industrial firms were well served by the investment banking houses (i.e., the haute banque), leaving the optimal bank size of French commercial banks relatively small. There were less than 150 joint stock banks in all of France by 1870, a lower level of bank density than in Scotland one hundred years earlier (Cameron 1967: 111).

Neither Norway nor Denmark underwent merger movements, although there were mergers in both countries. In Norway, the government engineered several mergers in the wake of a post–World War I slump, and in Denmark there were mergers among the *landsmansbanken* and *andelsbanken*, yet sustained merger movements in these countries did not arrive until after World War II. The absence of merger movements may be explained by geography, the state of industry, and the role of alternative intermediators, namely savings banks. Both Norway and Denmark had relatively small industrial sectors. Per capita crude steel and pig iron production, indicators of industrial output, were tiny—particularly in Denmark—compared with Sweden. Savings banks were more important in Scandinavia than in most countries at the time: Danish savings bank deposits exceeded total commercial bank assets prior to the early twentieth century and Norwegian savings bank lending exceeded that of Norwegian commercial banks until about the same time. Because they operated on a purely local basis, the persistence of small savings banks, particularly in many isolated towns in Norway, combined with relatively modest industrial demand for bank financing, may explain both the relatively small optimal size of commercial banks and the absence of a merger movement among commercial banks.

Merger movements played important roles in the consolidation of commercial banking during the pre–World War II period. Despite the difficulty of establishing a one-to-one correspondence between merger movements and their causes, several motivating factors stand out. Economies of scale played an important role. Economic growth and geographic spread, as well as demands for increasingly complex financial transactions by larger industrial firms, raised the optimal bank size. The greater the gap between the optimal and actual bank size, the greater the incentive to merge. Of course, banks could grow in more conventional ways—raising more capital, opening new branches, establishing new product lines, and expanding more gradually—however, where the gap was large, the incentive to grow quickly through mergers was more urgent.

Regulatory changes also played a key role in a number of instances, including several in which laws were changed specifically to induce mergers. In other times and places, the easing of regulatory constraints encouraged banks to grow through mergers. The more longstanding and severe the restrictions, the greater the gap between optimal and actual bank size, thus the stronger urge to merge when regulatory restraints were loosened. The desire for market power was no doubt an important factor in many individual mergers; however, there is less evidence to suggest that it was responsible for inaugurating merger movements on its own. Competitive pressures, too, were a powerful factor in mergers. Weakened banks made good acquisition targets, sometimes encouraged by government policy, since the price was reasonable. And rising stock market values also encouraged mergers. An interesting, if not fully satisfying conclusion is that time of both prosperity and economic downturns provided good environments for bank mergers.

Bank mergers in the pre–World War II period took place almost entirely within countries. Cross-border mergers, not to mention mergers across functions (i.e., commercial banks with insurance companies), were rare. That changed after World War II, particularly during the last quarter of the twentieth century, when substantial numbers of sizable cross-border and cross-industry mergers occurred. I will touch on these developments in chapter 10.

CHAPTER 6

Regulation

> Jostling against clerks going to post the day's letters, and
> against counsel and attorneys going home to dinner, and against
> plaintiffs and defendants, and suitors of all sorts, and against
> the general crowd, in whose way the forensic wisdom of ages
> has interposed a million of obstacles to the transaction of the
> commonest business in life. . . .
>
> —Charles Dickens, *Bleak House*

GOVERNMENTS HAVE LONG PLAYED an important—and varied—role in
shaping the banking system.[1] From defining the specie content of the
monetary unit, to the establishment of government banks, to setting the
rules and regulations under which commercial banks operate, governments have influenced the shape of the financial landscape for centuries.
Nor has that influence waned in recent years: governments and regulatory authorities in the industrialized, not to mention the industrializing,
world are hard at work building up, altering, and tearing down various
facets of regulation in what is already one of the world's most heavily
regulated activities (Möschel 1991: 3).

The phenomena examined in the three preceding chapters, banking
crises, rescues, and merger movements, suggest some factors that may
drive bank regulation. Crises encourage governments to enact regulations
aimed at improving safety and soundness. The more dramatic the crisis,
the more drastic the reforms: the banking crises of the Great Depression
led to some of the most sweeping banking reforms ever enacted, and the
subprime meltdown may do the same. Rescue operations, particularly
those that involve extensive state intervention—again, the subprime crisis
resonates—are also typically followed by regulatory changes. And merger
movements, when they threaten to lead to excessive concentration, can
bring about government intervention to slow the process.

Conducting a systematic analysis of regulation is complicated because
the rules governing banking are both numerous and multifaceted. Banking law restricts entry; sets capital, reserve, and other balance sheet requirements; limits the types of assets that banks can hold and the quantities in which they can hold them; specifies the collateral banks can accept

---

[1] The first three sections of this chapter draw heavily on Grossman (2001b).

as security for loans; restricts or encourages mergers; sets standards for liability, liquidation, and corporate governance; and determines the form of supervisory and regulatory institutions, as well as establishing countless other rules and regulations.[2] Given this variety, a comprehensive examination of all banking regulations is impossible. Instead, this chapter focuses on four aspects of regulation that are important from historical and contemporary perspectives.

First, I consider the regulations governing entry into banking. These are among the earliest—and most fundamental—banking regulations, and specify the conditions under which banks can be brought into existence. Second, I examine capital regulation, since the amount of capital held is widely perceived as being a key determinant of banking stability. Third, I consider the regulations governing the securities powers of banks (i.e., universal banking). Attitudes toward universal banking constitute a fundamental difference between the market-based financial systems of the United States and Britain and the bank-based financial systems of continental Europe and are at the center of a substantial literature on financial system design. Fourth, I look at the identity of the agency charged with banking supervision. Relative to the design of regulations themselves, the identity of the supervisor has received comparatively little attention from researchers. Recent changes adopted by a number of countries, however, have brought this issue to the forefront of modern regulatory policy.

MOTIVES FOR REGULATION

The impetus for regulation can be categorized as stemming from either purely economic or from political economy motives.[3] Purely economic reasoning has long guided economists in their study of regulation and has led to the conclusion that, in the presence of market imperfections, such as monopolies or incomplete information, government regulation can result in superior (i.e., more efficient) outcomes (Scherer 1980). Thus, regulation is merely a response by the authorities to an imperfect world. For banking, the purely economic motives for regulation center on promoting stability and efficiency. Because of the unique role that banks play in money creation, regulation may also be motivated by the government's desire to exert monetary control.

---

[2] The litany is from Allen et al. (1938: 3ff.). For a catalogue of modern regulations, see Barth, Caprio, and Levine (2006).

[3] Kroszner (1999b) separates these into five categories, the first of which (public interest) approximates the purely economic motive described above. I group his other four (private interest, ideology, institutions, and leviathan) under the category of political economy explanations.

An alternative explanation focuses on the political economy motives for regulation, that is the incentives faced by, and political power of, different actors, and views the evolution of regulation as the outcome of the interplay between different interest groups (Stigler 1971, Peltzman 1976, and Becker 1983). Groups with greater numbers, financial resources, and cohesion will have an advantage in securing regulations that are favorable to them. If the balance of power shifts, regulation may as well. This literature also considers politicians and regulators to be interest groups that may be motivated by the desire for such non-economic goals as larger budgets and more staff or to advance a particular ideological agenda.

Banking stability can yield both economic and political economy benefits. The high cost of banking crises highlights the substantial economic benefits of banking stability. On the political economy front, since bank deposits are a common and, for some part of the electorate, the major form of wealth-holding, policies aimed at preventing banking instability can bring electoral benefits for politicians who enact such rules. The stated purpose of federal deposit insurance in the United States, established by the Banking Act of 1933, was to protect small depositors. The initial level of deposit protection ($2,500) was, even after adjusting for inflation, far below the current level of depositor protection ($250,000, slated to fall to $100,000 in 2014) and underscores the aim of protecting small savers. Savers, small and large, are of course not the only parties affected: bank shareholders, borrowers, and the economy at large are all liable to suffer from banking crises. I emphasize small savers because they may comprise a larger portion of the electorate. The impact of crises on other groups may also have serious political consequences.

Government responses to banking crises include bailouts, lender of last resort operations, and more extreme measures. These are the most direct means of stopping a systemic crisis in its tracks. In addition to these tools, a variety of regulations are aimed at strengthening individual institutions in order to render them less likely to fail. These include capital and reserve requirements. Reserve requirements mandate that banks hold a certain minimum level of liquid reserves, making it less likely, other things being equal, that the bank will be forced to close due to an unexpected withdrawal of demand liabilities. Capital requirements provide enhanced assurance that if a bank's assets are impaired, sufficient shareholder equity will be available to redeem deposits, as well as other benefits. Other regulations that might enhance bank stability include balance sheet restrictions, such as those that limit the type of assets a bank might hold (e.g., prohibiting certain categories of risky investments), regulate the composition of assets (e.g., restricting the percentage of assets that might be loaned to an individual borrower), or impose restrictions on permitted liabilities (e.g., restricting certain types of bank borrowing). Requiring periodic publication of bank balance sheets, combined with an effective supervisory regime, can enforce balance sheet regulations, encourage market discipline, and reduce the likelihood of fraud-induced failures. The enforcement of enhanced (e.g., unlimited) liability, which increases the potential cost to shareholders of a bank failure, should also heighten the risk-aversion of bank managers and reduce the likelihood of failures.

Regulatory policy might also enhance banking stability by reducing competition. This can be achieved by limiting entry into banking, fostering mergers among existing banks, or by establishing capital requirements that are so high that they can be satisfied by only a small number of institutions. By preventing competition, regulators can reduce the likelihood of failure by fostering large, profitable institutions (Guiso, Sapienza, and Zingales 2007). Such measures could include exemptions from antitrust legislation, legal inducements to merge, and government-sanctioned or government-sponsored agreements to limit interest paid on deposits.

Although restricting competition could enhance stability, it conflicts with a second important economic goal of banking regulation: efficiency. Efficiency arguments are made in connection with the regulation of many industries, and are widely discussed in the literature on industrial organization (Scherer 1980: 482ff.). An efficiently functioning market is typically characterized by numerous buyers and sellers, where externalities (i.e., the costs of the byproducts of production) are borne by producers, and where consumers have relatively complete information about firms and products. Violations of this ideal can lead to outcomes that the government may have an interest in curbing.

One threat to efficiency is monopoly, a situation in which there is only one seller, or oligopoly, in which there are only a few sellers. A "natural monopoly" occurs when economies of scale are so persistent that a single firm can serve the market on a lower per-unit cost than two or more firms. Monopoly or oligopoly can occur because of barriers to entry, such as high start-up costs, proprietary information, or government restriction on entry, which limits the number of producers. Monopolies are costly for society because they restrict output and result in higher prices than would occur in a more competitive environment. Oligopolies can behave like a monopoly, either because of explicit collusion or because one of the firms acts as a price leader, with others following. Thus, government intervention in non-competitive industries to outlaw price-fixing and removing barriers to entry is warranted on economic grounds. Although a desire for stability might motivate regulations to stifle competition, the goal of an efficient banking system is best achieved with regulations that promote competition.

Market efficiency can also be compromised by imperfect information. The efficient functioning of a competitive market assumes that all participants are well informed about the consequences of their choices. However, there are a variety of circumstances in which individuals lack adequate information to make informed decisions. For example, government-mandated labeling of food products provides consumers with more information than they might otherwise have about additives. Financial disclosure requirements provide another example: since individual consumers do not have access to adequate information about financial institutions or the expertise to interpret the information that is available, government maintenance of standards and provision of information, such as the publication of balance sheets, can ameliorate information asymmetries (Goodhart et al. 1998, Meltzer 1967).

A third economic rationale for regulation revolves around banks' importance in the monetary system. Under fractional reserve banking, banks issue demand deposits (and, formerly, notes) on the basis of their holdings of reserves of currency (formerly, monetary metals) and deposits issued by the central bank. By setting a minimum proportion of reserves a bank must hold against its demand liabilities, the regulator establishes an upper limit on the total amount of notes and deposits banks can issue. This can help to control the rate of monetary growth and contribute to the maintenance of price stability.

A variety of non-economic goals can be met by means of regulation as well. Some political economy objectives may be public in nature: regulations can force banks to invest in government bonds, helping a fiscally strapped national, regional, or local government; they can also be used to promote the development of particular regions or industrial sectors by setting differential capital requirements for banks located in different areas or dealing with particular industries. Other political economy motives may be private in nature: governments can show favoritism toward politically powerful classes of banks (Economides, Hubbard, and Palia 1996). In most countries, prior to the enactment of laws governing the chartering of new banks, the decision to issue charters was left up to the discretion of the sovereign or legislature, which opened the way for chartering practices that favored certain suitors for non-economic reasons. Political economy motives could also be ideological in nature: Sweden's 1864 banking law, for example, mandated that holders of common equity be Swedish citizens.

Although these reasons for regulation are distinct, it is difficult in practice to disentangle multiple motivations for a particular reform. The National Banking Acts in the United States (1863–64), which established a new type of bank (national banks), a new regulatory authority (the Comptroller of the Currency), and a bond-backed bank-issued currency (national banknotes), could have been passed on any of those grounds. Since the acts established uniform and relatively strict guidelines for granting bank charters, they could be viewed as stability-enhancing. Since the acts also required publication of bank balance sheets, they could be viewed as ameliorating an information asymmetry and therefore be viewed as promoting efficiency. Alternatively, since the acts both established a new national currency and effectively drove notes issued by state banks out of circulation, they could be viewed as enhancing the government's monetary control. Finally, since banks chartered under these acts were required to secure banknote issues with holdings of government bonds, the acts could be viewed as serving the political economy goal of increasing the demand for federal government bonds during the fiscally demanding Civil War. The difficulty of disentangling the motives behind banking legislation also can be applied to Belgium's Banking Decree of 1935, England's Joint Stock Bank Act of 1844, Japan's National Banking Decree of 1872, and Sweden's Banking Code of 1846.

In some cases, it is relatively straightforward to identify the timing of the forces driving regulatory reform; in others, it is more complicated. Governments frequently enact stability-promoting measures following financial crises; the more severe the crisis, the more swift and far-reaching the reforms. In Belgium and the United States, for example, Depression-era reforms drastically curtailed commercial bank activities by preventing them from engaging in investment banking functions. Another instance in which the timing of reform is relatively easy to explain is when rules and regulations come with a built-in expiration date, necessitating the periodic revision or renewal of existing rules. Beginning in the second half of the nineteenth century, Canadian banking legislation was written so that it would have to be revisited every ten years. Nineteenth-century legislation in Japan and Sweden mandated that bank charters be of fixed duration, insuring that banks could be subject to new rules when their charters were renewed.

Although in some cases the timing of banking reform is clear, in many others regulations respond to more subtle and gradually evolving economic and political influences. These influences may be exogenous, such as wars or political instability, or endogenous, resulting from previous developments in the economy or banking system, that themselves may result from earlier regulatory changes. Such endogenous change can lead to cycles, both long and short, in which regulators and bankers constantly adjust to the actions of each other, with bankers trying to avoid regulatory constraints and regulators devising new regulations in an effort to impose their will. Kane (1977) aptly refers to this as the "regulatory dialectic."

The evolution of English banking demonstrates the interplay between economic and political economy forces. The Bank of England was chartered in 1694 in return for a large loan which helped the government prosecute war with France. Shortly thereafter, Parliament considered founding a second bank, which never got off the ground. In return for a second loan, the Bank of England was granted a new charter in 1697 which gave it a monopoly on joint stock banking in England and Wales that persisted for more than a century. The result of the bargain was a banking system composed of one large joint stock bank, the Bank of England, and many small private banks. The inability of these small banks to provide for the needs of business and their vulnerability during the frequent crises of the late eighteenth and early nineteenth centuries led to a gradual easing of the restrictions on entry into banking starting in 1826. It could be argued that ending the bank's monopoly reflected the economic necessity of allowing the growth of other large banks. It could also be argued that the monopoly's end may have reflected the diminished influence of the bank, which was by the early nineteenth century a less important source of government funds than credit markets.

Entry Regulation

The Emergence of Charters

The earliest form of financial regulation was not banking regulation per se, but monetary regulation, specifying the weight and fineness of metallic coins (Allen et al. 1938: 3ff.). Public interest in such regulation is clear enough: since it is difficult for individuals to accurately assess the specie-content of coins, government certification—backed up with penalties for non-compliance through counterfeiting or coin-clipping—increases the confidence of the population in the circulating medium. On the other hand, control over the weight and fineness of coins provides the government with a means of increasing its revenue by debasing the coinage (i.e., reducing the specie content), which can have inflationary consequences (Sussman 1993).

As the preeminence of coins gave way to banknotes, the emphasis of government regulation shifted in the same direction. First, and most simply, a banking license was made contingent on a bank's ability to maintain convertibility of banknotes into specie: Australia's Colonial Banking Regulations (1840) mandated that any bank that did not maintain convertibility of its notes into specie for six consecutive days, or a total of sixty days during the year, would lose its charter. Second, unlimited liability was frequently imposed on banks, making shareholders personally liable for the entire amount of losses on the note issue. English joint stock commercial banks, note-issuing and non-note-issuing alike, were subject to unlimited liability during much of the nineteenth century. In Sweden, note issue was concentrated in unlimited liability enskilda banks for most of the nineteenth century. In the United States, note-issuing banks in a half a dozen states were subject to unlimited liability at some point during the nineteenth century, and shareholders of banks in almost all other states and those of national banks were subject to some form of enhanced (e.g., double, triple) liability until the 1930s. Unlimited liability could have serious consequences. The 1878 failure of Scotland's City of Glasgow Bank led to the failure of the Caledonian Bank when the Caledonian was unable to pay the amount due on the four shares of City Bank it had acquired as security for a loan.

Finally, government regulations set limits on the amount of banknotes that could be issued. The Canadian banking law of 1841 and the 1846 revision of the Colonial Banking Regulations limited a bank's note issue to the amount of its paid-in capital. Free banking laws in various U.S. states and the U.S. National Banking Acts required that note issues be limited to the extent that they could be secured with a deposit of government bonds. The Japanese National Bank Decree of 1872, modeled on the U.S. National Banking Acts, similarly required banks' note issues—limited to a proportion of bank capital—to be backed by a deposit of government bonds.

As bank deposits grew in importance relative to banknotes, both as a store of value and as a means of payment, the focus of regulation shifted from notes to bank deposits, and therefore to the regulation of commercial banks (Allen et al. 1938: 3ff.). Among the most basic, and earliest, banking regulations were those on entry, which typically took on one of three forms: charters, banking codes, and corporation law.

The earliest form of entry regulation was through charters, explicit permission given by the legislature or sovereign for a firm to undertake banking business. Such charters sometimes provided the new company with limited liability; they typically set general conditions under which it could do business, such as setting minimum share capital and authorizing the bank to conduct certain types of business. The first institutions to receive such charters were government banks, such as those granted to the Swedish Riksbank (1668) and the Bank of England (1694). Subsequent acts granted charters to government banks in France (1800), the Netherlands (1814), Austria-Hungary (1817), Denmark (1818), Norway (1818), and Belgium (1850) (table 6.1). These banks were private profit-maximizing firms, not the public sector firms we associate with the central banks of today; however, they were special in that they were given rights as the government's banker and received certain privileges, such as a monopoly on note issue (table 6.2). In many cases, it was not necessary to provide these banks with exclusive banking privileges, since they were frequently the only commercial bank when founded (Capie et al. 1994: 4).

Although government banks were often the first to be chartered in a country, sovereigns and legislatures granted charters on a case-by-case

TABLE 6.1
Establishment of Central Banks

Country	Name	Year
Australia	Commonwealth Bank of Australia (Reserve Bank of Australia, 1959)	1911
Austria	Österreichische Nationalbank	1816
Belgium	Banque nationale de Belgique	1850
Canada	Bank of Canada	1934
Denmark	Danmarks Nationalbank	1818
England	Bank of England	1694
Finland	Suomen Pankki	1811
France	Banque de France	1800
Germany	Reichsbank	1876
Italy	Banca d'Italia	1893
Japan	Nippon Ginko	1882
Netherlands	De Nederlandsche Bank	1814
Norway	Norges Bank	1816
Sweden	Sveriges Riksbank	1668
Switzerland	Swiss National Bank	1907
United States	Federal Reserve System	1914

Source: Capie et al. (1994: appendix B).

Notes: Several central banks had predecessor institutions (e.g., Danmarks Nationalbank, Reichsbank, Banca d'Italia). The Federal Reserve Act became law in 1913, but the Federal Reserve System did not commence operation until 1914.

basis to other commercial banks as well. Legislative acts were the most common way of founding banks in British colonies. The British Parliament passed the Bank of Australia Act in May 1827. This charter served as the model for subsequent charters in New South Wales, Tasmania, and South Australia until the Colonial Banking Regulations made some adjustments to the model in the 1840s. Similarly, the British Parliament chartered the first commercial banks in Canada, including the Bank of New Brunswick, Bank of Upper Canada, and Bank of Montreal, during 1820–22.

The first chartered bank in Belgium not only predated the central bank, but also an independent Belgium. The Algemeene Nederlandsche Maatschappij ter Begunstiging van den Volksvlijt (Société Générale pour favoriser l'Industrie nationale) was granted a charter by William I of the Netherlands in 1822. Following Belgian independence in 1830, the Bank de Belgique was established by royal decree. Banks in the United States also operated under individually granted charters during the early years of the Republic. With the exception of the proto-central First and Second

Table 6.2
Centralization of Note Issue

Country	Year	Action
Australia	1910	The federal government authorized the Treasury to issue notes and placed a 10 percent tax on all private banknotes.
Austria	1816	The Privilegierte Österreichische Nationalbank was established with exclusive rights to issue banknotes, which were to be convertible into silver.
Belgium	1850	The Banque nationale de Belgique was established after the crisis of 1848 led to the suspension of convertibility. The largest note-issuing banks "were persuaded" (Capie et al. 1994: 159) to abandon their banknote issues in favor of the new central bank.
Canada	1934	The Bank of Canada was granted a monopoly on note issues upon its establishment. The preexisting banknotes of chartered banks and government-issued Dominion notes were gradually phased out.
Denmark	1818	The Kurantbanken (established 1736), which had been Denmark's sole note-issuer, folded. The Specie Bank (established 1791) failed in 1813. The Rigs-bank, the immediate predecessor to Danmarks Nationalbank, was also given sole right to issue banknotes upon its establishment.
England	1844	The Bank Charter Act (Peel's Act) began the process of centralizing note issue of England and Wales in the Bank of England by restricting the right to issue banknotes to banks that held it at the time of the act's passage and by specifying that lapsed banknote issues (due to closures, mergers, etc.) would revert to the Bank of England.
Finland	1886	The Suomen Pankki had been in existence since 1811, even though Finland did not have its own currency until 1860. It was given the sole right to issue banknotes in 1886.
France	1848	Permission was given for three banknote-issuing banks to be established in 1817–18. Six more were established by 1838. Following the crisis of 1848, these became branches of the Banque de France.
Germany	1876	Law limited the currency of non-Reichsbank banknotes to the state within which they were issued.

TABLE 6.2 (*continued*)

Country	Year	Action
Italy	1926	Law removed the authority to issue banknotes from the Banco di Napoli and the Banco di Sicilia, leaving the Banca d'Italia with a monopoly on banknote issue.
Japan	1883	Bank of Japan regulations centralized banknote issue.
Netherlands	1863	The Bank Act of 1863, which rechartered the Nederlandsche Bank, restricted the right of other institutions to issue banknotes.
Norway	1818	Norges Bank was granted a monopoly on banknote issue shortly after its founding.
Sweden	1897	Law eliminated the right of institutions other than the Riksbank to issue banknotes by 1904.
Switzerland	1905	A federal statute permitting the establishment of a national bank with monopoly note issue was enacted in 1891, but national bank legislation was not passed until 1905.
United States	1863–64, 1914	The National Bank Acts imposed a tax on state banknote issues, driving them out of circulation, resulting in the creation of a uniform national bank-issued currency. Establishment of the Federal Reserve System began the process of centralizing note issue in the new central bank.

Sources: Capie et al. (1994: 6, appendix B) and Willis and Beckhart (1929).

Banks of the United States chartered by Congress, neither of which out-lived its initial twenty-year charter, bank charters were all special acts of incorporation by state legislatures. Prospective bankers had to lobby the legislature in order to be granted a charter; they might be successful if they were, in the view of the legislature, of good character and if the legislature felt that the area needed another bank. The success of a petition might also depend on the ability of the potential banker, or the inability of existing banks opposing the petition, to persuade—or bribe—legislators (Hammond 1963: 7ff., Bodenhorn 2006).

In time, most countries moved away from the model of individually granted charters to one of two less discretionary methods of charter-granting: (1) banking codes; and (2) corporation law (table 6.3). Banking codes specified the conditions under which new banks could be chartered; corporation law specified those conditions for corporations, whether banking or non-banking. Although legislators or regulators may have retained some residual authority over granting charters, the establishment of banking codes and corporation law greatly reduced the discretion of chartering agencies, both to grant charters and to alter their terms. In countries where specific banking codes were not passed, banks were established under corporation law.

The first banking codes were introduced in England (1844) and in Sweden (1846).[4] These represented relatively detailed banking codes, which spelled out conditions of entry, form of charter, minimum capital standards, and requirements to publish balance sheets. Despite these details, elements of the chartering system remained: in both England and Sweden, the government retained the right to approve charters. The English banking code was not particularly long-lived: by 1857, the small number of banks chartered under the 1844 Joint Stock Bank Act led Parliament to replace the Act with the Joint Stock Banking Companies Act, which essentially subjected banks to the provisions of the commercial code. The Swedish code was amended several times in the nineteenth century (1848, 1850–51, 1855), and was eventually repealed and replaced with a new law in 1864.

In the United States, Canada, and Japan, the initial shift away from individually granted charters came in the form of free banking laws. Under free banking, which was introduced in Michigan in 1837 and in New York in 1838, rather than apply to the state legislature for a charter, individuals could obtain a charter by completing paperwork and depositing a prescribed amount of specified bonds with the state authorities. By 1860, over one-half of the states had enacted some type of free banking law (Rockoff 1975). In 1863–64, with the passage of the National Banking Acts, free banking was established for banks chartered by the federal government. The Canadian Free Banking Act, modeled on that of New York, was passed in 1850, although it was repealed in 1866 and replaced with another comprehensive banking law. The Japanese National Bank Decree, based on the U.S. National Banking Acts, similarly regularized the charter-granting process in 1872.

In other countries, no special banking law was passed and, with the decline of individual chartering acts, new banks were established, explicitly or implicitly, under company law. Four Australian states passed laws allowing banks to be established under general company law during 1863–74. In many countries, however, specific banking laws were not enacted until the twentieth century. Many of these laws were passed in the aftermath of the turbulence caused by World War I and the financial crises of the Great Depression: Austria (1924–25), Belgium (1935), Denmark

---

[4]These were not the first commercial banking laws passed in either country, although they were the first to establish a detailed banking code. An 1826 law in England allowed for the establishment of joint stock banks sixty-five miles or more from London; a royal decree in Sweden in 1824 also authorized the establishment of private banks.

TABLE 6.3
Establishment of a Comprehensive Banking Code

Country	Year	Description
Australia	1840	Until the Colonial Banking Regulations (1840, revised 1846) were promulgated, banks were granted charters on a case-by-case basis by the Crown or Parliament. Banks were subsequently permitted to be established under general company law in Queensland (1863), Victoria (1863), Tasmania (1869), and New South Wales (1874). A number of banks were headquartered in the UK and incorporated under British law. No comprehensive Australian banking code was in existence at the time of the Royal Commission Appointed to Inquire into the Monetary and Banking Systems at Present in Operation in Australia (1937).
Austria	1924	A banking commission was established in 1921. Key banking laws were enacted in 1924–25.
Belgium	1935	Prior to the Banking Decree (Decree 175) of July 9, 1935, there was no specific banking law.
Canada	1850, 1870–71	Prior to 1850, banks had been chartered primarily by legislative acts. Following a short period of free banking (1850–66), a more comprehensive banking code was enacted.
Denmark	1919	A savings bank law was enacted in 1880, although it explicitly excluded commercial banks from its purview. The first commercial bank legislation was enacted in 1919 and revised in 1930.
England	1844	The Joint Stock Bank Act set up procedures for the establishment and operation of joint stock banks in England and Wales. The provisions of this law were repealed in 1857 and banks were essentially governed by the commercial code.
Finland	1866	First commercial banking legislation enacted.
France	1941	Until the passage of the 1867 general incorporation law, banks were established by special charter. No specific banking law had been enacted as of 1936.
Germany	1931–34	The Banking Commission was established in 1931. A law enacted in 1934 established rules and strict control by the Banking Commissioner.
Italy	1926	Two decrees in 1926 established the basics of a banking code. Previously, the only law governing commercial banking was corporation law.

TABLE 6.3 (*continued*)

Country	Year	Description
Japan	1872	The National Bank Decree was based on U.S. National Banking Acts. It was replaced by the Ordinary Bank Regulations of 1890.
Netherlands	1952	Preliminary Bank Act of 1952 (revised 1956).
Norway	1924	Before 1918, general corporation law applied to banks. A temporary law of 1918 regulated entry and changes in bank capital. A full banking code was enacted in 1924.
Sweden	1846	A preliminary banking law was enacted in 1824. A full-fledged banking code was enacted in 1846.
Switzerland	1934	The Banking Act and a subsequent executive order established the Federal Banking Commission and a banking code.
United States	1837–, 1863–64	Prior to 1837, banks had been chartered by individual acts of state legislatures. Starting in 1837, states began to enact free banking laws. Under the National Banking Acts (1863–64), the federal government began to issue bank charters.

Sources: Allen et al. (1938), Butlin (1953), Enderle-Burcel (1994), Tamaki (1995), and Willis and Beckhart (1929).

(1919), Germany (1931–34), Italy (1926), Norway (1924), and Switzerland (1934). In France (1941) and the Netherlands (1952), explicit banking statutes were not enacted until even later. Interestingly, no new banking code was enacted between 1872 and 1919. This almost half-century hiatus may indicate that the process of enacting codes was essentially completed by 1872, and would not have continued in the absence of the turbulence following World War I and the Great Depression.

Banking Codes versus Corporation Law

The evolution away from individually granted charters raises two questions. First, what caused the shift to less discretionary means of charter issuance? Second, why did some countries enact banking codes, while others allowed banks to be formed under general corporation law?

When governments granted charters on a bank-by-bank basis, especially in the case of government banks, they usually received compensation, typically in the form of a loan (Capie et al. 1994: 7). For example, in return for its charter, which included limited liability and a monopoly on joint stock banking in England and Wales, the Bank of England extended a long-term loan to the British government, which was, along with the charter, periodically renegotiated (Broz and Grossman 2004). By supplying charters on a case-by-case basis, issuers were able to extract the maximum amount possible for each charter: banks with greater profit potential (i.e., higher charter values) could be more highly "taxed" than those with lower charter values. The rapid increase in the number of charters had two effects. First, it led to a decrease in average charter value, making the issuance of new charters less remunerative. Second, because governments were issuing more charters in areas where their values were high than where they were low, the disparity between high-value and low-value charters declined. Both of these effects reduced the incentive for governments to issue charters on a case-by-case basis.

In some countries, the demand for banks and banking services—and consequently the value of an individual charter—was so low that the chartering agency could not expect a substantial payment in return for the charter. When the government banks of Austria-Hungary, Denmark, Finland, the Netherlands, Norway, and Sweden were chartered, the new institutions were effectively the only domestic incorporated commercial bank. The demand for chartered banking in Denmark was so low, that after the establishment of the Danmarks Nationalbank in 1818, a second chartered bank was not founded for another thirty years. In the Netherlands, the presence of an active money market (*prolongatie*), private merchant houses, and cashiers (*kassiers*), reduced the demand for chartered banking ('t Hart, Jonker, and Van Zanden 1997: ch. 5, Jonker 1996a). In other places, including Scandinavia and Italy, the development of alternative intermediators during the nineteenth century, such as savings banks, may have reduced the charter value of commercial banks.

In the United States, on the contrary, the demand for bank charters was robust and the development of alternative intermediators was comparatively slow. Consequently, state legislatures maintained tight control of the bank chartering process until the beginnings of free banking in the 1830s, with more than a dozen state legislatures issuing charters individually as late as 1860. This shift occurred during 1837–63 for two reasons. First, the state legislatures' control of banking charters was seen as responsible for confining the banking franchise to well-heeled and well-financed elites, which ran against a populist grain (Hammond 1963). Second, the spread of free banking laws suggests that the period might have been one of a decline in both charter values and in the disparity between charter values. Because U.S. free banking laws served as the model for those in Canada and Japan, changes in U.S. charter values may have influenced banking laws abroad.

In other countries, the evolution from individually granted charters resulted from competition between jurisdictions, changes in corporation law, or from the prevailing economic ideology. In Australia, states that included banks within general incorporation laws may have done so to encourage more banks to secure charters domestically rather than from the British parliament. In France, a law of 1867 greatly simplified incorporation, replacing charters granted by a central authority with simple registration, which applied to banks as well as to other corporations. The French change can be traced, in part, to a desire to keep up with the liberal company law passed in Britain some years earlier (Freedeman 1979). In Germany, several attempts were made in the nineteenth century to regulate banking; however, these were forestalled by clauses in the constitution and a prevailing ideology supporting a laissez-faire economic environment (Honold 1956).

Why did some countries regulate banking with special banking codes while others allowed banks to be established under general corporation law? The first countries to centralize note issues within the central bank were among the last countries to enact detailed banking codes. Countries that centralized their note issue relatively early, such as Austria-Hungary, Belgium, Denmark, France, the Netherlands, and Norway, instituted banking laws relatively late—after World War I and, in the case of the Netherlands, not until after World War II. Countries that did not centralize note issues within central banks until later typically relied on currency issued by private banks. Because of the dangers of an over-issue, these countries, including Australia, Canada, Finland, Japan, Sweden, and the United States, enacted comprehensive banking codes earlier. These codes usually imposed strict restrictions on note-issuing. In the United States, for example, national banks could issue currency equal to 90 percent of the amount of bonds placed on deposit with the Comptroller of the Currency. Similar restrictions were placed on the free banks of Canada and Japan. Australian regulations predating the state acts mandated that any bank that did not maintain convertibility would lose its charter.

The relationship between the date of the centralization of the note issue and the establishment of a banking code is illustrated in figure 6.1. The statistically significant trend clearly indicates the negative relationship between the year in which the note issue was centralized and the year in which a banking code was enacted.[5] Despite the good fit suggested by the trend line presented in figure 6.1, Switzerland and England are obvious outliers. Given that the first Swiss banking code was not adopted until

---

[5] Assigning precise dates to the enactment of a banking code and note centralization is problematic in several cases. In the United States, the first banking codes were the free banking acts, which were enacted by different states between 1837 and 1860. Free banking on a national scale was only adopted with the National Banking Acts (1863–64). This is illustrated in figure 6.1 by showing a range of dates (1837–63) at which banking codes were enacted, with the midpoint (1850) adopted as the year in which a code was adopted for purposes of fitting the trend line.

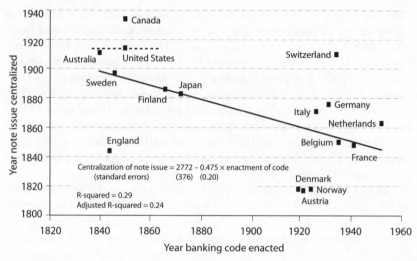

Figure 6.1. Centralization of note issue and enactment of banking code.
Sources: See tables 6.2 and 6.3.

1934, the centralization of the country's note issue in the Swiss National Bank in 1910 occurred later than would be predicted. This seeming contradiction may result from the fact that although the note issue was not centralized until 1910, a federal law regulating note issue had been enacted in 1881. Had the earlier date been adopted for the analysis, the point for Switzerland would be quite close to that of Germany and the trend line. Alternatively, it could be noted that an attempt to establish a central bank in Switzerland in 1897 was defeated in a referendum. Had it passed, and the note issue been centralized then, the point for Switzerland would also have been closer to Germany (Landmann 1906, Sandoz 1898: 304). The enactment of both note centralization and a banking code in England in 1844 places it far from the trend line. However, the Joint Stock Banking Act of 1844 was repealed thirteen years later, and as late as 1938 it was noted that, ". . . apart from a few special sections in the 1929 act, banking companies are subject to exactly the same regulations as other companies" (Allen et al. 1938: 233). Had a later date been adopted for the analysis, the point for England would have been near Belgium and France and close to the trend line.

Entry regulation passed through several stages from the earliest banking charters in the seventeenth century through World War II. At first, bank charters were granted on a case-by-case basis. These charters were usually given to government banks, which both provided public services and compensation to the chartering authority. To the extent that charter values—and the disparity between them—remained high, governments and legislators had an incentive to parcel out charters on a case-by-case basis. Declines in charter values and the disparity between them, changes in corporation law, and hardening of public attitudes toward banking encouraged the authorities to regularize the manner in which charters were granted. Once it was clear that the way in which charters were issued was to be changed, two options were available: banking codes and corporation law. For the most part, countries enacted banking codes when issuing money was the responsibility of private commercial banks. In countries where the central bank had been granted a monopoly on note issue relatively early, the need for a detailed banking code was less pressing and entry regulation was left to corporation laws. Although other factors may have played a part, monetary control was the dominant motive for entry regulation.

CAPITAL REQUIREMENTS

Capital requirements have been a key feature of banking regulation from the enactment of the first commercial banking codes in England and Sweden in the nineteenth century through the establishment of the Basel and Basel II accords in recent years. Policy makers emphasize the role of adequate capital in promoting bank "soundness and stability" (Basel Committee on Banking Supervision 1988, 2004). Even in the absence of an explicit government directive, the investing and depositing public has an interest in bank capital levels, what Berger, Herring, and Szegő (1995) refer to as "market capital requirements." This section provides evidence on the evolution of bank capital levels and assesses the relative importance of market and government capital requirements.

The Role of Capital

Among the first and most basic tasks to be undertaken by a prospective bank—or any other business, for that matter—is to raise funds with which to run the enterprise.[6] New firms, which cannot tap into retained earnings, have two sources: (1) borrowed funds (i.e., debt); and (2) funds invested by the owners/shareholders (i.e., equity, capital). Firm managers seek the optimal mix of debt and equity financing to maximize a firm's value. Modigliani and Miller's (1958) classic work concludes that in a world with an efficient capital market, no tax distortions, and no bankruptcy costs, firms should be indifferent to the debt-equity mix.

---

[6]This section relies heavily on Berger, Herring, and Szegő (1995).

Since one of their primary businesses is to take deposits, it would seem that banks could operate with almost no capital at all: managers could simply make loans and buy securities with the funds borrowed from depositors or note-holders. If the returns on loans and investments consistently exceed the interest paid to depositors, and there were no unforeseen deposit withdrawals, it would be in the shareholders' interest to finance as much of the bank's operation with borrowed money as possible: the less dispersed the ownership, the fewer shareholders with whom to share the profits. And, in fact, banks are among the most highly leveraged firms: the average debt-to-equity ratio in U.S. agriculture in the early twenty-first century was about one-to-one; the average in manufacturing was close to two-to-one; the average in banking was over nine-to-one (Troy 2004). Of course, exclusive reliance on debt has a downside. Although dividend payments to equity holders can be postponed or cancelled without an existential threat to the firm, if debt service obligations are not met the debtor may be forced into bankruptcy. Since a large proportion of bank liabilities (demand deposits, notes) is payable on demand, the inability to meet such withdrawals may lead to a sudden bank closure.[7]

Bank capital, then, serves several roles. First, it provides a buffer against a shortfall in cash flow. As noted above, dividends can be suspended without catastrophic consequences, freeing up money to pay depositors and other creditors. Second, if a bank is forced to close, capital serves as a reserve that can be called on to liquidate unpaid debts. Third, higher holdings of capital can encourage banks to undertake less risk: because capital is at risk in case of failure, banks have an incentive to avoid risks that might put them out of business. Fourth, because banks know more about the soundness of their operations than investors (i.e., information asymmetry), the decision to hold more capital and to subject owners to a greater loss in case of failure signals to depositors and potential investors that the bank will undertake less risk than it otherwise might. Finally, banks hold capital because government regulations force them to do so.

Although government-mandated capital requirements are common today, they were far from universal in the nineteenth and early twentieth centuries. A number of industrial countries had no specific commercial banking regulations before the twentieth century (e.g., France, Germany, Italy, the Netherlands), and consequently banks in many of these countries made capital decisions without input from the government for long

---

[7]The demandable nature of bank debt has also led governments to impose regulations establishing minimum liquidity ratios, that is, the amount of cash or cash-like assets that must be held against demand liabilities. Such requirements were imposed in the aftermath of banking difficulties in Denmark (1919), Germany (1934), Switzerland (1934), and Belgium (1935).

periods of time. Still, even in the absence of government-mandated capital requirements, banks will hold more than token amounts of capital. We will therefore begin by examining the impact of market forces in determining bank capitalization and then look at the influence of government regulation.

Market Capital Requirements

Even in the absence of government mandates, banks will hold capital for all the reasons outlined above: to reduce cash-flow needs, serve as a reserve of funds to pay creditors in case of failure, encourage more risk-averse behavior, and reassure depositors and investors.[8] Berger, Herring, and Szegő (1995) refer to the amount of capital required for these purposes as "market capital requirements," the amount of capital that banks will hold in order to maximize the value of their institutions. Holding less capital calls the bank's safety into question and will reduce its value; holding higher amounts of capital will be costly, since it dilutes the returns to shareholders, and will therefore also reduce its value.

Market capital requirements decline as a country's financial system matures for two reasons. First, as information about financial institutions becomes more widely available through the publication of balance sheets, and as reputations become established, depositors and shareholders will require banks, on average, to hold less capital. In other words, since banks hold capital in part to mitigate the information asymmetry, as information flows improve less capital will be necessary. Second, since the role of capital is largely tied to reducing the likelihood of bank failure and mitigating the effects of bank failures once they happen, as the risk of bank failure declines, market capital requirements will fall. Berger, Herring, and Szegő (1995: 402) document the decline in bank capital-to-asset ratios in the United States during the century-and-a-half following 1840, which they ascribe largely to a decline in the risk of bank failure.

The risk of failure declines with economic development for a variety of reasons. First, as money markets develop, banks are able to hold some fraction of their assets in liquid securities, rather than choosing between liquid cash and illiquid loans. This allows banks to hold lower levels of non-earning assets, which boosts cash-flow, while maintaining protection against sudden deposit withdrawals which can lead to failure. Second, as banking systems grow and individual banks increase in size and geographic spread, their ability to diversify increases and the risk of failure falls (Demsetz and Strahan 1997). Third, as financial systems prosper the stakes rise for all parties: managers, shareholders, depositors, and the

[8]This section draws heavily on Grossman (2007a).

public. These actors therefore have a greater incentive to develop ways and means of reducing the risk of bank failures. Such mechanisms might include the development of "conventional" (i.e., conservative) banking practices (Kennedy 1987, Collins 1989). They might also be reflected in the emergence of bankers' associations, which, among other things, would promote increased study and standardization of banking practices. Bankers' associations founded at this time include the Chartered Institute of Bankers in Scotland (1875), the Chartered Institute of Bankers in Great Britain (1879), the American Bankers Association (1875), the Canadian Bankers Association (1891), the German Zentralverband des deutschen Bank- und Bankiergewerbes (1901), and the Finnish Suomen Pankkiyhdistys (1914). A Bankers Library (Keizai Bunko) was established in Tokyo in 1897. Finally, failure-reducing mechanisms might also take the form of a bank safety net, encompassing formal government programs, such as bank inspection, double liability, deposit insurance, and lender of last resort facilities, as well as unofficial elements, such as clearinghouses.

Figure 6.2 presents the average capital-to-asset ratio for banks in eleven countries during 1834–1940. To the extent possible, the data represent the ratio of paid-in capital to total assets for all commercial banks and exclude central banks, savings banks, savings and loans, and credit cooperatives. Because state-level regulations varied widely, the U.S. data presented are for national banks only. Total asset data are not available for Japan; however, Japanese capital-to-deposit data show a similar pattern. Available data on capital-to-assets vary substantially in the completeness and accuracy of their coverage. And, since the early years of each series may well include only a few banks, it is possible that sharp fluctuations may be due to the entry of new banks. In Finland, for example, the capital-to-asset ratio dropped dramatically, from over 40 percent in 1862 to less than 20 percent in 1864, and fell consistently thereafter until 1873–74, when it tripled, from slightly over 9 percent to nearly 28 percent. This can be explained by the fact that there was only one commercial bank in Finland between 1862 and 1873. When a new bank with a substantially higher capital-to-asset ratio entered in 1874, the aggregate ratio rose substantially as well, before continuing the preexisting downward trend.

The data present a clear pattern: average capital-to-asset ratios dropped from 40 to 50 percent in the first half of the nineteenth century, to less than a third by the 1860s, to around 10 percent by World War I. Although the data are far from perfect, and not necessarily comparable across countries, the long-run downward trend is remarkably consistent across countries, suggesting that economic development indeed led to declining capital-to-asset ratios.

Despite the clear downward trend in capital-to-asset ratios during 1860–1940, two reversals stand out. First, average capital-to-asset ratios

Figure 6.2. Average capital-to-asset ratio, 1834–1940. *Note*: Countries (start-ing dates) and *sources*: Sweden (1834), Sveriges Riksbank (1931) and League of Nations (1938); Denmark (1846), Danmarks Statistik (1969) and Johansen (1985); Finland (1862), *Suomen Tilastollinen Vuosikirja* (various); United States, national banks (1863), U.S. Department of Commerce (1989); Canada (1867), Curtis, Taylor, and Michell (1931: 3–4), and League of Nations (1938); Belgium (1877, continuous from 1886), *Moniteur des Intérêts Matériels* (various); Germany (1883), Deutsche Bundesbank (1976); United Kingdom (1881), Sheppard (1972); Italy (1890), Cotula et al. (1996); Norway (1900), Norges Offisielle Statistikk (1948); and Australia (1908), Butlin, Hall, and White (1971).

rose during the mid-1870s, from just under 25 percent to just over 30 percent. This rise is not surprising, since crises in Austria (1873), Belgium (1876), Canada (1879), Denmark (1877–78), Finland (1878), Germany (1873), Sweden (1877–78), the United Kingdom (1878), and the United States (1873) prompted banks to hold higher levels of capital. Second, the period from the end of World War I until the early 1930s saw a lon-ger, and proportionally larger, rise in capital-to-asset ratios, from about 7 percent to about 11 percent. These data accord with our intuition about the relationship between capital-to-asset ratios and the risk of banking crises: the boom-slump following World War I led to a number of bank-ing crises in the early 1920s, as the onset of the Great Depression did in in the early 1930s. Statistical analysis of the data presented here demon-strates that the market response to crises was to insist on higher levels of capitalization. These results hold true not only across countries, but also across states of the United States, where higher levels of bank fail-ures led surviving banks to hold higher capital-to-asset ratios (Grossman 2007a).

Explaining Government Capital Requirements

Market capital requirements fell over time as a result of greater banking stability and improved information flows, although they rose during periods of crisis and financial uncertainty. Did the same forces drive government capital requirements? Of the four motives for regulation discussed earlier (stability, efficiency, monetary control, and political economy), it is unlikely that monetary factors drove government-imposed capital requirements. Although some countries, like the United States and Japan, limited banknote issues to a fixed proportion of bank capital, setting *minimum* capital requirements would not limit the size of the money supply. Further, since government capital requirements were altered only infrequently, they would not have been an effective tool for engineering changes in the total money supply or credit conditions.

Capital requirements could be efficiency-promoting if many banks were below some minimum efficient size. Without detailed data on individual bank cost functions, however, it is impossible to determine any efficiency threshold. Bank capital requirements were established or altered in England (1844), Sweden (1846, 1886, 1903), the United States (for national banks, 1863–64, 1900), Finland (1866), Canada (1871–72, 1890), Japan (1872, 1927), Denmark (1919), Norway (1924), Italy (1926), and Belgium (1935). The minimum capital requirement was typically well below the average level of capital held by banks at the time; however, it was often set above the levels held by the smallest banks.

Promoting stability has been by far the most frequently stated rationale for government-imposed capital requirements among contemporary policy makers and their predecessors. Although the market does impose capital requirements, if governments are more wary of financial crises than the private market—due to their concerns about bearing the political and economic costs of them—they may wish banks to be even more risk averse than the market requires and hence might enact higher capital requirements.

Political economy reasons also drive government capital requirements. The interest group most directly affected by such requirements is bankers themselves. One would expect that bankers, especially those commanding substantial amounts of capital, would favor high capital requirements to serve as a barrier to entry and to allow incumbents to earn monopoly profits (Rajan and Zingales 2003b). Prospective bankers, along with owners of smaller banks which might find themselves newly constrained by higher capital requirements, would likely oppose them. And since monopolies tend to restrict output and raise prices, those involved in sectors that employ bank services—trade, industry, and consumers, particularly in countries with limited alternatives to commercial banks—would oppose higher bank capital requirements that limited competition among banks.

It is difficult to systematically analyze government-imposed bank capital requirements because they were set in many different ways. Contemporary studies and modern regulation typically focus on the amount of capital held relative to the aggregate balance sheet (i.e., capital-to-asset ratios). In fact, nineteenth-century regulations almost never used this standard, but instead set capital requirements in one of three ways: (1) separately for each individual bank, which was more common when banks were chartered on a case-by-case basis; (2) one minimum standard for all banks; and (3) varying standards based on population density (Allen et al. 1938: 8ff.). A further complication in calculating capital requirements is the existence of "uncalled capital" (see note 5 in chapter 4). Government-mandated capital requirements frequently specified both minimum subscribed and paid-in capital, as well as the time period within which paid-in capital was due. Thus, comparing national capital requirements is complicated by the necessity of taking into account both nominal and paid-in capital, the length of time within which the capital needed to be paid in, as well as any exceptions for banks established in more or less populous areas.

The most common method of capital regulation adopted during the pre–World War I period was to set a fixed minimum level of capital for all banks. The early banking codes in England, Canada, Finland, and Sweden each fixed minimum levels of capital, as did the post–World War I Danish and Norwegian codes. If all banks are about the same size, establishing one minimum level of capital may be appropriate. However, the "one size fits all" approach might be problematic because it subjects all banks, big and small, urban and rural, diversified and undiversified, growing and shrinking, to the same capital requirement. Governments have sought to address this problem in two ways.

First, bank capital requirements were sometimes tailored to the population of the place where the bank was located. This route was taken in the United States, where the National Banking Acts specified different minimum capital requirements for localities with populations under 6,000, between 6,000 and 50,000, and over 50,000. State banking regulation in the United States was even more prone to such categorization, with some states adopting as many as eight different population-based capital categories. A similar approach was adopted under Japan's National Banking regulations (1872) and in the Bank Act of 1927, which specified higher capital requirements for banks located in Tokyo and Osaka. The Swedish (1886) and Norwegian (1924) banking codes empowered the chartering authority to issue charters to institutions with just one-fifth (Sweden) or one-quarter (Norway) of the statutory minimum capital, paving the way for the establishment of small banks in rural areas. Italy's banking law of 1926 specified different levels of capital for banks operating nationally, regionally, and within one province. Belgium's Banking Decree of 1935 specified different levels of capital for banking corporations and banking partnerships, as well as the amount of capital that foreign banks were required to assign to their Belgian operations.

Second, starting in the twentieth century, the minimum required capital was often specified as a proportion of total liabilities or of some component of liabilities. The Swiss banking law of 1934 established a variety of required capital ratios. The German banking decrees of 1931 and the Bank Act of 1934 empowered the Banking Commissioner to establish capital-to-liability ratios, although as of 1937 he had not done so. Denmark (1919), Italy (1926), and Sweden (1911) all imposed capital ratio requirements in addition to minimum capital levels. Modern capital requirements (Barth, Caprio, and Levine 2006), including those set under the Basel and Basel II accords (Basel Committee on Banking Supervision 1988, 2004), are typically set in this manner.

Despite the difficulties in comparing the details of capital requirements across time and countries, some patterns stand out. The highest capital requirements were set in England in 1844 (£100,000 subscribed) and in Canada in 1870–71 ($C500,000 subscribed, or the equivalent of about £86,000). It is perhaps not surprising that these countries had both high minimum capital requirements and no exceptions for banks in rural areas, since most English and Canadian banks were large and extensively branched relative to those in other countries at the time, and suggests that these requirements were merely meant to codify existing practices, rather than generate an increase in aggregate capital-to-asset ratios. The Canadian paid-in capital requirement was raised in 1890 in response to the closure of several smaller banks in the late 1880s, perhaps again merely codifying existing capital standards or further discouraging the entry of small banks. Japanese capital requirements (¥500,000, about £83,200) instituted in 1872 and effectively repealed in 1879, required a similarly high level of capital, but only for banks in the largest cities. Sweden's 1846 capital requirement (SKr 1 million, about £55,000) was high relative to the capital position of the six preexisting banks: four of these banks had started with less than SKr 1 million in capital and one was, at the time of the law's passage, below the mandated level.

Capital requirements set under the National Banking Acts in the United States were low relative to the amount of capital held by preexisting state-chartered banks. The average capital of all state-chartered banks in 1862 was $285,000—well over the $200,000 (approximately £41,000) minimum capital requirement set for banks in cities of 50,000 or more. Excluding the eight states that contained the nine cities in the United States with populations of more than 50,000 in 1860 (i.e., including states where the minimum capital requirement could have been no more than $100,000), average bank capital was still over $220,000. Low capital requirements may have been set in order to encourage the establishment of new national banks and to increase the demand for government bonds, which national banks were required to purchase. The capital requirement of national banks in the least populous locations (less than 6,000 inhabitants) was set to $50,000 in 1862; however, this was halved in 1900 in order to make the national banking system more competitive with state banking systems, which often had lower capital requirements.

Denmark's banking law of 1919 had its origins in the banking crisis of 1907–8, which led to the appointment of a parliamentary committee to revise the savings bank law and enact the country's first commercial bank law. Proposals were introduced into Parliament in 1913, but delayed by lobbying from the savings and commercial banks until 1919. The revised law of 1930, which raised capital requirements and reduced the amount of time within which the capital had to be paid in, had been introduced following the banking crisis of 1922, but was also delayed by competing interests (Hansen 2001). Although the minimum capital requirement (DKr 200,000, or less than £8,000 at pre–World War I exchange rates in 1919, raised to DKr 300,000 in 1930) was not high by the standards set by other countries in the nineteenth century, or by the average Danish bank capitalization in 1918 (which was nearly DKr 2 million), approximately one-third of all banks were below the prescribed minimum. Five years after the enactment of the 1930 legislation, one-third of all banks remained below the minimum capital requirement, although waivers of the requirement through 1939 were available. The Norwegian banking law of 1924 also came about following a banking crisis and, similarly, imposed capital requirements that were low by average preexisting capital standards: the average capital of the smallest 84 percent of banks was still five times the newly imposed minimum.

Relative to those of Denmark and Norway, the capital requirements imposed on the largest banks in Italy in 1926, Japan in 1927, and Belgium in 1935 were far higher in absolute terms, between eight and fifty-eight times those in Denmark. The Belgian capital requirements imposed in 1935 were part of an overall and far-reaching reform of the banking system. The Belgian decree of 1935 set high capital requirements for new banks, although preexisting banks were allowed to continue with a lower requirement. Although the average preexisting bank capital was nearly seven times the new minimum, the minimum was above levels of a handful of banks in existence in June 1930.

The Japanese banking law of 1927 continued a long trend on the part of the government to foster mergers among banks. Bank capital requirements had been gradually increased from the turn of the twentieth century, reaching a new peak in 1927. The 1927 law reflected in part a desire to speed consolidation, and was enacted in the aftermath of the financial distress following the Great Kanto earthquake of 1923. The law also fostered regional mergers, rather than encouraging a system of nationally branched banks as in the United Kingdom, which had been the policy in the early 1900s (Sawada and Okazaki 2004).

The Italian decree laws of 1926 imposed minimum capital requirements where none had existed before. The laws were part of a series of measures adopted by the fascists in order to maintain "Quota 90," Mussolini's determination to maintain the exchange rate at ninety lira to the pound sterling. The increase in the number of banks and the money supply in the preceding few years had put the exchange rate in jeopardy and the laws of 1926 were aimed at reining in the banks under the leadership of the Bank of Italy in order to achieve tighter monetary control. Bank of Italy Governor Bonaldo Stringher argued:

> There has been too much ease in creating new banks, large and small, and in multiplying their branches even in very small centers in order to collect deposits. The result has been that such deposits have not always been used wisely nor often invested in the communities where gathered. . . . It seems that in this delicate field, it would be advantageous to re-establish 'discipline' and 'hierarchy,' following the principles so forcefully fostered for other important matters by the eminent Chief of Government to whom the Banca d'Italia send with sincere admiration, its respectful homage. (Volpi, Stringher, and Pennachio 1927: 83–84)

Although the motivation for these laws was, in some sense, monetary control, they were, in fact, part of a larger plan to exert tighter control over the banking sector more generally.

The most common motive for imposing capital requirements was to promote banking stability, although political economy motivations were also at work. Many of the capital requirements discussed here were established as the result of investigations set in motion by banking crises. The English law of 1844 followed a period of banking instability in the 1820s and 1830s and committees of investigation in the late 1830s. Similarly, the Danish law of 1919 was the result of a decade of investigation following the banking crisis of 1907–8. The delay between the establishment of an investigative committee and the enactment of regulatory reform reflects, in part, the intervention of interest groups that attempted to slow down or alter the reforms. Canadian capital requirements were also aimed at maintaining banking stability, by codifying existing high capital standards, but also protected the banking establishment by discouraging entry.

In a number of instances, new capital requirements were an ancillary part of much broader banking reforms. In the United States (1863–64) and in Belgium (1935), capital requirements were introduced in the con-

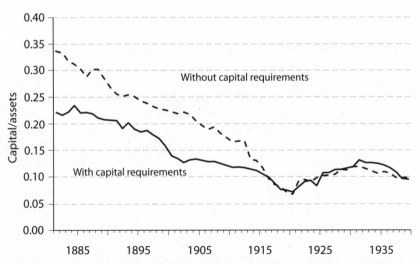

Figure 6.3. Average capital-to-asset ratios for countries with and without capital requirements, 1881–1939. Without capital requirements: Australia, Belgium (data available through 1912), Germany, Italy, and Norway (prior to 1924). With capital requirements: Canada, Denmark (from 1919), Norway (from 1924), Sweden, and the United States. *Sources*: See figure 6.2.

text of sweeping banking reforms, although the capital requirements themselves were not the most noteworthy aspect of those reforms. The change in U.S. capital requirements in 1900 was clearly the result of political economy motives, as the federal government tried to beat back competition from state-chartered banking systems. In Germany, Italy, and Japan, setting capital requirements was part of establishing a new order in banking—in Japan, encouraging and accelerating a process already under way toward consolidation, and in Italy and Germany, toward greater state control of the banking sector.

The Impact of Government Capital Requirements

Although it seems that government regulation should lead to higher capital-to-asset ratios, a cursory examination of the data suggests that it did not. Figure 6.3 presents average capital-to-asset ratios for countries with and without capital requirements. Before the end of World War I, banks in countries without specific capital requirements held *higher* capital-to-asset ratios than countries in which there were capital requirements; the averages converge during World War I and are not appreciably different during the interwar period. Further, changes in capital requirements do not have a statistically significant impact on capital-to-asset ratios (Grossman 2007b). There are at least three possible explanations for this result.

First, if government regulations were more likely to be established in countries which were perceived as having more stable banking systems—perhaps because of well-established conservative banking practices or a proven lender of last resort—the market might not have required banks to hold as high a proportion of their assets in capital as in countries perceived as being more susceptible to crisis. Second, because the market viewed smaller banks as more susceptible to failure, it required them to hold higher capital-to-asset ratios than large banks. Therefore, countries with high capital requirements, populated by large banks, would have had lower average capital-to-asset ratios. It is therefore possible that high minimum capital requirements did not result in higher capital-to-asset ratios, but instead discouraged entry, leading to banking systems characterized by fewer and larger banks with lower capital-to-asset ratios. Third, it is possible that in countries where parallel sets of institutions had different regulatory requirements (e.g., state and national banks in the United States, banks and savings banks, and private and chartered banks in many other countries), capital-to-asset ratios may merely reflect the presence or absence of alternative regulatory regimes.

Statistically assessing the effects of increased capital requirements on bank entry using cross country data from the nineteenth and early twentieth centuries is problematic for two main reasons. First, many countries had no capital requirements at all. Second, countries that had capital requirements altered them infrequently. Fortunately, the United States presents a gold mine of useful data: each state set capital requirements that were changed frequently for banks operating under their jurisdiction. Additionally, the change in the number of state banks in any year is readily available. Statistical analysis of the state-level U.S. data indicates that, although changes in capital requirements did not translate into changes in average capital-to-asset ratios, they did lead to changes in the growth rate of state banks (Grossman 2007b). That is, increased capital requirements did not raise average capital-to-asset ratios, but did have the effect of limiting entry into banking.

Capital regulation is far more complicated to analyze than entry regulation. In the case of entry, the authorities either grant or deny a charter: although firms denied can seek entry into a related field (e.g., as a savings bank) or operate without a charter as a private bank, the regulatory aspect of entry is straightforward. Capital regulation is more nuanced: regulations can affect subscribed capital, paid-in capital, the period within which capital must be paid in, and capital requirements for institutions located in different regions. Also, because capitalization is determined both by government regulation and market forces, discovering the causal factors underlying capital-to-asset ratios is more difficult. Market capital regulation was determined largely by the prospects for banking stability: as the risk of banking crises declined, so did the market's demand for banks to hold capital. Market capital requirements appear to have played a dominant role in determining aggregate capital-to-asset ratios.

Government capital requirements had a less important impact on capital-to-asset ratios, per se: banks in countries without capital regulation typically held more capital than those with capital regulation, and changes in capital requirements rarely led to substantial changes in capital-to-asset ratios (Grossman 2007b). There is, however, robust evidence that government-imposed capital requirements did have an important effect on the structure of the banking system. Higher capital requirements acted as a barrier to entry, slowing the increase—or leading to a decrease—in the number of banks in operation. There are two plausible explanations as to why authorities might have an interest in reducing the size (or growth) of the banking sector. First, as a stability-promoting measure: reducing the population of banks may promote stability if it leads to a banking system composed of larger, stronger, more profitable banks. Second, political economy motives were at work. Making entry more difficult was in the interest of incumbents, as well as those of competing regulatory systems (e.g., state versus national banks, commercial versus savings banks), although it was detrimental to the interest of trade, industry, and consumers.

OTHER REGULATIONS

The two sets of regulations discussed above constitute only a small portion of the constraints under which banks operate. A variety of regulations govern many other aspects of bank behavior. These include restrictions on the classes of assets that banks can own or hold as collateral for loans and a number of detailed balance sheet ratio requirements (e.g., mandated ratios of reserves to various categories of liabilities, maximum proportion of loans permitted to be made to one lender). Other common regulations require the publication of balance sheets and the establishment of regulatory agencies with varying degrees of regulatory and supervisory authority. Still other rules govern whether banks can establish branches and regulate a variety of aspects of corporate governance. Two of these are of special interest: (1) restrictions on the type of assets that banks can hold; and (2) the agencies assigned as supervisor.

Universal Banking

A major distinction between modern banking systems can be found in the extent to which they are market-based or bank-based. In Britain and the United States for most of the twentieth century, long-term corporate finance (i.e., corporate equity and long-term debt) was undertaken by specialized institutions (e.g., investment banks, merchant banks), which raised funds primarily from securities markets. Commercial banks in market-based systems focus on making relatively short-term loans. The alternative, common in continental Europe, is a bank-based system, in which universal banks engage in deposit-taking, short-term commercial lending, corporate bond and equity underwriting, as well as additional functions not generally undertaken by commercial banks in market-based systems (Fohlin 1999: 309). This section will focus on universal banks' role in providing long-term finance, although this is not the sole defining characteristic of universal banking, and will examine how these distinctions developed and what role legal restrictions played in maintaining them.

Alexander Gerschenkron (1962) asserted that the structure of the financial system was largely dependent on economic development. The more economically backward a country, he argued, the scarcer and more diffuse was its capital. Hence, the mobilization of capital in amounts sufficient to finance industrialization required the development of specialized institutions (Fishlow 2003). In Britain, the first to industrialize and the most economically advanced country through much of the nineteenth century, the early and gradual development of industry allowed a great deal of industrialization to be financed with internally generated funds (i.e., retained earnings). Mobilization of capital was also facilitated through the development of a national money market.[9] In Germany, and indeed throughout much of continental Europe, the absence of substantial retained earnings and lack of integrated and liquid securities markets necessitated the emergence of a new type of institution, the universal bank, which not only took deposits, but also made long-term loans and underwrote debt and equity securities.

Universal banking first emerged in Belgium during the first half of the nineteenth century. Founded in 1822, the Société Générale pour favoriser l'Industrie nationale was the first bank of any sort in the territory that would soon become Belgium. The Société's investment in industry resulted from the illiquidity of its short-term debtors, primarily coal mining operations. When these partnerships ran into difficulties around the time of the 1830 revolution, the Société required that the debtors convert their firms into joint stock companies and convert their debts into shares that the Société kept in its portfolio. The decision of the new Belgian state to

---

[9]Jonker (2003) argues, in a similar vein, that the presence of liquid markets in the Netherlands removed the need for the early development of universal banking.

build a railway system further stimulated the Société's place as a universal bank (Teichova 1997: 7, Chlepner 1943: 8, Durviaux 1947).

Universal banking has been a distinctive feature of the German economy from about the middle of the nineteenth century (Edwards and Ogilvie 1996). This development was due in large measure to the demands of industry and the relative scarcity of concentrated sources of capital. According to an 1856 monograph (Riesser 1911: 6–7):

> When industrial development has reached the stage at which great industries are forced to acquire their capital largely through the gathering of small capitals, special economic organizations must develop on which special functions regarding the initiative in stock transactions devolve. Banks for the promotion of such enterprises meet this need.

Universal banking came into existence without official government encouragement or sanction: in fact, banking law—when countries had any banking law at all—was largely silent on the issue of universal banking, with the possible exception of central banks which were often prohibited from participating in non-financial enterprises. Universal banking evolved in response to a variety of factors: economic backwardness, the development of the joint stock company form of organization, the pace at which securities markets and alternative intermediators emerged, as well as laws regulating those intermediators.

The emergence or non-emergence of universal banking in the nineteenth century was usually not directly tied to government regulation. The countries in which universal banking appeared in the nineteenth century, including Austria-Hungary, Belgium, France, Germany, Italy, and Switzerland, placed almost no restrictions placed on commercial banks. In England, Japan, and the Netherlands, where universal banking did not emerge in the nineteenth century, the absence of universal banking was also generally not the result of legislation. In the United States, the National Banking Acts discouraged—but did not completely prohibit—national banks from engaging in the securities business. Nonetheless, before World War I, few national banks did so (White 1986). In Japan, as early as the 1890s, stocks served as collateral for more than a quarter of all bank loans; however, banks did not become directly involved in equity underwriting until later. Japan migrated from a market-based system to a bank-based system prior to World War II when the government wanted to take greater control of the capital allocation mechanism so as to direct funds toward the military buildup (Hoshi and Kashyap 2001).

The desirability of universal banking was much debated during the 1990s (Saunders and Walter 1996, Shull 1999, Canals 1997) for two main reasons. First, as the formerly socialist economies of eastern Europe began the process of privatizing and liberalizing their economies, deciding on the most appropriate financial model to adopt became an important policy issue. Second, as the process of financial deregulation progressed in the West, countries in which universal banking had been outlawed by Depression-era reforms began to consider whether restrictions on commercial bank involvement in investment banking activities should be loosened. On the positive side, it was argued that permitting banks to undertake securities activities would allow them to achieve greater diversity and economies of scale and scope. Proponents of expanded bank powers also argued that restrictions on these activities put commercial banks at a competitive disadvantage vis-à-vis foreign competitors that were not so constrained. Arguments against universal banking emphasized three main points: (1) the potential conflict of interest between universal banks in their role as protectors of depositor's interests and in their desire to place new equity with investors (Crockett et al. 2003); (2) the retardation of the development of liquid securities markets, arguably a more efficient capital allocation mechanism, due to the dominance of universal banks; and (3) increased instability, since the equity held by universal banks is inherently more risky than short-term loans which make up the a larger proportion of commercial bank loans in non-universal banks. Historically, legislative changes curbing commercial banks' securities powers have come in response to crises, particularly those perceived as caused by universal banking. In France, universal banking was ushered in by the establishment of the Crédit Mobilier by the Péreire brothers in 1852, and was ushered out around the time of the firm's failure (1868) and the crisis of 1870. These disturbances, plus the banking failures of the 1880s led a number of large deposit banks to decide not to engage in investment banking activities (Plessis 1994: 188–90).

In many countries, the onset of the Great Depression signaled the end of universal banking. In Belgium, sweeping legislation to this effect was enacted in 1934 and 1935. Belgian banking difficulties were exacerbated by the dramatic fall in the value of bank-owned shares: the index of 120 stocks on the Brussels exchange fell by 70 percent between 1929 and 1934. Socialists in the national government that had been formed to deal with the financial crisis urged that the government take full control of the banking system, while other parties looked for less dramatic reforms. The end result was a compromise measure that ended universal banking (Chlepner 1943: 83–84). Similarly, in the United States, the widespread bank failures of the Great Depression led to the passage of the Banking Act of 1933, which included provisions that prohibited banks and their securities affiliates from engaging in securities transactions, despite White's (1986) argument that the investment banking activities of commercial banks' securities affiliates had not been, in fact, destabilizing.

In Italy, the end of universal banking came with the banking crisis of the early 1930s (Ciocca and Toniolo 1984: 131ff.). The Italian banking system underwent an extensive reorganization during this time, including the transfer of the equity holdings of the two largest universal banks to separate holding companies. The Istituto Mobiliare Italiano (IMI) was created in 1931 to take over commercial banks' long-term advances to industry (Allen et al. 1938: 259). In 1933, the Istituto per la Riconstruzione Industriale (IRI), a state-owned holding company which raised money by issuing government-guaranteed long-term bonds, was created and took over the industrial equities of the universal banks. By 1934, IRI became the majority shareholder in the three big formerly universal banks (Banca Commerciale, Credito Italiano, and Banco di Roma). Subsequent banking legislation required that ordinary banks restrict their lending to short-term commercial lending, while IRI, which was declared a permanent institution in 1937, was to provide long-term funds.

In Germany too, where universal banking had been central to banking for a half-century, the banking crisis of the 1930s led to legal changes that constrained banks, although the reforms did not hit at the heart of universal banking as they had in Belgium, Italy, and the United States. The German banking crisis was seen, in part, as the result of banks having invested too much to one particular borrower (e.g., Danat-Bank and Nordwolle). The Bank Act of 1934 set limits on the amount of credits (as a proportion of capital) that could be granted to one borrower, although exceptions were possible. Despite these changes, German universal banking remained fundamentally intact.

Swedish banking law and practice underwent several changes during the half-century prior to the Great Depression. The banking law of 1846 allowed enskilda banks to hold corporate equity—except for that of other enskilda banks—as security for the unpaid part of their capital and as collateral for loans, although they were forbidden to deal directly in shares. The 1886 law that established limited liability incorporated banks forbade these institutions to own or lend against the security of shares (Flux 1910). Nonetheless, Swedish banks were actively involved in industrial finance prior to World War I. As private merchant houses declined during the last third of the nineteenth century, commercial banks, operating through private consortia, became deeply involved in industrial finance (Larsson and Lindgren 1992: 339ff.).

Following the banking crisis of 1922–23, the Banking Commission was appointed to assess the relationship between banks and industry in Sweden. The Commission's 1927 report recommended "far-reaching" alterations in the bank law; however, by the time of the report, industrial recovery was well under way and the report's recommendations were shelved (Allen et al. 1938: 337ff.). Following the collapse of Ivar Kreuger's industrial empire in March 1932, the government passed a new banking law which clearly defined the circumstances under which banks could acquire equities.[10] The new restrictions appeared to be more severe than they actually were. Bank share ownership actually increased after the law was enacted, perhaps due to a loophole which allowed banks a grace period of several years within which to be divested of industrial participations. By 1934, Larsson and Lindgren (1992: 352) argue, the personal and economic bonds between the larger banks and their industrial customers were too strong to be dissolved without greater political will than existed at the time.

Where universal banking grew, it grew largely without government sanction: in most countries the law was silent on the topic. Not so for the end of universal banking: this frequently came about as part of a stability-promoting package of reforms during the turbulent interwar years. The extent of the suppression of universal banking varied across countries. Suppression was strongest in Belgium, Italy, and the United States: laws and agreements enacted in the 1930s fundamentally ended universal banking in these countries. Elsewhere, especially in Germany and Sweden, the financial instability of the 1920s and 1930s gave the government cause to move against universal banking; however, these were more cosmetic. This difference in experiences can be attributed to both the severity of the banking crises, the extent to which they were seen as being tied to universal banking, and to how well established universal banking had been prior to the crises that motivated the reform.

Identity of the Banking Supervisor

Although the form and specifics of banking regulations have been extensively studied, until recently there has been very little research on *who* should be entrusted with their implementation. Interest in this issue has been heightened by recent moves in several countries to establish unified financial supervisory authorities with powers to oversee insurance and securities firms, as well as banks. These contemporary developments will be discussed in chapter 10; the remainder of this chapter will focus on the factors that have historically determined the identity of the main banking supervisor.

Although bank regulation is ubiquitous, there is no consensus view on which institution—or combination of institutions—should be responsible for banking supervision. Historically, bank supervision typically has

---

[10]The government also formed AB Industrikredit to take the place of some bank financing, similar to Italy's IRI, although on a much smaller scale.

been undertaken by central banks, government ministries (e.g., finance, economics), subnational jurisdictions, independent commissions, or by a combination of two or more of these. The focus here is on the evolution of central banks as banking supervisors, and how these ostensibly private, profit-maximizing institutions, evolved into public institutions that were frequently entrusted with banking supervisory responsibilities. As central banks developed a multifaceted and non-competitive relationship with the commercial banking sector, they became well situated to act as supervisors.

Among the first tasks that central banks undertook was the discounting of financial instruments, primarily bills of exchange. As domestic and international commerce grew, banks and other financial houses became more involved in issuing and discounting bills of exchange, and central banks became convenient rediscounters. This frequently led to close cooperation between the central bank and other participants in the discount market. For example, the Bank of England maintained a close relationship with discount houses, institutions which financed their holdings of acceptances (bills of exchange) with call loans from the joint stock banks, prior to a falling out after the crisis of 1857. Similarly, because of the growth of new credit institutions in the Netherlands in the 1840s, the Netherlands Bank's rediscounting facilities grew substantially. By the time of the passage of the bank's charter renewal in 1863, which established new branches throughout the Netherlands, the bank was already interacting primarily with financial firms.

As banking systems developed, informal, then formal, clearing networks evolved to settle accounts between individual banks. Since central banks were large, often well-branched institutions, they were strategically placed to be a key member of these clearing systems, which further strengthened their role in holding the banking reserves of the country and acting as the bankers' bank. The earliest known clearinghouse was established by London private bankers, probably around 1770, although the precise circumstances of its origin "seems to be shrouded in doubt and uncertainty" (Cannon 1900: 321). London joint stock bankers were admitted to the clearinghouse in 1854, country bankers in 1858, and the Bank of England in 1864 (Clapham 1945, II: 250–51). The Swedish Riksbank established a clearing institution in 1899, the Bank of France helped to found one in 1901, and the Bank of Finland established an interbank clearing in 1906.

Finally, and perhaps most important in terms of marking the decline in competition between central and commercial banks, was the evolution of central banks into lenders of last resort. That evolution, discussed at length in chapter 4, was pioneered in England, although it spread during the late nineteenth century. The Swedish Riksbank, for example, which

TABLE 6.4
Year Central Banks Undertook Role in Banking Supervision (through 1948)

Country	Central bank	Year
Australia	Commonwealth Bank of Australia (from 1959, Reserve Bank of Australia)	1945
Austria	Österreichische Nationalbank	Never
Belgium	Banque nationale de Belgique	Never
Canada	Bank of Canada	Never
Denmark	Danmarks Nationalbank	Never
England	Bank of England	1946
Finland	Suomen Pankki	Never
France	Banque de France	1945
Germany	Reichsbank	1934
Italy	Banca d'Italia	1926
Japan	Nippon Ginko	1928
Netherlands	De Nederlandsche Bank	1948
Norway	Norges Bank	Never
Sweden	Sveriges Riksbank	Never
Switzerland	Swiss National Bank	Never
United States	Federal Reserve System	1914

Average year of establishment
  Central banks that did not become supervisors: 1828
  Central banks that did become supervisors: 1848

Source: Capie et al. (1994: appendix B).

was explicitly prohibited by law from supporting private banking, nonetheless engaged in lender of last resort activities in 1897. Capie et al. (1994) chronicle similar lender of last resort actions by central banks in France (1889), Norway (1899), and Denmark (1908).

Table 6.4 presents data on the year in which the central bank was given supervisory responsibility for some part of the banking system, if indeed it was ever given such responsibility. The data presented in this table are problematic for a number of reasons. First, the table does not include the date from which a central bank took informal responsibility for banking supervision. The Netherlands Bank, for example, acted as informal supervisor of the Dutch banking system for some years prior to World War II, although formal supervisory authority was not granted to the bank until 1948 (Capie et al. 1994: appendix B, Jonker 1996b).

Second, the table merely includes the date at which supervisory authority was granted to the central bank, and does not take into account any subsequent change—strengthening or weakening—in that supervisory authority. For example, the Reichsbank was granted supervisory authority over the German banking system under the commercial banking

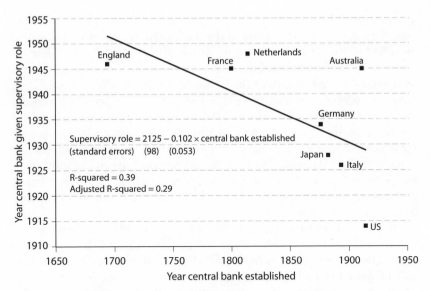

Figure 6.4. Establishment of central bank and year in which it became banking supervisor. *Sources*: Appendix table 2.1 and table 6.4.

code of 1934. Five years later, however, most supervisory and regulatory authority was transferred to the Ministry of Economics under a revised banking law. Figure 6.4 presents the data from table 6.4 along with information on the year central banks that were eventually granted such authority were established. The data suggest that the central banks that eventually became supervisors were younger than those that did not and also that younger central banks took on supervisory roles earlier than older central banks.

In no country did the central bank gain formal responsibility for banking supervision until the twentieth century. In fact, aside from the U.S. Federal Reserve, which assumed some supervisory functions when it opened its doors in 1914, no central bank was given supervisory authority prior to the end of World War I. Thus, by the time supervisory authority was entrusted to central banks, most had already acted as lender of last resort and were no longer in active competition with the institutions that they would regulate.

Considering the countries in which the central bank never had responsibility for banking regulation, two patterns stand out. First, none of the Nordic countries ever entrusted banking supervision to their central banks. Second, central banks that did become banking supervisors were, on average, established twenty years later than central banks that would not become banking supervisors.

The Nordic experience can be partially explained by the history of the evolution of the Swedish central bank, explained more fully in chapter 8.

The Riksbank had its origins in a private bank founded in 1656. At the time King Karl X Gustav granted the bank's charter, he also established an office of the Chief Inspector of Banks to supervise the new institution.[11] The bank failed during the regency of the King's young son and the Diet, taking advantage of the Crown's weakness, took control of the bank. In succeeding years, there was a struggle over control of banking and finance between the Diet and the Riksbank, on the one hand, and the King on the other. A result of this struggle was the reluctance of the executive to cede financial power—including the power to supervise banks—to the Riksbank. The next Nordic central bank to be established, the Suomen Pankki (Bank of Finland), was patterned on the Riksbank, and it is not surprising that it also took no significant role in supervising banks.

Another reason that central banks were not involved in bank supervision in the Nordic countries was the presence of well-developed savings banks systems. Savings banks, which were established during the first half of the nineteenth century, were completely distinct from the more primitive commercial banks and the well-established national banks. Because of their importance to a large segment of the population, governments had more incentive to regulate the activities of savings banks than commercial banks. Later in the nineteenth century, both Denmark and Norway adopted systems of savings bank regulation (neither adopted commercial bank regulation prior to the twentieth century), including the establishment of a bank inspectorate. In Norway, the savings bank inspectorate was given authority to supervise commercial banks when the first law regulating commercial banks was enacted in 1924.

Central banks that eventually became banking supervisors were established, on average, twenty years later than those that did not become supervisors and younger central banks generally became banking supervisors before older central banks. This may have occurred because younger institutions were more flexible and better able to adapt to include the role of banking supervisor. This, along with the United States' peculiar dual state and federal banking systems, might explain why the Federal Reserve, which was created in the aftermath of the crisis of 1907, was given some supervisory powers upon its establishment. By contrast, the Bank of Canada, also established in the aftermath of a severe crisis (the Great Depression), did not come into being with any supervisory powers, probably because the Canadian banking system, although not the economy as a whole, was quite stable during the Depression (Bordo and Redish 1987).

[11]Finansinspektionen (Swedish Financial Supervisory Authority) web site (http://www.fi.se/Templates/Page____3127.aspx).

Of the next three youngest central banks, Switzerland (1907), Italy (1893), and Japan (1882), those of both Italy and Japan were eventually given responsibility for banking supervision, although the Swiss National Bank was not. Switzerland's experience may be explained by the failure of an earlier attempt to establish a central bank. A proposal for a publicly-owned central bank was defeated in a referendum held on February 28, 1897, by a vote of 255,984 to 195,764 (Landmann 1906). Among the reasons for its defeat was the fear of creating a centralized and too-powerful institution (Sandoz 1898: 304), so when the Swiss National Bank was eventually created by less ambitious legislation enacted in 1905 (the bank opened its doors in 1907), it was created with relatively circumscribed powers.

The data support two conclusions. First, younger central banks were more likely to be called on to become banking supervisors than their older counterparts. Second, among central banks that were entrusted with banking supervision, younger central banks were typically given this task earlier than older ones. These results can be explained by the fact that younger central banks were less entrenched in their means of operation, and were flexible enough to adapt to the dual role of monetary policy maker and banking supervisor. Because younger central banks were more likely established in response to financial instability, they may have acquired supervisory oversight as a result. Older central banks were less adaptable and required more time to be brought into this new role—indeed, a number were not brought in at all.

Summary

Regulation has been a key element of the banking industry for centuries, and continues to exert an important influence over banking today. Although we conventionally think of regulation as a set of government-imposed rules, in fact, banking regulations have been imposed both by governments and by the market. Before the advent of incorporated commercial banking where entry was controlled by governments, private banking was governed primarily by market forces. Similarly, market regulation was an important factor in determining bank capital-to-asset ratios, even in the presence of government regulations. There were also market-based incentives—which frequently trumped government regulations—for banks to engage, or not engage, in investment banking activities.

This discussion of regulations demonstrates the complex combination of motives (stability, efficiency, monetary control, and political economy) and forces (government and market) that drive regulation. The regulation of entry, the earliest form of regulation, was driven primarily by the desire of governments to establish monetary control: commercial banks that were responsible for issuing money were more likely to be regulated than banks in countries where the central bank had a monopoly on money supply.

Market capital regulation was driven largely by a changing evaluation of banking stability: capital-to-asset ratios fell during the period leading up to World War I and then rose during the turbulent years of the interwar period. Increases in banking distress led to higher capital-to-asset ratios. Although some of these changes resulted from the failure of banks with low capital-to-asset ratios, they suggest that in times of greater uncertainty, the market demands that banks hold higher levels of capital. Government capital requirements had both stability and political economy motives: although government-imposed capital requirements did not have the effect of raising aggregate capital-to-asset ratios, they did act as a barrier to entry into banking. Such a barrier might have been set up in order to promote stability; alternatively, it could have been set up for the benefit of banking incumbents, enabling them to achieve greater profitability at the expense of economic efficiency.

The presence or absence of universal banking was also primarily market-driven. Economically backwards countries and those without alternative intermediators were more likely to develop universal banking than economies with developed financial markets. Hence, the introduction of universal banking was essentially independent of government policy. Not so the end of universal banking, which frequently was imposed in the wake of a financial crisis. And even then, where universal banking had strong institutional roots, complete abandonment was unlikely. The choice of supervisor, on the other hand, was largely a function of institutional history, and depended on the extent to which the central bank was entrenched, political economy motives, institutional squabbles, and historical accident.

CHAPTER 7

Banking Evolution in England

> The establishment of the Bank of England can be treated, like
> many historical events both great and small, either as curiously
> accidental or as all but inevitable.
>
> —John Clapham (1945, I: 1)

PREVIOUS CHAPTERS HAVE TAKEN a comparative approach to banking evolution, focusing on the forces generating banking crises, bailouts, merger movements, and regulatory reform across the industrialized world. Broadly speaking, this is akin to what economists call "cross-section" analysis: comparing similar events across countries. The strength of this approach is that the same phenomena can be compared in different settings and common elements can be isolated. Its weakness is that it may ignore important "time-series" elements: since developments may be causally connected to preceding and subsequent events, an exclusive focus on cross-section analysis may overlook important temporal interactions. For example, if crises lead to regulatory reforms, which encourage banks to develop regulation-avoiding practices, which then result in further reforms or crises, comparing regulations or crises across countries might miss this important dynamic. In order to better assess the interplay between the different factors that affect banking structure, this chapter focuses on the evolution of banking in one country: England. The subsequent two chapters focus on Sweden and the United States.

England provides many advantages as a case study with which to examine banking evolution. First, as the earliest industrialized country, it presents the longest possible time series over which to observe banking evolution in a developed economy. Second, England was among the first countries to develop many of the institutional structures that were crucial to banking evolution: the Bank of England is the world's second oldest central bank; England established the gold standard—de facto in 1717, de jure in 1819, although specie payments were not resumed until 1821—well before its trading partners; and England enacted the world's first joint stock banking code in 1844. Because England developed so many of these financial structures early in its history, we can be relatively certain that they were not imported wholesale from abroad. In contrast, Japan adopted a variant of the U.S. National Banking Acts as its first banking code and the Reichsbank (Wikara 1929: 817) or Bank of Belgium (Tamaki 1995: 63) as the model for the Bank of Japan. Because these key institutional developments were largely imported, Japan may be a less useful case with which to study banking evolution. Similarly, Canada's free banking law in the 1850s was based largely on the U.S. example. This is not to say that English banking institutions developed in complete isolation from developments elsewhere. Certain aspects of English banking were influenced by the banking systems of Sweden, Scotland, Hamburg, Amsterdam, and Italy. There is, however, little evidence of wholesale importation of practices or institutions. Finally, because of its colonial empire, the evolution of English banking may well have had implications for other countries.

THE BANK OF ENGLAND AND BRITISH GOVERNMENT FINANCE

The first joint stock bank in England was the Bank of England, which was founded in 1694. Prior to that, banking services had been rendered by a number of different agents, notably scriveners, goldsmiths, money-lenders, and participants in the daily meetings of London merchants. Perhaps those most closely identified with banking were the goldsmiths, who became an important force in finance sometime during the first half of the seventeenth century (Powell 1915 [1966]: 40, 58–59). According to F. G. Hilton Price's 1876 *Handbook of London Bankers*, there were forty-four goldsmith bankers in London in 1677 (Crick and Wadsworth 1936: 11). None, however, had received any charter, sanction, or official recognition from the government.

The establishment of the Bank of England was one of the many important fiscal reforms that followed the Glorious Revolution of 1689 (Broz and Grossman 2004). Prior to the Revolution, the king had been sovereign in fiscal matters—borrowing when needed and repaying when it suited him. During the "Stop of the Exchequer" in 1672, for example, Charles II unilaterally ceased all repayment of principal to his creditors (Dickson 1967: 44–45). Among the reforms instituted by Parliament following the Glorious Revolution, termed "the financial revolution," was a replacement of unsecured short-term debt with long-term debt secured by specific sources of revenue, or, in the terms of the day, the replacement of "unfunded debt" with "funded debt." By 1720, the funded debt accounted for more than 90 percent of all British government debt. North and Weingast (1989) argue that making government finances subject to Parliamentary control and the rule of law was responsible for a substantial decline in interest rates in England; Sussman and Yafeh (2004) contest that view. Among the most important sources of funded debt were three chartered corporations, namely the Bank of England, the New East India Company (chartered in 1698), and the South Sea Company (1711). In each of these cases, in return for a loan, the government promised shareholders an annual payment secured by some specific source of revenue and granted a charter that conferred a monopoly in the company's sphere of economic activity.

The Bank of England, then, ". . . owed its birth mainly to the needs of the Public Treasury" (Thomas 1934: 4), primarily those generated by war with France, rather than any desire to foster the growth of banking or to promote monetary stability. In return for a loan of £1,200,000, the government promised the investors an annual payment of £100,000, or 8-1/3 percent, construed as 8 percent interest and one-third of 1 percent management fee, secured by duties, and a charter as the Governor and Company of the Bank of England. The original charter did not grant the bank a privileged position as the government's banker, as it would later become, nor did it grant the bank a monopoly on joint stock banking, which was accomplished in a subsequent charter, nor did it make the bank's notes legal tender, which they would later become. The main accomplishment of the original charter was to secure a long-term loan in return for a predetermined annual payment secured by a discernable source of revenue.

The law did not establish the bank permanently, but guaranteed it a life of at least eleven years. After that time, with one year's notice, the government could repay the principal and cancel the bank's charter. In fact, the government did not do so, and instead renewed the charter nine times at intervals ranging from three to thirty-three years until 1844, when the Bank Act restructured the Bank of England and effectively continued its existence indefinitely. Charter renewals were frequently enacted well before the guaranteed life of the previous charter expired. Of the nine rechartered between 1697 and 1844, four were enacted with a year or less remaining before the expiration of the previous charter, while the others took effect with five, eight, eleven, twelve, and nineteen years left before the expiration of the preceding charter. Statistical analysis of the timing of charter renewals suggests that the government offered the bank a charter renewal under two sets of circumstances: (1) when the government was fiscally strapped, it offered to extend the bank's charter in return for an additional loan; and (2) when the bank appeared to be too profitable, the government attempted to renegotiate the contract on more favorable terms (Broz and Grossman 2004).

Although written evidence of the recharter negotiations between the government and bank is scarce, it is clear that the bank was not just a passive actor but responded to competitive challenges. In 1695, for example, Parliament chartered a rival Land Bank that never began operation because its promoters failed to raise the capital needed for a loan to the government (Horsefield 1960). The Land Bank challenge prompted the Bank of England to negotiate an exclusive privilege in the recharter of 1697. In return for additional loans to the government, the 1697 Continuance Act stated that "no other Bank or Constitution in the nature of a bank be erected or established, permitted or allowed by Act of Parliament during the Continuance of the Bank of England." In the words of John Clapham (1945, I: 47), the bank "wanted no more Land Banks."

In 1708, during the War of Spanish Succession and again in exchange for a fresh loan, the bank obtained from Parliament its most significant protection from competition: the legal prohibition of associations of more than six individuals from conducting a banking business (i.e., issuing banknotes) in England. This was a crucial component of restricting competition, since issuing banknotes was the major source of banks' funds in this era (White 1989: 73). The Act of 1708 thus gave the bank a monopoly on note issues by joint stock banks. Although the act did not explicitly ban joint stock deposit banking, "the intention was to give the Bank of England a monopoly of joint-stock banking, and had any other institution of more than six partners attempted to carry on a banking business in England . . . it would have been suppressed" (Feaveryear 1963: 167–68). The 1742 chartering act, the first such act not connected to a tax bill, enunciated the bank's "privilege of exclusive banking" (Crick and Wadsworth 1936: 11, Thomas 1934: 15). Thus, the bank's founding as the only joint stock bank in England and Wales rested on the fiscal needs of the government. According to one nineteenth-century observer (Thomas 1934: 4):

> So the Bank of England, the first English joint stock bank and destined to be first among all banking institutions, was brought into being, not so much as an instrument to promote national industry and to encourage commerce, as a device for getting an unpopular king out of a financial hole.

Not only was the bank founded to serve fiscal goals, but its continued privilege as the only joint stock bank in England and Wales depended on its fiscal usefulness. Within six years of its establishment, the government's debt to the bank exceeded 15 percent of the total outstanding debt of the British government; as late as fifty years after its foundation, debt to the bank represented approximately one-fifth of total government debt. From the mid-eighteenth century onward, as the government began to rely on other forms of borrowing, particularly bonds, the debt owed to the Bank of England fell as a proportion of total debt outstanding: from 20 percent in 1743, to less than 10 percent in 1762, to less than 5 percent in 1784, and to less than 2 percent in 1808. Not surprisingly, as its fiscal usefulness diminished during the second half of the eighteenth century, the bank's leverage to maintain its monopoly on joint stock banking fell. By this time, however, the bank had become a well-established institution. Speaking of the bank in 1781, Lord North—the Prime Minister and Chancellor of the Exchequer—said that it was "... from long habit and usage of many years ... a part of the constitution" (Clapham 1945 I: 174, citing *Parliamentary History* XXII, 516: 13 June 1781).

The establishment of the Bank of England stands in sharp contrast with developments in Scotland. The first Scottish joint stock bank, the Bank of Scotland, was chartered by the Scottish Parliament in 1695. Despite the similarity of their names, the Bank of Scotland had no fiscal connection to the government: it was forbidden to lend to the state by its charter, it had no role as the government's fiscal agent, and no connection to the management of the public debt (Kerr 1918, Checkland 1975: 24). In order to promote the new institution, it was granted a monopoly on Scottish joint stock banking for twenty-one years, as the Bank of England would later obtain in England, and its dividends were to be tax-free for the same period. Since the government derived no particular fiscal benefit from the bank, it is not surprising that after twenty-one years the monopoly privilege was not renewed. The Royal Bank of Scotland was established in 1727, over the protests of the Bank of Scotland, and the British Linen Company in 1746, which, despite its name, was more important as a bank than as a textile company. Despite periodic efforts by these institutions to secure a banking monopoly, free incorporation characterized Scottish banking for much of the eighteenth and nineteenth centuries (Checkland 1975: 118ff.).

PRIVATE BANKING IN LONDON AND THE PROVINCES

From 1694 until the early nineteenth century the Bank of England was the only bank in England, note-issuing or not, with more than six partners. The legislation restricting the banking franchise had different consequences for banking in London, already the country's commercial center, and the provinces. Although Bank of England notes were not made legal tender until 1833, due to its superior resources its notes nonetheless drove the preexisting note issues of London private bankers out of circulation soon after its establishment. Since note issue had been an important source of funds for private bankers, they bitterly opposed the new institution (Thomas 1934: 7, Crick and Wadsworth 1936: 12). In time, though, the private bankers accommodated themselves to the bank, as the growing use of deposits against which written orders of payment could be made gave private banks an important alternative source of funds.[1] By the 1770s, the London private banks had established a clearinghouse to more easily clear checks. They also began to deposit spare balances with the Bank of England, viewing them as reserves, and applying to the bank for loans when they needed funds.

Banking was not nearly as well established outside of London in the eighteenth century. In *Regicide Peace*, Edmund Burke wrote that when he came to England from Ireland in 1750 there were not more than a dozen "bankers' shops" outside of London (Pressnell 1956: 4). In the provinces, banking functions were undertaken by merchants who extended credit and bought and sold local bills of exchange.

> To a flourishing trade as a draper, brewer, merchant, or manufacturer would be added the task of transmission of funds and dealing in local bills of exchange. In course of time his newly developed functions would give him prestige enabling him to issue notes—and sometimes even token coin—in his own name and establishing himself as a custodian of spare funds. The final stage would be a complete severance of the two businesses, leaving for the one part a banking firm freed from direct connection with trade. . . . Thus it came about that cattle drovers of Wales, wool broggers of Yorkshire and corn bodgers of provincial England developed into bankers. (Crick and Wadsworth 1936: 12–13)

Unlike their London counterparts, provincial bankers did not face competition from the Bank of England, which had not established branches in the provinces.

Although precise data are not available, it is clear that private banking expanded rapidly during the second half of the eighteenth century. From Burke's dozen "bankers' shops" in 1750, the number grew to more than a hundred in 1784, to more than 200 in 1797, and to between 600 and 800 in 1810 (Thomas 1934: 65, Crick and Wadsworth 1936: 13). In 1821, Thomas Richardson, a leading bill broker, testified before Parliament that "I should conceive there are bankers, or bankers' agents within ten miles of every place, almost . . ." (Pressnell 1956: 11).

The spread of country banking reflected increased demand coming from the rapid growth in commerce and industry in the industrializing North and Midlands. Growth in private banking was also encouraged by the relatively loose restrictions placed on them. These included: (1) to have no more than six partners; (2) to issue no notes of small denominations; (3) from 1804, to pay a stamp duty on notes; and (4) from 1808, to pay for a license fee of £30 for the privilege of issuing notes. No specific application or official approval was required for a bank to issue notes.

----

[1]See, however, Capie (2004).

Increased demand for banking services due to the growth of trade and industry, combined with ease of note issue, lack of regulation, and the suspension of the gold standard during the Napoleonic wars, led to a substantial growth in both the number of banks as well as the circulation, which increased by more than 250 percent between 1797 and 1814. Not surprisingly, because of the over-issue, many banks became temporarily unable to redeem their notes (i.e., "stopped payment"); others went bankrupt. About a hundred banks stopped payment in 1793, an equal number in 1810, and even more in 1812. During 1814–16, 360 banks stopped payment and ninety-two went bankrupt. The period 1780–1820 saw approximately 261 bankruptcies and 1,000 stoppages (Thomas 1934: 47). Failures were particularly severe during the crises of 1793, 1797, 1814–16, and 1824–25.

JOINT STOCK BANKING REGULATION, 1826–57

The crises of the late eighteenth and early nineteenth centuries led politicians and pamphleteers alike to turn their attention to the Bank of England. The bank was attacked for increasing its note issue too rapidly during economic expansions and feeding inflationary booms, and for contracting its note issue too dramatically during economic downturns and exacerbating the severity of the ensuing contraction and boom-bust banking crisis. According to one 1832 pamphlet:

> The Bank of England has been the main cause of the commercial and pecuniary difficulties which took place in those years (1783, 1793, 1797, 1816, 1818, 1825), and produced them in each case by precisely the same means; that is, increasing its issues under circumstances which justified no increase. The consequences of so doing, it appears, has been a greatly redundant currency; and when this has taken place, the Bank has, unfortunately, not proceeded to cure the evil gradually, by beginning in time to diminish its paper; but waited until great commercial distress and panic have taken place, and then suddenly contracted it, and thus led to the most disastrous results. (Thomas 1934: 59)

> Sir Henry Parnell, in his *Observations on Paper Money, Banking, and Overtrading* (1827), blamed these failures in policy on the bank directors' "ignorance of the principles of currency and banking" (Thomas 1934: 60). A consequence of this, according to Thomas, was the call for periodic publication of the bank's balance sheet. Clapham (1930: 271) notes that Ricardo denounced the directors of the bank in 1822 as "ignoramuses in currency."

Others ascribed banking instability to the Bank of England's monopoly on joint stock banking, which left the majority of English banking in the hands of small, private banks, many of which, it was argued, had insufficient funds to survive a severe crisis. The Prime Minister, Lord Liverpool, expressed concern:

> . . . that the country has grown too large, that its concerns had become too extensive, to allow the exclusive privileges of the Bank of England . . . Any small tradesman, a cheesemonger, a butcher, or a shoemaker, might open a country bank, but a set of persons, with fortune sufficient to carry on the concern with security, were not permitted to do so. (*Parliamentary Debates*, XIV, col. 462, cited in Thomas 1934: 65)

Robert Peel and Thomas Joplin, among others, argued that England ought to look no further than Scotland, where the joint stock banking system survived the 1825 crisis far better than that of England. According to Joplin's 1822 *Essay on Banking*:

> I believe that trade is pretty much the same in both nations, or if there is any difference, that the merchants of Scotland are the most speculative, and least stable of the two. But the true cause of the difference is to be found in the nature of their respective banking establishments; the Scotch banking being joint stock companies, while the English banks are private concerns. (Thomas 1934: 66)

Following the expiration of the Bank of Scotland's monopoly, other chartered banks with limited liability were chartered, including the Royal Bank of Scotland (1727) and the British Linen Company (1746). The second half of the eighteenth century and first quarter of the nineteenth saw the establishment of a number of Scottish joint stock banks. Although the 1825 crisis did extend to Scotland, ". . . her fully developed joint-stock banks, her new joint stock banks, and all Edinburgh and Glasgow banks" survived (Clapham 1930: 272). Their relative success during the crisis was ascribed to the fact that because they were joint stock, not private banks, Scottish banks had greater resources with which to defend themselves. Additionally, because of the clearing system in Glasgow and Edinburgh, banknotes were rapidly returned to their issuer, making it more difficult for banking firms to over-issue currency.

The Bank of England's charter was renewed in 1800, during the early years of the Napoleonic Wars. In return for a six-year interest-free loan of £3 million, Parliament reaffirmed the bank's monopoly position and renewed the charter for thirty-three years. Even before the crisis of 1824–25, however, there was pressure to end the bank's monopoly. In 1796–97, a group of London merchants and bankers led by Sir William Pulteney agitated for the establishment of an opposition bank; however, their proposal was voted down in Parliament. In the Supplementary Observations to the third edition of his *General Principles and Present Practice of Banking* (1822), Thomas Joplin argued that the bank's monopoly applied only to note issue and not deposits, and proposed opening a joint stock bank in Newcastle.

In April 1822, the Treasury suggested that the Bank of England's charter, which had been extended until 1833, be extended by ten years in return for loosening the restriction on joint stock banking. Specifically, the government proposed allowing joint stock banking outside a fifty-mile radius of London. The Bank was reluctant to give up its privilege, however, given the attacks from inside and outside Parliament—along with implied threats to terminate the charter following its 1833 expiration—the bank agreed to the extension on condition that the proposed fifty-mile radius was expanded to sixty-five miles. Legislation reflecting the government's agreement with the bank was announced; however, due to strenuous objections from country bankers and their allies, who feared competition from joint stock banks, the government decided not to proceed with the legislation (Clapham 1930: 271, Clapham 1945, II: 88, Acres 1931: 41, Crick and Wadsworth 1936: 16).

The banking disturbances of 1825–26 led to the passage of "An Act for the Better Regulation of Co-Partnerships of Certain Bankers in England" (7 Geo. IV, c. 46), which became law on May 26, 1826, and marked the beginning of the end of the Bank of England's monopoly on joint stock banking. Although the act was viewed as something of a watershed at the time, its provisions were quite modest. Most importantly, it allowed the establishment of banking corporations of more than six partners outside of a radius of sixty-five miles from London. Although the sixty-five-mile radius was enshrined in law, the definition of "London" was not. Consequently, country bankers asserted their right to set up branches sixty-five miles from the boundaries of the City of London, while the bank argued that the boundary of London encompassed a larger metropolitan area. In 1836, the bank warned the North Wiltshire Bank that its Hungerford branch was only sixty-four miles from Hyde Park Corner; that bank ignored the warning, arguing that it was sixty-five miles from the Post Office and Temple Bar, on the boundary of the City (Thomas 1934: 167, Acres 1931, II: 500). In Ireland, a fifty-mile exclusion zone for the Bank of Ireland was similarly complicated by the completion of a new highway that reduced the distance from Lowry to Dublin from just over fifty miles to just under fifty miles (Thomas 1934: 235).

The act did not grant banking corporations limited liability, nor did it specify minimum capital or reserve requirements, nor did it require any financial data to be filed with the authorities or published. In fact, the law did not impose any substantive regulatory burden on banks beyond the

178 • Chapter 7

requirement that they file annual returns of a prescribed form under oath. These returns were to include the name of the firm, place of business, and names and addresses of all the partners and of at least two officers, in whose name the firm could be sued. This last provision was important for at least two reasons. First, before the law's passage, suits involving banking partnerships were required to correctly name all partners in order for it to be valid: the death of one partner or sale of a partner's shares would render pending lawsuits invalid. Under the act, partners' liability for bank losses was to persist for three years after the sale of their shares and the death of a partner would have no substantive affect on pending lawsuits. Second, the law removed the obstacle to banks with partners in common to sue each other. The act also explicitly authorized the Bank of England to open branches outside of London, which it immediately began to do: Gloucester, Manchester, Swansea, and Birmingham branches opened in the year that the act was passed and eight more were opened by 1834.

Although the act did lead to the formation of new joint stock banks and the conversion of several private banks to joint stock form, the immediate impact on the number of joint stock banks was not dramatic (figure 7.1). The first bank formed under the act, the Bank of Liverpool, was founded in 1826, although it did not start business until 1831. Later in 1826, Vincent Stuckey joined his private bank at Langport, Somerset with four other banks to form a joint stock bank with nineteen branches and thirty-nine proprietors. Only three banks were established in 1826, three more in 1827, and none in 1828 (Thomas 1934: appendix M). The numbers increased more rapidly thereafter, with the total number of joint stock banks rising to fourteen by 1830, and twenty-eight by 1832 just prior to the renewal of the Bank of England's charter in 1833.

Notwithstanding the emergence of a number of banks during 1826–32, several impediments constrained the growth of joint stock banking: proprietors of these new banks did not enjoy limited liability, discouraging investment by all but those prepared to take an active role in monitoring their affairs; banks were not permitted to open branches in London, which was the most important commercial center in the country; and the Bank of England and established private bankers tried to persuade clients and others not to become shareholders in or customers of the new institutions. Despite these impediments, the new banks flourished. In 1835, shares prices were at 50 to 300 percent premiums over their paid-in amount and were paying "respectable" dividends of between 7 and 13 percent (Thomas 1934: 94–95, 98).

Discussions about the 1833 recharter of the Bank of England reopened the debate over the bank's privileged position as London's only joint stock bank. Predictably, the bank, as well as local private bankers, opposed allowing new joint stock banks to be established in London. The

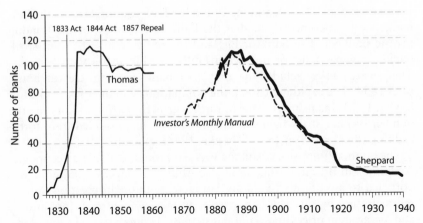

Figure 7.1. Number of banks in England, 1826–1939. *Sources: Investor's Monthly Manual* (various), Sheppard (1972), and Thomas (1934: appendix M).

efficacy of the bank's resistance was diminished on several counts. First, the relative success of the non-London joint stock banks established since 1826 argued in favor of allowing the franchise to expand to London. Second, the government's fiscal position in 1833 was healthy, having run seventeen consecutive budget surpluses of between 1.7 and 8.3 percent of the sum of revenues and expenditures, and allowed the repayment of one-quarter of the government's debt to the bank. At the time of the previous bank charter in 1800, the government had run seven consecutive deficits of between 2.6 and 45 percent of the budget, and had received an additional loan from the bank of £3 million, interest-free for six years, in return for the charter renewal. Finally, the government's lawyers were of the opinion that establishing a non-note-issuing bank in London was permissible under existing statutes (Clapham 1945, II: 128).

The Bank Charter Act of 1833 explicitly allowed the formation of joint stock banks within London. These banks, unlike their counterparts outside London, were not allowed to issue banknotes. As compensation, in addition to a new charter, the Bank of England's banknotes were given the status of legal tender. No other requirements were established, aside from reporting requirements on the part of the Bank of England and all note-issuing banks.[2] Although the law led to the opening of several new banks, including the London and Westminster Bank (1834), the London

---

[2]The law did not give London joint stock bankers the right to sue and be sued in the name of one or more corporate officers, which their non-London joint stock counterparts did have, perhaps to maintain parity with London private bankers. The London and Westminster attempted to get this changed through private legislation, which its enemies killed in the House of Lords. Clapham (1945, II: 134).

Joint Stock Bank (1836), and the Union Bank of London (1839), the new banks were welcomed by neither the Bank of England nor the London private bankers. The Bank of England refused to grant the joint stock banks drawing rights or to discount bills payable at joint stock banks. The private banks excluded the joint stock banks from the clearinghouse until 1854. The rapid increase in the population of joint stock banks following 1833 was primarily due to further growth outside of London: the number of joint stock banks in England more than doubled from forty-eight in 1834 to 111 in 1836 (Thomas 1934: appendix M).

The boom in joint stock banking was symptomatic of overall economic conditions in Britain during 1832–36. Abundant harvests and grain exports led to an inflow of gold and an increase in credit creation though rediscounting by the new banks, substantial new company formations, and increases in prices and economic activity. Economic conditions worsened during the second half of the 1830s. Andrew Jackson's 1836 specie circular in the United States, which required that purchases of public lands be made in specie, combined with poor domestic harvests and political trouble on the Continent beginning in 1838, led to substantial gold outflows and to a commercial and financial crisis during the second half of the 1830s. The crisis was marked by the failure of a number of banks—nearly thirty disappeared during 1839–43 (Andréadès 1966: 269)—among them several prominent joint stock banks. These failures included the Northern and Central Bank of Manchester, which failed in 1836 with total liabilities of £3.3 million (shareholders eventually lost £600,000), and the Commercial Bank of England, which failed in 1840 with £2.1 million in liabilities.

The disturbances of the 1830s, combined with the impending expiration of the eleven-year extension granted under the Bank of England's 1833 charter, led to the appointment of no less than three committees (1836–38, 1840, 1841) as well as a great deal of public debate over the consequences of the banking laws of 1826 and 1833 and the role of the Bank of England in the monetary system. The discussion centered on two main issues: (1) the fate of the outstanding note issues of the Bank of England, the private banks, and the provincial joint stock banks, in particular whether they should be consolidated within the Bank of England, and the rules governing future note issues;[3] and (2) the extent to which joint stock banking should be fostered. Two major pieces of banking legislation emerged as a result.

The more famous of these was entitled "An Act to regulate the Issue of Bank Notes, and for Giving to the Governor and Company of the Bank

---

[3]See Andréadès (1966: 269ff.) and Thomas (1934: 342ff.) on the Banking and Currency Schools.

of England certain privileges for a limited period" (7 & 8 Vict. c. 32), although it was widely referred to as "Peel's Act," after the Prime Minister, Sir Robert Peel. This was the last rechartering act prior to the bank's nationalization in 1946 and split the bank into two departments, the Issue Department and the Banking Department. The Issue Department was to be responsible for the bank's note issue and was authorized to issue £14 million of banknotes against securities (the so-called "fiduciary issue"); any additional notes could only be issued with 100 percent specie backing. The law also provided for the gradual extinction of all other note issues within England, centralizing the note issue in the Bank of England.[4] The Banking Department was to take over the remainder of the bank's business, which would continue to operate as a profit-making joint stock bank. Weekly returns of both departments were to be presented to the government and published in the London Gazette. The main importance of Peel's Act for commercial banking was to signal the beginning of the end of private banknote issue.

The second major piece of legislation enacted in 1844 was the Joint Stock Banking Act (7 & 8 Vict. c. 113), which established England's first banking code. Passed in the same year as a similar revision in non-banking company law,[5] this act prescribed a detailed set of regulations for the establishment and management of joint stock banks, addressing many of the issues raised by the 1836–38 committee (Thomas 1934: 217ff.). The committee had complained that there were no barriers to entry into banking other than the payment of a license fee and the registration of shareholders at the Stamp Office, and that banks' deeds of settlement (partnership agreements) were not subject to governmental review. The act mandated that all new joint stock banks with more than six partners could only be formed by letters patent granted upon petition

[4]The provisions were as follows: (1) If a country bank ceased issuing notes, the Bank of England was empowered to replace two-thirds of the lapsed note issue; (2) If any bank failed, its right of note issue expired automatically; (3) Country banks that had been entitled to issue notes were allowed to continue issuing notes, although the maximum note issue was prescribed based on the average quantity issued during the twelve weeks prior to the law's enactment; (4) No new banks were to have the power to issue notes; (5) If a private bank increased its partners to more than six, it would lose the right to issue; (6) Two country banks, one with and one without the right of note issue, might merge without losing the note issue; (7) If two joint stock note-issuing country banks merged, only the note issue of the absorbing bank would continue; (8) Any amalgamation involving a bank within a sixty-five-mile radius of London, or any note-issuing bank that opened an office within a sixty-five-mile radius of London, would forfeit its note issue. Sykes (1926: 19).

[5]The Act for the Registration, Incorporation and Regulation of Joint Stock Companies (7 & 8 Vict. c. 110) specified some of the same requirements for non-banking joint stock companies. Like the Joint Stock Banking Act, this law did not offer limited liability status to joint stock companies. Maltby (1998).

to the Privy Council, which had the authority to impose additional conditions (banks that already had more than six partners were given a year to reregister). Prospective bankers had to submit a deed of partnership in a particular form that specified details about the firm (e.g., names and addresses of partners) and its governance, such as timing of shareholder meetings, directors' qualifications, plans for the performance of audits, and the publication of monthly balance sheets.[6] These provisions filled a void since neither law nor custom specified such basic elements of firm governance. New charters would be valid for twenty years and banks would continue to operate with unlimited liability.

The committee had also expressed concern about the quantity and composition of bank capital. Prior to 1844 there had been no specified minimum amount of capital required to open a bank, suggesting that banks might be formed with insufficient resources. Moreover, there had also been no minimum requirement for the fraction of a firm's subscribed capital to be paid in prior to commencing business, which made it easy for banks to declare a high nominal capital without actually raising the declared amount. Additionally, preexisting law did not prohibit banks from reserving shares for bank directors or their friends or from selling them at a discount. The new act specified a minimum nominal capital of £100,000 and that no charter was to be issued until all the shares were subscribed and one-half of the nominal value was paid in.[7]

Between the restrictions on bank establishment imposed by the Joint Stock Banking Act and the limitations on note issues of new and newly merged banks established by the Bank Charter Act, there was little incentive to form new joint stock banks in the years following 1844. Indeed, critics argued that the purpose of the Joint Stock Banking law was to limit joint stock banking (Thomas 1934: 415). No new joint stock bank was formed until the Royal British Bank was established in 1849 (it failed in 1856). During the life of the new law (1844–57), only seven new joint stock banks were established, compared with well over one hundred banks during the previous thirteen-year period. Although there were two full-fledged financial crises during 1844–57 (1847, 1857) which involved the failure of several prominent banks, the 1844 banking code was not

---

[6]The auditors were to be chosen by the shareholders and not the directors, while the form of the published accounts was left entirely up to the bank. The returns had to be signed by the manager or a director and had to be authenticated by a declaration in front of a justice of the peace.

[7]The law also specified a minimum nominal share value of £100. Witnesses before the committee had argued that a higher minimum share value would ensure that shares were only purchased by the well-heeled, who would understand—and could afford—the associated risk and would be able to meet additional calls for capital. For that reason, many deeds of settlement gave bank directors the authority to approve share sales and transfers, preventing shareholders from selling to the impecunious. Hickson and Turner (2003).

seen as having been responsible for either the crises or the downfall of the individual banks.

The slow development of joint stock banking during 1844–57, combined with rapid developments in corporation law, led to a reversal of the joint stock banking regulations imposed in 1844.[8] The 1855 Limited Liability Act (18 & 19 Vict. c. 133) allowed companies to register with limited liability, while the 1856 Joint Stock Companies Act (19 & 20 Vict. c. 47) withdrew some of the registration and accounting requirements, making it easier to establish limited liability joint stock companies. In 1857, the Joint Stock Banking Companies Act (20 & 21 Vict. c. 49) repealed the detailed code of 1844, leaving banks subject to the joint stock companies law, aside from the limited liability provisions; a brief law passed in the following year allowed banks to register with limited liability (Crick and Wadsworth 1936: 27ff., Maltby 1998). From this time on, banks were essentially governed by corporation law.[9]

The period 1826 through 1857 saw dramatic changes in English banking law. Prior to 1826, largely due to the government's fiscal position, the Bank of England maintained a monopoly on joint stock banking in England and Wales. As the demands of industry increased and the government's dependence on the bank decreased, the acts of 1826 and 1833 gradually eroded the bank's monopoly position. More detailed regulations were passed in 1844. These had a stultifying effect on banking and, by the end of the 1850s, in parallel with developments in corporation law, the banking code of 1844 was scrapped and replaced with corporation law. This legal framework would govern English banking into the twentieth century.

MERGERS

There is evidence that bank mergers took place in England as far back as the latter part of the seventeenth century (Sykes 1926: vii). With the legalization of joint stock banking in 1826, mergers became a common feature of English banking—and remained so for the next century. Data

---

[8]The changes in banking law were somewhat parallel to those in corporation law. See Levi (1870), Evans (1908), Formoy (1923), Todd (1932), and Maltby (1998) on the evolution of company law.

[9]Although limited liability became readily available for banks by 1862, Sykes (1926: 38) suggests that the failure of the City of Glasgow Bank in 1878 and the fact that it brought down the West of England and South Wales Joint Stock Bank, among others, encouraged banks to register with limited liability. The Companies Act 1879 (42 & 43 Vict. c. 76) created "reserved liability," requiring that one-half of banks' uncalled liability be available solely in case of bankruptcy.

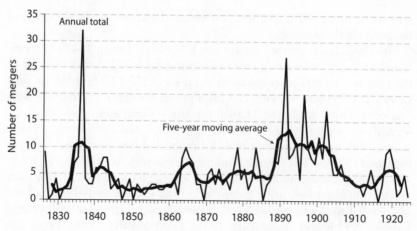

Figure 7.2. Bank mergers in England, 1826–1924. *Source*: Sykes (1926: appendix I).

on the annual number of bank mergers during 1826–1924 are presented in figure 7.2.

The first period of heightened merger activity took place from 1826 to about 1844. The 1826 act, which legalized joint stock banking by firms of more than six partners, and the 1833 Bank of England recharter, which codified the right to establish joint stock banks in London (albeit without note issue), dramatically increased the scope of permitted bank activities. Given the robust industrial and commercial growth starting in the second half of the eighteenth century, the increasing needs of commerce and industry almost certainly raised the optimal bank size beyond what could have been supported by banks with six partners.

In addition to the liberalization of joint stock banking and the long-term growth of the British economy during the previous half-century or so, the second quarter of the nineteenth century was conducive to mergers for other reasons. This period included years of high economic prosperity and rapid growth (1834–36), as well as years of economic crisis (1825, 1836–39, 1841), both of which provided incentives for banks to merge. Healthy banks—both private and joint stock—could increase their potential for growth by merging with a joint stock bank with greater resources. Joint stock banks hoping to create a foothold in a region and to develop branch networks likewise had an incentive to undertake acquisitions. The National Provincial Bank, for example, was established after the 1833 legislation and managed to absorb twenty banks in the subsequent decade (Sykes 1926: 6). Weak or failing banks were frequently acquired by existing joint stock banks; new joint stock banks were sometimes established with the express purpose of taking over the business of a recently failed private bank.

As hospitable as the years 1826–44 were toward mergers, a complete reversal of this pattern took place during the subsequent decade and a half. Like the earlier period, the years from 1845 to 1860 saw periods of boom and bust, culminating in financial crises in 1847 and 1857. The absence of mergers in the later period was due almost completely to the Bank Charter Act of 1844 and the Joint Stock Banking Act of 1844. The Joint Stock Banking Act's stringent restrictions discouraged the formation of new banking institutions (mergers frequently resulted in the formation of new corporate entities), establishing a detailed set of requirements governing establishment of new institutions. The Bank Charter Act was, perhaps, even a stronger deterrent, since most merging banks would have been required to forfeit all or part of their banknote issue, which was still a profitable part of the banking business. For example, any bank merging with a London joint stock bank would lose its right to issue banknotes; the merger of two joint stock banks with note issues would involve the loss of the absorbed bank's note issue. The repeal of the Joint Stock Banking Act in 1857, the continued development of the check as a form of payment, and the financial troubles that accompanied the Overend, Gurney crisis (1866), led to a rebound in the number of mergers in the 1860s.

Merger rates rose again in the 1890s. Although the data in figure 7.2 shows that the number of mergers fell around the turn of the century, this decline is deceiving, since the number of banks was much smaller than it had been earlier in the century. In fact, banking concentration ratios rose with few interruptions during the half-century prior to 1920. Figure 7.3 presents data on the concentration of market capitalization among English banks during 1870–1925. Table 7.1 shows the concentration of total deposits among the five and ten largest banks at ten-year intervals from 1870 to 1920.

Mergers were a constant feature of the 1880s, picking up in the years following the City of Glasgow Bank failure in 1878, and became even more common in the 1890s. This later increase was encouraged by the general uneasiness felt as a result of the failure of Baring Brothers in 1890 and by the low interest rate environment, reinforced by a large British government debt conversion in 1888, which encouraged banks to look to mergers as a way of increasing their returns. The increase in mergers was accompanied by a distinct change in their character: where local and regional mergers had once dominated, by the late nineteenth century large joint stock banks began to consolidate their holdings and develop nationwide networks of branches. These large banks began to compete with each other, both over size and geographic spread: "If by nothing

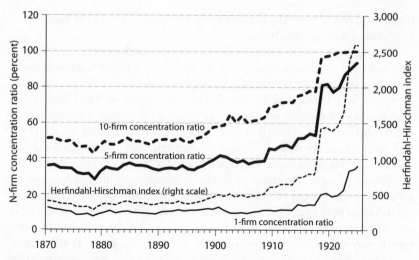

Figure 7.3. Concentration in English banking, 1870–1925. *Source: Investor's Monthly Manual* (various). *Notes*: N-Firm concentration ratio is the total share of market capitalization within the largest N banks. Herfindahl-Hirschman index is the sum of the squared percentage of market capitalization of all banks.

else, this is shown by the occasional militant and proud speeches by bank chairmen at the annual meetings, and especially at meetings called to sanction amalgamations" (Sykes 1926: 49).

The trend toward greater concentration in banking was widely noted, occasionally with apprehension, from the late nineteenth century. *Bankers' Magazine* reported on the amalgamation movement as early as May 1889 and in 1910 sponsored an essay contest on the subject, with prizes of ten and five guineas. One observer, noting the role of provincial banks in fostering local trade, agriculture, and industry, calls the movement, ". . . a process perhaps inevitable, but [one] whose march it is scarcely desirable to accelerate" (Martin 1891: 543–44). Others noted the distress of the mercantile community in Scotland caused by the monopolization of the banking business there prior to the turn of the century (Williams 1898: 4, Withers and Palgrave 1910: 49). And still others worried that excessive concentration would lead to an American-style "money trust" which would victimize bank customers and the public (*Bankers' Magazine*, August 1918: 77). Chisholm (1910: 332) notes that public opposition succeeded in preventing one merger, implying that there was periodic public opposition to such mergers.[10]

---

[10]In fact, increasing concentration did boost bank profitability during 1870–1913; however, this increase was overwhelmed by declines due to greater competition from equity markets and increasing conservatism among bankers. Grossman (1999).

TABLE 7.1
Concentration in British Banking, 1870–1920

	Ten largest banks		Five largest banks	
	UK	England and Wales	UK	England and Wales
1870	31.0	32.8	19.6	25.0
1880	32.5	36.2	20.6	26.4
1890	32.0	38.0	21.0	26.5
1900	41.0	46.3	25.5	31.0
1910	56.0	64.7	35.5	43.0
1920	73.7	96.6	65.5	80.0

Source: Capie and Rodrik-Bali (1982: 287).

The banking community, perhaps not surprisingly, was largely san-guine about the merger movement. Even while mourning the inevitable loss of many long-standing private banks, bankers focused on the numer-ous benefits of amalgamation, including an enhanced ability to accom-modate the needs of larger firms, more professional management, and the extension of banking facilities through the creation of new branches (Chis-holm 1910: 333–40, Lavington 1921: 57, Steele 1897: 122–23). Chan-cellor of the Exchequer George Goschen endorsed the benefits of large banks, complaining that the cash reserves of the ". . . Private Banks and of other financial institutions is inadequate to the necessities of the country, too small as compared with the gigantic liabilities which are in-curred . . ." (Sykes 1926: 49). Bankers did note, however, that the exten-sion of branch networks was costly, and suggested that it led to increased competition and greater costs (Sykes 1925, 1926).

The potential dangers posed by the monopolization of the banking sys-tem were frequently noted—and dismissed (Chisholm 1910, Jones 1910: 620). Steele's (1896: 541) argument is typical:

Apprehension has been expressed in some quarters lest the rapid de-crease in the number of banks resulting from the fusions of the last few years should lead to something in the nature of a banking monopoly, that the conveniences now afforded by banks may be restricted, and that we may even see a 'corner' in loans. This fear is surely chimerical. It is true that banking is getting into the control of fewer hands, and that the difficulties in the way of establishing new banks are so great as to be almost insuperable, but there are some banks which will never amalgamate, and there is no more likelihood of a cessation of competi-tion among the surviving concerns than in the case of any other class of commercial institutions.

More than twenty years later, before the Treasury Committee on Bank Amalgamations (the Colwyn Committee), a majority of bankers called to testify rejected the notion that mergers posed a threat to banking competition. In its May 1918 report, the committee was more circumspect, concluding that, "[w]hile we believe that there is at present no idea of a Money Trust, it appears to us not altogether impossible that circumstances might produce something approaching to it at a comparatively early date." The committee therefore recommended that further mergers, especially those involving large joint stock banks, be discouraged. The government subsequently established a standing committee to rule on proposed bank mergers. Whether it was due to the influence of these recommendations or the fact that the banking system had already reached a high degree of concentration by 1918 is unclear; however, merger activity slowed considerably in the post–World War I period.

Many factors influenced bank mergers in England during the nineteenth and early twentieth centuries. Long-term economic growth had increased optimal bank size well above what it had been during the second half of the eighteenth century; however, the deal struck between the fiscally strapped government and the Bank of England prevented banks from reaching that optimal size. With the end of that monopoly in 1826 and 1833, other banks were able to expand, both via internal growth as well as by absorption of smaller banks. With the passage of the Bank Charter Act 1844 and the Joint Stock Banking Act 1844, the legal impediments and disincentives to merger grew more severe and the pace of mergers slowed.

Macroeconomic fluctuations also contributed to merger movements, with both extremes—booms and slumps—particularly conducive to merger activity. Booms allowed banks to expand via acquisitions and encouraged sellers to take advantage of generally favorable terms. Slumps not only forced poorly performing firms to merge or to have their business acquired upon failure, but also encouraged smaller banks to consider the dangers inherent in such fluctuations and made them more likely to agree to being acquired.

There were dramatic changes in the structure of English banking during the nineteenth century. In 1800, banking was dominated by relatively small, older firms that relied primarily on banknote issues to finance their operations. As the century progressed, newer, deposit-funded joint stock banks increased both the size and geographic reach of individual banks. During the closing years of the nineteenth century and the beginning of the twentieth, competition between the large banks intensified as they solidified their national networks and attempted to garner greater market power. The increase in concentration encouraged the government to act. In 1918, the Treasury Committee on Bank Amalgamations urged that the pace of mergers be slowed, specifically recommending that the large banks each be allowed to make one more acquisition. Of course, by this time, there had already been a substantial number of mergers: by 1920, the "Big Five" banks held approximately 80 percent of all deposits in England and Wales, and the merger movement may have already reached its natural limit (Capie and Rodrik-Bali 1982: 287).

CRISES AND RESPONSES

Banking and financial crises were a common feature of the English economy well before the legalization of joint stock banking in 1826. Among the earliest of these crises was that associated with the collapse of the South Sea bubble in 1720. Historical accounts place other eighteenth century crises in 1763, 1772, 1783, 1788, 1793, and 1797, although for some of these it is difficult to pinpoint if they were banking—as distinct from financial—crises. Nineteenth-century crises include those of 1810, 1825, 1836, 1847, 1857, 1866, and 1890, although the identification of these is also subject to some dispute.[11]

Because the focus of this book is on joint stock banking, it might be preferable to ignore all banking crises prior to 1826, since at that time there were no joint stock banks in England, aside from the Bank of England. Nonetheless, it will be instructive to extend the discussion back at least to the 1790s for three reasons. First, bank failures became increasingly common in the years following 1790: the vast majority of bank failures in the years 1710–1825 took place after 1790,[12] therefore the period may provide additional insight on—and an interesting contrast with—the crises that followed. Second, the causes of the crises of the late eighteenth and early nineteenth centuries had much in common with

[11]Although neither Clapham (1945) nor Pressnell (1956) identify a crisis as having occurred in 1836, Kindleberger (1996: appendix B) does. Thomas (1934) argues that the period 1836–39 included two separate crises (1836–37 and 1839), while Crick and Wadsworth (1936) refer to one 1836–39 crisis. Given the authors' different concerns—financial crises (Kindleberger), the Bank of England (Clapham), country banking (Pressnell), and joint stock banking (Thomas)—these differences in definition are not surprising. Similarly, Schwartz (1986) argues that 1866 was Britain's last "real" financial crisis: because her definition is largely based on monetary factors, she excludes the City of Glasgow Bank crisis of 1878 and the Baring Crisis of 1890.

[12]According to Pressnell (1956: appendix 20), over ninety percent of country bank failures that took place between 1710 and 1826 occurred after 1790 (there were, of course, relatively few country banks earlier in the period); the corresponding figure for London banks is close to fifty percent (fifty-two percent, if the failures that took place in the aftermath of the collapse of the South Sea bubble are excluded). Data on failures of brokers and scriveners tell a similar story.

those that occurred after 1825. Finally, since the Bank of England's evo-lution into a lender of last resort began in the 1790s, it will be useful to consider crises from this period.

Chapter 3 described three crisis-generating mechanisms: boom-bust fluctuations, shocks to confidence, and bank structure. Of these, boom-bust were the most consistently important in precipitating banking crises during the century following 1790. Recall the model of crisis espoused by Fisher (1932, 1933), Kindleberger (1978), and others: economic ex-pansion results in an increase in bank lending and in the indebtedness of non-bank firms beyond what is justified by underlying economic condi-tions. When the expansion ends, over-indebted marginal firms are unable to meet their debt service obligations, leading to loan defaults, declines in securities and commodities prices, and commercial and banking failures.

English crises of the late eighteenth and nineteenth centuries were characterized by these boom-slump conditions. Each followed increased speculation; although the object of speculation varied across crises, it was present in almost all of them: canals in 1793 and 1797, overseas trade in 1825, cotton and railroads in 1836, grain and railroads in 1847 and 1857, limited liability companies in 1866, and South American securities in 1890. The speculative booms were frequently fed by gold inflows due to abundant harvests, just as slumps were exacerbated by poor harvests.

Although boom-slump conditions were the most consistently impor-tant factor in generating English crises during 1790–1890, shocks to confidence, particularly related to war, or the threat of war, were also fre-quently present. The crises of 1763, 1783, and 1793 were, for example, "demonstrably connected with, if not solely due to, the beginning or end-ing of a war" (Clapham 1945, I: 225). Panic withdrawals from country banks during the crisis of 1797 were set off by the invasion of approxi-mately 1,400 French troops at Fishguard, Wales, on the evening of Feb-ruary 22–23 (they surrendered to a much smaller force on February 25). A shock to confidence also contributed to the panic following the failure of the firm of Overend, Gurney which, according to the *Times* of London (May 11, 1866), could "rightly claim to be the greatest instrument of credit in the country."

Bank structure was also an important determinant of stability dur-ing the nineteenth century. Prior to the legislation of 1826, banking was effectively restricted to firms of no more than six partners, essentially guaranteeing that banks would not have adequate resources to defend themselves in case of a generalized panic. Even after the 1826 act, the ab-sence of limited liability constrained the resources available to joint stock banks. Given these structural realities, it is perhaps not surprising that English banking suffered crises in the 1830s, 1840s, 1850s, and 1860s. As banking became more concentrated during the nineteenth century, banking structure may have been at least partially responsible for the remarkable banking stability that reigned in England following the Baring crisis of 1890. Many industrialized countries experienced banking crises in the years following 1907, others during the immediate post–World War I years (especially 1920–21), and even more during the crisis-laden 1930s. England's banking system, by contrast, weathered these crises without major incident.

England responded to crises primarily with bailouts or lender of last resort operations. The most famous English bailout of the nineteenth or twentieth century was that of Baring Brothers in 1890, although there were others.[13] More extreme measures, in the form of a government takeover, bank moratorium, or bank holiday were never employed in England for the simple reason that such extreme measures were primarily a product of the first third of the twentieth century, and English banking was remarkably stable during the fifty years following the Baring crisis.

By far the most common response to banking crises in England was that of a lender of last resort. A lender of last resort provides liquidity by buying, or lending money against, securities that might have no other market in the case of a financial panic. The obstacles to the Bank of England's evolution into a lender of last resort revolved around two dichotomies: the bank's status as a private institution, albeit one with public responsibilities and privileges; and the bank's responsibility to maintain the gold standard and the consequences of that for its responses to domestic and international drains of liquidity.

The first of these conflicts seemed to impair the bank's actions as a lender of last resort in 1793, when, according to Baring (1797 [1993]: 20–21), ". . . the Directors caught the panic; their nerves could not support the daily and constant demand for guineas; and for the purpose of checking that demand, they curtailed their discounts." That is, the bank reduced its lending and discounting in order to preserve its gold holdings.[14] In the end, the lender of last resort facility was provided by the government, which issued Exchequer bills to merchants on the security of commodities of all kinds.[15]

---

[13]Sir James Sanderson, M.P., the Lord Mayor of London in 1793, was promised funds because of, " . . . the 'mischief' that might result from a Lord Mayor's bankruptcy." Clapham (1945, I: 261).

[14]Clapham (1945, I: 261) notes that the Bank advanced £40,000 to banks in Liverpool, but rejected a loan against the bonds of the corporation (i.e., city) of Liverpool because of its practice not to loan against anything other than two-month notes of "respectable gentlemen of London."

[15]Thomas (1934: 26). These became known as "commercial Exchequer Bills," according to Clapham (1945, I: 265). See also Lovell (1957).

The conflict between internal and external goals was highlighted by the crisis of 1797 (Hawtry 1918). Contrary to the bank's 1694 charter, which forbade it to lend to the government without the consent of Parliament, Chancellor of the Exchequer William Pitt resorted to the bank for funds, as the newly issued notes were exchanged for gold. The continual borrowing led the bank's gold reserve to fall from over £6 million in 1795 to about £1 million in 1797. With the outbreak of the crisis in February 1797, the government issued an order prohibiting the bank—against its wishes—from redeeming its notes in gold. The suspension of the gold standard would last until 1821. Similarly, the suspension of the gold standard at the outset of World War I freed the bank to undertake extensive lender of last resort operations.

The Bank of England's response to the crisis of 1793 was tentative, but Bagehot (1924: 52) describes the response to the crisis of 1825 as being more sure-footed:

> The way in which the panic of 1825 was stopped by advancing money has been described in so broad and graphic a way that the passage has become classical. 'We lent it,' said Mr. Harman, on behalf of the Bank of England, 'by every possible means and in modes we had never adopted before; we took in stock on security, we purchased Exchequer bills, we made advances on Exchequer bills, we not only discounted outright, but we made advances on the deposit of bills of exchange to an immense amount, in short, by every possible means consistent with the safety of the Bank, and we were not on some occasions over-nice. Seeing the dreadful state in which the public were, we rendered every assistance in our power.' After a day or two of this treatment, the entire panic subsided, and the 'City' was quite calm.

Despite the Bank of England's acceptance of the lender of last resort function in 1825, it backed away from that role in 1836. As financial pressure increased in 1835, the bank decided not to make advances on bills that had been endorsed by note-issuing joint stock banks. This was no doubt caused in part by the bank's displeasure at the provision in its charter of 1833 legalizing the establishment of other joint stock banks in London. During the summer of 1836, the bank further decided to substantially reduce the amount of its holdings of bills accepted by the major merchants in Anglo-American trade (Collins 1972: 52). Upon a deputation from the Bank of Liverpool, the Bank of England relaxed the ruling, and again agreed to permit the discounting of American bills drawn against actual transfers of goods.

The Bank of England became much less hesitant as a lender of last resort in subsequent crises, particularly those following the enactment of the Bank Charter Act (Peel's Act) of 1844. This act should have made it more difficult for the bank to serve as lender of last resort, since any notes beyond the £14 million backed by securities (the so-called "fiduciary issue") would have to be backed one-for-one with the Issue Department's gold holdings.[16] Peel understood the constraints of the new law and privately acknowledged that it might be necessary to suspend it in time of emergency. Yet a new pattern emerged after 1844: during the crises of 1847, 1857, and 1866, the Government encouraged the Bank of England to violate Peel's Act by exceeding its fiduciary limit and, in return, sent the bank a letter promising that it would ensure the passage of a bill in parliament indemnifying the bank for any violations of the law. The lack of flexibility in the law itself can be seen as a protection against moral hazard. Peel's view was, however, that despite the law, it would be possible for the bank to engage in lender of last resort activities. Following the crisis of 1847, Peel congratulated the Government on their handling of the crisis with:

> My confidence is unshaken that we are taking all the precautions which legislation can prudently take against the recurrence of a monetary crisis. It *may* recur in spite of our precautions, and if it does, *and if it be necessary* to assume a grave responsibility for the purpose of meeting it, I daresay men will be found willing to assume such responsibility. (Andréadès 1966: 329n)

The Bank of England occasionally did bail out troubled firms. A prominent example of this was the rescue of Baring Brothers in 1890. Baring, which had been founded by Sir Francis Baring in 1763, had long been an influential member of the London financial community. The specifics of the rescue were presented in chapter 4: upon hearing of the impending failure of Barings the Governor of the Bank of England, William Lidderdale, first had an audit of the firm made, ascertaining that Barings was solvent. He also approached the Prime Minister and the Chancellor of the Exchequer, receiving assurance from them that the Government would bear part of the risk of any rescue that the bank would undertake. Lidderdale then set about assembling a guarantee fund among London financial institutions, with the notion that the fund would only be called on if the liquidated assets of Barings were not sufficient to cover its liabilities. Before the news of Baring's difficulties became public, the guarantee fund was in place and panic was avoided.

---

[16]Opponents to the act raised this during the debate. Fetter (1965: 187–91) discusses the objections of Thomas Tooke and John Fullarton. Fullarton argued that an increase of notes should be permitted in time of emergency, warning that the arrangement "must have the very effect of disabling [the Bank of England] for the performance of what has hitherto been considered the duty of the Bank in time of difficulty and pressure."

The rescue of Baring Brothers stands in sharp contrast to the failure of another prominent firm, Overend, Gurney, in 1866. Overend was widely acknowledged to be among the most important financial firms in England: when questioned about the extent of his firm's business before a House of Lords committee in 1848, Samuel Gurney conceded that it was about equal to that of all their competitors combined (King 1936: 117).

Overend, Gurney, and Company was floated as a limited liability company in August 1865. With money rates at comparatively low levels following the end of the American Civil War, there was much enthusiasm for an investment opportunity which promised a high return. Although the *Bankers' Magazine* trumpeted the flotation, in which the firm's goodwill was valued at £500,000, as "the greatest triumph of limited liability," the *Economist* was less optimistic, welcoming the change only because it would force Overend to periodically publish its balance sheet. The failure of Overend was:

> . . . as the shock of an earthquake. It is impossible to describe the terror and anxiety which took possession of men's minds for the remainder of that [Thursday, May 10] and the whole of the succeeding day [Black Friday]. No man felt safe. A run immediately commenced upon all banks, the magnitude of which can hardly be conceived. (King 1936: 243)

The Bank of England's decision to intervene on behalf of Baring Brothers, but not in the case of Overend, Gurney can be explained by several factors. Overend's relations with the bank were poor (see chapter 4). Given Overend's dire financial position, its failure was likely seen as inevitable, so that any rescue attempt would have generated moral hazard. Further, the banking and financial community was far more diffuse at the time of the Overend, Gurney failure than at the time of the Baring failure: it was easier to assemble a substantial guarantee fund with fewer institutions in 1890 than in 1866. A final important difference was the firms' orientations: Overend, Gurney was purely a domestic firm, dealing in domestic bills of exchange, while Baring Brothers engaged in a far more international business. The failure of Overend, Gurney led to a panic and massive domestic drain of money. As the creator of domestic liquidity in the form of Bank of England notes, the bank was able to provide the needed liquidity to meet this drain. Baring Brothers, by contrast, was an international firm, and its failure could well have led to an external drain on gold from the Bank of England. An increase in Bank of England's discount rate might well have stemmed this outflow, although it is not certain that the bank could have maintained the gold standard in the case of an external drain set off by the failure of Baring Brothers.

FISCALLY DRIVEN EVOLUTION

One of the outstanding features in the evolution of English banking through the eighteenth and nineteenth centuries is the extent to which it was shaped by the fiscal demands of the British government. The Bank of England, established in 1694, was not created to act as the nation's central bank, which it would later become. Nor was it created to serve as the guardian of the currency, a role it would also acquire. Nor was it established to be England's lender of last resort, a role it would also later adopt. It was, in short, given a charter as England's only joint stock bank in return for a large loan to the government. The charter itself did not permanently establish the bank in law but was an explicitly temporary charter that was renewed nine times between 1694 and 1844, frequently with the bank's privileges extended in return for further loans to the government. Despite the need of this first industrial country for financial services, the government's dependence on the bank led it to suppress commercial banking for more than a century. However, as alternative sources of government funding developed and the weakness of a banking system composed of small banks became apparent, the security of the bank's privileged position as the country's sole joint stock bank was eroded.

The end of the bank's monopoly in 1826, bolstered by additional liberalizing legislation in 1833, led to a rapid expansion of joint stock banking. Continued banking instability, combined with a desire to centralize the note issue in the Bank of England, led to a reversal in 1844 when expansion of joint stock banking was again halted, this time until 1857. The start-stop nature of the evolution of English banking during the nineteenth century illustrates the forces at work: as alternative government funding sources arose, the demands of commerce and industry became more politically potent than those of the bank, leading to the expansion of the joint stock banking franchise. The haphazard nature of the liberalization of 1826 and 1833—and the instability that ensued—led authorities to adopt a more restrictive joint stock banking regime in 1844. By 1857, and certainly by 1862, the pendulum had swung again and banks, which had by then lost their distinctive role in note issue, began to be governed by the same rules that governed non-financial corporations.

All three crisis-generating mechanisms were at work in England; however, as elsewhere, boom-bust cycles were primarily responsible for the frequent banking crises during the eighteenth and nineteenth centuries. As banking grew more concentrated and the Bank of England took on the role of as the lender of last resort, crises became notably less frequent, and the serious and widespread banking crises of the early twentieth century—1907, 1921–22, and the Great Depression—largely bypassed England. Although bailouts and government takeovers were pioneered elsewhere, the development of the lender of last resort can truly be considered an English innovation, developed both in theory and in practice from the late eighteenth century and reaching its most definitive statement in Walter Bagehot's *Lombard Street*, published in 1873.

It is instructive to note the differences between banking development in England with that in other parts of Great Britain and the empire. English politicians saw the greater stability of the Scottish joint stock banking system and wondered aloud if Scotland could serve as a model for reform in England. Scottish banking had developed differently from that in England primarily for fiscal reasons: because the state had no fiscal interest in the Bank of Scotland, it had no need to suppress other joint stock banks. As the fiscal benefits of the Bank of England for the government waned, England adopted the joint stock model. The absence of an official "state" bank with a monopoly on joint stock banking was of tremendous importance. By the middle of the eighteenth century, the joint stock banking principle was already established in Scotland, allowing the development of banks with many shareholders and extensive branch networks.

The absence of a government bank was also characteristic of Canadian and Australian banking. The earliest joint stock banks in these countries were established prior to the legalization of joint stock banking in the mother country and, although these early banks (especially the Bank of Montreal and the Bank of New South Wales) enjoyed some privileges, they did not play as central a role in government finance or in the management of the money supply, and had no monopoly to impede the growth of joint stock banking. Neither the Commonwealth Bank of Australia (later the Reserve Bank of Australia) nor the Bank of Canada was established until the twentieth century. The banking systems of these countries, like England's, were characterized by a relatively small numbers of large, well-branched national banks. Unlike England, however, their process toward this pattern was not impeded by a century-long suppression of joint stock banking.

CHAPTER 8

Banking Evolution in Sweden

> A daler is the size of a quarto page . . . many carry their money
> around on their backs, others on their heads, and larger sums
> are pulled on a horsecart. Four riksdaler would be a terrible
> punishment for me if I had to carry them a hundred steps; may
> none here become a thief. I shall take one of these dalers back
> to you unless it is too heavy for me; I am now hiding it under
> my bed.
>
> —Jacob Bircherod, Danish diplomat, letter home
> on the Swedish coinage, 1720[1]

IF EARLY INDUSTRIALIZATION is the sole criterion for conducting a case
study of banking evolution, England is an obvious choice. Sweden is not.

> . . . in Sweden so many developments appear to come late: by west-
> ern standards the whole history of Sweden seems to be retarded. Man
> came late to Sweden; the Romans never came at all; Christianity did
> not finally triumph till half a millennium after St. Augustine came to
> Britain. The founding of the University of Uppsala comes more than
> two centuries after the time when Oxford had emerged as one of the
> great centres of European scholarship. . . . Even more remarkable, to
> an English observer, is the slowness with which the country emerged
> from a relatively primitive economic condition. (Roberts 1967: 2)

Despite the fact that it industrialized at least a century after Britain,
that its per capita GDP lagged behind much of western Europe prior to
World War II, and that it has not been among the first rank of commercial, industrial, military, or financial powers in modern times, Sweden
is an appropriate subject for an in-depth study of banking evolution.
Sweden was among the first countries to rely primarily on paper money,
rather than a "commodity money," such as gold or silver. Sweden's central
bank, the Riksbank, is the world's oldest, having its origins in a private
bank founded in 1656. Along with England, Sweden was one of the first

---

[1]Heckscher (1954: 90), quoting *Jacob Bircherods Reise til Stockholm 1720*, ed.
G. Christensen (København, 1924: 60). Heckscher goes on to say that: "In Viborg some
burglars who had broken into a cellar and found there a small sum of money had to leave
it behind because they could not lift it."

countries to establish a comprehensive banking code. England's banking code, however, was short-lived: the 1844 Joint Stock Banking Act was repealed in 1857; Sweden's 1846 banking code, by contrast, was amended on numerous occasions, allowing an assessment of the evolution of more than a century of Swedish banking law. By contrast, many countries that might be considered more appropriate for a case study of banking evolution because of their greater size or superior commercial, industrial, or military prowess have much shorter regulatory histories: neither France, nor Germany, nor the Netherlands enacted any significant banking legislation, aside from that governing the central bank, prior to the 1930s.

THE RIKSBANK AND THE BEGINNINGS OF SWEDISH BANKING

Sweden's central bank has its origins in a private bank, Stockholms Banco (Bank of Stockholm), which was granted a charter by King Karl X Gustav in 1656. The name of the bank's founder is given in most historical accounts as Johan Palmstruch, although he was born Hans Wittmacher in Riga (in what is now Latvia) of Dutch descent and took the name Palmstruch upon being ennobled. Prior to his arrival in Sweden he had spent five years in a Dutch prison, ". . . quite unjustly, in his own opinion" (Heckscher 1934: 162). Palmstruch's was not the first to attempt to establish a bank in Sweden: proposals had circulated during the preceding fifty years and, in fact, a charter had been issued ten years earlier—although that bank never commenced operation. The government had wanted to start a bank itself but had been unsuccessful, so when Palmstruch, who was the head of the Merchants' Guild, petitioned the Crown, his request was readily granted and the new institution granted a monopoly on banking for thirty years (Flux 1910, Olsson 1994, Jensen 1896, Melin 1929).

Modeled on the banks of Amsterdam and Hamburg, Stockholms Banco was permitted by its charter to grant loans against securities and to receive money on deposit against which drafts could be written. The plan was to create a bank with two departments: the Exchange Bank (*Wexelbank*, a literal translation of the Dutch *Wisselbank*), to take deposits and make transfers, and a Lending Bank (*Länebank*, from Amsterdam's *Huys van Leening*), to make collateralized loans.[2] The idea of an ex-

---

[2]In fact, the Dutch *Wisselbank* and *Huys van Leening* were separate institutions founded five years apart by the City of Amsterdam. "Palmstruch is the first to have mentioned the connection between the two institutions (*Wisselbank* and *Huys van Leening*); but he is far from being the last." Heckscher (1934: 163, 169) also notes the close resemblance of this division to the "Issue Department" and "Banking Department" at the Bank of England

change bank, by which transactions in cash could be avoided, was particularly welcome. Sweden was Europe's preeminent copper producer. Early in the seventeenth century, in an effort to increase the demand for copper and therefore to raise its price, King Gustav II Adolf established a bimetallic copper and silver standard which was, de facto, a copper standard. Because the legal value of copper was high relative to its market value, vis-à-vis silver, Swedes used copper in transactions and hoarded silver: this is an example of Gresham's Law, under which "bad" (cheap) money is used in transactions and drives "good" (expensive) money out of circulation. Heckscher (1954: 88ff.) explains that this policy was ultimately unsuccessful in raising the price of copper. Because silver was nearly one hundred times as valuable as copper, copper coins were both large and heavy: the ten-daler piece weighed 19.7 kilograms (forty-three pounds), the two-daler piece (the standard coin) measured about twenty-four centimeters (9.5 inches) across (Heckscher 1954: 89). This situation rendered large-scale transactions all but impossible without the use of a cart and horse; hence, the idea of a bank that would facilitate payment through bank transfers, rather than in cash, was welcome. Although the charter did not empower the bank to issue notes, by 1661 it was doing just that, issuing receipts (called "credit notes") for amounts on deposit, which—due to the inconvenience of copper—soon gained acceptance as currency.[3] Moreover, because of its added convenience, paper money was typically valued at a premium over the equivalent amount of copper currency.

The popularity of the notes, which were loaned out at interest, not surprisingly led to their over-issue. Within a few years notes had been issued well in excess of the bank's ability to redeem them: the notes depreciated and a run ensued (Sandberg 1978: 658). The government intervened in 1664, revoking Palmstruch's charter and undertaking to settle the bank's business, including redeeming the outstanding notes within one year, although this time limit was repeatedly extended. In the meantime, notes were required by law to be accepted at face value in both public and private transactions.

In 1668 the bank was reconstituted under the ownership of Parliament (the Diet of the Estates of the Realm), and the name was changed to Riksens Ständers Bank, or Estates of the Realm Bank. The Diet was composed of four assemblies: the nobility, clergy, burghers, and peasants

established under Peel's Act of 1844. He argues that the Swedish equivalent was about half the size of the Wisselbank, even though the volume of trade and commerce in Holland was far greater than that in Sweden.

[3]Flux (1910: 14). Heckscher (1954: 91) suggests that these notes may have been modeled on "copper bills" that the mining association at Stora Kopparberg had used to pay miners.

(Scott 1977: 185). The peasants were not in favor of the new bank and refused to be associated with its management until 1800.[4] It is notable that when the bank foundered, it was taken over by the Diet, not King Karl XI, who was by then still only twelve years old, having inherited the Crown upon the death of his father, Karl X Gustav, in 1660. Because the legislature was politically stronger than the Crown during the Regency, when the bank failed, the Diet took sole possession of both ownership and management—a privilege it jealously guarded.

Although the newly rechartered institution was prohibited from issuing notes, by 1701 a system of endorsable transfer notes of not less than one hundred dalers was established for special classes of accounts. These notes circulated at a 3 percent premium over copper coins—that is, they were more highly valued in transactions than copper coins with an equivalent face amount—although they were not issued in large quantities for several years.

Unlike the Bank of England, the Riksbank and its predecessor appear not to have been established primarily for fiscal reasons, but rather to ameliorate the inconvenience of the copper standard as well as to promote commerce. This is not to say that the government had no fiscal incentive or interest in the bank: one month after the charter was issued a royal decree ordered the division of the new institution's profits between the bank, the Crown, and the city of Stockholm.[5] Additionally, the bank was the custodian of a variety of public revenues, including customs and revenue of the city of Stockholm, which generated some income.

It does not appear that the growth in the demand for the Riksbank's services was especially vigorous during the late seventeenth and early eighteenth centuries. Three new branches had been established between 1692 and 1694, and all had closed by 1705. Three other branches that had been planned never opened for business. Part of the reason for the bank's lackluster performance was its practice of not changing its rate of interest in order to attract more deposits or make more loans. Rather than vary the rate, the bank merely closed its doors to prospective depositors or borrowers, depending on whether the bank's funds were plentiful or not.[6]

---

[4]Flux (1910: 16). The Estates of the Realm gave way to a bicameral Parliament (the Riksdag) in 1865, which was subsequently replaced in 1974 by a unicameral legislature. Shortly after the Diet was reconstituted, the bank's name was officially changed to the Riksbank, although I use this term to describe the bank from 1668.

[5]Heckscher (1934: 163) cites Palmstruch, no doubt promoting the enterprise, as writing: "The City [of Amsterdam] earns a monstrously great profit from this bank of exchange [the Bank of Amsterdam]."

[6]Heckscher (1934: 174) does not explain why this was the case. He suggests that because the bank rolled over loans automatically and gave credits at any time upon certificates of deposit, the bank had little control over the flow of funds into or out of the bank. Sandberg

Another reason for the absence of growth was the limit on the types of securities against which loans could be given: loans on personal security were forbidden and those against commodities were difficult to arrange. This meant, in practice, that the majority of loans were made to nobles on the security of land and, later, to the state (Heckscher 1934: 175).

The Riksbank soon became an instrument of government policy. During the Age of Liberty (1718–72), when the Diet was politically dominant, the bank was used to advance the economic policies of the competing political parties, the Hats and the Caps (Heckscher 1934: 177ff., Heckscher 1954: 138, 197). The bank extended subsidized loans to the Manufacturer's Discount Office (*Manufacturdiskontot*) and the Association of Swedish Miners (through the *Järnkontoret*, the Iron Office) which, in turn, loaned the funds to favored firms and industries. Foreign trade, especially iron exports, was financed largely by the purchasers; these credits were used for advances to iron producers, so export production was financed largely by foreign capital (Heckscher 1934: 176–77). The Riksbank also dealt in foreign bills of exchange, further providing financing for international trade, although the amount of credit granted was small relative to that of foreign purchasers (Flux 1910: 21).

Around 1770, the government developed an interest in creating private banks to increase the supply of credit to domestic commerce and industry. The new institutions that arose were "discount companies" which were created with private share capital and the assistance of low interest loans from the Riksbank and the National Debt Office (Sandberg 1978: 658–59). In 1773 a twelve-year charter was granted to a discount company in Stockholm; a second was established in Gothenburg in 1783. Neither institution's charter was renewed on expiration. More discount companies were established in subsequent years, although the last of these closed in 1817.

Since there were no banking institutions per se, outside of the Riksbank and the discount houses, banking functions were increasingly being taken on by other institutions, such as merchant houses and money brokers (Gasslander 1962: 7–8, Sandberg 1978: 660). Even when banks were first established in the 1830s, legal limits on interest rates put them at a competitive disadvantage vis-à-vis preexisting institutions, which were more easily able to avoid these ceilings. For example, although merchant houses might be forced by interest rate ceilings to lend money at the same interest rate at which they borrowed it, they could require debtors to purchase other services (Sandberg 1978: 660).

(1978: 657) implies that the inability or unwillingness to alter either borrowing or lending rates may have resulted from legal limitations.

The Riksbank and the Bank of England were both established in the seventeenth century, more than one hundred years before the oldest of their counterparts, and are the two oldest central banks in the world. The circumstances surrounding their establishments, however, were completely different. At the time of the Bank of England's establishment, London already had an active private banking system; in return for continued financing, the government protected it from competition by granting it a monopoly on joint stock banking and an effective monopoly on note issue in London. Although the Crown and Diet surely planned to reap fiscal advantage from the Riksbank, its ostensible purpose was, like the public banks of Amsterdam and Hamburg, to facilitate exchange and commerce.

From the beginning, the Bank of England was construed as a private institution, albeit one with special rights and obligations. These rights and obligations were periodically renegotiated, although they essentially involved providing government finance in return for regular payments and a continuation of the bank's privileges. Although the relationship was important, it was nonetheless arms' length: the government did not become involved in the bank's day-to-day management, but merely set the general terms of the relationship via legislation. If the government's fiscal position deteriorated, it offered the bank a new charter in return for fresh loans; if the bank became more profitable, the government tried to engineer a new deal on more favorable terms. By contrast, the relationship between the Swedish government and the Riksbank was more intimate. From its founding as Stockholms Banco, the Crown was, quite literally, a shareholder in the new enterprise. After its reestablishment in 1668, when the Diet took over as owner and manager, the Riksbank became an important actor on the political landscape.

Bank Politics and Legislation: Enskilda Banks

The Age of Liberty ended with the accession of the autocratic Gustav III to the throne in 1771 and with the enactment of a new constitution in 1789 that made him "more nearly absolute" (Roberts 1967: 282, Roberts 1986). His successor, Gustav IV Adolf, lost Finland, which represented over one-third of Sweden's land and total population, to Russia, which led to a coup d'état and the adoption of a more liberal constitution in 1809 that divided power more evenly between the king and the Diet.[7]

---

[7]According to Andersson (1957: 311): "The constitution incorporated a division of powers on the lines laid down by Montesquieu: an executive with full powers within its prescribed limits; the legislature, the Riksdag, which was slow to act but powerful in obstruction . . ."

The king retained a monopoly on financial legislation, while the Diet held unrestricted power over the national budget, as well as retaining exclusive control over the Riksbank.[8] The ensuing political tug-of-war between the king and the Diet was reflected in, among other things, banking legislation. For the next half-century, the Crown advanced banking legislation that promoted the creation of private banks with note issues that competed with that of the Riksbank. The Diet supported quasi-public institutions, like the discount houses, that both used the notes of, and received credit on favorable terms from, the Riksbank.

With the closure of the last of the discount houses in 1817, Swedish banking was largely in the hands of the Riksbank and non-banking institutions, such as the merchant houses and the private loan market, the majority of which was concentrated in Stockholm. In 1823 the Diet raised the possibility of creating private institutions to supplement the work of the Riksbank, as well as to spread banking facilities to other sectors of the economy and geographic locations. In response to these discussions, a royal decree on January 14, 1824, authorized the establishment of enskilda ("private" or "individual") banks. Despite employing the word private, these banks should not be confused with private bankers in the British sense. Enskilda banks were to be publicly chartered, though not publicly managed, institutions. To acquire a charter, prospective bankers had to apply to the Crown, including proposed articles of association, rules governing the conduct of business, and a statement of the resources that would be at the bank's disposal. Banks were to have unlimited liability and were to make a public declaration that they were— and would remain—completely independent of the State and would receive no government aid under any circumstances. The Crown could then issue (renewable) charters of up to ten years.[9] The application, conditions, and declaration were to be published in the Official Gazette. Banks could make loans of up to one year. Although the decree was silent on the note-issuing powers of these new enskilda banks, in practice, almost all of the new institutions issued notes.

The response to the new legislation was far from overwhelming: the first bank formed under the new law was not chartered until 1830 and did not commence business until 1831. Additional banks were chartered in 1832, 1835, and 1837, although this was followed by a lull of nearly a

[8]Nygren (1983: 30) continues: "Banking policy and banking questions thus became a key item in the power-struggle waged between these two centres of authority over their jurisdictions and at the same time was a vital issue between mutually conflicting interest groups in the government and Riksdag."

[9]According to Flux (1910: 31) the charters were renewable "at the end of the ten-year term." Ögren (2003: 9) argues that the charters were not quite renewable, but that the banks had to wind up operations and then apply for a new charter.

decade—and another piece of banking legislation—before a seventh was established. None of the initial six enskilda banks was established in Stockholm. Flux (1910: 32) asserts that the slow growth of enskilda banking suggests that "the development of the country did not call very urgently for a widespread system of bank offices at that time," although Sandberg (1978) argues that the legal limits on interest rates, which persisted until 1863, was responsible for the absence of banking growth.

The law of 1824 was revised by royal decree in 1846, which established a detailed code for the establishment and operation of enskilda banks. The new law specified minimum amounts of nominal and paid-in capital, quantitative limits on note-issuing, as well as provisions for quarterly reporting to the Crown.[10] The government could order a bank inspection and, in theory, the Crown could annul the charter of a bank that was in violation of the rules. The previous decree's provision on unlimited liability remained in force and the law specified that shareholders could only transfer their shares with the consent of the company. The first bank created under the new legislation was founded in 1847; others were established in 1848, 1856, and three in 1857.

Although the number of enskilda banks rose slowly, they soon grew sufficiently in size and stature to rival the Riksbank—and to worry the Diet (see figures 8.1 and 8.2).[11]

The Diet responded in 1851 by adding a third branch of the Riksbank and by authorizing a new type of bank, called *filialbank* ("branch" or "affiliated bank").[12] These were to be established with private capital and were have no note-issuing authority, but would instead use Riksbank notes. To make up for the disadvantage of not being able to issue their own notes, the filialbanker were supported by the Riksbank with grants and subsidized credit.[13] Twenty-five filialbanker were chartered between 1852 and 1862, but since they were not profitable, the Diet withdrew the Riksbank's support, without which none survived past 1875. Many

[10]Minimum capital was to be Kr 1 million, with 10 percent paid in prior to the bank's opening and another 15 percent within one year. The law also specified what assets banks could hold as security for the unpaid portion of the capital.

[11]Sandberg (1978: 661) estimates that by 1850, the combined note issue of the enskilda banks equaled about 45 percent of that of the Riksbank and that their combined assets were equal to nearly 54 percent of those of the Riksbank. Nygren (1983: 31) argues that the enskilda banks' share of the note issue was closer to 28 percent of that of the Riksbank. The data presented in figure 8.2 suggests that enskilda assets were equal to 80 percent of Riksbank assets and enskilda note issues were equal to two-thirds of that of the Riksbank.

[12]Sandberg (1978: 662) argues that enskilda banks were unpopular in rural areas, which gave further impetus to the formation of filialbanker.

[13]The establishment of filialbanker was the work of the Diet, although the regulations governing them were enacted through a royal decree of September 30, 1851. Flux (1910: 43–44), Nygren (1983: 31).

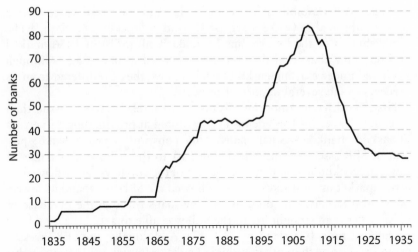

Figure 8.1. Number of banks in Sweden, 1834–1937. *Source*: Sveriges Riksbank (1931).

filialbanker were absorbed by enskilda banks; others disappeared when their charters expired.

Despite the growth in the absolute number and size of enskilda banks during the quarter-century following 1824, they were, for the most part, established in provincial towns of administrative importance. The first

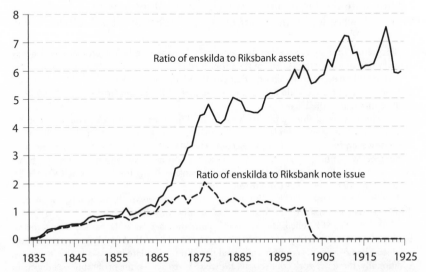

Figure 8.2. Assets and note issues of enskilda banks and the Riksbank, 1834–1924. *Source*: Sveriges Riksbank (1931).

enskilda banks established in commercial and industrial centers were those established in Gothenburg (1848) and in Stockholm (1856).[14] The establishment of the Stockholms Enskilda Bank (SEB) in 1856 marked an important change in the evolution of Swedish banking.[15] Although chartered under existing enskilda banking law, the SEB differed from its predecessors in several important respects.

First, the SEB relied more heavily on deposits, relative to note issue, than its counterparts: by 1860 deposits constituted approximately 13 percent of enskilda bank assets nationally, while constituting more than 65 percent of SEB assets.[16] This was due in part to the relative abundance of funds in Stockholm compared to the rest of the country—as evidenced by lower market interest rates—which allowed the SEB to expand its operations substantially.[17] Second, by making loans through the purchase of bills, rather than straight loans, the SEB was able to avoid the legal limit on interest rates (Gasslander 1962: 17). Additionally, the SEB invested greater resources than other enskilda banks in foreign trade finance: this is not surprising since its founder, A. O. Wallenberg, was involved in shipping and timber exports and occupied an important place in Sweden's international trade.

The four decades following the passage of the first enskilda banking law constitute the infancy of banking in Sweden, and constituted the first step toward chartered, limited liability banking. Previous experiments with discount houses had not lasted long and the development of enskilda banking was hampered by the tug-of-war between the Crown and the Diet. The initial law of 1824 established the principle of unlimited liability note-issuing banks; however, the details of how these banks were to be run were left almost entirely to the individual bank charters and,

[14]Nygren (1983: 45) argues that the early enskilda banks ". . . conducted a primitive type of credit operation for the benefit of the propertied classes, hostile to the borrower, rigid in approach and financed by banknotes that circulated among the less well-to-do." He argues that the future of the enskilda banks was threatened by the hostile attitude of the Estate of the Peasants within the Diet.

[15]The idea of establishing a private bank in Stockholm had been under consideration for several years. The bank's founder, A.O. Wallenberg, had applied for a filialbank charter in 1852; however, the application was rejected. The Minister of Finance, C. O. Palmstierna, encouraged Wallenberg to apply for a charter as a non-note-issuing limited liability bank. Eventually, the SEB was chartered as an enskilda bank, opening for business on October 15, 1856. Gasslander (1962: 12–15), Olsson (1997).

[16]Sveriges Riksbank (1931: 176) reports aggregate private bank totals; Gasslander (1962: 41) reports totals for the SEB. See also Sandberg (1978: 663).

[17]Although the SEB relied less on note issue than other enskilda banks, it nonetheless developed its note issue. One of the bank's founders had been the Stockholm agent for three provincial banks and this connection helped the SEB to circulate its notes in the provinces. Additionally, these network connections allowed SEB to act—quite profitably—as the agent for many provincial banks in Stockholm.

therefore, to the Crown. The 1846 revision clarified a number of issues by defining where a bank could be established, setting minimum amounts of nominal and paid-in capital, specifying what assets could be accepted as security for the unpaid portion of the capital, defining what businesses could be undertaken, limiting the size of the note issue, mandating a rudimentary form of supervision in the form of a quarterly accounting, and establishing a mechanism for bank inspection and, potentially, cancellation of a charter.

Legislation enacted in 1855, which incorporated some aspects of the 1851 filialbanker law, further clarified the rules of enskilda banks, setting a minimum number of shareholders, mandating uniform currency denominations and issue size, limiting the activities that a bank could undertake, and shortening the maximum term of loans from one year to six months (Allen et al. 1938: 327). Thus, by 1855, enskilda banking law was well developed.

Despite these advances in banking law, two legal impediments stifled the development of banking: a ceiling on interest rates; and the absence of limited liability. The Stockholms Enskilda Bank demonstrated that these obstacles need not prevent the growth of large incorporated commercial banks. By making loans via discounting bills, the SEB was able to charge interest rates above the legal limit. Additionally, because of the easier credit conditions in Stockholm, the SEB was better able to accumulate deposits and grow, even though it did not have limited liability. Both impediments fell away in the 1860s, paving the way for the emergence of a modern banking system.

THE EMERGENCE OF MODERN BANKING

The first of these impediments to fall was the ceiling on interest rates, which was repealed in 1863. The Stockholms Enskilda Bank had already found a way to evade this limit by making loans via discounting bills. As a practical matter, the enforcement of the maximum lending rate of 6 percent had been relaxed during the panic of 1857 when market interest rates were substantially above the legal limit.

The rules preventing the establishment of limited liability banks began to be breached around the same time. Since before the establishment of the SEB in 1856, there had been political support for the establishment of limited liability banks (Gasslander 1962: 12–13). The Diet had approved legislation permitting the establishment of limited liability non-note-issuing banks during its 1862–63 session; however, the law was not enacted until 1886. Even in the absence of specific legislation, limited liability non-note-issuing banks began to be established under general corporation law at about this time. The first such bank was established in Gothenburg in 1863; others were established in 1864, 1869, two in 1871, and two in 1872 (Flux 1910: 103–4).

The principle of limited liability was also made available to enskilda banks. A decree of May 20, 1864, repealed the laws of 1824, 1846, and 1855, and replaced them with a new code. One of the new law's provisions was that one-third of the capital of enskilda banks could be issued with limited liability, and that limited liability shares were to be more easily transferable than unlimited liability shares. Although several banks did issue limited liability shares, they never became an important part of enskilda bank capital (Flux 1910: 68–69). Additional features of the 1864 law and the 1874 revision made further attempts to bolster the soundness and security of enskilda banks. The 1864 law specified that all of a bank's capital had to be paid in within one year of the start of business. It also specified that if the annual audit showed that as much as 10 percent of a bank's capital was impaired, it would be required to either liquidate or call a special general meeting of shareholders to subscribe additional capital. It further reduced the government's discretion over issuing charters. The 1874 law increased the frequency of reports to the Crown from quarterly to monthly and established an inspector of banks; an inspector was first appointed by the Ministry of Finance in 1877. Following the adoption of the gold standard in 1873, the 1874 law additionally required that banks hold at least 10 percent of their capital in gold coin.

The first limited liability bank appeared in 1863, when a bank in Gothenburg incorporated under general company law. Legislation specifically permitting non-note-issuing banks, however, was not enacted until 1886. This law stipulated twenty-year renewable charters, a minimum capital of Kr. 1 million to be paid in within one year.[18] Like enskilda banks, these limited liability banks were prohibited from either owning or lending against shares or real estate (Allen et al. 1938: 329). The growing importance of deposits as a source of funds gave further impetus to the creation of limited liability banks: no new enskilda banks were established after 1893, and by 1900 there were forty limited liability banks and only twenty-six enskilda banks.

Another important influence on banking structure during this period was the decision to centralize Sweden's note issue in the Riksbank. This decision had been under active consideration since the middle of the nineteenth century and, for a time starting in the 1880s, all enskilda bank charters were set to expire in 1893 (i.e., those renewed after 1883

---

[18]Banks conducting a more local operation might be chartered with as little as Kr. 200,000. Subsequent Banking Acts (1911 and 1920) established minimum capital to "own funds" ratios, as well as other liquidity ratios.

were issued for periods of less than the customary ten years), when it was thought that these note issues would be relinquished. This did not materialize, however, and it was not until 1897 that a law was enacted that called for the elimination of enskilda banknote issues by the end of 1903. Because only a few enskilda banks had voluntarily surrendered their note issues by 1901, the process of centralization was hastened by a 1901 law that granted long-term low-interest Riksbank loans to enskilda banks that voluntarily surrendered their note issues. The month following its enactment, one of the largest enskilda banks, with a note issue equal to about one-eighth of all enskilda issues, surrendered its issue. Three months later, four other banks followed suit, and by the middle of 1903 all banks had made arrangements to surrender their note issues. The alternative for them would have been for their note issues to be subject to taxes after 1903. According to Flux (1910: 77), the enskilda banks "chose rather to be bought out than taxed out of their privileges." Of the twenty-seven enskilda banks issuing notes in 1897, seventeen continued as unlimited liability banks; the rest were either converted to limited liability banks or absorbed by institutions.

With the end of the note issuing rights of the enskilda banks in 1903, the only practical difference between enskilda banks and banks that had been non-note-issuing from the outset was the limitation of liability. This was recognized by the passage of virtually identical laws for both types of banks in 1903. Allen et al. (1938: 330) notes that, from 1903, "for all practical purposes, the distinction between enskilda banks and joint stock banks disappears." The Bank Act of 1934 mandated that the remaining enskilda banks be converted into limited liability banks.

MERGERS, CRISES, AND GOVERNMENT INTERVENTION, 1903–39

The liberalization of banking rules and interest rates in the early 1860s contributed to a dramatic growth in Swedish banking. Bank assets equaled only about 10 percent of Swedish GDP prior to 1864, but grew almost unabated during the subsequent half-century, reaching 120 percent of GDP prior to World War I (figure 8.3).[19] This growth was not achieved via mergers nor was it accompanied by the development of extensive branch networks. Rather, it came as the result of the foundation of new banks and the growth of existing institutions.

Aside from the acquisition of a number of filialbanker by enskilda banks in the 1860s and the first half of the 1870s, bank mergers and acquisitions were not especially common in the nineteenth century. Starting

---

[19]Larsson (1992: 342) ascribes some of the growth to the decline of private money lenders during financial disturbances of the 1860s.

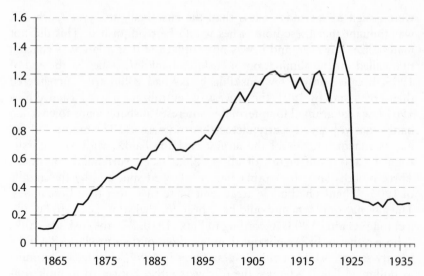

Figure 8.3. Ratio of bank assets to GNP in Sweden, 1861–1937. *Sources:*
Sveriges Riksbank (1931) and Mitchell (1978).

around the turn of the twentieth century, however, a steady stream of
mergers, as well as liquidations and reorganizations, began among small
banks, averaging about three per year in the years preceding World War I
(figure 8.4); mergers accounted for about two-thirds of these (Melin 1929:
1048–49). Much of this activity in the first decade of the twentieth century was due to the end of the enskilda banknote-issuing privilege, which
led to mergers as well as to liquidations and reorganizations.

In 1910, the two largest banks in the country, Skånes Enskilda Bank
and Skandinaviska Kredit AB, merged, setting off a wave of competitive
amalgamations between other large banks. These mergers were fueled by
a surge in industrial mergers, which increased optimal bank size, as well
as by the Bank Act of 1911 which raised minimum capital requirements
for smaller banks to Kr. 500,000 from Kr. 200,000 (the minimum capital
for larger banks remained at Kr. 1 million). Mergers became even more
common, averaging nearly ten per year, during the prosperous period
around World War I. As banks became larger, their desire for market
power increased. According to Melin (1929: 1050), many of the mergers
following 1910:

> ... showed how a growing bank might outstrip its competitors through
> means scarcely realized before, and many of the amalgamations of the
> last ten or fifteen years have had their origin in the banks' natural
> desire to outdo their competitors. This fact is particularly true of a

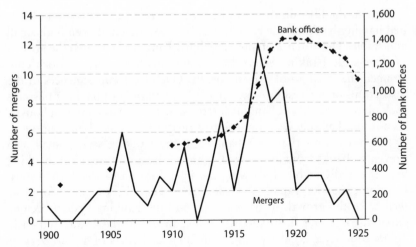

Figure 8.4. Mergers and branching in Sweden, 1900–1925. *Source*: Melin (1929: 1049).

number of amalgamations which occurred during the prosperous years 1916–1919.

The mergers of the 1910s not only led to a halving of the number of banks (from eighty in 1910 to forty-one in 1920), but also to a dramatic increase in the number of bank offices (from 584 to 1,410), as banks established nationwide branch networks. The average number of offices per bank, which had been about four during the period 1880–1900, rose to 7.3 in 1910 and 34.4 in 1920 (Melin 1929: 1048).

As in Britain, the trend toward consolidation in Sweden led to concerns about the concentration of banking power. These fears were especially strong in the provinces, where a number of established local banks had been acquired by banks with nationwide networks, and where there were worries that the credit needs of these regions were not being met (Melin 1929: 1052). These concerns were addressed by the Bank Act of 1918, which mandated that no new branches could be opened without the sanction of the government, and that new branch offices would only be approved when it was shown that they would prove useful to the community in which they were to be situated. A 1919 amendment directed that no further mergers be allowed without the approval of the government, and that they should only be approved if they were not prejudicial to the community where they took place. The total number of branches fell from a peak of 1,410 in 1920 to 1,091 in 1925 (Melin 1929: 1049, 1052–53). As in England, the total number of banks continued to decline for more than a decade following the decision to limit mergers.

Prior to the liberalization of interest rates and the legalization of limited liability banking, the banking sector in Sweden had been both small and stable. The absence of limited liability banking prevented the growth of large-scale banking enterprises, while interest rate restrictions constrained the freedom of existing banks. One of the consequences of the restrictions on interest rates was that a large amount of banking business took place through non-banking intermediaries, such as merchant houses. As a result, banking was confined to a relatively few small institutions.

The restrictions that kept banks and the banking sector small also prevented banks from overextending themselves: prior to 1864, banking was essentially stable. Following the liberalization of the early 1860s, banking expanded rapidly, both in terms of numbers of institutions as well as in the growth of bank assets, and the banking system became exposed to greater fluctuations. The expansion of the 1860s and early 1870s soon ended, culminating in the financial crisis of 1878–79. This crisis was characterized by a substantial fall in prices and resulted in distress for many banks and merchant banks (Olsson 1994: 964, Olsson and Jörnmark 2007). In December 1878 the general public withdrew more than one-third of all deposits from Stockholms Enskilda Bank, which nearly suspended (Olsson 1997: 45). Separately, one bank failed due to fraud and was struck off the list of banks (Flux 1910: 65).

The Swedish banking industry experienced rapid expansion from the late 1870s through World War I. After remaining stable at about forty banks from 1878 through the early 1890s, the banking population increased, peaking at eighty-four in 1908, before falling off due to mergers. Additionally, the aggregate assets of the banking sector grew impressively during this period, increasing from about one half of GDP in 1878 to nearly 125 percent of GDP in 1909.

The end of the post–World War I boom was especially severe for Sweden: during the period 1920–22, wholesale prices fell by more than half and real GDP fell by more than 16 percent. The downturn of 1920–22 was slightly more severe than that experienced by Sweden during the Great Depression.[20] The postwar slump led to significant banking distress, during which a number of banks had to be closed, reorganized, or merged. Frothingham (1924: 53) estimates the losses of the eighteen largest banks during this crisis to have been slightly over one-half their total capital and reserves.

---

[20] Given the substantial inflation that had occurred during the World War I boom (prices more than tripled between 1914 and 1918), it is perhaps not surprising that deflation (slightly over 20 percent between 1929 and 1931) was more severe during the earlier period. The decline in real GDP in 1930–32 was approximately 12 percent. Mitchell (1978: 391–415).

Sweden's banking distress during the 1920s stands in marked contrast to its banking stability during the subsequent decade, as well as to the widespread banking crises that swept Europe during the 1930s. One possible explanation of this extraordinary stability is that the mergers and liquidations that occurred following the banking difficulties of the early 1920s left remaining Swedish banks in a much stronger position going into the Great Depression than they had been going into the post–World War I slump. A similar contrast can be seen between Belgium and the Netherlands: following a severe shock in the early 1920s, Dutch banking went through a period of consolidation and retrenchment during the second half of the 1920s and emerged from the banking crisis of the 1930s relatively unscathed; Belgian banking, which had not faltered as severely after World War I, was hit much harder in the early 1930s (Vanthemsche 1991).

Sweden's first Social Democratic-led government put the issue of bank nationalization on the agenda when it assumed office in 1920 (Larsson and Lindgren 1992: 349). The plight of Swedish banking in the 1920s led to further interest in direct state ownership, either through the takeover of an existing bank or the establishment of a new institution. Proposals on establishing a public partnership were made to the two largest banks in October 1922, but they were turned down by the banks' boards of directors in January 1923.

The collapse did, however, lead to greater direct state involvement in banking. For example, the Jordbrukarbanken (Agrarian Bank) was formed almost entirely with government funds in 1923 in order to replace AB Svenska Lantmännens Bank (Swedish Farmers Bank), which had recently failed (Larsson 1992: 141). Government assistance of a more widespread nature took the form of the foundation of the A.B. Kreditkassen av 1922 (Credit Bank of 1922), which was established in April 1922 (Frothingham 1924: 52–54, Melin 1929: 1055–57). The Kreditkassen was funded by the government and the members of the Swedish Bankers Association (Svenska Bankföreningen) with a capital of Kr. 55 million: Kr. 5 million from the banks and Kr. 50 million from a government guarantee which could be drawn in the form of credit from the National Debt Office (Riksgäldskontoret) (Frothingham 1924: 53). The funds initially committed were not sufficient and by the following year the institution's capital was doubled to Kr. 110 million (Larsson 1992: 138–39). The Kreditkassen guaranteed the share issues of new banks created to acquire the businesses of failed institutions, loaned funds against the shares of those new banks, and guaranteed the subscription of new shares. During the course of the reconstructions the six largest institutions were forced to write off Kr. 294 million in assets, and the eighteen largest banks to write off Kr. 530 million(Frothingham 1924: 53, Larsson 1992: 143).

Government intervention in the banking sector was also dramatic during the downturn of the 1930s. This slump, which featured the collapse of Ivar Kreuger's industrial empire in 1932, was marked by the creation of A. B. Insustrikredit which was established, in part, to relieve the banks of their long-term industrial assets. The government similarly stepped in— with Kr. 215 million—to assist the Skandinaviska Kreditaktiebolaget, which was threatened with failure following the Kreuger collapse (Allen et al. 1938: 337–38).

The Swedish government had long been actively involved in the banking system. The clearest and earliest examples were the Diet's role in the foundation and management of the Riksbank, as well as in the foundation and subsidization of the filialbanker. The government also regulated specific aspects of bank operation as early as the banking decree of 1824 and continued to do so in the more detailed banking laws enacted subsequently. The crises of the 1920s and 1930s led to even more dramatic state intervention: in order to rescue failing banks the government, alone and in combination with the banking industry, directly and through specially created institutions, stepped in with resources needed to facilitate a bailout.

Additional government involvement in the banking sector, in the form of inspection and supervision, began as early as 1846, when banks were required to submit quarterly accounts to the Crown. The king's local representative (the district governor) was to have a part in making up these accounts and was entitled to inquire into the affairs of any bank at any time; the Crown could annul the charter if the bank was found to be in breach of the law. In 1874, the frequency of required reporting was increased from quarterly to monthly, and in 1877 an officer within the Ministry of Finance was appointed inspector of banks.[21]

The enskilda bank law was revised in 1903 and, in addition to centralizing Sweden's note issue in the Riksbank, created a unified authority for bank inspection and supervision. Previously, supervision had been the shared responsibility of the Ministry of Finance and district governors. However, as banking grew more complicated, supervisory authority was transferred to the Bank Inspection Board, a civil service department with enforcement authority (Larsson 1989: 41). The Bank Act of 1911 further empowered the Bank Inspection Board by requiring more detailed monthly reporting.

The Bank Inspection Board was harshly criticized—for overzealousness on the one hand, and ineffectiveness on the other—in the wake of the banking crisis of the early 1920s; however, an investigating committee

---

[21]Flux (1910: 64). According to Allen et al. (1939: 345), monthly reporting began in 1871.

in 1924 concluded that the board had intervened appropriately (Larsson 1989: 57–58). The Parliamentary investigation of 1932 did not call for any broad changes in the Bank Inspection Board's authority; however, it did recommend more frequent audits of bank activities and appointment of an auditor for each bank.[22]

Strikingly, the consolidation of regulation and control of banking occurred at the same time that the note issue was centralized in the Riksbank. Hence, these increases in regulatory and supervisory stringency do not appear to have been made for monetary control reasons, but instead represented a reaction to an increasingly unstable banking environment.

UNIVERSAL BANKING

The framers of nineteenth-century Swedish banking law did not envision that enskilda banks—or their non-note-issuing limited liability counterparts—would engage in universal banking activities. The banking code of 1846 specifically prohibited enskilda banks from trading in goods other than gold or silver (Larsson 1989: 57–58). Subsequent legislation (1855) broadened the scope of permitted activities to include dealing in bills of exchange and interest-bearing paper; however, the law explicitly forbade banks to own real estate beyond their own premises (Flux 1910: 34, 51). And when the limited liability bank law was passed in 1886, it explicitly prohibited these non-note-issuing banks from either owning shares or using them as collateral for loans. The imposition of these prohibitions may have stemmed from the authorities' conviction that limiting the scope of bank activities would limit their scope for excessive risk-taking (Larsson and Lindgren 1992: 343).

Despite these prohibitions, Swedish commercial banks became increasingly involved in long-term financing. The decline of the merchant houses following the turbulence of the 1860s and the increasing industrialization of Sweden in the subsequent decades drew commercial banks into medium- and long-term lending, although Samuelsson (1958: 178) argues that commercial banks' contribution to industrial finance prior to the 1870s was "negligible" and did not become significant until just before the turn of the twentieth century. Banks funded long-term finance in a variety of ways:

[22]Larsson (1989: 60) notes the Parliamentary investigation of 1932 suggested that bank audits take place at least every other year; Allen et al. (1938: 344) writes that these audits included two auditors chosen by bank shareholders and one by the Bank Inspection Board.

Executives, leading managers and members of the bank boards organized themselves into private consortia or syndicates, to which the bank made the necessary advances to make share underwriting and industrial restructuring operations possible. Investment and issuing companies were formed, legally separated from, but totally financed by and working in close collaboration with their parent-banks. (Larsson and Lindgren 1992: 344–45)

Perhaps recognizing this reality, the Bank Act of 1903 again broadened the scope of permitted universal banking functions. Banks now had fewer restrictions on their lending and investment activities, although they were still not allowed to purchase real estate for investment purposes, to acquire or receive their own shares as collateral, or to acquire the shares of any other bank. However, with special approval, banks could carry on a stock exchange commission business.

Banks continued to take a greater role in industrial finance in the years leading up to World War I (Samuelsson 1958: 180). The Investment (Emissions) Banks Act was passed in 1909 to allow banks to set up investment banking facilities, although the restrictions imposed on these institutions were so severe that none were established. The Bank Act of 1911 formally made it easier for banks to purchase shares, with the extent to which a bank could engage in this activity limited by the size of its capital (Larsson and Lindgren 1992: 346).

The period 1911–22 was the high water mark for universal banking in Sweden. Following the banking crisis of 1922–23, a commission was appointed to assess the relationship between banks and industry. The commission's 1927 report recommended "far-reaching" alterations in banking law; however, by 1927 industrial recovery was under way and the main recommendations of the report were ignored (Allen et al. 1938: 337ff.). Following the collapse of Ivar Kreuger's industrial empire in March 1932 and the subsequent Kr215 million bailout of Skandinaviska Kreditaktiebolaget, the government passed a new Bank Act in 1933, which clearly defined the circumstances under which banks could acquire shares in non-financial firms. The restrictions imposed by this legislation appeared more severe than they actually were: the law allowed banks a grace period of several years within which to divest themselves from industrial participations; in fact, bank share ownership actually increased after the law's passage (Allen et al. 1938: 339, Larsson 1992: 352). By 1934, the personal and economic bonds between the larger banks and their industrial customers were too strong to be easily dissolved.

Universal banking grew in importance in Sweden during the rapid industrialization prior to World War I. With the decline of the merchant houses and increasing liberalization of interest rates, long-term industrial finance became more and more the province of commercial banks and the law gradually recognized this reality. With the end of the post–World War I boom and the collapse of the Kreuger industrial empire, the pendulum swung away from universal banking. Unlike the United States and Belgium, however, where the transition away from universal banking was quick and decisive, the shift in Sweden was less dramatic, with universal banking continuing to exist in fact, if not in law, for some time.

SWEDEN IN A NORDIC CONTEXT

Sweden was among the first countries in the world to use paper money, to establish a government bank, and to enact a detailed banking code. The fact that England established a government bank and a banking code at about the same time suggests parallel financial development in the two countries; however, despite these superficial similarities, there were important differences between Swedish and English banking development.

Although England and Sweden shared some characteristics of banking development, the differences in their economic and financial development make the comparison of the evolution of banking institutions problematic. For example, GDP per capita in the UK was roughly double that of Sweden in 1850. Other measures of economic and financial development (e.g., trade, extent of monetization) similarly show England to have been far more developed than Sweden through the early twentieth century. Denmark, Finland, and Norway provide more appropriate comparisons. Without presenting extensive economic and financial histories of these other Nordic countries, it is safe to say that their economic development was broadly similar to that of Sweden. GDP per capita approximately doubled in all four countries during the period 1850–1930. Denmark had the highest output of the countries throughout this period, with about twice the GDP per capita of Finland; Sweden (slightly above three-quarters of Danish GDP) and Norway (slightly below three-quarters of Danish GDP) were somewhere in between. Each country began industrialization during the second half of the nineteenth century.[23] Despite the many important differences between these countries' economic development, those differences are probably less pronounced than those between the any of the Nordic countries and England.

---

[23]Jörberg (1975) asserts that Swedish industrialization began during the 1850s, paused for a decade and began again during the 1870s, or roughly comparable with his characterizations of industrialization in Denmark (1860s), Finland (1860s–70s), and Norway (1870s).

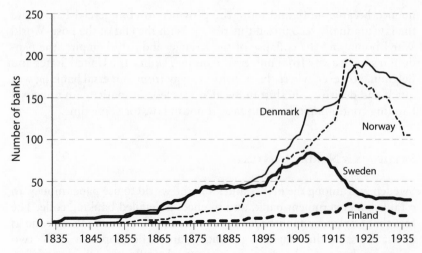

Figure 8.5. Number of banks in the Nordic countries, 1834–1939. *Sources*: Denmark: Danmarks Statistik (1969) and Johansen (1985); Finland: *Suomen Tilastollinen Vuosikirja* (various); Norway: Norges Offisielle Statistikk (1948); Sweden: Sveriges Riksbank (1931) and League of Nations (1938).

Among the Nordic countries, Sweden's banking history stands out.[24] The Riksbank, established in 1668, predates the government banks of Finland (1811), Norway (1816), and Denmark (1818) by well over a century. Sweden's first commercial bank, founded in 1830, predates by more than fifteen years those of Denmark (1846), Norway (1848), and Finland (1862). A look at the rise and fall of banking populations in the Nordic countries (figure 8.5) confirms that Sweden's banking system saw the characteristic peak and decline in its banking population a dozen or more years before those in the other Nordic countries.

Compared to its Nordic neighbors, Sweden was early in establishing a framework for banking regulation and supervision. The earliest commercial banking legislation came to Sweden in the first half of the nineteenth century. Finland did not enact any banking legislation until 1866, and neither Denmark (1919) nor Norway (1924) enacted any commercial banking law until after World War I. The most straightforward explanation for these differences is the relatively early emergence of the Riksbank. Sweden's inconvenient copper money fairly cried out for the establish-

[24]By contrast, savings bank developments were roughly parallel in all four countries, with the first savings banks established in the 1820s and rising to prominence in the second half of the nineteenth century. See Hansen (1982), Egge (1983), Nordvik (1993), Kuusterä (1994).

ment of mechanism to issue banknotes. Although Stockholms Banco collapsed, it demonstrated the benefits of a note-issuing bank. In Denmark, Finland, and Norway, the establishment of a government bank came in response to monetary or political crises. Denmark's Kurantbanken, which held a monopoly on note issue, had been established in 1736, but collapsed due to an over-issue of notes as a result of financing government deficits. The successor Specie Bank, founded in 1791, collapsed under similar circumstances that culminated in the *Statsbankerot* (State Bankruptcy) in 1813. Five years later, the Danmarks Nationalbank was established, again as the country's sole note issuer. In Norway, the end of the union with bankrupt Denmark in 1814 led to the establishment of a government bank in 1816, also as the sole note issuer. And two years after Finland became a quasi-independent grand duchy under the Russian Empire, a government bank was established (1811) in order to drive Swedish notes out of circulation.

The relatively late development of commercial banking is related to the events surrounding the establishment of the government banks. In Denmark, the Statsbankerot led to a quarter-century of deflation. This presented an inhospitable climate for the establishment of new banks; in fact, the Danmarks Nationalbank refused several requests from the provinces to set up branches during this period. As the notes of the Nationalbank neared par in the 1830s, increasing demand for banking services led to the establishment of new branches in 1837 and 1844. The rise of a less absolutist government after 1848 led to a general liberalization of economic policy, including a more favorable view toward the establishment of new banks (Hansen 1982: 576–78, Capie et al. 1994: 148–49). In Norway, the Norges Bank had been established as the sole note issuer in 1816. This note monopoly, combined with interest rate ceilings and a general absence of demand for banking services slowed the emergence of other joint stock banks.[25] In Finland, as in other Nordic countries, the greatest demands for credit emanated from the trade in raw materials, which was largely financed by foreign banks and lessened the need for the development of domestic commercial banks prior to industrialization.

The enactment of legislation regulating the conduct of banking affairs can be traced to the role of banks as note issuers. In Denmark (1818) and Norway (1816), the government banks were granted a monopoly on note issue from the time of their establishment, no doubt inspired in part by the effects of the over-issue of notes during the Danish Statsbankerot. Because note issue was not an option for commercial banks in

---

[25]Egge (1983: 275–76) also notes that the greatest demand for financing in Norway during the first half of the nineteenth century was for mortgage loans, rather than commercial lending.

these countries, banking legislation was not adopted until after World War I. In Finland, due to the lack of demand for banking services at the time, the Suomen Pankki was not granted a monopoly on note issue. When the first commercial bank was established in 1862, the authorities at first declined its request to issue notes; however, this right was granted in 1866—the same year that a commercial banking code was enacted.

Sweden's financial development outpaced those of its Nordic neighbors, as well as its own commercial and industrial needs. Two factors were crucial to that development. The acceptance of paper currency, which can be directly traced to the adoption of a copper standard, led to the development of credit-creating banking by the Riksbank and, subsequently, by the enskilda banks. The enskilda bank note-issuing privilege, and the development of detailed bank regulation, emanated from the power struggle between the King and the Diet. The Diet, which controlled the Riksbank, worked to prevent the spread of the note-issuing franchise, while the Crown encouraged the spread of note-issuing banks and kept banking supervision out of the hands of the Riksbank. Had the Diet secured a monopoly for the Riksbank's note issue, the development of the legal and regulatory institutions of Swedish banking would not have occurred until much later.

CHAPTER 9

Banking Evolution in the United States

> The financial center of the world, which required thousands of years to journey from the Euphrates to the Thames and the Seine, seems passing to the Hudson between daybreak and dark.
>
> —John Hay (1906: 165)

> I've had it up to my keister with the banking industry . . .
>
> —Ronald Reagan[1]

IN SOME WAYS, banking in the United States is considerably younger than in England and Sweden. The Bank of England and Riksbank were founded during the second half of the seventeenth century, predating the first attempt at establishing a government bank in the United States by a century. London private banking emerged even earlier, an additional half-century prior to the establishment of the Bank of England and well before such institutions emerged in the United States. In other ways, banking in the United States is not so young. Aside from the Riksbank and Bank of England, commercial banks did not appear in either England or Sweden until the first third of the nineteenth century. In the United States, by contrast, the first commercial banks appeared around the time of the Confederation, with the establishment of the Bank of North America (1782), the Bank of Massachusetts (1784), and the Bank of New York (1784, chartered 1791).[2]

The United States presents a third useful case study of banking evolution for several reasons. The United States has one of the longest continuous histories of commercial banking in the world. Since the first commercial bank in the United States was established in 1782, more than four decades before such banks emerged in either Sweden or England, there is a relatively long time series over which to observe the evolution of commercial banking.

Other important reasons for focusing on the United States are the durability, stringency, and variety of its regulations. Among the countries

---

[1]Sen. Bob Dole, quoted in the *New York Times*, March 23, 1983, p. A16.

[2]Sumner (1896), Gras (1937), and Fenstermaker (1965). There is some doubt about whether an earlier bank, the Bank of Pennsylvania (1780), was, in fact, a commercial bank. Myers (1970: 41).

studied here, few have had banking regulations for as long as the United States: state banking codes were established as early as the 1830s; Belgium, Denmark, France, Germany, Italy, the Netherlands, Norway, and Switzerland, among other countries, had no banking codes at all, and therefore no specific banking regulations, prior to the twentieth century. Further, banking regulations in the United States were, by both nineteenth- and twentieth-century standards, quite restrictive, resulting in a banking system characterized by a large number of small banks. This regulatory stringency can be seen by comparing bank densities (i.e., banks per million inhabitants) across countries. In 1900, the United States had nearly 170 banks for every million inhabitants. No other country considered in this study comes close to this figure: the corresponding numbers in Norway and Denmark, which had no banking regulation at the time, was about thirty-three banks per million inhabitants. Density was substantially lower in Australia and Canada (between five and six banks per million inhabitants), Germany (between three and four), and the United Kingdom (about two). Finally, a unique feature of U.S. banking regulation is its great variety. The federal government and each state established banking codes, which specified the rules and regulations governing bank behavior, as well as supervisory regimes. Analyzing the content and timing of these regulatory enactments allows greater insight into the political and economic forces responsible for regulation.

The First and Second Banks of the United States, 1791–1836

In England and Sweden the first and, for a long time, the most important chartered bank was the government bank. The establishment of the Riksbank and Bank of England constituted major turning points in the financial development of Sweden and England. By contrast, the first two attempts by Congress to establish a similar institution in the United States were short-lived: each resulted in a bank that lasted no more than twenty years. A permanent institution, the Federal Reserve System, would not be established until the twentieth century.

Congress's first attempt at a government bank, the Bank of the United States (BUS), was established by legislation enacted in 1791. The BUS was the brainchild of Secretary of the Treasury Alexander Hamilton, who had suggested the formation of a national (i.e., government) bank to financier Robert Morris as early as 1779.[3] In December 1790, Ham-

---

[3] He again suggested such a bank to Morris in 1781, shortly after Morris was appointed Superintendent of Finance. See Holdsworth (1910: 9–17) on Hamilton's involvement in the

ilton submitted a report to Congress outlining his plans for a bank.[4] He argued that national banks contribute to the "augmentation of the active or productive capital of a country," by promoting currency circulation and capital creation. He also argued that they afford, "[g]reater facility to the government, in obtaining pecuniary aids, especially in sudden emergencies."

A bill to establish the BUS was introduced in the Senate on December 23, 1790, where it passed with a majority and was sent to the House on January 20, 1791 (Holdsworth and Dewey 1910: 17). Neither Senate votes nor debates were recorded, so we do not know the extent of the division of opinion in that chamber (Meyers 1970: 67). Much of the debate in the House centered on whether the federal government had the constitutional authority to charter a bank: Hamilton and other Federalists, who favored a strong central government, supported it; Anti-Federalists, including Jefferson, Madison, and others who believed that the powers not explicitly granted to the federal government should be the reserved to the states and who believed in a weaker central government, opposed it.

The House passed the bill on February 8 by a vote of 39 to 19 and it was signed into law by Washington on February 25.[5] The vote was not strictly along partisan lines: eleven of those who voted to establish the BUS were anti-Federalist Republicans, while six Federalists voted against it. The geographic pattern of voting was more striking: only three votes in favor came from southern states (two from North Carolina and one from South Carolina) and only one vote against came from a northern state (Massachusetts). The six votes from Delaware and Maryland were split evenly. The bank's supporters were of the commercial and moneyed classes and believed in a strong central government; the opponents were mainly agrarians who mistrusted business interests and expansive federal authority (Hammond 1957: 118–19).

In designing the bank's charter, Hamilton borrowed extensively from that of the Bank of England (Holdsworth and Dewey 1910: 21–22).

Bank of the United States. Hamilton had also written the constitution of the Bank of New York in 1784 and was one of its first directors. Domett (1902).

[4]Reprinted in Clarke and Hall (1832 [1967]: 15–35). Much of the report is devoted to defending banks, and therefore the proposed national bank, against charges "That they increase usury; That they tend to prevent other kinds of lending; That they furnish temptations to overtrading; That they afford aid to ignorant adventurers, who disturb the natural and beneficial course of trade; That they give to bankrupt and fraudulent traders a fictitious credit, which enables them to maintain false appearances, and to extend their impositions; and, lastly, That they have a tendency to banish gold and silver from the country."

[5]Clarke and Hall (1832 [1967]: 85) record the roll call vote in the House, as well as the written opinions Washington requested from Attorney General Edmund Randolph, Secretary of State Jefferson, and Secretary of the Treasury Hamilton. The first two advised Washington that the bill was unconstitutional.

Hammond (1957: 129) notes that the Bank of England charter "had influenced the measures which had already incorporated the Bank of North America, the Massachusetts Bank, and the Bank of Maryland, but nowhere near the extent the act was to influence the charter of the Bank of the United States." For example, the bank's prohibition on trading in "goods, wares, merchandise, or commodities" was virtually identical to the Bank of England's bar on trading in "goods, wares, and merchandise." Like the Bank of England, the Bank of the United States was forbidden to purchase land (aside from what it might need for premises) or government debt, or to lend to the states or federal government beyond a set limit without the express consent of the legislature. Also, like the Bank of England following the recharter of 1697, the charter of the Bank of the United States prohibited the federal government—but not state governments—from chartering another bank during the lifetime of the BUS.

Intentionally or not, the Bank of the United States synthesized several characteristics of both the Riksbank and the Bank of England. For example, the motivation for the formation of the Bank of England had been strictly fiscal; the Riksbank was established out of a desire to enhance trade, as well as to cope with the inconvenient copper currency. Both of these goals—fiscal, as well as trade promotion—were among Hamilton's reasons for the establishment of the Bank of the United States. Similarly, although the Bank of England was a strictly private institution—albeit one with public responsibilities and publicly granted privileges—and the Riksbank an explicitly publicly-owned institution, the Bank of the United States was a private institution in which the government was entitled to, and did, purchase a 20 percent share. Finally, the banking environment into which the BUS was born was neither as barren as that of Sweden, nor as fertile as that of England. At the time of the Riksbank's establishment, there were essentially no private banks in Sweden, whereas the Bank of England was launched into a well-established private banking community. By 1790, the United States already had several chartered banks, as well as unincorporated private banks; however, the banking community was nowhere near as well populated nor the banking business as well developed as in England.

A crucial difference between the Bank of the United States and both the Bank of England and the Riksbank is that the initial charter of the BUS was limited to twenty years: without an explicit renewal, the Bank's charter would expire in March 1811. In Sweden, the Riksbank's charter was not subjected to any such time limit and could, in theory, continue indefinitely. The Bank of England's charter was guaranteed to continue for a minimum period of time, ranging from eleven to thirty years, depending on the particular rechartering legislation, after which the government could, with one year's notice, repay the loan and revoke the charter. Still, neither the Swedish nor English chartering legislation required that the bank be rechartered: in the absence of any legislation to the contrary, both the Riksbank and the Bank of England would have continued indefinitely.[6]

The Bank was headquartered in Philadelphia and branches were almost immediately established in New York, Boston, Baltimore, and Charleston. By 1804 additional branches had been opened in Norfolk, Savannah, New Orleans, and Washington, DC. Despite the generally friendly relations between the BUS and state-chartered banks, by returning outstanding state banknotes in exchange for specie, the bank "undoubtedly had an influence in restricting the circulation of state banks. This was admitted by these institutions, and by many of them regarded as a benefit" (Holdsworth and Dewey 1910). That is, by returning banknotes to the issuing banks in return for specie, the BUS prevented state banks from over-issuing notes.

Three years before the charter was to expire, shareholders in the BUS sent a request to Congress asking for an extension. The political landscape nearly two decades later was, however, quite different from that in 1791: the Federalist-inclined administrations of Washington and Adams gave way to anti-Federalist (Democratic Republican, known as Republican) administrations of Jefferson and Madison; with the exception of New England, the House and Senate, were now dominated by Republican forces. Jefferson and Madison, as well as Federalists in Congress, recognized the benefits of the bank and were in favor of its recharter. Republicans, however, were split. Business interests were wary of the bank's restraining influence on state banks, some of which they either controlled or had a financial interest in. The legislatures of Massachusetts, Pennsylvania, and Maryland "instructed" their senators to vote against the renewal of the bank's charter and Samuel Taggart, a representative from rural Massachusetts, argued that virtually all the representatives from the great commercial towns had opposed the bank (Hammond 1957: 209ff.). The results differed from the earlier vote as well: the BUS lost in both the House and the Senate by one vote.[7]

The period during which the Bank of the United States operated was one of near constant expansion of banking. The first state-chartered

---

[6]Charters of limited life were not unusual: the Massachusetts Bank's initial charter did not have a limited life, but subsequent charters were granted for twenty years. The Bank of New York's initial charter—which came some years after it was organized—was also granted for twenty years.

[7]The vote in the House was 65–64 in favor of indefinitely postponing consideration of the recharter. The vote in the Senate was tied, with the deciding vote against the bank cast by Vice President George Clinton.

banks, the Bank of North America (1782) and the Bank of Massachusetts (1784), received their charters prior to the BUS; several more, including the Bank of New York, Bank of Maryland, and Providence Bank, received charters in the same year as the BUS. From these five state-chartered banks in existence by the end of 1791, the number of banks rose to more than 110 by 1811 (figure 9.1) and paid-in bank capital increased nearly fifteen times. Banks were present in only five states at the end of 1792; by the end of 1811, they had spread to twenty-one states and territories and the District of Columbia. The dramatic growth of banking reflected the country's expanding area, population, and inter-regional and international trade: from 1790 to 1810, the U.S. population increased by 75 percent and total land area doubled.

The demise of the Bank of the United States marked the beginning of a period of rapid expansion of the banking system, both in terms of numbers and note issue: from 1811–16 the number of banks approximately doubled while the value of notes in circulation increased by nearly 250 percent, from $28 million to $68 million (Hammond 1957: 227). Albert Gallatin (1879, III: 285), Secretary of the Treasury from 1801 to 1814, places the blame for this excessive expansion squarely on the failure to renew the charter of the Bank of the United States:

> [T]he creation of new state banks in order to fill the chasm was a natural consequence of the dissolution of the Bank of the United States. And, as is usual under such circumstances, the expectation of great profits gave birth to a much greater number than was wanted. They were extended through the interior parts of the country, created no new capital, and withdrew that which might have been otherwise lent to the government, or as profitably employed. From the 1st of January, 1811, to the 1st of January, 1815, not less than one hundred and twenty new banks were chartered and went into operation, with a capital of about forty, and making an addition of nearly thirty millions of dollars to the banking capital of the country. That increase took place on the eve of and during a war which did nearly annihilate the exports and both the foreign and coasting trade. And, as the salutary regulating power of the Bank of the United States no longer existed, the issues were accordingly increased much beyond what the other circumstances already mentioned rendered necessary.[8]

The rapid banking expansion, combined with the fiscal strains of war with Britain, rendered the banking system and public credit more vul-

---

[8]Timberlake (1978: 12–26) argues that the increase in liquidity and inflation was due to the expansion of U.S. Treasury note issues and not the demise of the "restraining hand" of the BUS. He blames the retirement of these notes after 1815 for the downturn that led to the panic of 1819.

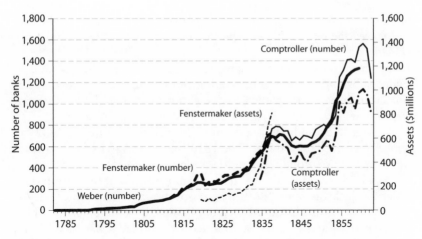

Figure 9.1. Number and assets of banks in the United States, 1782–1861. *Sources*: Fenstermaker (1965: 111), U.S. Comptroller of the Currency (1876: 94), and Weber (2005).

nerable to crisis. When the British raided Washington and threatened Baltimore in August 1814, there was a general banking panic (Hammond 1957: 227ff.). Even before the panic, proposals had been made for the establishment of a new national bank. A charter was enacted in 1816, incorporating many features similar to those of the 1791 charter. Hammond (1957: 243) notes that the new charter, ". . . differed from the old mainly in terms of verbosity, being about treble the length." Like the first bank, the second Bank of the United States (2BUS) was to have 20 percent government ownership, a twenty-year charter, and one-fifth of the bank's capital was to be in the form of specie. The 2BUS had a larger paid-in capital ($35 million in $100 shares versus $10 million in $400 shares for the BUS). The BUS had been the Treasury's depository, de facto; the 2BUS filled this role by law (Holdsworth and Dewey 1910: 164–75). Political support for the new bank had been:

> . . . geographically like that of 1791, with the sentiments of both sides reversed. In 1791, with the Federalists in power, the North had established the Bank, and the South had opposed it. Now, in 1816, with the Republicans in power, it was the South and West that reestablished it, and the North opposed it. (Hammond 1957: 240)

Republican support may have reflected the pragmatic interest of those in power in having a useful instrument in the form of a national bank. Opposition from representatives of northern states may have reflected the greater number—bank density in the New England and the Middle Atlantic states in 1810 was about four times that in southern and western states—and, presumably, influence of bankers in these states, who may have feared the restraining influence of a second bank (Hammond 1957: 443–44).

Aside from the decline associated with the crisis of 1819,[9] banking expanded substantially during the lifetime of the 2BUS: approximately 230 banks were in existence at the bank's creation in 1816 and more than 650 twenty years later; paid-in capital increased nearly five times.

The election of Andrew Jackson in 1828 and his reelection in 1832 cast a cloud over the bank's future. The 1816 charter was to expire before the end of Jackson's second term and Jackson made no secret of his opposition to the bank. In his address to the opening session of the Twenty-First Congress, Jackson said: "Both the constitutionality and expediency of the law creating this bank, are well questioned, by a large portion of our fellow-citizens; and it must be admitted by all, that it has failed in the great end of establishing a uniform and sound currency" (Clarke and Hall 1832 [1967]: 734). The demise of the Second Bank of the United States can be ascribed to a number of factors: the resentment of state banks, business enterprise, and agriculturalists of its restraint on state bank credit creation; states' rights sentiment; mistrust of banks and, especially, banking corporations; the inability of Jackson's administration to extract political "spoils" from the bank; and New York's determination to overtake Philadelphia as the nation's financial center (Hammond 1957: 443–44, Holdsworth and Dewey 1910: 248ff., Gatell 1966, Temin 1968).

Congress passed a recharter bill in 1832 with comfortable majorities in both houses; however, Jackson vetoed the bill on July 10. The attempted override and subsequent attempts to pass a new charter failed, and the 2BUS's federal charter expired in 1836. The following year, Jackson ordered that federal government deposits be placed in state chartered banks (called "pet banks" by his political opponents), further weakening it.[10] The Bank of the United States continued to operate with a Pennsylvania charter until 1841, when it closed in the aftermath of the panic of 1837.

---

[9]This crisis has been blamed on a variety of factors, including the resumption of specie payments and the accompanying reduction in the money supply, poor management of the bank, and misguided Treasury policy. Timberlake (1978: 13). Conant (1896: 298) argues that the bank was poorly managed by its first president, William Jones, who brought it to the brink of failure. Perkins (1983) argues that Jones's successor, Langdon Cheves, brought about the panic through his reform efforts.

[10]The subsequent inflation, followed by the recession and panics of 1837 and 1839, has been blamed on Jackson's veto of the bank's charter renewal and the removal of the bank's restraining hand upon state bank credit creation. Temin (1968) takes issue with this view, arguing that the crisis and panic were due to a variety of other factors which led to an outflow of specie from the United States.

A bill was passed in 1841 to charter a third federal bank; however, the legislation was vetoed by President John Tyler. The American experiment with central banking was over for the next three-quarters of a century: the necessity to renew the charter, combined with partisan and sectional interests, made the first two attempts at establishing a central bank short-lived. It would take another quarter-century and the Civil War for the federal government to enact major banking legislation.

From Chartered to Free Banking, 1837–62

From the earliest days of the Republic, banks had been chartered by special acts of incorporation passed by state legislatures and, in the case of the First and Second Banks of the United States, Congress. Like those of the First and Second Banks of the United States, these charters were often quite comprehensive, specifying in detail issues such as par value of shares, number of directors, minimum note denomination, maximum note issue, dividend policy, and any periodic payments that might be due to the state—aside, of course, from any bribes necessary to smooth the passage of the charter through the legislative and executive branches (Bodenhorn 2006).[11] Legislation in some states forbade conducting banking functions without a charter, giving chartered banks monopoly status (Bodenhorn 2003: 183ff.).

Starting with Michigan in 1837 and New York and Georgia in 1838, states began to enact "free banking" laws. Under free banking, rather than apply to the state legislature, individuals could obtain a charter and the right to issue notes by completing some paperwork and depositing a prescribed amount of bonds—frequently state bonds—with the authorities. Free banking did not exactly take the country by storm: nearly all the banks chartered under Michigan's law failed and the law was repealed in 1839—although a second free banking law was enacted in 1857—and no other state enacted free banking for more than a decade. Free banking did not spread rapidly until the 1850s, when legislation was enacted in Alabama (1849), New Jersey (1850), Massachusetts, Vermont, Ohio, Illinois (1851), Connecticut, Tennessee, Indiana, Wisconsin (1852), Louisiana, Florida (1853), Minnesota, Iowa (1858), and Pennsylvania (1860) (Rockoff 1975).

It is difficult to discern a particular pattern in the adoption of this innovation: free banking laws were adopted in all regions of the country and by more and less economically developed states. A formal statistical analysis of the timing and pattern of free banking adoption is hampered

[11]For examples of early bank charters, see Gras (1937) and Domett (1902).

by the paucity of accurate annual state-level data on banking and economic conditions going back to the 1830s. Broadly speaking, average bank size, average levels of capitalization, specie holdings, and growth in bank assets are not particularly good predictors of whether a state adopted free banking.

Free banking emerged in the 1830s and caught on in the 1850s because a substantial increase in the demand for charters made it impractical for state legislators to continue issuing charters on a case-by-case basis; if so, regularizing the process was a way of dealing with the backlog of charter requests (Bodenhorn 2003: 186ff.). Also, because the demand outstripped supply in the 1830s, the high and rising market value of charters made state legislators reluctant to give up their hands-on control of—and ability to profit from—bank chartering. By the 1850s the banking population had increased sufficiently so that legislators had less incentive to micromanage the process. Finally, state legislatures' control of banking charters was seen as contributing to the concentration of banking among the elite, which ran against a populist grain and increased popular support for free banking. By 1860, over half the states had enacted some type of free banking law. The National Banking Acts, passed in 1863 and 1864, institutionalized a form of free banking at the federal level.

THE NATIONAL BANKING ERA, 1863–1913

Prior to the outbreak of the Civil War, the federal government had not enacted any major banking legislation since it chartered of the Second Bank of the United States almost fifty years earlier. The National Banking Acts (originally called the National Currency Acts) of 1863–64 established a new kind of bank, the national bank. National banks were to be chartered and supervised by a new Treasury agency, the Comptroller of the Currency. For the first time in U.S. history, incorporated commercial banks in different states would operate with uniform charters and be subject to the same set of regulations.

National banks were empowered to issue national banknotes backed by U.S. Treasury securities deposited with the Comptroller. Banknotes were of uniform design and, in fact, were printed by the government. The value of banknotes a national bank was allowed to issue depended on the its capital, which was also regulated by the acts, and the value of bonds on deposit with the Comptroller. The relationship between bank capital, bonds held, and note issue was changed by laws enacted in 1874, 1882, and 1900 (Cagan 1963, Krooss 1969).

As its original title suggests, one of the main objectives of the legislation was to provide a uniform national currency. Prior to the establishment of the national banking system, the national currency supply consisted of a confusing patchwork of banknotes issued under a variety of schemes by banks chartered under different state laws. Notes of sound banks circulated side-by-side with notes of banks in financial trouble, those of banks that had failed, and forged notes. In fact, banknotes frequently traded at a discount, so that the notes of a smaller, less well-known bank, or of a bank located some distance from the transaction, would have been valued in trade slightly below face value. The confusion was such as to lead to the publication of magazines that specialized in printing pictures, descriptions, and prices of various banknotes, along with information on whether the issuing bank was still in existence. The acts also placed a tax on state banknotes, effectively eliminating them from circulation and giving a monopoly on note issue to national banks. Another important objective of the National Banking Acts was fiscal. Since note issue was a major source of funds for banks at this time, tying national banknote issues to deposits of Treasury bonds increased demand for those bonds and assisted the Union government's finances.

The national banking system grew rapidly at first (figures 9.2 and 9.3). Much of the increase came at the expense of state banking systems which, deprived of note-issuing powers, contracted over the same period as state-chartered banks applied for federal charters. The expansion of the new system did not lead to the extinction of the old: the growth of deposit-taking, combined with less stringent capital requirements, convinced many state bankers that they could do without a note issue or a federal charter, and led to a resurgence of state banking in the 1880s and 1890s.

Under the original acts, the minimum capital requirement for national banks was set at $50,000 for banks in towns with populations less than 6,000, $100,000 for banks in cities with populations ranging from 6,000 to 50,000, and $200,000 for cities with populations exceeding 50,000. By contrast, the minimum capital requirement for state banks, which varied widely across states, was often as low as $10,000. The difference in capital requirements may have been an important difference in the resurgence of state banking: in 1877 only about one-fifth of state banks had capital of less than $50,000, while by 1899 the proportion was over three-fifths. Recognizing this competition between states and the federal government, the Gold Standard Act of 1900 reduced the minimum capital necessary for national banks.[12]

----

[12] The relatively high minimum capital requirement for national banks may have contributed to regional interest rate differentials in the post–Civil War era. The period from the Civil War through World War I saw a substantial decline in interregional interest rate differentials. Sylla (1969) argues that the high minimum capital requirements established by the National Banking Acts represented barriers to entry and left many country bankers in "relatively monopolistic positions," leading to persistence in interest rate differentials. James (1976b) contends that more liberal banking laws encouraged the growth of state banks and led to the reduction of interest rate differentials. See also James (1976a, 1978).

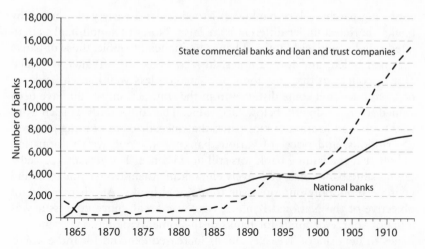

Figure 9.2. State and national banks in the United States, 1863–1913. *Source*: U.S. Comptroller of the Currency (1931: 3).

Contemporary observers, including Secretary of the Treasury Franklin MacVeagh, complained of both the persistence and ill effects of bank failures under the national banking system (Goodhart 1969: 108). O.M.W. Sprague (1910) classified the main financial crises during the era as occurring in 1873, 1884, 1890, 1893, and 1907, with those of 1873, 1893, and 1907 being regarded as full-fledged crises and those of 1884 and 1890 as less severe. Data on the number and assets of state and national bank failures during the national banking era are presented in figures 9.4 and 9.5.[13]

The largest number of failures occurred during and immediately following the crisis of 1893. The number and assets of national and non-national bank failures remained high for four years following the crisis before returning to pre-1893 levels. Other crises were also accompanied by an increase in the number and assets of bank failures. The earliest peak during the national banking era accompanied the onset of the crisis of 1873. Failures subsequently fell, but rose again in the trough of the downturn that followed the 1873 crisis. The panic of 1884 saw a slight increase in failures, while the financial stringency of 1890 was followed by a more substantial increase. Failures peaked again following several minor panics around the turn of the century and failures—and,

---

[13]Suspensions—temporary closures of banks unable to meet demands from their creditors—frequently exceeded outright failures during times of financial distress.

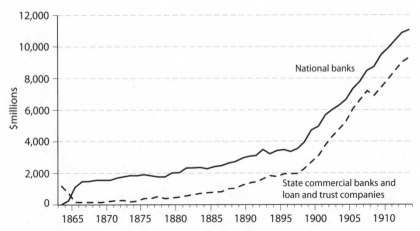

Figure 9.3. Assets of state and national banks in the United States, 1863–1913.
Source: U.S. Comptroller of the Currency (1931: 5).

even more dramatically, assets of failed institutions—peaked again at the time of the crisis of 1907.

Each of the crises was brought about by a unique set of circumstances. The crisis of 1873 was preceded by a collapse in speculative activity in railroads and housing. The crisis of 1893 may have been set off by a shock to confidence caused by doubts about the continued convertibility of the dollar into gold brought about by popular agitation for Free Silver. And the 1907 crisis was closely related to speculation and a rapid economic expansion associated with the activities of trust companies.

Despite these distinct elements, it is clear that macroeconomic fluctuations played an important part in generating the banking crises of the national banking era. All three of the major crises—and four of the five that Sprague catalogues—occurred within several months of a business cycle peak, suggesting that boom-slump conditions contributed to the crises. Side-by-side comparisons of business cycles marked by a banking panic with those that were relatively free of banking disturbances confirms this: cycles marked by banking crises were, on average, preceded by more exaggerated expansions in pig iron production (as an indicator of industrial activity), urban construction, stock prices, interest rates, than those that were free of banking crises (Grossman 1993: 303ff.). Moreover, crisis-cycles were typically followed by steeper-than-normal cyclical contractions, supporting the boom-bust explanation of banking crises.

Structural factors, including an insufficiently elastic money supply and a system of pyramided reserves, also contributed to crises under the

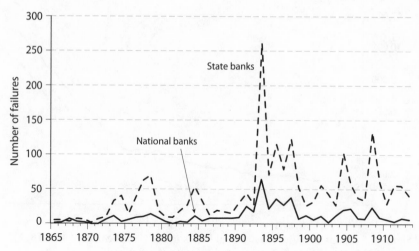

Figure 9.4. State and national bank failures in the United States, 1865–1913. *Source*: U.S. Comptroller of the Currency (1931: 6).

national banking system. Under the National Banking Acts, a portion of banks' required reserves could be held in national banks in larger cities ("reserve city banks"). Reserve city banks could, in turn, hold a portion of their required reserves in "central reserve city banks," national banks in New York, Chicago, and St. Louis. In practice, this led to the buildup

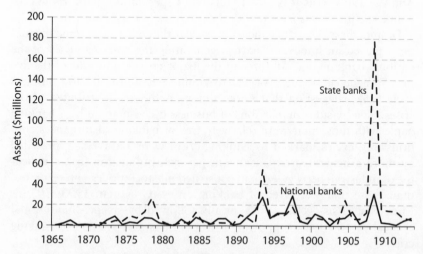

Figure 9.5. Assets of state and national bank failures in the United States, 1865–1913. *Source*: U.S. Comptroller of the Currency (1931: 8).

of reserve balances in New York City. Increased demands for funds in the interior of the country during the autumn harvest and spring planting seasons led to substantial outflows of funds from New York, which contributed to tight money market conditions and, sometimes, to panics (Miron 1986).

The frequency of disruptions during the national banking era led bankers and policy makers to develop new methods, and to refine old methods, for responding to crises. One response was for the bankers of a city to pool their resources through the local clearinghouse and to jointly guarantee the payment of member bank liabilities. The origins of clearinghouse loan certificates can be traced to a predecessor instrument that had been employed by the banks of the New York clearinghouse during the panic of 1857. The certificates soon gained popularity with clearinghouses in the rest of the country and, "[a]fter 1873 the issue of clearinghouse loan certificates in time of emergency became a matter of routine (although in 1893 the application was still limited to a few large clearinghouses)" (Redlich 1947, II: 166ff.).

In 1893, the Atlanta clearinghouse issued small-denomination certificates to satisfy the demand of cotton merchants who needed the currency to move the cotton crop. During the crisis of 1907, as many as fifty-one clearinghouses issued certificates, and the practice of issuing small-denomination circulating certificates spread.[14] The issue of, in effect, illegal currency led the federal government to enact the Aldrich-Vreeland Act (1908), which instituted government regulation of any issues of "emergency" currency (Kemmerer 1914). The Aldrich-Vreeland Act was superseded by the Federal Reserve Act (1913), which permanently ended the monetary role of the clearinghouses. In addition to the private *ex post* actions by the clearinghouses, federal and state governments enacted rules and regulations designed, in part, to reduce the *ex ante* risk of banking crises. The most important of these were capital requirements, double liability, deposit insurance, and branching regulations.

Next to entry requirements, capital requirements are among the most basic type of banking regulation. Mandating that bank shareholders must put up a minimum amount of capital serves several purposes: it provides a buffer in case of a shortage of cash flow, since shareholder dividends can be postponed or cancelled, while creditors' (i.e., depositors') demands for cash cannot; it provides a reserve from which to pay creditors if the bank fails; by forcing shareholders to commit more of their money, it can encourage banks to undertake less risk; and, because of asymmetric information, greater levels of capital can signal potential depositors and

---

[14]An additional element of the private response to the banking crisis of 1907 was a bankers' pool (headed by J. P. Morgan) of $25 million in loans. Herrick (1908: 309).

stockholders that the bank is less likely to undertake excessive risk. Although only a half-dozen or so state banking codes plus the National Banking Acts had established minimum capital requirements for banks by the end of the Civil War, the number rose steadily during the next six decades. By 1926, thirty-one states had established some sort of minimum capital requirement.

It is difficult to accurately summarize minimum capital requirements because they typically varied on more than one dimension. Although many states specified one minimum level of capital for all banks, it was more common for state law to specify different capital requirements for banks in cities and towns of different sizes. For example, in Alabama during 1880–1911, all state chartered banks were required to have $25,000 (1880–87, 1903–11) or $50,000 (1887–1903) in capital. During 1911–31, state-chartered banks in towns with populations below 1,000 were required to have $10,000 in capital; those in towns with populations of between 1,000 and 2,500 people were required to have $15,000; and those in with populations above 2,500 people were required to have $25,000. In 1931, the schedule of capital requirements was altered to include four different population categories. In 1906, seven states had a minimum capital requirement of $10,000; however, in one of these states $10,000 was the minimum for any and all banks, in others it was the minimum for banks in towns of less than 1,500 (one state), less than 2,000 (one state), less than 5,000 (three states), and less than 150,000 (one state). For a time, Michigan and Maryland had seven different population categories and minimum capital requirements; Nebraska had eight. Summarizing capital requirements after the Civil War is more difficult, since the average number of capital categories tripled between 1865 and 1922, from 1.25 to 3.7 categories per state.

Although it is difficult to construct a precise summary of capital requirements, the general downward trend in capital requirements is easy to spot (figure 9.6). The average capital requirement for banks in cities and towns with the smallest populations fell dramatically during the period, from nearly $57,000 in 1865 to about $28,000 by the early 1880s, to just over $17,000 during World War I, before rising to about $24,000 by the beginning of the Great Depression. Much of the early decline is due to a lowering of capital requirements in southern states from, on average, $100,000 in 1865, to $50,000 in 1880, to $20,000 in 1882. Nonetheless, the decline persists even if the southern states are excluded. Some of this decline in capital requirements was attributable to regulatory competition—that is, keeping requirements low enough to discourage banks from leaving for other regulatory systems (White 1982). This regulatory competition was most obvious between the state and federal governments: in response to growth of state banking systems, at the expense of the national banking system, the Gold Standard Act of 1900 halved (from $50,000 to $25,000) the capital requirement for national banks located in cities and towns with populations of less than 3,000. The decline also reflects improvements in information flows, which mitigated information asymmetry and reduced the market's capital requirement. Finally, the decline may have reflected the perceived, if not actual, increase in safety of the banking system due to the spread of potentially risk-reducing measures such as double liability, deposit insurance, and branching.

Additional capital can be made available by giving management and, in case of failure, the courts, recourse to the personal wealth of shareholders via some form of extended liability. Most major corporations in the United States today are incorporated with limited liability: when such corporations fail, the most that shareholders can lose is the amount of their initial investment. Creditors have no recourse against shareholders to make up any debts not paid for by the liquidation of company assets. This differs from an older corporate form, the partnership, in which partners are typically subject to unlimited liability, meaning that if the firm fails owing money, creditors can sue the individual partners for recovery of unpaid claims. In this case, partners' liability is not limited to the initial amount invested in the firm, but can include the partner's personal assets.

For much of the national banking era, a number of states and the federal government imposed "double liability" on holders of bank shares (Grossman 2001a, 2007a). Under double liability, shareholders of failed banks, in addition to losing their initial investment, could be called on to pay an additional amount approximately equal to the amount they had invested in the bank.[15] Double liability was the most common form of liability law for bank shareholders during the period: all but a handful of states implemented it for at least some of the national banking era (figure 9.6). Double liability was also the rule for national banks. According to the chief sponsor of the National Banking Acts, Senator John Sherman, the provision tracked the laws of "most of the States of the Union" (Macey and Miller 1992, 1993). Half a dozen states instituted triple liability (i.e., shareholders in failed banks could be called on to pay twice the par value of shares) for some portion of time, while other states enacted unlimited liability for banks chartered in their jurisdiction.[16]

---

[15]Strictly speaking, the law made shareholders liable for an additional amount equal to the par value of their shares. Shares at that time were typically issued with a par value, which approximated the value of the shares when first issued. By the time a shareholder had purchased the shares, their market value might no longer be close to the par value. Hence, the term "double liability" is something of a misnomer.

[16]Several states instituted so-called "voluntary liability," under which the choice of liability regime was up to individual banks.

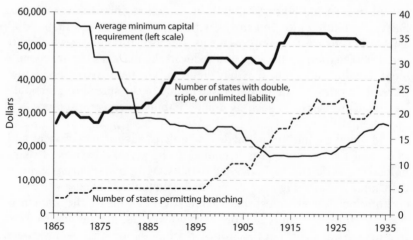

Figure 9.6. Capital requirements, branching, and double liability in the United States, 1865–1935. *Source*: Various state statutes.

Two main arguments support the imposition of double (or triple, or unlimited) liability: by enhancing shareholder liability, additional moneys become available to satisfy the creditors of failed banks; further, since shareholders suffer greater loss if their bank fails, they should be more reluctant to pursue—or allow managers to pursue—risky enterprises and, hence, be less likely to fail in the first place. Looking back on the National Banking Acts, Senator Sherman explained that in addition to providing security for creditors, the double liability provision "tends to prevent the stockholders and directors of a bank from engaging in hazardous operations."

By 1870, double, triple, or unlimited (i.e., multiple) liability was the rule for state banks in eighteen states, principally in the Midwest, New England, and Middle Atlantic regions, as well as for national banks. By 1900, multiple liability was the law for state banks in thirty-two states. By this time, the main pockets of single liability were in the south and west. By 1930, only four states had single liability.

Why would states institute double liability for state-chartered banks? Why might they prefer single liability? I find two motives: fear and greed.

Policy makers justified the adoption of double liability on the grounds that it reduced risk-taking and therefore enhanced banking stability. This can be thought of as "fear-induced" double liability. Why would lawmakers in some states have been especially fearful of excessive risk-taking on the part of banks? One explanation might be that the state's principal economic activities were inherently high-risk—such as agricultural sectors that are highly susceptible to fluctuations in temperature, rainfall, pests, etc.—and therefore bank failures were more likely. Alternatively, if a state's economy was not particularly well diversified, it might have been more susceptible to bank failures due to a downturn in an important sector than a state in which the economy was more diversified.

Even if a state's economic environment was not inherently high-risk—and therefore bank failures were no more likely than in any other state—lawmakers in states that were more economically developed might have had heightened concerns (i.e., fear) about the *costs* of bank failures. First, more economically developed states would have more to lose from a severe downturn than less developed states, and would therefore take greater precautions against banking crises, in the same way that industrialized countries typically have both more sophisticated financial systems and crisis prevention mechanisms (e.g., lender of last resort, deposit insurance) than their less-developed counterparts. Even if more economically developed states were characterized by large and relatively healthy banking sectors, the risk of contagion arising from one or two failures might encourage politicians in those states to adopt more stringent measures to contain risk-taking than politicians in states where banking systems were neither as large nor as stable. Second, politicians overseeing a well-developed financial system that was already adequately serving the needs of the state might be inclined to err on the side of caution in terms of encouraging entry into banking. If imposing double liability discouraged further entry into banking, it might also have the political backing of established bankers, a group that would have been especially prominent in an economically developed state (Rajan and Zingales 2003c).

Why might a state's lawmakers opt for single, or limited, liability, which, other things being equal, would lead banks to undertake more risk? Although it would not seem to be in the interest of any state to encourage excessive risk-taking, it could be argued that some states could benefit from more aggressive bank behavior. This might be the case in economically less developed states or in states with fewer banks, which might benefit from a policy that encouraged expansive—and riskier—banking practices or easier entry into banking (i.e., greed). Lawmakers in the postbellum South, which was relatively starved for capital and hampered by high minimum capital requirements, may have opted for single (i.e., limited) liability in an attempt to facilitate the spread of banking services (Davis 1965, Sylla 1969).

Analysis of the timing and pattern of the adoption of double liability supports the fear and greed hypothesis (Grossman 2007a). Rapidly growing and less developed states tended to adopt single liability, which encouraged more expansive banking. Economically developed states, with more to lose, and states with a history of economic and financial instability, were more likely to adopt double liability, which would encourage more circumspect banking practices.

Although double liability was in fact successful in generating more risk-averse behavior on the part of banks, it did not ensure banking stability. During 1890–1930, state banks that were subject to multiple liability typically undertook less risk than their counterparts in single liability states. However, during crises, banks in multiple liability states were more likely to fail than banks in limited liability states. This may have resulted from the fact that banks in crisis-prone states were more likely to have already adopted double liability, and so when a severe financial turbulence erupted, banks in multiple liability states were disproportionately affected (Grossman 2001a).

The Great Depression did not spare banks in either single or double liability states, and by 1941 virtually every state had repealed double liability. Macey and Miller (1992: 38) ascribe the demise of double liability to three factors: (1) the bankruptcies of many shareholders who had taken no part in the management of failed banks generated political pressure to repeal double liability laws; (2) the substantial waves of bank failures during 1929–33 made it clear that double liability had not been adequate as a stability promoting mechanism; and (3) the establishment of federal deposit insurance in 1933 made double liability redundant. Capital regulation and double liability are, in part, aimed at protecting the creditors of failed banks; their incentive effects may also help to stabilize a banking system *before* it runs into trouble. Although deposit insurance might have stabilizing effects on the banking system by engendering confidence and therefore preventing panic-induced runs, one can argue that deposit insurance, which guarantees that the claims of creditors of failed banks are met, is more of an ex post remedy to banking crises.

The first deposit insurance system in the United States was the New York Safety Fund, which was established in 1829. Other systems were introduced in Vermont (1831), Indiana (1834), Michigan (1836), Ohio (1845), and Iowa (1858). Three of these systems were "safety fund" systems, in which insurance funds were generated by periodic assessments, that is, deposit insurance premia; the other three were mutual guarantee systems, where no assessments were made unless a bank suspended. Some of the systems made insurance mandatory for all state-chartered banks, while in others participation was voluntary (Calomiris 1989). Of these systems, the mutual systems of Indiana, Ohio, and Iowa fared better than those of New York, which lasted until 1866 but needed several rounds of recapitalization, and Michigan, which failed shortly after it was founded. All of these deposit insurance systems were dismantled by 1866.

Deposit insurance petered out in the 1850s and 1860s for two reasons. First, the spread of free banking, since free banks were primarily financed with bond-secured note issues rather than deposits, were generally exempt from deposit insurance systems. Second, the passage of the National Banking Acts and the introduction of a tax on state banknotes caused many state banks to switch to federal charters and to become ineligible for state deposit insurance (Golembe 1960).

Following the banking crisis of 1907, eight states established deposit insurance systems: Oklahoma (1907); Texas, Kansas, Nebraska, South Dakota (1909); Mississippi (1914); North Dakota and Washington (1917). Each of these deposit insurance systems followed the safety fund format: banks contributed annual assessments to a deposit insurance fund. These systems suffered from several flaws. First, all contained provisions allowing some banks to escape from the system and the assessments. As a result, healthy banks opted out by becoming national banks, leaving the weaker, more failure-prone banks within the system.[17] Second, because the economies of many states were not well diversified, they were vulnerable to failures concentrated within the state's main sectors. All of these systems ceased operation prior to the Great Depression (Federal Deposit Insurance System 1998). Branching regulation was another important component of regulation during the national banking era. Although the motives for allowing or barring bank branching may be varied (Kroszner and Strahan 1999), much has been made about the consequences of bank branching for bank stability (Calomiris and Gorton 1991, Laderman, Schmidt, and Zimmerman 1991). In theory, extensively branched banks should be less likely to fail than unit banks for three reasons: banks with an extensive branch system are likely to have a more diversified loan portfolio than unit banks which make loans in one location only; branched banks may have a more geographically diversified deposit base and, therefore, may be less likely to fail due to purely local deposit runs than unit banks; and, a branch system provides seasonal diversification, eliminating the stringency in money centers caused by the flow of funds to agricultural areas at harvest time.[18] Recent work, however, suggests that extensively branched banks did not fare as well as theory predicts (Carlson 2004, Carlson and Mitchener 2006).

Branching was not widely permitted in the years after the Civil War, with no more than five states permitting branching as late as the middle of the 1890s. The number grew steadily through the early 1920s, when

[17]A Comptroller of the Currency ruling in 1908 prohibited national banks from participating in state deposit insurance systems, and so a bank that wished to avoid deposit insurance needed only to secure a federal charter. Calomiris (1989: 20).

[18]Miron (1986), Sprague (1910), Noyes (1909a), and others ascribe many instances of financial instability in the United States to the seasonal demands of agriculture. Madden and Nadler (1935: 114) argue that the branch systems of Europe were more adept at handling the seasonal movement of funds than the correspondent system in the U.S.

about half of the states allowed branching (figure 9.6). The battle over branching involved regulatory competition between federal and state authorities, and typically pitted small, but numerous and politically influential, unit banks against larger urban banks (White 1982, 1983, Economides, Hubbard, and Palia 1996, Dehejia and Lleras-Muney 2003).

Capital requirements, double liability, deposit insurance, and branching each had important effects on the structure of banking across the United States. And although it is useful to examine each of these individually, in fact, legislators may have considered them jointly. As noted, the spread of double liability and branching coincided with a sustained decline in capital requirements. Can we find other interactions between these rules?

If double liability states were more concerned about bank risk-taking, one would expect those states to also allow branching. Alternatively, it could be argued that states which had enacted single liability were more inclined to allow branching, in order to compensate for the higher risk associated with single liability.[19] Simple statistical tests suggest that states with single liability were more likely to allow branch banking (Grossman 2007a). This may have resulted from a conscious effort by state authorities to compensate for stricter liability law; alternatively, this could have resulted from lobbying on the part of bankers.

Higher capital requirements could have been used to stem bank risk taking, discourage entry into banking, or to encourage the development of larger banks. The ratio of the average minimum capital requirements (in the smallest location) in single-to-double liability states, along with the average minimum capital requirement, reveals no consistent pattern: in the 1870s, single liability states had higher minimum capital requirements; the situation was reversed in most of the 1880s, before switching back in 1887. Capital requirements remained higher in single liability states through 1902, after which those in double liability states were higher. Given both the variability of the ratio and the difficulty in summarizing capital requirements in one number, the data do not suggest any straightforward conclusions about the relationship between capital requirements and double liability.

Eight states had deposit insurance systems in place during some part of the period 1907–31, the stated goal being to protect depositors in case of bank failure.[20] An often-noted drawback of deposit insurance is

---

[19]Equivalently, it could be argued that states without branching were more inclined to enact double liability to compensate for the higher risks associated with unit banking. However, since liability laws on average predated branching laws (only seven states had branching laws in 1870, while twenty-eight had multiple liability laws), it seems more reasonable to consider the consequences of liability law for branching law.

[20]White (1981) argues that states characterized by small unit banks were more likely to enact deposit insurance because of their greater vulnerability to panics.

moral hazard, that is, that it may encourage the insured to take on more risk. Thus, one might expect to find double liability and deposit insurance enacted in the same states, assuming that legislators wanted to dampen the moral hazard of deposit insurance with double liability. Interestingly, every state that adopted deposit insurance in the twentieth century also adopted double liability. With the exception of Mississippi, which enacted both double liability and deposit insurance at the same time, however, most of these states had enacted double liability a decade or more prior to the introduction of deposit insurance. Consequently, although double liability may have influenced the decision to enact deposit insurance, as it appears to have done in Mississippi, it did not generally do so immediately.[21] It could be that establishing double liability, in a sense, raising the "deductible," gave policymakers greater confidence about enacting deposit insurance. Given the small number of states that enacted deposit insurance during this period, a closer inspection of the debates surrounding its enactment may be the best way to understand the connection between deposit insurance and double liability.

THE CRISIS OF 1907 AND THE FOUNDING OF THE FEDERAL RESERVE

The crisis of 1907, which had been brought under control by a coalition of private banks led by J. P. Morgan, along with action by the clearinghouses, led policy makers to reconsider the country's banking and monetary institutions. Congress established the National Monetary Commission in 1908, which undertook a massive study of banking and monetary arrangements in the United States and in other economically advanced countries (Dewald 1972). An eventual result of this investigation was the Federal Reserve Act (1913), which established the country's first central bank since the demise of the Second Bank of the United States, more than three-quarters of a century earlier.

The First and Second Banks of the United States, like all government banks founded in the nineteenth century or earlier, had been established as a single institution. That is, each bank had one set of shareholders, directors, and executives. Branches, if they existed, were under the control of the management of the bank itself. By contrast, the Federal Reserve Act provided for a system of between eight and twelve quasi-independent regional reserve banks. The Federal Reserve Board Organization Committee, charged with setting up the districts and locations of the regional banks, finally settled on twelve districts, although during debate over the

---

[21]By contrast, in the pre-1867 period four of the six states with deposit insurance (New York, Michigan, Indiana, and Ohio) adopted it prior to enacting double liability. Only one state (Iowa) enacted at nearly the same time (one year apart).

act, some had called for as many as one reserve bank per state (Hammes 2001). The establishment of a decentralized bank, like the rejection of the First and Second Banks of the United States, resulted in part from American wariness of concentrating too much financial authority within one institution.

The stated goals of the Federal Reserve Act were: ". . . to furnish an elastic currency, to furnish the means of rediscounting commercial paper, to establish a more effective supervision of banking in the United States, and for other purposes." Furnishing an "elastic currency" was an important goal of the act, since none of the components of the money supply (gold and silver certificates, national banknotes) were able to expand rapidly enough to meet periodic monetary tightening. This inelasticity, along with the seasonal fluctuations in money demand, was seen to be responsible for many of the panics of the national banking era. These panic-inducing seasonal fluctuations resulted from the large flows of money out of New York and other money centers to the interior of the country to pay for the newly harvested crops. If monetary conditions were already tight before the drain of funds to the nation's interior, the autumnal movement of funds might precipitate a panic.

The act also fostered the growth of the bankers' acceptance market. Bankers' acceptances were short-dated IOUs, issued by banks on behalf of clients that were importing or otherwise purchasing goods. These acceptances were sent to the seller who could carry them until they matured and receive the face value, or could discount them, that is, receive the face value minus interest charges. By allowing the Federal Reserve to rediscount commercial paper, the act facilitated the growth of this short-term money market and provided an important mechanism—along with direct loans—for the Federal Reserve to act as a lender of last resort (Warburg 1930, Broz 1997).

The establishment of the Federal Reserve did not end the competition between the state and national banking systems. While national banks were required to be members of the new Federal Reserve System, state banks could also become members of the system—and gain access to Federal Reserve facilities such as discount window lending—on equal terms with national banks. Further, the Federal Reserve Act, bolstered by the amendment of June 21, 1917, ensured that state banks could become members without losing any competitive advantages they might hold over national banks. Depending on the state, state banking law sometimes gave state banks advantages in the areas of branching, trust operations, interlocking managements, loan and investment powers, safe deposit operations, and the arrangement of mergers (Kent 1963: 48–51). Where state banking laws were especially liberal, national banks had an incentive to give up their national bank charters and seek admission to the Federal Reserve System as a state-chartered member bank.

The McFadden Act (1927) addressed some of the competitive inequalities between state and national banks. It gave national banks charters of indeterminate length, allowing them to compete with state banks for trust business. It expanded the range of permissible investments, including real estate, and allowed investment in the stock of safe deposit companies. The act granted national banks the right to establish branches (in cities with populations above 25,000) when such right of establishment was also available to state banks.

Legislation in the post–World War I period also encouraged mergers. The Bank Consolidation Act of 1918 provided for the merger of two or more national banks: prior to its enactment, a merger would have required both banks to liquidate and reincorporate. Additionally, in 1927 the McFadden Act provided a mechanism for state and national banks to merge. Combined with a booming stock market, this legislation encouraged the bank merger movement of the 1920s (White 1985).

THE GREAT DEPRESSION

The Great Depression was "the great economic catastrophe of modern times" (Eichengreen 1992: 3). Throughout the world, output and prices fell at unprecedented rates, unemployment rose to record heights, and financial systems—banking and financial markets—began to disintegrate. Nowhere was the economic downturn of the Great Depression more severe than in the United States: between 1929 and 1933, real GDP fell by nearly 30 percent,[22] prices fell by more than 20 percent, the unemployment rate reached nearly 25 percent, and the industrial unemployment rate reached nearly 38 percent.[23] The United States also suffered a dramatic stock market crash and three banking crises: national bank suspensions, which had averaged about 85 per year during most of the 1920s, averaged 580 per year during 1930–33, including 1,475 suspension in 1933 alone. The suspensions among non-national banks were even more dramatic: during 1921–29 non-national bank suspension averaged 635 per

[22]This decline was similar to that in Canada and greater than that in Austria (approximately 20 percent), France, and Germany (approximately 15 percent). Annual declines in U.S. real GDP were: 9.6 percent (1929–30), 7.7 percent (1930–31), and 13.8 percent (1931–32). By comparison, there were three consecutive declines of between 6 and 7 percent during the period 1919–22, one decline of more than 8 percent following the crisis of 1907, and two declines between three and five percent in 1893–94. Balke and Gordon (1986).

[23]Data on industrial unemployment in the U.S. are from Lebergott (1964), as cited in Eichengreen and Hatton (1988). German industrial unemployment reached nearly 44 percent in 1932; other industrialized countries saw less significant unemployment.

year; during the period 1930–33, the average was 2,573, including 5,190 in 1933 (Bremer 1935).

The origins and propagation of the Great Depression, including the source of the initial shock, the relationship between the banking and financial crises and the onset and deepening of the Great Depression, and the relationship between the economic downturn in the United States and other industrialized countries are the subject of a substantial literature and are beyond the scope of this chapter. Many scholars argue that banking and financial crises contributed to the length and depth of the Great Depression, particularly the three banking crises that struck the United States in the 1930s.[24]

The first banking panic erupted in October 1930. It began with failures in Missouri, Indiana, Illinois, Iowa, Arkansas, and North Carolina, and quickly spread to other areas of the country. During November 1930, 256 banks with $180 million of deposits failed; 352 banks with over $370 million of deposits failed in the following month, the largest of which was the Bank of United States (not to be confused with the First or Second Bank of *the* United States) which failed on December 11 with over $200 million of deposits. The second banking panic began in March 1931 and continued into the summer. The third and final panic began at the end of 1932 and continued into March 1933 (Wicker 2000). During the early months of 1933, a number of states declared banking holidays, allowing banks to close their doors, temporarily freeing them from the requirement to redeem deposits. By the time President Franklin Delano Roosevelt was inaugurated on March 4, 1933, bank holidays had been declared in a number of states; the following day, the new president declared a national banking holiday. Beginning on March 13, the Secretary of the Treasury began granting banks licenses to reopen.

The first major piece of banking legislation was the Emergency Banking Act of 1933, enacted on March 9. This legislation granted ex post sanction to Roosevelt's declaration of a bank holiday. It also allowed (section 203) the Comptroller of the Currency to appoint "conservators" of national banks, "whenever he shall deem it necessary in order to conserve the assets of any bank for the benefit of the depositors and any other creditors . . ." Conservators were to have the broad powers previously granted to receivers of insolvent banks, that is, to run the banks on a day-to-day basis. Conservators were to devise reorganization plans under which their banks, with the approval of depositors, stockholders, and other creditors, could be removed from conservatorship and returned to normal operation. Additional portions of the act provided for national banks under conservatorship to issue preferred stock, for the

---

[24]Important sources on this include Fisher (1933), Friedman and Schwartz (1963), Kindleberger (1973), Temin (1976, 1989), Bernanke (1983), and Eichengreen (1992).

Federal Reserve Banks to issue more currency, and to make advances in "exceptional exigent" circumstances to member banks on the security of the bank's time or demand notes.

More long-lasting reforms were contained in the Banking Acts of 1933 and 1935. The most important of these reforms were the introduction of federal deposit insurance, the separation of commercial and investment banking, and the enactment of interest rate ceilings.[25]

Federal deposit insurance was established under the Banking Act of 1933, enacted just three months after FDR's inauguration. Although fourteen state deposit insurance systems had been established prior to the Great Depression (the last of which had folded in 1930) and Congress had considered federal deposit insurance in one form or another for at least fifty years (Golembe 1960: 182, Flood 1992), 1933 marked the first time that deposit insurance was enacted on a national level. The act established the Federal Deposit Insurance Corporation (FDIC), which was to insure commercial bank deposits up to $2,500 (raised to $5,000 six months later). Originally envisioned as a temporary measure, the program was made permanent by the Banking Act of 1935. Deposit insurance was mandatory for member banks of the Federal Reserve System and optional for non-member banks; however, within six months of the 1933 act, 97 percent of commercial bank deposits were covered by deposit insurance.

Deposit insurance was anticompetitive in that it both limited entry into banking and made entry more discretionary, since federal banking authorities were required to consider capital adequacy, earnings prospects, managerial character, and community need before allowing prospective banks to commence operations with deposit insurance (Spong 2000: 24). It was also widely considered to have been responsible for the low level of bank failures suffered in the United States during the four decades following its introduction. According to Friedman and Schwartz (1963: 434) "Federal insurance of bank deposits was the most important structural change in the banking system to result from the 1933 panic ... and ... the structural change most conducive to monetary stability ..."

A second major reform contained in the Banking Act of 1933 was a provision, known familiarly as Glass-Steagall, separating commercial and investment banking. Despite recommendations in 1913 by the Pujo Commission and in 1920 by the Comptroller of the Currency, no specific

---

[25]Because monetary policy was seen as being in part to blame for the crises, the 1935 act also reorganized the Federal Reserve, centralizing power in Washington and relegating the heads of the individual reserve banks to a more consultative role. Symptomatic of this reorganization, the heads of the individual reserve banks were downgraded from "governors," as European central bank heads were typically styled, to "presidents," while the Washington-based establishment became the "Board of Governors of the Federal Reserve System."

restrictions on commercial bank security underwriting existed in 1933 (Carosso 1970, Ang and Richardson 1994). The collapse of the American securities market in 1929 led to an extensive reevaluation of the banking system in general and the system of securities affiliates in particular.[26]

The chairman of the Senate subcommittee examining these practices was Carter Glass, a vehement opponent of the affiliate system, under which banks conducted investment banking (i.e., securities) activities through affiliated, and often wholly-owned, institutions. Glass's persistence led to the enactment of provisions in the 1933 Banking Act prohibiting member banks after June 16, 1934, from being affiliated with any company engaged in the, ". . . issue, flotation, underwriting, public sale, or distribution at wholesale or retail or through syndicate participation of stocks, bonds, debentures, notes, or other securities (other than Treasury securities)." It also prohibited securities dealers from taking deposits or allowing corporate connection between banks and securities dealers (Burns 1988: 56). Aside from Belgium, which instituted a similar reform in 1934, no other country erected such a thorough separation between commercial and investment banking.

Research suggests that the abuses of the affiliate system highlighted by its opponents may not have been as dire as contemporaries believed. White (1986) argues that the securities affiliates of national banks, which were spun off into separate entities as a result of the Banking Act of 1933, had not destabilized the U.S. banking system during the Great Depression. White focuses exclusively on whether the presence of securities affiliates destabilized the banking system, and does not consider whether banks or their affiliates engaged in share manipulation, one motive for the law. Nor does he consider whether banks "pushed" securities on unsuspecting customers, another reason given by lawmakers, although he argues that further research is needed on this subject. Kroszner and Rajan (1994) find that the securities underwritten and sold by the securities affiliates of commercial banks were no less sound than those issued by independent investment banks.

A third component of Depression-era banking reform was the imposition of interest rate ceilings. The Banking Acts of 1933 (for national banks) and 1935 (for federally insured banks) prohibited the payment of interest on demand deposits and gave the Federal Reserve the power to set interest rate ceilings on time and savings deposits under Regulation Q (Gilbert 1986: 22–23). Interest rate ceilings were meant to address two main concerns. First, they would encourage rural banks to lend funds locally and leave less on deposit with banks in large financial centers. The

---

[26]U.S. Senate Committee on Banking and Currency (1934), Willis and Chapman (1934), Pecora (1939), Peach (1941), and Bentson (1990).

migration of funds, it was argued, had contributed to speculation and aggravated the already existing seasonal movement of funds into and out of the nation's financial centers, which many believed had contributed to the banking crises. Second, interest rate ceilings would reduce competitive pressures, making banks more profitable and less likely to fail.

The Regulation Q ceiling was initially set to 3 percent in November 1933 on all types of savings and time deposits, and lowered to 2.5 percent in February 1935. Rates on time deposits of less than ninety days and between 90–179 days were further lowered to 1 and 2 percent in January 1936 (Winningham and Hagan 1980). These ceilings would not change for the next twenty years; Regulation Q itself would not be dismantled for another thirty years after that.

Summary

A distinguishing feature of the United States is its federal character. The dichotomy between federal and state authority has shaped the debate over, policy toward, and the evolution of banking in the United States since the earliest days of the Republic. Much of the debate over the establishment and recharter of the First and Second Banks of the United States focused on whether it was the proper role of the state or federal government to charter banks, although debates over these principles often merely masked partisan, sectional, and private interests. The shift from chartered to free banking similarly can be attributed to both matters of high political principle (sentiment in favor of broadening the banking franchise) and low economic calculation (declining charter values).

From the beginning of the national banking era, when the federal government entered the banking arena after an absence of more than a quarter-century, regulatory competition characterized the relationship between banks chartered by the federal and state governments. From branching, to deposit insurance, to double liability, to capital requirements, banks responded to changes in regulation, in part, by switching to different regulatory jurisdictions—and adopting other methods of circumventing regulations—which, in turn, led to further regulatory changes. Thus, the United States presents a good example of what Kane (1977) terms the "regulatory dialectic."

Another distinctive feature of American banking was its instability. Banking crises occurred on a regular basis in the nineteenth and early twentieth centuries. It could be argued that the absence of a central bank for much of this period contributed to instability and that such an institution could have ameliorated the seasonal drains of funds from the money centers, which triggered or aggravated many of the banking crises. It seems unlikely that, based on the experience of other countries, even an effective central bank could have moderated the macroeconomic fluctuations that played the dominant role in generating banking instability. Structural factors were also important in nineteenth- and early-twentieth-century banking crises: regulation—influenced by the political power of various interest groups—kept U.S. banks small, which contributed to their vulnerability in the face of macroeconomic fluctuations.

A final important feature of U.S. banking prior to World War II was the severity of the regulations imposed following the banking crises of the Great Depression. These wide-ranging reforms restricted the ability of banks to compete—and to get into trouble. Keeping banks on a tighter leash was a common policy response to the Great Depression across the industrialized world, although nowhere were the regulations more severe than in the United States. These Depression-era strictures were also long-lived, many of them lasting for more than a half-century, when a new era—an era of deregulation—began.

CHAPTER 10

Constrained and Deregulated Banking in the Twentieth Century and Beyond

> Seek neither license, where no laws compel,
> Nor slavery beneath a tyrant's rod;
> Where liberty and rule are balanced well
> Success will follow as the gift of God,
> Though how He will direct it none can tell.
> —Aeschylus, *The Eumenides*

No matter where banking systems were within their evolutionary life cycle, the Great Depression and World War II stopped the process dead in its tracks. In response to financial devastation and wartime needs, governments enacted strict rules and regulations aimed at stabilizing the banking system and directing credit toward favored sectors. These constraints—a sort of financial "lockdown"—combined with low, stable interest rates and robust economic growth, led to a period of unprecedented banking stability. The gradual rise in market interest rates that began in the 1960s, the liberalization of banking regulation during the 1970s and 1980s, and the economic slowdown associated with oil shocks in 1973 and 1979, however, contributed to growing instability which, in turn, led to renewed cycles of crises, bailouts, mergers, and regulatory reform, which continue until the present day. The banking history of the period covered by this chapter warrants a volume of its own. Given that the focus of this book is primarily historical, this chapter presents an abbreviated version of developments since the Great Depression.

CONSTRAINED BANKING

The economic collapse that accompanied the Great Depression and World War II left indelible marks on the banking systems of the industrialized world. Many countries were struck with severe banking crises during the 1920s and/or 1930s. It is safe to say that few industrialized countries emerged from the interwar period with their banking systems completely intact. The unprecedented severity of these crises led policy makers in many countries to adopt wide-ranging reforms aimed at both reducing the likelihood of a recurrence and mitigating the costs of any crises that nonetheless occurred. In countries where banks had operated under general company law prior to World War I and which enacted their initial banking codes during this time (e.g., Belgium, Denmark, France, Germany, Italy, Norway, and Switzerland), the change in the regulatory environment was especially dramatic. Major reforms typically fell into three categories. First, governments introduced more extensive regulation, such as interest rate ceilings and limitations on the scope of permitted bank activities. In addition to their other consequences, these reforms often had the effect of reducing competition among banks. Second, governments developed more stringent supervisory mechanisms, including the establishment of new agencies with broad powers. Third, many countries substantially reorganized bank ownership.

On the international level, the post–World War II Bretton Woods system created a system of fixed exchange rates and capital controls, with lending facilities provided by the newly created International Monetary Fund to support the exchange rate arrangements. These reforms were established to avoid some of the problems of the international monetary system of the interwar period, which had been characterized by misaligned exchange rates, capital flight, and imbalances in international reserve holdings.

As a result of these changes, the economic and financial environment in the quarter-century following World War II was far less liberal than that at the beginning of the twentieth century—or that which came to exist by its end. According to Eichengreen (1996: 94), "This was a period when governments intervened extensively in their economies and financial systems. Interest rates were capped. The assets in which banks could invest were restricted. Governments regulated financial markets to channel credit toward strategic sectors."

As in the United States, authorities in Belgium drastically curtailed the scope of permitted bank activities. Prior to the Great Depression, Belgium had no specific banking legislation: banks operated under the same rules and regulations that governed non-financial firms and had long participated in universal banking (i.e., operated as both commercial and investment banks). Laws dated August 22, 1934, and July 9, 1935, forced universal banks to split into deposit banks and holding companies, and forbade bankers from taking part in the operation of a non-financial company or from receiving loans from their bank, although these reforms were not completely implemented by the end of 1936 (Allen et al. 1938: 94). The laws also established capital and reporting requirements and prohibited banks from using their resources to influence public opinion (Allen et al. 1938, Chlepner 1943, Kurgan-van Hentenryk 1995). The later law established the Banking Commission with wide-ranging powers over all deposit-taking institutions, including private banks. The commission was empowered to limit entry into both banking and the banking profession, to set interest rates and liquidity ratios, and to establish reporting and auditing requirements.

In Switzerland, where no commercial banking law had existed prior to the Depression, a full-fledged banking code was enacted in November 1934, supplemented by detailed regulations adopted by the Federal Council in February 1935. The law established detailed capital and liquidity regulations, each of which had an element of risk-weighting,[1] specified certain rules of corporate governance,[2] gave savings depositors a prior claim on all bank assets, held managers liable for intentional damage to creditors and shareholders, and allowed for the possibility of a moratorium (Allen et al. 1938, Cassis 1995: 69–70). The law also established the Federal Banking Commission, which was empowered to regulate entry, approve articles of association, certify auditing associations, and set required financial ratios, and gave the Swiss National Bank the authority to veto the conditions of certain bank undertakings.

Elsewhere, the crisis led to greater government ownership in the banking sector. In Germany, virtually all important commercial banks received an infusion of capital from the state in the aftermath of the 1931 banking crisis. As a result of the reorganization following the crisis, the government was left in control of the Dresdner Bank, the Commerz- und Privatbank, and a number of other institutions; the quasi-public Golddiskontbank became a large shareholder in Deutsche Bank. It was estimated that in 1932 the state held 50 percent of the capital of the large commercial banks and the Golddiskontbank an additional 14 percent (Allen et al. 1938).

In addition, the crisis led to a variety of banking reforms embodied in a series of decrees during 1931–33, culminating with the adoption of Germany's first full scale banking code in 1934. Engineered largely after the Nazi takeover, the new laws gave government authorities broad powers of control over the banking system. The reforms established the Supervisory Board, largely under the authority of the President of the Reichsbank (later, the Economics Minister), and a Banking Commissioner with wide-ranging powers to set balance sheet ratios, limit the amount of loans to individual creditors, enforce interest rate ceilings set

---

[1] The reserves required to be held against any liability depended upon the character (e.g., maturity, type) of the liability. This method was adopted by the Basel Committee on Banking Supervision in establishing capital requirements on an international basis half a century later.

[2] The law required banks to separate the management from the board of directors, and forbade the chairman of the board from taking on management responsibilities except with the explicit consent of the Banking Commission.

by the bankers' association, and to intervene in the affairs of individual banks. The regulations empowered the supervisory bodies to determine which institutions—not just banks, but also the financial departments of industrial companies—would be under their supervision and to revoke charters. The law also required banks to report the total credit extended to individual borrowers, which the authorities could share with other banks in order to stifle competition.

The 1931 crisis in Italy led to substantial government participation in the banking industry through the creation of the Istituto Mobiliari Italiano (IMI) in 1931 and the Istituto Ricostruzione Industriale (IRI) in 1933.[3] These institutions took over the industrial participations, loan portfolios, and, in some cases, the lending operations of distressed Italian banks. For example, IRI took over the industrial participations previously held by the three leading banks, Banca Commerciale Italiana, Credito Italiano, and Banco di Roma, as well as a number of smaller banks (Gerbi 1954: 487ff., Allen et al. 1938, Zamagni 1993: 299), effectively marking the end of universal banking in Italy.

As in Germany, Italian law subjected banking to greater administrative control by an authoritarian state. Italy had operated without any commercial banking laws, except those governing note issuing banks, during the first quarter of the twentieth century. A stock exchange crash in 1925 led to the passage of a banking code the following year (Zamagni 1993: 294). The new law set minimum capital requirements and established a supervisory system led by the Banca d'Italia, subject to supervision by the Ministry of Finance. Decree laws of 1936 and 1937 further strengthened the government's administrative control. Like the German legislation of 1934, the Italian law encompassed many different types of institutions and set out the general principles of bank regulation, but left the details to administrative decree (Allen et al. 1938: 260). Interest rate controls were established in 1932 (Gerbi 1954).

In some ways, an even more dramatic shift occurred in Japan. Prior to the 1930s, the Japanese financial system had been characterized by substantial securities (in particular, equities) markets, with banks playing a secondary role as intermediators. Japanese stock market capitalization peaked at 122 percent of GDP in 1936, below modern figures for the United States (164 percent in 1998) and the United Kingdom (175 percent), but well above those for France (69 percent), Japan (66 percent), and Germany (51 percent). During the military buildup of the 1930s, the

---

[3]Government ownership was not limited to the banking sector. In discussing public enterprises such as IRI and IMI, Cohen (1988), citing R. Romeo, *Breva storia della grande industria in Italia* (Rocca San Casciano, 2ⁿᵈ edition, 1963), writes, ". . . through such institutions by 1936 the Italian government owned a greater share of domestic industry than any other European country, with the exception of the Soviet Union."

government enhanced the role of banks, at the expense of securities markets, in order to better channel national savings toward military production. Hoshi and Kashyap (2001: 15–89) argue that the American postwar occupation solidified the bank-based model in Japan, albeit one in which banks became "informed lenders" rather than agents of the state.

Even in countries where banking systems remained essentially intact, important Depression-era changes in the regulatory environment were enacted. In Canada, following the recommendations of the Macmillan Commission, the Government established the Bank of Canada. Bordo and Redish (1987: 417) argue that the Bank was founded because of the government's desire to be perceived as doing something in response to the Great Depression, rather than from any pressing economic need for a central bank. Sweden's banking system also weathered the 1930s without a serious crisis, despite the collapse of the Kreuger industrial empire in 1932, although it enacted legislation in 1933 making it more difficult for banks to own industrial shares. Sweden also established A/B Industrikredit which, like IMI and IRI in Italy, was created to take industrial shares off the hands of banks.

World War II led to the introduction of additional legislative and administrative measures on the uses and cost of bank credit, as governments harnessed the banking industry to finance the war effort. Many of these reforms persisted long after the conflict ended. In February 1942 the Commonwealth Bank of Australia was given powers to set maximum interest rates as a wartime measure. At the war's end, these powers were continued by the Banking Act 1945 and lasted until the 1980s (Australia. Parliament 1991: 20–21). Similarly, in Germany, interest rates on deposits during World War II had been set by the Zentralverband des Deutschen Bank- und Bankiergewerbes (i.e., bankers' association) in "authoritative consultation with the Reich Control Office for Banking" (Irmler 1954: 322). Following the war, the job was taken over by West German state governments, which maintained control until interest rate deregulation in 1967. Sweden introduced credit controls at the beginning of World War II and interest rate controls at the war's end, both of which remained in force for nearly a half-century (Jonung 1993). Even more dramatically, France nationalized its large deposit banks in 1945 (Myers 1949).

As an indicator of the pervasiveness of government control of the banking sector, and of the magnitude of the deregulation that was to follow, consider interest rate regulation. In 1960, interest rates in all twenty-two industrialized countries of the Organization for Economic Cooperation and Development (OECD) were set by official government policy or by state-sanctioned bankers' cartels. By the end of 1980, interest rates in eighteen of those countries were still controlled. By the end of 1987, the number of countries with controls had fallen to nine. By the end of the twentieth century, interest rate controls and cartel arrangements had disappeared from the OECD countries.

The constraints on banking were supposed to reduce the risk of financial instability and were, in fact, effective in that regard. Compared with the preceding century, banking was remarkably stable between the end of World War II and the onset of the first oil crisis in 1973: the first important bank failure of the postwar era did not occur until 1974, when West Germany's Bankhaus Herstatt collapsed (Bordo et al. 2001b). The regulatory regimes established by the end of World War II and, indeed, the practice of banking itself, remained largely unchanged during the next quarter-century. According to Steinherr (1992: 1), "In most countries the business of banks did not change significantly from the late 1940s to the 1970s. The products offered, the management and sales techniques applied showed great consistency."

Despite the generally constrained nature of banking, several countries did experience substantial changes in their banking populations. The most dramatic fluctuation came in West Germany, where by 1948 the occupation authorities had split up the country's three largest banks into approximately thirty regional banks. The banks, with the cooperation of the government, reversed this trend during the 1950s (Tilly 1994: 308). The number of West German commercial banks continued to fall, but only slightly, declining by about 1 percent per year between 1957 and 1973. Denmark saw an increase in merger activity during the 1960s. As industrial activity spread to smaller towns and rural areas, local banks could not finance growing industry without exceeding the banking law's 35 percent limit on loans to a single borrower, which encouraged mergers. And in the Netherlands, the rise of foreign industrial competition and the loss of colonial Indonesia led to the merger of the Twentsche Bank and the Nederlandsche Handel-Maatschappij into ABN in 1964, which, in turn, encouraged the merger of Amsterdamsche Bank and Rotterdamsche Bank into AMRO. These two banks merged into ABN-AMRO in 1991 (Van der Werf 1999: 82).

These exceptions aside, banking structure in the industrialized world did not change much during the quarter-century or so following the end of World War II. In the United States, the banking population rarely varied by more than 1 percent per year. The number of Australian trading banks, seventeen in 1950, fell by about one per decade between 1950 and 1980, and in 1980 Australia saw the first new domestically authorized bank since the 1920s. Similarly, the banking populations of England, Canada, Japan, and Sweden remained remarkably stable.

Despite the relatively static nature of the banking business, banking assets grew substantially, both absolutely and relative to overall economic output. Table 10.1 presents data on the ratio of bank assets to gross

TABLE 10.1
Bank Asset-to-GDP Ratios, 1953 and 1973

	1953	1973
Australia	0.58	0.50
Austria	0.31	0.79
Belgium	0.21	0.62
Canada	0.32	0.50
Denmark	0.29	0.34
Finland	0.39	0.48
France	0.22	0.58
Germany	0.37	1.01
Italy	0.07*	1.05
Japan	0.43	1.04
Netherlands	0.04**	0.80
Norway	0.51	0.43
Sweden	0.59	0.65
Switzerland	1.37	1.97
United Kingdom	0.47	1.28
United States	0.47	0.52
Average	0.47	0.78

Source: International Monetary Fund, *International Financial Statistics*.
* Data for 1963
**Data for 1956

domestic product in 1953 and in 1973. This ratio more than doubled in Austria, Belgium, France, Germany, Japan, the Netherlands, and the United Kingdom. On average, the ratio increased from slightly less than one-half to more than three-quarters. And banking was profitable, at least relative to later in the century: although data on banking profitability are notoriously unreliable, those presented in figure 10.1 suggest that banking was more profitable in the 1960s and early 1970s than in the 1980s and 1990s.

Given the "static" and "constrained" nature of banking, how can we account for its remarkable growth and profitability? In part, it can be explained by the historically robust economic growth experienced during the quarter-century following World War II (Temin 1997, 2002). Annual real GDP per capita growth rates, which averaged between 1.5 and 2 percent both between 1870 and World War I and after 1973, were more than double that in the 1950s and 1960s, averaging 3.59 percent during 1950–72 (table 10.2), and more than 4 percent during 1946–72. Still, why would an increase in economic activity lead to a disproportionate growth in banking?

Figure 10.1. Bank profitability, 1964–2003. *Notes*: Norway (1990–92) and Finland (1991–95) excluded due to Nordic banking crisis; some countries represented by all banks, others by all commercial banks, others by large banks, depending upon data availability. *Sources*: 1964–77 (ratio of pre-tax profits to total capital): Revell (1980: 122); 1978–82 (ratio of pre-tax profits to capital plus reserves): Revell (1985a,b); 1982–86 (ratio of pre-tax profits to capital plus reserves): Organization for Economic Cooperation and Development (OECD) *Bank Profitability* (1988); 1979–2003 (ratio of pre-tax income to capital plus reserves): OECD Bank Probability Statistics database, accessed November 2005.

Banking growth can be attributed, in part, to the anticompetitive nature of regulation. Governments restricted entry and capped the interest rates that banks were permitted to pay on their liabilities, which reduced competition. Additionally, because interest rate caps were stable for much of the period, while market rates on bank assets were gradually rising, banks with substantial deposit bases became more profitable. Former Federal Reserve Chairman Arthur Burns (1988: 6) sums up the effects of competition-reducing regulation as follows:

In the later 1950s banks were not chafing under the restraints imposed on them by the regulators. While many of the regulations prevented banks from exploiting opportunities for larger profits—and were in that sense onerous—the regulations that limited competition and that provided a safety net were clearly a boon. The law marked out a protected domain in which banks could profitably operate, and the banks tended to stay in that domain.

Banking growth was also spurred by the increasing internationalization of commerce and the corresponding growth in cross-border finan-

TABLE 10.2
GDP Per Capita Growth Rates (percent)

	1870–1913	1950–72	1973–2001
Australia	1.22	2.39	1.99
Austria	1.48	5.33	2.21
Belgium	1.06	3.54	2.10
Canada	2.39	2.74	1.88
Denmark	1.58	3.28	1.89
Finland	1.49	4.14	2.37
France	1.55	4.14	1.82
Germany	1.63	5.65	1.71
Italy	1.33	5.03	2.24
Netherlands	0.95	3.40	1.91
Norway	1.32	3.25	2.87
Sweden	1.50	3.10	1.61
Switzerland	1.77	3.15	0.80
United Kingdom	1.04	2.14	2.03
United States	1.90	2.58	1.98
Average	1.48	3.59	1.96

Source: Maddison (2001).

cial transactions. This trend was especially strong in Europe, where the European Coal and Steel Community (1952) evolved into the European Economic Community (EEC) (1957) consisting of Belgium, France, Italy, Luxembourg, the Netherlands, and West Germany. During 1950–72, the average ratio of exports plus imports to gross domestic product rose substantially, from about 40 percent to about 50 percent. Growth in cross-border trade was strongest among the EEC members, somewhat less among other European countries, and least among the non-European, non-EEC countries of Australia, Canada, Japan, and the United States.

Despite the impressive growth and stability of banking during the 1950s and 1960s, the strict constraints retarded banking development. In the absence of barriers to entry, economic theory suggests that profitable sectors should attract new firms. However, for the most part, there was little entry into banking. Similarly, the activities in which banks engaged did not change very much, despite obvious complementarities between banking and other financial services, such as insurance, pension fund management, and, for countries without universal banking, investment banking services. Nonetheless, with strong economic growth and government protection against competition, banking companies prospered and pressure from bankers and policy makers to change the status quo was muted.

THE ERA OF DEREGULATION BEGINS

The close of the 1960s marked the beginning of the end of the era of tightly controlled domestic banking and financial markets which had been ushered in by the Great Depression and World War II. Financial liberalization can be traced, at least in part, to the exigencies of inflation-induced high and volatile market interest rates. Important components of liberalization included the gradual elimination of interest rate controls on bank lending and deposit rates, the growth of market-oriented mechanisms for the allocation of capital, such as the development of money markets and auction techniques for the issue of government debt securities, and the elimination of direct controls on bank lending (Bröker 1989: 162–67). Many countries made substantial strides toward liberalizing other aspects of bank regulation as well, including blurring the lines between securities firms, savings banks, and commercial banks, and relaxing rules that restricted branching and foreign entry into domestic banking markets.

Inflation contributed to, and was exacerbated by, the demise of the Bretton Woods system. The agreements were concluded by representatives of forty-four countries in Bretton Woods, New Hampshire in July 1944 and laid the framework for the postwar international monetary system. Among their provisions, the agreements called for the establishment of a system of fixed exchange rates (Bordo and Eichengreen 1993: 465–66). After these collapsed during 1971–73, the U.S. dollar depreciated dramatically, exchange rates became more volatile, and there was an increase in the volume of international capital flows.

During the 1970s the post–World War II period of rapid economic growth in the developed world came to an end. The oil shocks of 1973 and 1979, combined with the 1979 reversal in previously expansionary U.S. monetary policy engineered by Federal Reserve Chairman Paul Volker, contributed to stagflation: recession (i.e., reduction in economic growth) combined with high inflation (figures 10.2, 10.3). Although the oil shocks of the 1970s were dramatic, the sharp increases in inflation and interest rates (reflected in the government bond yields displayed in figure 10.4) followed a period of about twenty years during which these had been gradually rising. In part, the upwards pressure on prices and interest rates resulted from rapid economic growth during the 1950s and 1960s. In the United States, these increases were further stimulated by expanded government spending on Great Society programs and on the Vietnam War.

These macroeconomic events led to important changes—and, in some cases, accelerated changes already under way—in the banking system. Banks had been profitable as long as economic growth was robust

Figure 10.2. Average real GDP growth rate, 1953–96. *Note*: Average of Australia, Austria, Belgium, Canada, Denmark, Finland, France, Germany, Italy, Japan, the Netherlands, Norway, Sweden, Switzerland, the United Kingdom, and the United States. *Source*: Maddison (2001).

Figure 10.3. Average consumer price inflation, 1953–2001. *Note*: Average of Australia, Austria, Belgium, Canada, Denmark, Finland, France, Germany, Italy, Japan, the Netherlands, Norway, Sweden, Switzerland, the United Kingdom, and the United States. *Source*: International Monetary Fund, *International Financial Statistics* online, accessed February 2003.

Figure 10.4. Government bond yields, 1950–2001. *Note*: Average of Australia, Austria, Belgium, Canada, Denmark, Finland, France, Germany, Italy, Japan, the Netherlands, Norway, Sweden, Switzerland, the United Kingdom, and the United States. *Source*: International Monetary Fund, *International Financial Statistics* online, accessed February 2003.

and interest rates were low and stable. Consistently moderate interest rates were important, because banks profited from the spread between government-mandated low deposit rates and higher lending rates. As the spread between these rates increased, however, depositors began to look for alternatives to low-interest-rate bank deposits. The subsequent drain of funds from banks—disintermediation, as famously occurred during the U.S. credit crunches of 1966 and 1969 (Wojnilower 1980)—weakened banks and made them more susceptible to failure.

The new stresses and strains on bank profitability were met, in part, by deregulation. Interest rate caps were loosened, and eventually eliminated, and the scope of permitted bank activities was substantially broadened. Policy makers hoped that by giving banks greater freedom to expand into new, and potentially profitable, product lines, they would be able to meet the macroeconomic challenges of the 1970s and 1980s. An unintended consequence of this newfound freedom was greater instability.

Among the most pervasive regulations limiting competition among banks were those on interest rates. Until the early 1960s, virtually all developed countries imposed some sort of interest rate caps on demand, time, and savings deposits; many also limited the interest rates that could be charged on loans. Interest rate restrictions took on a variety of forms, ranging from formal or informal agreements among banks in Austria, Belgium, Denmark, Germany, Italy, Sweden, Switzerland, and the United

Kingdom, to direct control by the government in France, Japan, and Norway, to government-mandated interest rate ceilings in Australia, Finland, and the United States (Bröker 1989).

As long as market interest rates remained low and stable, interest rate ceilings had little or no impact and their effects were benign. As market interest rates increased, however, interest rate caps generated a substantial gap between market interest rates and those banks were allowed to pay, which had two consequences. First, it encouraged both depositors and banks to find ways of avoiding interest rate ceilings. This resulted in disintermediation, as individual and corporate depositors removed funds from banks in order to find more favorable returns elsewhere, such as in securities markets. It also led to non-price competition among banks, such as offering toasters and other prizes for opening new accounts, establishing new branches in order to make banking more convenient for customers, greater expenditures on advertisements, and bundling services (Baltensperger and Dermine 1987: 85). Second, it exerted pressure on policymakers to loosen interest rate controls.

Alternatives to bank deposits existed in the form of newly developing markets for short-term government and private debt, where yields were not limited by law. By 1960, Treasury bill markets existed in Britain, Canada, and the United States, and commercial paper markets existed in Canada and the United States. A market for bankers' acceptances developed shortly thereafter in Australia. The growth in these markets was dramatic. In the United States, the volume of outstanding commercial and finance company paper grew from about $4 billion in 1960 to over $33 billion by the end of 1970, or by more than 20 percent per year. During the same period, the total amount of outstanding Treasury bills more than doubled, and the share of Treasury bills of the national debt nearly doubled (Board of Governors of the Federal Reserve System 1976: tables 12.11, 13.2). In Canada, the value of Treasury bills outstanding increased by about 30 percent between 1961 and 1967, when interest rate ceilings were abolished, while the amount of outstanding commercial paper doubled during the same period—a 15 percent average annual rate of increase (Leacy 1983: section J).

Yet another alternative available to depositors, developed primarily in Canada and the United States, surfaced around 1960: the negotiable certificate of deposit (CD). Although CDs had been in existence for some time, the negotiable certificate of deposit, also called a "transferrable term note" in Canada (Neufeld 1972: 128–29) was introduced by the Bank of Nova Scotia in 1960 and by the First National City Bank in New York in 1961 (Greenspan 2004). Certificates of deposit, typically in large denominations, were available with a variety of maturities. Interest rates on these instruments in Canada were not subject to the deposit rate ceiling set by the Canadian Bankers Association, although they were not outside the scope of Regulation Q in the United States. In both cases, the introduction of CDs marked the beginning of a more aggressive bank strategy to compete for funds.

In the United States, as Regulation Q ceilings began to bind in the mid-1960s, banks and their customers turned their attention to Eurodollar markets, that is, dollar-denominated deposits and loans issued outside of the United States.[4] Eurodollar deposits originated after World War II when the Soviet Union wanted to hold dollar balances but feared that funds held in the United States would be subject to seizure, as they had been by the Alien Property Custodian during the war (Friedman 1971: 17). Eurodollar markets were attractive to American customers because they were not subject to Federal Reserve interest rate ceilings (Regulation Q) or reserve requirements (Regulation D). The Eurodollar market grew substantially in its early years, from between $4 and $5 billion in 1962 to $216 billion in 1973.[5] Another avenue open to banks in the United States was repurchase agreements, whereby they sold securities (i.e., borrowed funds) which were subsequently repurchased (i.e., repaid with interest). These transactions were considered by law to be securities transactions rather than loans and were therefore not subject to interest rate ceilings. Repurchase agreements amounted to about $4 billion in 1969, the first year for which data exist, and reached $50 billion ten years later (Federal Reserve Statistical Release H6, table 4).

Outside North America, a variety of wholesale, typically interbank markets, in which rates were not subject to the same stringent control as bank borrowing and lending rates, took off in the 1960s and 1970s. Such markets appeared in Sweden (wholesale time deposits) in 1968, Denmark (interbank money market) in 1970, Japan (bill discount market) in 1971, and Finland (call and wholesale money markets) in 1975 (Bröker 1989: 162–66).

In addition to giving bankers and their customers an incentive to discover ways and means of avoiding the strictures of interest rate regulation, the increase in market interest rates led policy makers to reconsider and, eventually, eliminate interest rate controls. Public and private inquiries in Australia, Canada, and the United States took up the question of financial sector liberalization and concluded that it was in the national

---

[4]In fact, Euromarkets came to mean any deposits or loans issued in a currency other than that of the country in which it was issued.

[5]Altman (1961: 328) argues that, ". . . the size of the Euro-dollar market can be nothing but a guess—perhaps a very wild guess." Nonetheless, in subsequent work (1963: 89) he estimates the world total at $4–5 billion. Data from 1973 come from United States President (1975: 215).

interest to move toward a system of deregulated interest rates.[6] Interest rate deregulation came first to Canada and Germany (1967), followed by the Netherlands (1980), United Kingdom (1981), Denmark (1982), Italy (1983), Australia, Norway, Sweden (1985), Finland (1986), and Japan (1994) (OECD 2000: 173, Williamson and Maher 1998).

Despite the impression of precision in the dating of interest rate liberalization given above, in fact, the timing is approximate at best. Interest rate ceilings were eliminated by a variety of methods and at varying speeds in different countries. Some countries (e.g., Canada, Germany) liberalized quite rapidly; in others (e.g., Denmark, Japan) the process was much slower. In some countries, ceilings were first eased on large deposits (e.g., Belgium, Germany, and the United States); in others liberalization was enacted by type or maturity of deposit (e.g., Australia, France, and Germany). A brief review of the history of interest rate regulation and deregulation in the United States sets the stage for the discussion on crises and rescues, mergers, and regulation that follows.

The Regulation Q ceiling on time and savings deposit rates was initially set at 3 percent in November 1933 on all types of savings and time deposits, and was subsequently lowered to 2.5 percent in February 1935. Rates on time deposits of less than ninety days and of from ninety to 179 days were further lowered to 1 and 2 percent in January 1936. These ceilings were not changed for the next twenty years. With the gradual rise of market interest rates in the 1950s and 1960s, Regulation Q ceilings were raised on five separate occasions during the subsequent eight years.[7] Savings deposit ceilings were raised from 2.5 percent to 4 percent, while time deposits of various maturities were raised to 5.5 percent in 1965 (Winningham and Hagan 1980).

Starting in 1966, the schedule of interest rate ceilings became more complex, differentiated by size and maturity of deposit, and by type of institution. In 1966, the ceiling on small certificates of deposit (those of less than $100,000) was lowered by 0.5 percent, leaving the maximum rate on large CDs unchanged.[8] In 1968, different ceilings were set

---

[6]These included the Australian Financial System Inquiry (Campbell Committee) in 1981, the Australian Review Group (Martin Committee) in 1984, the Royal Commission on Banking and Finance (Porter Commission) in Canada in 1964, and the Commission on Financial Structure and Regulation (Hunt Commission) in the United States in 1971.

[7]January 1, 1957; January 1, 1962; July 17, 1962; July 17, 1963; November 24, 1964; and December 6, 1965.

[8]Mayer (1982). The ceiling on large CDs with maturities of less than ninety days was eliminated in 1970; the ceiling on other large CDs was eliminated in 1973. Winningham and Hagan (1980: 8) argue that the goal of this policy change was to differentiate consumer from money market funds.

for large CDs with different maturities (longer maturities were allowed to pay higher rates); maturity-linked ceilings were applied to small CDs in 1970. In 1966, the authorities began to differentiate between different types of financial institutions. Because savings and loan association (S&L) assets consisted primarily of fixed-rate long-term loans, which were funded with relatively liquid deposit liabilities, these institutions were even more vulnerable to increases in short-term interest rates than commercial banks. Because of this threat, interest rate ceilings were adjusted to allow S&Ls to pay slightly higher deposit rates than commercial banks and give them a slight advantage in competing for funds.

Both the private Commission on Money and Credit (1961) and the President's Commission on Financial Structure and Regulation (1972) had recommended that interest rate controls be phased out (Aliber 1972, Commission on Financial Structure and Regulation 1972). The increases in interest rate ceilings starting in the 1950s can be seen as constituting the beginnings of interest rate liberalization in the US. To be sure, this liberalization came with many exceptions, each with its own particular political economy or economic reason. Nonetheless, the movement toward relatively unfettered interest rates was discernable. The Depository Institutions Deregulation and Monetary Control Act of 1980 mandated the phase-out of interest rate ceilings. The last remaining interest rate ceiling was eliminated in 1986.

CRISES AND RESCUES

Deregulation was a liberating experience for banks, allowing them to broaden the range of activities in which they engaged, to increase flexibility in setting interest rates, and to compete for new and different types of business. The growth in international transactions due to the collapse of the Bretton Woods system and the improvement in the technology for making these transactions also provided outlets for bank expansion. This liberation came at a cost, however: banking, which had been constrained but safe, became freer but more vulnerable to crisis.

The industrialized world's banks became much more vulnerable after 1973. Bordo et al. (2001) look at the incidence, duration, and severity of banking and currency crises during 1880–1997. They find that the probability of a banking crisis occurring was similar during 1880–1913 and 1973–97, approximately double this rate during the turbulent interwar period of 1919–39, and essentially zero during 1945–71.

Although the banking crises of the last quarter of the twentieth century were like their predecessors, caused mainly by boom-bust cycles, shocks to confidence, and structural weakness, two additional powerful and complementary factors emerged. The collapse of the Bretton Woods system led to enhanced opportunities for engaging in high-risk international transactions, and improvements in technology allowed larger risks to be undertaken more quickly and easily than ever before. Also, the roll-back of Depression-era regulations gave banks more freedom to engage in other risky transactions.

The stories of two important bank failures in 1974, Bankhaus I.D. Herstatt in Germany and Franklin National Bank in the United States, il-lustrate the new sources of risk in the post-1973 environment. These were the first substantial bank failures of the post–World War II era, although they were soon overshadowed by more severe banking difficulties.

Herstatt and Franklin National

Among the first banking disruptions of the post–Bretton Woods era was the failure of a Cologne private bank, Bankhaus I.D. Herstatt, which collapsed on June 24, 1974. Herstatt lost an estimated US$200 million in currency trading prior to the collapse—a substantial sum, considering that the bank's total assets had been estimated at $800 million just six months prior to its failure. Herstatt was closed by West German authori-ties around 3:30 pm local time, after foreign counterparties had made substantial irrevocable Deutsche mark payments to Herstatt but before those counterparties had received dollars in return. This was particu-larly problematic for U.S. banks, where the business day was not yet half over when Herstatt was closed (Galati 2002). The failure reverberated throughout the world banking system; injured counterparties included Seattle National Bank (which had been involved in a $22.5 million trans-action with Herstatt), Hill Samuel of London ($21.5 million), and Mor-gan Guarantee Trust Company ($13 million). The failure of Herstatt demonstrated the dangers inherent in the new world of volatile exchange rates and capital flows combined with improved technology for moving large sums of money quickly.[9]

On the same day it reported the failure of Herstatt, the *New York Times* noted that, "In a somewhat similar situation, the Franklin National Bank of New York had foreign exchange losses of $45.8 million in the first five months of 1974." By October 8, 1974, Franklin had closed—at the time, the largest bank failure in American history (Kotsopoulos 1981: 322).

---

[9]It also demonstrated the risk inherent in many financial transactions when the exchange of securities or funds is not simultaneous. This is generally known as "settlement risk," or, in foreign exchange transactions, as "Herstatt risk." Although Herstatt risk was frequently discussed by policy makers, a widely-used continuous linked settlement institution was not established until 2002.

International expansion constituted an important, but not the only, source of Franklin's problems.[10]

Located on Long Island, New York, Franklin Square National Bank was chartered in 1926.[11] The bank expanded rapidly during the 1950s, primarily through mergers and acquisitions: between 1950 and 1958, Franklin merged with or acquired thirteen other banks in Nassau County, where it was headquartered. Franklin's prosperity was aided by robust economic growth on Long Island during the 1950s and also because New York State banking law prohibited banks from branching across county lines, protecting Franklin from competition from banks in neighboring New York City. A 1960 law allowed banks to operate in contiguous counties and Franklin soon opened an office in New York City. Subsequent growth brought offices in the Bahamas and London, where Franklin entered the Eurodollar market, although it never became a major player (Spero 1980: 41). Franklin's expansion into the international arena mirrored the increasing trend of internationalization exhibited by U.S. banks generally: in 1965, thirteen U.S. banks had 211 overseas branches with $9.1 billion in assets; by 1975, 126 U.S. banks had 762 foreign branches with $145.3 billion in assets (Spero 1980: 1). In addition to the incentives for overseas expansion generated by Regulations D and Q, several government programs aimed at curbing the growing U.S. balance of payments deficit by limiting credit extended by American banks to foreign borrowers also encouraged the opening of overseas branches, since such branches were exempt from the restrictions on U.S. banks.[12]

The failures of Herstatt and Franklin National highlight several sources of banking instability in the post–Bretton Woods world. Volatile exchange rates and capital flows, the latter supported by improved technology for moving money quickly, led to greater opportunities for profit—and potential for risk-taking. In addition, overseas expansion provided a straightforward way of avoiding domestic banking regulation. In the case of Franklin National, regulatory avoidance through offshore operations dovetailed with a liberalization of domestic regulation, both of which allowed Franklin to grow rapidly and to expand into more risky endeavors. The loosening of regulatory constraints, combined with the

[10]Michele Sidona, owner of a controlling interest in Franklin, was subsequently convicted for fraud in connection with his dealings with Franklin. He was later murdered in an Italian prison while serving a sentence for murder.

[11]The bank's name was changed to Franklin National in August 1949, to Franklin National Bank of Long Island in October 1957, and back to Franklin National Bank in October 1962. Kotsopoulos (1981: 323).

[12]These included the Voluntary Foreign Credit Restraint Program, the Foreign Direct Investment Program, and the Interest Equalization Tax. Spero (1980: 42ff.).

macroeconomic fluctuations of the time, led to the downfall of Franklin, as well as other banks (Fabozzi 1981).

The U.S. Savings and Loan Crisis

Because U.S. banking problems during the 1980s and early 1990s were intertwined with those of savings and loan associations (S&Ls, also known as thrifts), a short digression on the thrift industry in the United States is in order. The first S&L was established in the Philadelphia area in 1831. Similar institutions were established in New York (1836) and South Carolina (1843), and soon spread to the rest of the country. Although the organization of these early associations differed in a number of ways, they shared an underlying principle: depositors pooled their savings and, as money accumulated, loans were made so that individuals could build, buy, or refurbish a house (Bodfish 1931). During the next century S&Ls evolved into institutions that resembled banks, in the sense that they both made loans and took deposits that could be withdrawn on relatively short notice. However, S&Ls differed from banks in that their assets consisted primarily of fixed-rate long-term mortgage loans.[13]

If the inauguration of tighter monetary policy in October 1979 had serious consequences for banks, the results for S&Ls were catastrophic. Because of the term mismatch—that is, long-term assets funded with short-term liabilities—the increase in market rates put S&Ls in an interest rate squeeze. Higher market interest rates encouraged thrift depositors to withdraw their funds, despite the slightly higher Regulation Q ceilings on S&L deposits than on commercial banks deposits. Because S&L loan portfolios consisted of relatively low-yielding mortgages, even if they had been free to pay higher deposit interest rates, to do so would have been too costly. And, had a market for their loan portfolios existed, the high prevailing market interest rates meant that these low fixed-interest rate loans could only have been sold for a substantial loss.

The response to this squeeze by both state and federal governments was, for the most part, to broaden the powers of savings and loans, in the hope that S&Ls could earn their way out of trouble. The Depository Institutions Deregulation and Monetary Control Act of 1980 and the Garn-St. Germain Depository Institutions Act of 1982 allowed S&Ls to issue demand and money market deposit accounts, to make personal and credit card loans, as well as loans for the acquisition and development of real estate. Real estate development partnerships—and loans to

---

[13]Federally chartered S&Ls were not granted the right to issue adjustable rate mortgages until 1979, although some state-chartered S&Ls did make such loans earlier.

them—were made more desirable by tax changes adopted in 1981, which increased the investment credit and doubled the allowed depreciation on real estate (Starbuck and Pant 1997, FDIC 1997: 10). National bank powers were also liberalized, allowing banks to undertake real estate lending and relaxing limits on the amount that could be loaned to one borrower. All of these changes encouraged the rapid expansion of banks and S&Ls into new—and not necessarily safe—areas of lending. This expansion of lending contributed to real estate booms and busts in various parts of the country.

The deposit insurance system also contributed to banking difficulties. Deposit insurance for commercial banks had been established in 1933 with the creation of the Federal Deposit Insurance Corporation (FDIC) and for S&Ls in 1934 with the creation of the Federal Savings and Loan Insurance Corporation (FSLIC). Unlike most types of private insurance, federal deposit insurance did not distinguish between institutions that engaged in especially risky activities and those that did not: all paid the same premium per dollar of deposit. The ensuing moral hazard encouraged more risk-taking on the part of banks and thrifts. Moral hazard effects were enhanced by an increase in the deposit insurance limit to $100,000 from $40,000 in 1980 and by a federal hiring freeze in the late 1970s and early 1980s, which led to a decline of about 20 percent in the number of federal bank examinations and removed another potential constraint on greater risk-taking (FDIC 1997: 57).

Moral hazard-induced problems were also exacerbated by technological innovations. Because deposits were insured, banks and S&Ls in need of funds could raise virtually unlimited sums by offering above-market interest rates on insured certificates of deposit. The improved technology of money transfer made it possible for a national market in brokered deposits to develop, removing the need for banks and S&Ls to raise funds locally. These innovations encouraged troubled institutions to raise additional funds and to employ them in ever-riskier activities in, what Barth, Bartholomew, and Labich (1989: 25) aptly term "gambling for resurrection."

The confluence of deregulation, less frequent bank examination, fixed-rate deposit insurance, and developing technology contributed to a series of regional and sectoral fluctuations, which further weakened banks. The energy sector was particularly hard-hit. In the aftermath of the Yom Kippur war and resulting OPEC embargo, oil prices rose dramatically in the 1970s: the price of Saudi Arabia light rose from about $2 per barrel in 1973 to nearly $10 in 1974 and from $13 in 1979 to over $30 by 1981. The rise in oil prices led to rapid economic growth, including a boom in real estate values and in banking, in oil-rich Texas, Oklahoma, Louisiana, New Mexico, and Arkansas. By 1987, the price of oil had fallen to about half of its 1981 level and banks in these areas were particularly hard hit. Nearly three-quarters of all bank failures in the United States during 1987–89 took place in the southwest; in Texas, where the crisis was particularly severe, nine of the ten largest bank holding companies failed. Similar regional and sectoral boom-bust cycles—with similar consequences for banks—occurred in agriculture, largely in the Midwest and south central states, in the mid-1980s and in technology, centered in the northeast, in the early 1990s.

The surge in bank and thrift failures took a toll on both FDIC and FSLIC funds. The 1987 Competitive Equality Banking Act chartered a new entity (the Financing Corporation) to raise money to recapitalize the FSLIC. By 1988, the FSLIC was reported to be $75 billion in the red; the 1989 Financial Institutions Reform, Recovery, and Enforcement Act (FIRREA) abolished it and created a new S&L deposit insurance fund, the Savings Association Insurance Fund (SAIF), administered by the FDIC, and established the taxpayer-funded Resolution Trust Corporation (RTC), also initially administered by the FDIC.[14]

The FDIC, FSLIC, and RTC employed a variety of methods to deal with insolvent banks and S&Ls, with a key objective being getting the assets off their books as rapidly as possible (Klingebiel 2000). The most popular technique was a purchase and assumption (P&A) transaction, in which a healthy financial institution purchased some or all of a troubled institution's assets and assumed responsibility for all insured deposits, as well as some other liabilities. If a healthy institution could not be found for a P&A, the insurance agency might just pay off depositors ("straight deposit payoff") and take on the assets itself for sale as soon as practical. In the case of other institutions, a notable example being Continental Illinois in 1984, the FDIC supplied "open bank assistance," providing funds for the bank to remain open as a going concern.

One complaint lodged against deposit insurers was in their use of "regulatory forbearance," that is, allowing insolvent institutions that did not meet established safety and soundness standards to remain open, possibly with open bank assistance. It was argued by some that in their desire to maintain overall banking system stability, regulators favored large institutions such as Continental Illinois, allowing the too-big-to-fail criterion to overwhelm other considerations, or otherwise misused forbearance. In response, the Federal Deposit Insurance Corporation Improvement Act of 1991 imposed prompt corrective action provisions, which were aimed at reducing the discretion of regulators to use forbearance.

[14]The FDIC's financial situation was far better than that of the FSLIC and hence was a natural choice to take over deposit insurance for S&Ls as well as to take the lead in the resolution process. FIRREA also abolished the Federal Home Loan Bank Board, which had been the thrift industry supervisor and replaced it with a new bureau within the Treasury, the Office of Thrift Supervision.

The S&L crisis was, at the time, the most costly faced by the United States since the Great Depression. By the time it was over, the number of federally insured banks had declined by more than one quarter and the number of insured S&Ls by about a half. During 1980–94, the FSLIC and RTC managed the resolution of nearly 1,300 S&Ls with over $620 billion in assets at a cost of more than $160 billion; during the same period, the FDIC managed the resolution of nearly 3,000 banks with assets of more than $900 billion at a cost of almost $200 billion (FDIC 1997, Curry and Shibut 2000).

The Nordic Crises

Like the savings and loan crisis in the United States, the Nordic banking crises of 1987–94, which centered on Finland, Norway, and Sweden, resulted from a series of boom-bust cycles, which were amplified by banking deregulation.[15] From the end of World War II until the late 1970s, the Nordic countries tightly regulated their banking, credit, capital, and foreign exchange markets. Although these countries were industrially advanced, their stock and bond markets were not well developed and banks were the primary intermediators. Banks, however, were tightly constrained by regulations designed to channel credit to favored sectors of the economy. For example, Swedish financial institutions were subject to lending ceilings, which limited the rate of growth of lending to low priority sectors (e.g., household loans, except for those to purchase newly constructed homes), and were required to hold a certain percentage (over 50 percent in 1980) of their assets in bonds issued by the government and mortgage institutions. In Norway, a number of government lending institutions were responsible for allocating funds to the housing, manufacturing, and agriculture and fisheries sectors (Steigum 2004: 35). Banks in all three countries were subject to interest rate ceilings and in Finland the central bank set ceilings on each bank's average and top lending rates (Englund and Vihriälä 2003: 4–5).

Restrictions on credit allocation led to unfulfilled demands for funds in many sectors. Excess demand was exacerbated by high inflation, low interest rate ceilings, and the generous tax treatment afforded to interest payments, which was particularly important in light of the high tax rates in the Nordic countries. After adjusting for taxes and inflation (i.e., the

---

[15]This section draws on descriptions of the Nordic banking crises by Koskenkylä (1994), Nyberg and Vihriälä (1994), Drees and Pazarbaştioğlu (1995), Englund (1999), Knutsen (2002), Englund and Vihriälä (2003), Moe, Solheim, and Vale (2004), Jonung, Kiander, and Vartia (2006), and Jonung (2008).

real after-tax interest rate), the interest rate on loans was negative in all three countries during the 1970s and during some or all of the 1980s. In Norway, the real after-tax interest rate on mortgage loans became positive during 1982–83 (Steigum 2004: 36); in Finland, the real after-tax rate on ten-year loans turned positive in 1984; in Sweden, the real after-tax rate on five-year loans became positive around 1990 (Englund and Vihriälä 2003: 5).

All three countries began to loosen financial restrictions in the 1980s. Norway was the first to make substantial progress in deregulation, dismantling many credit regulations by 1984–85, although some were briefly reintroduced after a decline in oil prices and revenues in 1986 (Steigum 2004: 35–36). Sweden made strides toward deregulation by 1985 and Finland did so by 1988. Deregulation consisted of removing interest rate ceilings on loans and deposits, permitting the development of CD, bond, and money markets, easing foreign exchange controls and allowing foreign banks to operate domestically, and removing quantitative controls on bank lending.

At the same time that regulations were being eased, all three countries reorganized their supervisory systems. In Norway, the Inspectorate of Banks shifted from an on-site to a document-oriented approach to supervision: the number of on-site inspections fell from fifty-seven in 1980, to eight in 1985, to one in 1986, and two in 1987 (by 1989, the number had increased to forty-four). Norway's Banking Inspectorate was merged with insurance and securities regulators to form a unified Financial Supervisory Authority (Kredittilsynet) in 1986, the first industrialized country to create a unified financial supervisor. In Sweden, the bank, savings bank, and insurance regulators were unified into the Financial Supervisory Authority (Finansinspektionen) in 1991; in Finland, a unified authority, excluding the insurance industry, was created in 1993 (Finanssivalvonta). The timing of the switch in the organization of supervision was unfortunate. Englund and Vihriälä (2003: 12) argue that supervision in Finland and Sweden was too passive and that the reorganization, ". . . may have contributed to diverting the attention of the supervisors away from the emerging systemic crisis to issues of internal organization."

The response to deregulation was dramatic. Household and corporate indebtedness grew substantially and bank lending expanded rapidly following deregulation through the early 1990s: the ratio of bank loans to gross domestic product more than doubled in Norway (to 65 percent from slightly over 30 percent), and rose by about 150 percent in Sweden and Finland (Drees and Pazarbaştioğlu 1995: 13). Aggressive lending policies increased the extension of credit to the real estate, construction, and services sectors, and the prices of stocks and real estate rose dramatically: real estate prices doubled over the second half of the 1980s in all three countries, while stock prices more than tripled in Sweden and more than quadrupled in Finland.

The bubbles in real estate and other assets were generated, in part, by the expansion in bank lending and by accommodating fiscal and monetary policies (Gerlach 1997: 236); however, other factors contributed to the boom-bust scenario among the Nordics. Like the American southwest, Norway was adversely affected by the boom-bust in energy prices, particularly following the 1986 decline in oil prices. The oil price collapse may have been partially responsible for Norway's shorter and less severe crisis, relative to those in Finland and Sweden, since the decline in oil prices brought about a premature end to the lending boom in Norway (Sandal 2004: 84). An increase in paper and pulp prices contributed to longer expansions in Finland and Sweden, which were hurt by declines in these prices later in the 1980s, as well as by reduced trade with the former Soviet Union.

In contrast to the turbulence in Finland, Norway, and Sweden, the banking situation in Denmark was calm due to a variety of macroeconomic and structural factors. On the macroeconomic side, Denmark experienced more moderate credit growth during the business cycle upswing of the 1980s than the other Nordic countries and implemented a sounder fiscal policy. On the structural side, Denmark's situation was helped by smoother—and earlier—banking deregulation, more prompt recognition of loan losses, and a substantial number of mergers. The consolidation of the 1960s may also have helped in this regard (Gerlach 1997, Hagberg and Jonung 2002, Vastrup 2009).

By the time the U.S. banking crisis emerged around 1980, virtually all affected banks and S&Ls were covered by federal deposit insurance. The situation in the Nordic countries was different: Sweden had no deposit insurance system prior to 1996, while Norway and, to a lesser extent, Finland, had private industry-run deposit guarantee funds. As the crises developed, it soon became clear that these funds had insufficient resources. Governments soon stepped in.

In Norway, the crisis began in 1988 when several smaller banks and savings banks found themselves in distress. The Commercial Banks' Guarantee Fund and the Savings Banks' Guarantee Fund provided money to facilitate mergers of these ailing banks with stronger institutions; however, by the winter of 1990–91 these funds were essentially depleted (Drees and Pazarbaştioğlu 1995: 27, Sandal 2004: 87–88). Early in 1991, the government established the Government Bank Insurance Fund (GBIF), which provided assistance via loans to the private funds. Later on, when the scale of the required rescue operation became clear, the GBIF began to provide capital directly to banks. By the autumn of 1991, the three largest Norwegian banks, Fokus Bank, Christiana Bank, and Den norske

Bank, representing more than half of all Norwegian bank assets, were in serious trouble. The GBIF effectively took over these three banks, writing down the existing capital to zero, and infusing them with new funds. In 1995, all the shares of Fokus Bank were sold by the government, and the bank was subsequently purchased by Danske Bank of Denmark. Christiana Bank was also sold, although the government retained one-third ownership for several years. The bank subsequently became part of Finland-based Nordea. Shares in Den norske Bank were also sold and the bank merged with the Union Bank of Norway in 2003–4, although here, too, the government retained one-third of the new bank, this time in an effort to insure that it remained headquartered in Norway.

The Finnish banking crisis began in September 1991 with the failure of Skopbank, a major commercial bank that had acted as a central bank for Finnish savings banks. Skopbank, which had been the subject of heightened interest by bank supervisors since the fall of 1989, was restructured with additional capital provided by a group of savings banks in the fall of 1990, and was finally taken over by the Bank of Finland in the fall of 1991. The cost of the Skopbank operation was FIM 15 billion (FIM 4 billion of which was not recovered), or about 3 percent of GDP. Skopbank's bad assets were transferred to two new asset management companies owned and capitalized by the Bank of Finland, and the shares of Skopbank were subsequently sold to the newly created Government Guarantee Fund (GGF). Existing shareholders were bought out for a nominal sum (Sandal 2004: 85–86), in contrast to Norwegian shareholders, who had received nothing. The GGF subsequently took an active role in reorganizing troubled banks and savings banks.

In order to support other troubled banks, the government offered a capital infusion by agreeing to purchase preferred shares in the amount of FIM 8 billion, or about 1.6 percent of GDP, which could be converted into ordinary voting stock if certain conditions were violated. Virtually all banks applied for, and received, a share of this open-bank assistance. In August 1992 the government announced that the stability of the Finnish banking system would be secured under all circumstances, and in January 1993 Parliament issued a blanket creditor guarantee, which was maintained until December 1998.

In Sweden, the vast majority of direct government support was given to the third and fourth largest banks, Nordbanken and Gota Bank. In the autumn of 1991 Nordbanken reported heavy losses. The state already owned more than two-thirds of the equity of this bank, and Parliament authorized the use of Kr. 20 billion, or 1.3 percent of GDP, for restructuring. The assets were transferred to a separate asset management company (Securum), which was funded by the state. Private shareholders were eventually bought out, and therefore suffered minimal loss. In

April 1992 Gota Bank failed. Gota's bad assets were transferred to an asset management company (Retriva) and the rest of the bank was sold to the state-owned Nordbanken and a new agency, the Bankstödsnämnden, created to manage the government's support of Nordbanken and Gota Bank.[16] As in Finland, Sweden's government issued a blanket creditor guarantee in 1992, which remained in force until 1996.

Like the U.S. S&L crisis, the Nordic crises of the late 1980s and early 1990s were the most severe financial crises experienced by Finland, Norway, and Sweden since the interwar period. Similarly, like the S&L crisis, the Nordic crises were generated by boom-bust cycles combined with ill-timed regulatory changes. One of the distinguishing characteristics of the extreme measures adopted was the blanket—and long-lived—creditor guarantees in Finland and Sweden: the Swedish guarantee was extended until 1996, while the Finnish guarantee was extended until 1998, in both cases well beyond the end of the emergency.[17] These, like federal deposit insurance in the United States, dramatically reduced the risk of further panic withdrawals, but at the risk of generating additional moral hazard. Norway did not give such a blanket guarantee, which may have lessened the severity of the crisis there (Bergo 2003).

Japan's "Lost Decade"

Like those of the Nordic countries and the United States, the Japanese financial system had been severely constrained in the period from the end of World War II until the mid-1970s.[18] Stock and bond markets had been kept "deliberately underdeveloped" and foreign securities markets were off-limits, forcing both borrowers and lenders to rely on the domestic banking system. The banking system was used as an instrument of government policy to channel domestic savings towards investment in export-oriented industries, which contributed to Japan's robust growth during the 1950s and 1960s. Interest rates were fixed and the spreads between borrowing and lending rates were kept high, contributing to bank stability and profitability. The banking system operated under what was

[16]Klingebiel (2000) argues that Securum and Retriva were successful in both managing their assets and selling them within a relatively short period of time.

[17]Although no intervention was necessary in Denmark, it is clear that the government would have intervened if necessary: in 1992, the Danmarks Nationalbank announced that it stood ready to support the country's second largest bank with liquidity, following rumors of bankruptcy. Vastrup (2006).

[18]This section draws on Amyx (2004), Caballero, Hoshi, and Kashyap (2008), Cargill (2000), Cargill, Hutchison, and Ito (2000), Hartcher (1998), Hoshi (2001, 2006), Hoshi and Kashyap (2000, 2001), Hoshi and Patrick (2000), Packer (2000), Patrick (1999), Kawai (2003), and Vogel (1996).

known as the "convoy system," in which all banks were allowed to grow at approximately the same speed, and none was allowed to fail. Banks that found themselves in trouble were typically merged—often with the assistance and at the behest of government authorities—with healthier institutions (Teranishi 1994: 32, Hoshi 2002: 159ff.).

A distinguishing characteristic of the Japanese banking system was the relationship between the Ministry of Finance (MoF) and the banking sector, which Amyx (2004: 257) characterizes as: ". . . personal . . . informal . . . opaque . . ." Banks maintained a personal relationship with the Ministry of Finance through their *mofutan* (variously translated as "MoF liaison" or "MoF handler"), whose job it was to establish a rapport with a relatively junior civil servant at the Ministry, and by hiring MoF officials upon their retirement. Although Japanese law established detailed banking regulations, officials within the Ministry of Finance had great latitude to direct banks though "administrative guidance." That is, Ministry officials could "suggest" that a bank pursue a particular course of action, including making business decisions that might not have been in the firm's interest. Although these suggestions did not have the force of law, failure to follow them had subtle and not-so-subtle consequences (Vogel 1996: 171).

The tight-knit relationship between the banks and the Ministry complicated a system that was already characterized by weak oversight and a lack of transparency. Due to limited resources, the MoF's Banking Bureau conducted few bank examinations, which tended to focus on banks' compliance with administrative rules rather than on the composition of bank assets and liabilities, which were more germane to bank solvency. Solvency data were often not gathered during examinations, but provided to the Ministry by the banks themselves. Such figures were later found to be incomplete and inadequate.

Deregulation began in the mid-1970s, starting with the bond market. Prior to 1975, the bond market was quite small and dominated by banks and securities firms through the *kisaikai*, or bond committee. The kisaikai determined whether a firm would be allowed to issue bonds and, if so, in what quantities and to what extent the issue needed to be collateralized.[19] Starting in 1975, the kisaikai adopted a policy of approving all bond issues and amounts and, subsequently, unsecured bonds were permitted. Other changes in the 1970s and 1980s liberalized money, debt, equity, and foreign exchange markets, each of which had been under formal or

[19]All bonds had to be collateralized at this time. Since only banks could manage collateral, they were able to collect fees from firms borrowing on securities markets. Hoshi and Kashyap (2001: 102), Ramseyer (1994: 238).

informal control.[20] The motivation for liberalization was in part fiscal: the oil shock-induced fiscal deficits of the 1970s heightened the government's desire to sell more bonds (Hoshi and Patrick 2000: 9).

The liberalization of the bond market opened up alternative funding sources for corporations; deregulation aimed at expanding the options of depositors was slower to develop. Banks that still had substantial deposit bases began to lose their large corporate customers to the bond market. This led banks to expand their lending—typically collateralized by real estate—to small- and medium-sized businesses, which could not as easily or cheaply borrow money in the bond market as large firms. The resulting boom in real estate prices—which rose spectacularly during the closing years of the 1980s—was further supported by expansionary monetary policy undertaken by the Bank of Japan. The boom in land and stock prices collapsed in the early 1990s, with stock prices falling by 60 percent from their 1989 peak within three years and land prices falling by roughly 50 percent from their 1992 peak within the next ten years (Caballero, Hoshi, and Kashyap 2008: 1493). The sharp decline in land prices made it difficult for real estate and construction firms to service their debts, leaving banks with substantial portfolios of bad loans, which threatened to bring down the entire banking system.

One of the first signs of the crisis came with the downfall of a number of mortgage lending institutions, or *jūsen*. These institutions were first set up in the early 1970s by large commercial banks as a way to tap into the home mortgage market; loans to individuals constituted 95 percent of jūsen loans in 1980. The loss of corporate customers brought about by bond market liberalization led commercial banks to make inroads into the home mortgage market and the jūsen began entering other areas, particularly corporate real estate lending. By 1990, more than three-quarters of jūsen loans were to corporations and their loan portfolios had increased to four times their 1980 levels. It took three rescue attempts and four years before the jūsen crisis was resolved. Approximately ¥6.41 trillion of assets were written off, with ¥672 billion of public funds (1.3 percent of GDP) used in the resolution (Hoshi and Kashyap 2001: 269–71). Banking conditions continued to deteriorate as the 1990s progressed.

Although the MoF was well aware of the seriousness of the banks' problems, it used all the tools in its arsenal—from changing accounting rules and permitting (even encouraging) shady accounting practices, to intervening in the stock market, to engineering lower interest rates—to

---

[20]The trend towards liberalization came to a climax with the announcement in 1996 of "Big Bang," a relatively complete liberalization of the Japanese financial system, which was to be completed by 2001.

keep news about the banking problems under wraps in hopes that re-bounding real estate and stock markets would come to the rescue. The *Economist* (June 10, 1995: 96) summarized the Ministry's strategy:

> The mandarins of Japan's Ministry of Finance used to pride themselves on artful cover-ups. They concealed weakness in the stockmarket by propping up security prices. They threw a veil over the weakness of the banking system by discouraging the disclosure of bad loans. By these ploys the ministry hoped to conceal the true awfulness of the troubles plaguing Japan's financial system after the popping of the financial bubble in 1990. Time and economic recovery would, it thought, heal all. But half a decade after the bubble burst the economy has yet to recover, the banks' woes are getting worse, and the cover-up increasingly hard to sustain.

Banks themselves had little incentive—and were certainly not pressured by the MoF—to acknowledge problem loans, since by doing so they would be forced to recognize the need to raise additional capital. Instead of pressing troubled borrowers for repayment or cutting off the flow of loans, banks often continued to lend to these firms, in effect throwing good money after bad, in order to forestall the day of reckoning. These "living dead," or "zombie," firms had little or no hope of recovery but nonetheless avoided failure—at least temporarily—due to continued bank support, further worsening the eventual fallout from the crisis (Caballero, Hoshi, and Kashyap 2008).

The government undertook a number of cosmetic fixes during the first half of the decade, none of which made fundamental changes to the financial system or imposed any penalties upon bankers, bank shareholders, or uninsured depositors.[21] For example, with the erosion in bank capital, the MoF "encouraged" insurance companies—which the Ministry also regulated—to take on bank capital, bolstering bank capital ratios at the expense of the insurance industry.

By the second half of the decade it had become obvious that propping up unsound banks was not a viable strategy. On November 18, 1996, Federal Reserve chairman Alan Greenspan told the Japanese Federation of Bankers, "Our goal as supervisors should not be to prevent all bank failures, but to maintain sufficient prudential standards so that banking

---

[21]Resources from the Deposit Insurance Corporation were first employed in 1991. A bank-organized Credit Cooperative Purchasing Company (CCPC) was founded in 1992 for the purpose of purchasing real estate held by banks as collateral on non-performing loans. The CCPC was not especially effective. Banks were fearful of drawing attention to their bad loans; since CCPC could only purchase loans that were offered by banks, it acquired a limited number of loans. Packer (2000).

problems which do occur do not become widespread."[22] Three days later Hanwa Bank was allowed to fail; however, the Ministry of Finance continued to engineer "convoy" operations, such as the 1997 restructuring of Nippon Credit Bank, which, along with Long Term Credit Bank, was nationalized the following year.

The Asian financial crisis, which had erupted in the summer of 1997 in Thailand, Malaysia, and Indonesia, reached Japan in November, when Sanyo Securities, Hokkaido Takushoku Bank, Yamaichi Securities, and Tokyo City Bank failed. The Asian crisis threw a spotlight on the precarious position of Japanese banks, which was reflected in the emergence of a "Japan premium," or higher interest rate charged to Japanese banks than to European and U.S. banks because of their greater perceived risk of failure.

By March 1998, the Diet enacted the Financial Function Stabilization Act, which authorized the Bank of Japan and Deposit Insurance Corporation to provide as much as ¥30 trillion (approximately 6.25 percent of GDP) to protect depositors (¥17 trillion) and to inject capital into "undercapitalized, but presumably healthy" banks (¥13 trillion). Although a much larger expenditure was authorized, only ¥1.8 trillion of capital was, in fact, provided. The plan injected the same amount of capital into each bank, with the amount based on what the strongest bank requested (Hoshi 2008). This small injection proved to be inadequate and, one year later, the Rapid Recapitalization Act led to an injection of ¥8.6 trillion. Although this was inadequate to solve the long-term capital shortage among Japanese banks—estimates place the cumulative losses to Japanese banks from bad loans during 1992–2006 at about ¥96 trillion, or approximately 19 percent of GDP—it was seen as a more serious attempt to calm the market and led to the elimination of the Japan premium.

As in the United States and the Nordic countries, the Japanese crisis was characterized by the confluence of a boom-bust cycle and structural (i.e., regulatory) changes. The uneven pace of deregulation, particularly the liberalization of debt markets while deposits were still tightly regulated, was an important contributing factor to the boom-bust that followed. A distinguishing feature of the Japanese banking crisis was the length of time it took for the authorities to confront banking problems. This delay made the crisis longer and more costly than it would otherwise have been, and resulted in slow growth and high unemployment throughout the 1990s, which has subsequently been dubbed Japan's "lost decade."

[22]Greenspan's words were eerily reminiscent of those uttered two years earlier by Bank of Japan Governor Yasushi Mieno, who said: "It is not the business of the central bank to save all financial institutions from failure. On the contrary, failure of an institution that has reasons to fail is even necessary from the viewpoint of nurturing a sound financial system" (Nakaso 2001: 4).

Crises and Rescues: Summary

The interwar period was the most turbulent that commercial banking has ever experienced. The post–World War I boom-slump led to widespread crises during the early 1920s. Less than a decade later, the Great Depression, the worst economic and financial crisis the industrialized world had ever known, erupted. Both of these events encouraged governments to institute tight controls on banking in an effort to promote stability. The outbreak of World War II and the desire to channel domestic savings to war-related needs gave governments further incentive to constrain banks and financial markets. Thus, the response to depression and war was a financial "lockdown": the imposition of dramatic and, as it turned out, long-lasting controls over many aspects of the banking business.

The post–World War II financial lockdown had two important results. First, it contributed to near-perfect banking stability between the end of World War II and the early 1970s. Second, it prevented any substantial evolution of the banking system. Banking was controlled, competitive forces were stifled, and banking development was stunted.

Many factors contributed to the end of the post–World War II period of banking stability. The breakdown of the Bretton Woods system was accompanied by exchange rate volatility and increased capital flows. Even in the absence of any other developments, this would have introduced a new element of risk into the business of banking. Technological developments increased the ability of financial institutions to undertake more risk: inappropriately priced government guarantees in the United States, Nordic countries, and Japan gave financial institutions greater incentives to do so. The oil shocks of 1973 and 1979, combined with sometimes misguided monetary and fiscal policies, exacerbated the preexisting trend of gradually rising inflation and contributed to greater macroeconomic instability. As inflation pushed interest rates higher, interest rate ceilings and other regulations, which had been omnipresent but not especially burdensome to banks' day-to-day operations, became more onerous.

An additional complicating factor was deregulation, brought about, in part, by the now-binding constraints of financial regulation. Deregulation made banks better able to compete with each other—and to engage in risky behavior. In the United States, the deteriorating banking situation led regulators to widen the scope of permitted banking activities even further, often unwisely, allowing banks and S&Ls to "gamble for resurrection." In the Nordic countries, banking regulation combined with tax incentives generated negative after-tax real interest rates and contributed to a substantial boom in asset prices, particularly real estate. As these booms were in full swing, the Nordic countries began to deregulate their banking systems and reorganize their supervisory regimes. In Japan, the uneven pace of deregulation left banks with a substantial deposit base, but declining outlets for their funds, as business turned from banks to securities markets, leading to a boom in real estate.

Many of the same macroeconomic and regulatory forces were at work in the run-up to the subprime mortgage crisis. Expansionary fiscal and monetary policies, combined with unhelpful government intervention in the mortgage market and weak regulatory oversight fuelled a speculative boom in U.S. real estate. The boom was exacerbated by the growth—and misuse—of new and complex financial instruments which, due to increasing globalization and improvements in communication, facilitated worldwide participation in both the boom and the subsequent bust.

The resolution methods adopted during the last quarter of the twentieth century had several common elements. First, regardless of whether countries had a deposit insurance system or other bank safety net measure in place, none was adequately prepared for the crises. Each dealt with the early phases of the crisis in an ad hoc manner, and only gradually developed resolution strategies, much as in the more recent subprime crisis. Second, many of the crises were made worse by adverse incentives of the various rescue schemes. In the United States, the flat-rate deposit insurance system contributed to the length and depth of the crisis. In Finland and Sweden, long-lived unconditional creditor guarantees opened the government up to potentially enormous contingent liabilities. Finally, prompt action was necessary to minimize the cost of the crisis and bailout. In Japan, the prolonged delay in closing insolvent banks led to a longer, costlier crisis than would otherwise have occurred.

MERGERS

Banking instability during the last quarter of the twentieth century contributed to an increase in mergers throughout the industrialized world, particularly during the 1980s and 1990s (Bank for International Settlements 1996: 86, Group of Ten 2001). Although mergers involving failing banks have been common in all eras, government promotion of such mergers has been more extensive during the post-1973 period than ever before. This is not to say that governments played no role in promoting mergers in earlier periods. Official and quasi-official bodies did promote the occasional absorption of ailing banks, such as the Bank of England's support of the Royal Bank of Scotland's takeover of Williams Deacon's in 1929–30, and the Canadian Bankers Association's support of the takeover of the Bank of Ontario in 1906 and of Sovereign Bank in 1908 (Johnson 1910: 104–27). Japanese officials explicitly promoted bank mergers starting in 1900 and did so even more forcefully starting in 1927. Nonetheless, the increase in banking instability during the 1980s and 1990s led governments, regulators, and supervisors to promote mergers more actively than ever before.

Regulators confronted with stability-threatening bank failures have several options, each of which was tried on different occasions in the closing decades of the twentieth century. They can do nothing and run the risk of a costly crisis. They can provide open bank assistance, an injection of funds to help the bank overcome the worst of the threat, in hopes that it will return to solvency (e.g., Continental Illinois). This option, if not applied to all troubled banks, may lead to complaints of favoritism against government regulators. Additionally, unless the regulator is willing and able to make the assistance conditional upon changes in bank policy or a management reshuffle, such assistance may not only not increase the probability of a healthy institution emerging at the end of the process, but may also lead to increased moral hazard. Another option is for the government to take over the ownership and management of the institution, injecting such public moneys as needed until the resulting institution is healthy enough to be sold off (e.g., Nordbanken). The downside of this approach is that the regulator may not be a particularly efficient owner or manager and it may take some years to sell off the institution, which may increase the cost of this policy (Blass and Grossman 2001). Finally, the government can arrange mergers between ailing and healthy banks (e.g., Japan), which may allow the regulator to bring about a change in management at the ailing institution without taking part in management of the new institution itself. This option may prove to be less costly than nationalization, both in terms of direct taxpayer cost as well as in longer-term efficiency costs. Such mergers are generally accomplished with an infusion of government funds and have been a common method of facilitating rescues. This approach may be even more attractive in smaller countries if regulators hope to create a "national champion," that is, an institution that can compete effectively in the international arena (Group of Ten 2001: 67).

Financial instability was by no means the only reason for bank mergers after World War II. In a massive study of financial consolidation in the 1990s that included both quantitative analysis of merger trends and interviews with market participants, the G-10 (Group of Ten 2001) found that many of the same motives at work prior to the Great Depression remained important in the late twentieth century: enhanced profitability through cost savings, economies of scale and scope, and increased market share (i.e., market power).[23] Booming stock markets and the growth of debt markets provided greater funding sources for mergers. Some of

---

[23]Other motives include those that benefit managers, rather than shareholders, such as controlling a larger organization or higher compensation. Group of Ten (2001: 66–68).

the incentives found for modern mergers were less important in earlier merger movements. For example, technological advances and their accompanying high fixed costs have increased incentives for consolidation as banks attempt to spread these costs over more consumers. Technological advances have also allowed institutions to offer a broader range of products to the same consumer base, which has encouraged mergers across product lines (e.g., securities, insurance).

The ability to consolidate across product lines and borders has also resulted from changes in the regulatory environment. Although the rules and conventions governing the ability of institutions to offer multiple product lines differ across countries, banks in most countries can buy and sell other financial products—either on their own or through subsidiaries or otherwise related firms. Nowhere has regulatory change opened up cross-border mergers more than in the European Union. The introduction of a common currency, a single market in financial services, and integrated securities markets have made cross-country European mergers more feasible—and common—than ever before.

REGULATION

The worldwide trend toward deregulation, which began in the 1960s and 1970s, was essentially uncoordinated: each country determined its own path and pace of deregulation. During the last quarter of the twentieth century, two important multilateral initiatives aimed at harmonizing banking regulation began to take shape: a European strand, under the aegis of the European Union, and a broader initiative, the Basel Accords, guided by the G-10.

Progress toward a united Europe began with the 1951 Treaty of Paris, which established the European Coal and Steel Community, consisting of Belgium, France, Italy, Luxemburg, the Netherlands, and West Germany, and the 1957 Treaty of Rome, which created the European Economic Community among the same countries. Denmark, Ireland, and the United Kingdom joined the EEC in 1973, Greece in 1981, Spain and Portugal in 1986, and Austria, Finland, and Sweden in 1995. A total of twelve more, mostly eastern European, countries joined in 2004 and 2007, and more are projected to join in the near future. Following the Maastricht Treaty, which took effect in 1993, the economic component of the EEC became the European Community, while the combined economic and non-economic components of the community became the European Union.

Among the goals set out in the 1957 treaty was to create a zone with free movement of goods, labor, capital, and services, to be completed within twelve years (Benink 2000, Dermine 1996). Although that objective was not achieved within the projected time period, progress toward integration was made. In June 1973, the Council of the EEC adopted a directive promoting the principle of equal supervisory and regulatory treatment of all banking firms within a country.[24] Further progress in harmonization came with the adoption of the First Banking Directive (FBD) in 1977.[25] The FBD espoused the principle of "home country" regulation, that banks should be supervised and regulated by the authorities in their home countries, although the directive did not legislate home country regulation. In the United States, by contrast, out-of-state banks are supervised by the local banking authorities (i.e., "host state" regulation). In terms of promoting integration, the FBD removed barriers that prevented banks from setting up branches in other member states, although it required branches to be separately capitalized from its parent bank, and called for greater collaboration among national banking supervisors.[26]

The Second Banking Directive, which was adopted in 1989 and came into force in 1993, established the concept of the "single passport" and home country regulation in European law.[27] Banks open for business in one country were permitted to establish branches in any other member country and would be subject to home country rules and regulations. Subsequent banking directives established accounting and monitoring rules and set capital and other balance sheet requirements. Additional measures enacted during the 1990s included establishing complete freedom of capital movement and, in 1999, the adoption of a single currency.

The process of integration liberalized banking in Europe in a fundamental way. The establishment of free capital mobility and a single currency encouraged increased cross-border transactions and competition among banks. The adoption of home country regulation gave a competitive advantage to banks based in countries with less strict regulation and contributed to a general loosening of bank regulation, although this trend was mitigated by coordinated efforts toward regulatory harmonization. The push toward the creation of a single market provided the impetus for

[24]73/183/EEC: The abolition of restrictions on freedom of establishment and freedom to provide services for self-employed activities of bank and other financial institutions. Dermine (1996: 339).

[25]77/780/EEC: The coordination of laws, regulations, and administrative provisions relating to the taking up and pursuit of credit institutions.

[26]The First Banking Directive required bank branches in foreign countries to apply to local authorities for permission to operate, but that national authorities "may not require the application for authorization to be examined in terms of the economic needs of the market."

[27]89/646/EEC: The coordination of laws, regulations and administrative provisions relating to the taking up and pursuit of the business of credit institutions.

the harmonization of regulatory standards in Europe, including a capital adequacy directive adopted in 1993 and amended in 1998.[28]

A broader approach to capital standards began in 1974 when the G-10, meeting at the Bank for International Settlements in Basel, formed the Committee on Banking Regulations and Supervisory Practices.[29] The committee had been formed in the wake of the failures of Herstatt and Franklin National Bank. Because of heightened fears in the United States, which had borne the brunt of the Herstatt and Franklin failures, and the United Kingdom, which was host to a large number of foreign banks, these countries took the lead in establishing the group (Kapstein 1989, Simmons 2001).

The committee, later renamed the Basel Committee on Banking Supervision, has no supranational authority and does not engage in banking supervision. It has, however, helped to develop a consensus view among the members on banking supervision issues. For example, a report issued in 1975 (known as the "concordat") asserted that "the basic aim of international cooperation . . . should be to ensure that no foreign banking establishment escapes supervision." Extensions of the original concordat recommended consolidated supervision, strengthened cooperation among regulators, and shared supervisory responsibility for international banking groups.

The LDC debt crisis of the early 1980s led to a deterioration in the capital ratios of banks with large international exposures, leading the committee to focus its efforts on standardizing measures of capital and developing guidelines for capital adequacy. The Basel Accord, released in July 1988, defined two measures of capital: core (or tier 1) capital, consisting of shareholder equity and reserves, and supplementary (or tier 2) capital, including various types of reserves (undisclosed reserves, asset revaluation reserves, loan-loss reserves), and other debt and equity instruments (e.g., certain types of preferred shares, subordinated debt). The accord called for banks to hold 8 percent capital (at least half of which in core capital) against risk-weighted assets. Risk-weights between zero and 100 percent were assigned to various components of assets. For example, safe assets, such as cash and government bonds, received a risk-weighting of zero percent: increases in bank holdings of these assets did not require banks to hold additional capital. Other asset categories, such as claims on banks incorporated in OECD countries, claims on in-

---

[28] 93/6/EEC (amended by 98/31/EEC): Capital adequacy of investments firms and credit institutions.

[29] The Group of Ten is a misnomer. The original group consisted of a dozen countries: Belgium, Canada, France, Italy, Japan, Luxembourg, the Netherlands, Sweden, Switzerland, the United Kingdom, the United States, and West Germany. Spain subsequently joined in 2001.

ternational development banks, fully secured mortgage loans, and other types of loans and securities, received risk-weightings of between 20 and 100 percent (Basel Committee on Banking Supervision 1988). By 1993, all banks with substantial international banking business in the G-10 countries had met the minimum requirements laid down by the accord. The application of the framework was not limited to banks in G-10 countries, but was introduced into virtually all other countries with active international banks (Basel Committee on Banking Supervision 2009: 2).

Although the Basel Accord was viewed as a contribution to the harmonization of definitions and capital adequacy ratios, there were acknowledged shortcomings. For example, since the asset categories were relatively crude, banks found it profitable to increase holdings of the riskiest—and, therefore, highest returning—components within each category. Additionally, since the Basel Accord took account of credit risk in the risk-weighting of assets, banks found ways to take on other types of risks such as market risk and interest rate risk (Chami, Khan, and Sharma 2003: 9). In June 1999, the committee circulated a new proposed framework of capital regulation, which went through a consultative process and was finalized in 2004–5 (Basel Committee on Banking Supervision 1999, 2005). This new accord, dubbed Basel II, based regulation on three pillars: (1) minimum capital requirements; (2) supervision; and (3) market discipline.

The first pillar, minimum capital regulation, kept the general framework of the original Basel Accord by requiring banks to hold capital equal to 8 percent of risk-weighted assets, however, with refined risk-weighting. Risk-weights under Basel II were to be calculated on the basis of external ratings produced by independent credit ratings agencies, with separate schedules for central banks and sovereign debtors, commercial banks, and the corporate sector (standardized approach). Alternatively, banks with sufficient resources to develop their own models of credit risk (the internal ratings based approach) were allowed to employ these models, subject to the approval of supervisors. The subprime crisis that erupted in 2008 led to increased doubts about both of these approaches. Ratings agencies are subject to a conflict of interest, since they are paid to make ratings. They have also been criticized for not having downgraded securities rapidly enough, in much the same tone that regulators have been criticized for not having recognized the subprime problem or intervened at an earlier stage. The internal ratings based approach may also be suspect because risk-weights are generated by the banks themselves.

The second pillar (supervision), required banks to have adequate internal mechanisms for evaluating risk and calculating the appropriate amount of capital (e.g., stress testing). Supervisors were to have responsibility to monitor and evaluate these mechanisms and intervene at an early stage if they judge capital ratios to be insufficient. The events of 2008–9 raised concerns that supervisors, like credit ratings agencies, may not be able to evaluate evolving circumstances rapidly enough to be able to intervene at an early stage.

The third pillar (market discipline) recognized the ability of the market to consistently monitor financial institutions and enforce good behavior. Because supervisors and ratings agencies do not have adequate resources to continuously monitor bank performance, by instituting enhanced disclosure requirements, Basel II aimed to give depositors and shareholders more and better information about the condition of a bank's capital and assets, so that they could withdraw funds and reduce equity holding if capital was insufficient. However, as financial institutions grow more complex, it may become more difficult to specify precise disclosure requirements that banks can satisfy in a timely manner.

Banking regulation following the Depression and World War II was motivated by the economic goal of banking soundness and stability, and the political economy goal of directing credit toward economic sectors that were deemed to be crucial. These goals were achieved, in part, by anticompetitive regulations which protected banking stability and profitability; their cost was an absence of financial innovation. Because the regulatory regimes—far stricter than at any other time in the history of commercial banking—left banks both stable and profitable, there was little incentive for the governments or bankers themselves to agitate for deregulation.

The gradual rise in inflation and market interest rates during the 1960s led to a host of changes in domestic and international financial arrangements. The Bretton Woods system of fixed exchange rates collapsed into general floating, international capital flows became more volatile, and pressure for domestic financial liberalization grew. The uneven pace of liberalization combined with improved technology allowed banks to take more risks than ever before and made it easier to evade regulatory restraints. The ensuing instability led to renewed cycles of crises and bailouts; liberalization and instability contributed to the rise of mergers, as did booming stock markets.

Surprisingly, perhaps, governments did not respond to the crises of the last quarter of the twentieth century with a wholesale repeal of the liberalized regulatory regime, but with more concerted multinational approaches to the harmonization and strengthening of regulations. The reemergence of banking instability during the 1970s, its intensification during the 1980s and 1990s, and its eruption during the first decade of the twenty-first century has not, as yet, led governments to reinstate the financial lockdown that characterized the quarter-century following World War II. Why has it not done so?

First, the disruptions of the late twentieth century were not serious enough to warrant such extensive reregulation: in comparison with the Great Depression, these crises were neither as severe, nor as widespread, nor as chronologically compressed. The subprime crisis comes closer to—although at the time of this writing has not yet equaled—the depth and breadth of financial devastation experienced during the Great Depression. Second, the process of globalization and improvements in technology make a renewed lockdown nearly impossible without a coordinated effort by the major economies. Unless the subprime crisis leads to a complete and long-lasting financial meltdown, it is hard to imagine a successful multinational effort to roll back deregulation. Finally, by the late twentieth century, a consensus had emerged that the trade, capital account, and financial liberalization—among other economic and financial reforms of the preceding quarter-century—were in the national self-interest. James (2001: 208) describes this consensus as "an order built in sustained reflection about appropriate policy—and the gains to be derived from it." It would take a sustained and severe depression to change this consensus.

Regulation alone cannot protect the banking system from the type of crises seen at the end of the twentieth century and the beginning of the twenty-first. No matter how carefully crafted and enforced, regulations and the people who enforce them cannot be as nimble as market participants driven by the pursuit of profit. Thus, a primary defense against crises should be the implementation of monetary and fiscal policies that are not conducive to boom-bust fluctuations. Because the central bankers and politicians responsible for these policies have missions that may at times conflict with maintaining banking stability, the role of banking supervisor should be filled by an agency that is independent of the central bank and, to the extent possible, the political process.

The above should not be taken to imply that effective regulation of financial institutions and new products is impossible or unnecessary. Regulations should be designed to align the interests of market participants with stability-promoting behavior. A regulatory authority with powers to enforce existing rules and propose new ones to meet a rapidly changing financial environment, and with sufficient independence to approach politicians and central bankers on an equal footing, will contribute to banking stability. Whatever regulations are eventually enacted, the likely response of bankers will be to devise techniques to circumvent the most costly aspects of them. If the historical experience is any guide, the *pas de deux* between the regulator and the regulated will continue to be a central feature of banking in the twenty-first century.

Appendix to Chapter 2

Country	Year	Description
Australia	1912	The Commonwealth Bank of Australia Act was enacted in 1911. The Commonwealth Bank was given some central banking powers in 1924, and its powers were strengthened in 1945. It became the Reserve Bank of Australia in 1959.
Austria	1816	The Privilegierte Österreichische Nationalbank was modeled on the Banque de France. It was supposed to take over the existing government note issue and was given exclusive right to issue banknotes (convertible into silver), accept deposits, and discount bills. It did not initially serve as the government's bank. Its charter was renewed in 1841 and 1862, and it became the Austro-Hungarian Bank in 1878. (Wirth 1896)
Belgium	1850	The Banque nationale de Belgique was established after the crisis of 1848. Other banks were persuaded to give up issuing banknotes. Although technically privately owned, the government appointed its officers. Its charter set limits on the amounts and types of securities that were eligible for discount.
Canada	1934	The Bank of Canada was established during the Great Depression, despite Canada's banking and monetary stability during the period. The bank was granted a monopoly on note issue, which was implemented gradually.
Denmark	1818	Kurantbanken (Currency Bank), with sole right to issue notes (convertible into silver), was established in 1736 but later folded. The Specie Bank was founded in 1791 but collapsed during the *Statsbankerot* (1813). The Rigsbank, established in 1813 as the country's sole note-issuer, became the Nationalbanken i Kjøbenhavn (subsequently Danmarks Nationalbank) in 1818.

APPENDIX TABLE 2.1 (*continued*)

Country	Year	Description
England	1694	The Bank of England was the first joint stock bank in England and Wales. The charter was renewed—for periods of eleven to thirty-three years—nine times between 1697 and 1844.
Finland	1811	Suomen Pankki was the only chartered bank in Finland until 1861. It was established two years after Finland was annexed to Russia as a Grand Duchy, and spent the next thirty years driving Swedish money out of circulation in favor of Russian money. It was modeled, in part, on the Bank of Sweden.
France	1800	The Banque de France was formed out of the discount and note-issuing Caisse des Comptes Courantes.
Germany	1765, 1846, 1876, 1957	Königliche Giro- und Lehn-Bank zu Berlin (Royal Giro and Loan Bank of Berlin) was established in 1765 by Frederick the Great. It was one of several note-issuing banks that were amalgamated into the Bank of Prussia in 1846. It was reorganized as the Reichsbank in 1876, the Rentenbank in 1923, and the "new" Reichsbank in 1924. It was succeeded by the Deutsche Bundesbank in 1957.
Italy	1893	Four early note-issuing banks (dating from 1860s and 1870s) were consolidated into the Banca d'Italia.
Japan	1882	Nippon Ginko (Bank of Japan) was established in the wake of the failure of the National Banking system (which was modeled on U.S. system of the same name) to limit its note issue. It was subsequently granted a monopoly on banknote issue.
Netherlands	1814	De Nederlandsche Bank was established as a private company, with both shareholders and the Sovereign appointing management, to discount bills, make secured advances, receive accounts for the government, and, although not explicitly in its charter, issue notes. The original charter was for twenty-five years. (Van der Borght 1896, Bosman 1987)
Norway	1816	Norges Bank, the first Norwegian-owned bank in Norway, was established shortly after independence from Denmark.

APPENDIX TABLE 2.1 (*continued*)

Country	Year	Description
Sweden	1668	Riksens Ständers Bank (Bank of the Estates of the Realm) was named for the Diet of the Four Estates (parliament), which took over ownership of the private note-issuing Stokholms Banco (Stockholm Bank), which had foundered in 1664. The new bank was forbidden from issuing notes, but began doing so in 1701. After the Diet of the Four Estates was replaced with a bicameral parliament, the bank was renamed Sveriges Riksbank.
Switzerland	1907	Individual note-issuing banks had been in existence since 1836. The federal government was granted authority to regulate banknote issuers in 1874. Legislation enacted in 1881 set a limit on total banknote circulation, and legislation enacted in 1891 conferred a note-issuing monopoly on the federal government, although the Swiss National Bank was not established until 1907.
United States	1791, 1817, 1914	The Bank of the United States, modeled in part on the Bank of England, was established in 1791. The government was entitled to purchase 20 percent of the share capital. The bank issued notes and acted as depository and banker for the government. It failed to obtain a new charter upon expiration of the original in 1811. The Second Bank of the United States was established in 1817. It also failed to secure a charter renewal when the original twenty-year charter expired. The Federal Reserve Act (1913) brought about the establishment of the Federal Reserve System in 1914.

Sources: Conant (1927), Capie et al. (1994), and other references as cited.

APPENDIX TABLE 2.2
Commercial Bank Origins

Country	Year	Description
Australia	1817	Bank of New South Wales established.
	1835	The conditions under which the London-headquartered Bank of Australasia would be granted a charter were first stated in December 1833; it began business in Australia in 1835.
Austria	1853	The Niederösterreichische Escomptegesellschaft (Lower Austrian Discount Company), the first incorporated commercial bank, was established in 1853. The Österreichische Credit-Anstalt was established in 1855. Two more banks were established in 1863, two more in 1864, two more in 1869, and four more during 1871–73.
Belgium	1822	The Algemeene Nederlandsche Maatschappij ter Begunstiging van der Volksvlijt (Société Générale pour favoriser l'Industrie nationale) was established by William I of the Netherlands. Following Belgian independence in 1830, the Bank of Belgium, Banque Liégoise (1833), and Bank of Flanders (1841) were established.
Canada	1820	The Bank of Montreal, which had operated without a charter since 1817, was chartered by the province of Lower Canada. The Bank of New Brunswick was chartered in 1820. In 1822, three other banks began operating under charters: the Bank of Canada (Montreal) and Quebec Bank (Quebec), both of which had operated privately since 1818, and the Bank of Upper Canada (York, now part of Toronto).
Denmark	1846	Discount Bank of Feyen established. Approximately fifteen banks were established during the prosperous 1850s. Privatbank (1857) was the first "real credit-creating bank."(Hansen 1982: 582)
England	1826	A law authorized the establishment of joint stock banks in England and Wales outside a sixty-five-mile radius of London. A law enacted in 1836 permitted the establishment of non-note-issuing joint stock banks in London.

APPENDIX TABLE 2.2 *(continued)*

Country	Year	Description
Finland	1862	Suomen Yhdys-Pankki (Union Bank of Finland) was established. The next incorporated bank was established during the 1870s by Germans. Only three incorporated banks were in existence for most of the 1880s.
France	1859	Although the short-lived Caisse d'Escompte (1776–93) discounted bills, issued notes, and collected deposits, commercial banking began in earnest with the establishment of Crédit Industriel et Commercial (1859), Crédit Lyonnais (1863), and Société Générale pour favoriser le Développement du Commerce et l'Industrie en France (1864).
Germany	1848	A. Schaaffhausen'scher Bankverein in Cologne, successor to a failed private banking house, became Germany's first incorporated commercial bank. It was soon followed by Disconto-Gesellschaft (1851), Darmstäder Bank (1853), and Berliners Handels-Gesellschaft (1856).
Italy	1843	Two of the earliest incorporated commercial banks in Piedmont, the Banca di Genova (1843) and Banca di Torino (1847), merged to form the Banca Nazionale degli Stati Sardi (1849). (Hertner 1994: 562)
Japan	1873	The National Bank Decree, modeled on U.S. National Banking Acts, permitted the establishment of incorporated commercial banks issuing bond-backed banknotes.
Netherlands	1861	Associatie Cassa was established in 1806, but its foray into commercial banking was short-lived. 't Hart et al. (1997: 115) argue that incorporated commercial banking began in 1861. Nederlandsche Handel-Maatschappij, a trading company specializing in the Dutch East Indies, was established in 1824 and moved into banking in the later part of the nineteenth century. Other joint stock banks founded at the time include Twentsche Bank (1861), Rotterdamsche Bank (1863), Amsterdamsche Bank (1871), and Incasso Bank (1891).

APPENDIX TABLE 2.2 (*continued*)

Country	Year	Description
Norway	1848	Christiana Bank og Kreditkasse was established in 1848, followed by Bergens Privatbank (1855) and Den norske Creditbank (Oslo, 1857).
Sweden	1830	The first enskilda (incorporated, note-issuing) bank was chartered in Ystad. Further enskilda charters were issued in 1832, 1833, 1835, and 1837 (three). Non-note-issuing incorporated commercial banks were established in 1863, 1864, 1869, 1871 (two), and 1872 (two).
Switzerland	1856	Crédit Suisse established in Zurich. Seven other large commercial banks soon established in Zurich, Geneva, Basel, and Berne.
United States	1782	Several short-lived note-issuing banks existed during the colonial period. The Bank of North America was chartered in 1782, the Bank of Massachusetts in 1784, and the Bank of New York (founded in 1784) in 1791. Free incorporation of banks was permitted in several states, starting in 1837. National bank charters were authorized starting in 1863. (Conant 1896: 286–87)

Sources: Willis and Beckhart (1929), Pohl (1994), and other references as cited.

Appendix to Chapter 3

SEVERAL AUTHORS HAVE COMPILED catalogues of banking, financial, and currency crises. Kindleberger (1978, 1996) presents a chronology of financial crises extending back to 1618, although his focus is on financial, rather than banking crises. Lindgren, Garcia, and Saal (1996) and Caprio and Klingebiel (1996, 1999 [revised 2003]) compile catalogues of modern banking crises. Bordo et al. (2001) catalogues banking, currency, and banking and currency crises from the early 1880s through the mid-1990s.

The following tables present two catalogues of banking crises using the definition presented in this chapter. The first focuses on a group of sixteen industrialized countries from North America, western Europe, Australia, and Japan prior to 1929. The second focuses on a larger sample of countries during the Great Depression, including all countries in the first sample, plus several from more southern and eastern Europe.

APPENDIX TABLE 3.1
Banking Crises prior to 1929

Country	Year(s)	Category: causal factor	Description and sources
Australia	1826	Boom-bust: land; confidence: currency; structural: bank war	A long pastoral expansion led to a boom-bust in land prices. This was accompanied by a drain of dollars resulting from doubts about the value of the currency (due to a return to a sterling currency). Further, the launch of a new competitor (the Bank of Australia) led to the near failure of the Bank of New South Wales. (Butlin 1953)
Australia	1843	Boom-bust: sheep and wool	The downturn following the boom of 1836–41 resulted from the exhaustion of opportunities for profitable expansion and increases in costs in banking. This led to the closure, failure, and forced absorption of five of the fifteen

APPENDIX TABLE 3.1 (*continued*)

Country	Year(s)	Category: causal factor	Description and sources
			banks then in existence. Two more banks were weakened to the point that they closed by the end of the decade. (Butlin 1953)
Australia	1893	Boom-bust: land	Collapse of the land boom of the late 1880s led to the suspension of fifteen (of about twenty-five) banks, including three failures/closures in 1891–92. (Copland 1929)
Austria	1857	Boom-bust: railroads and related industries, international factors	Failure of several important private banks following international financial crisis. (Rudolph 1976: 69)
Austria	1873	Boom-bust: railroads, securities	Banking crisis following stock market crash of 1873. Number of banks and banking firms fell from 141 in 1873 to forty-five in 1878. (Sokal and Rosenberg 1929)
Belgium	1838–39	Confidence: war, politics; structural: bank war	The breakdown of diplomacy between the Netherlands and the newly independent Belgium led to worries about the outbreak of hostilities, which were accentuated by a bank war between the country's two preeminent banks (one of Dutch lineage, one Belgian). In the space of one week in December 1838, Société Générale presented 1.4 million francs' worth of banknotes to its rival, the Banque de Belgique, forcing the latter to suspend payment. Parliament (and later the government) extended loans of 5 million francs, which allowed the Banque de Belgique to reopen three weeks later. (Chlepner 1943: 20–21)

APPENDIX TABLE 3.1 (*continued*)

Country	Year(s)	Category: causal factor	Description and sources
Belgium	1848	Confidence: war, politics	The Paris Revolution of 1848 and the accompanying international financial disruption, combined with bad harvests and high unemployment in Flanders, led to panic withdrawals by depositors. The Banque Commerciale d'Anvers was forced to suspend payments and the Antwerp and Brussels stock markets closed. The Société Générale survived only because the government passed a law authorizing it to increase its fiduciary banknote issue (i.e., notes not backed by specie). (Durviaux 1947: 47–50)
Belgium	1876	Boom-bust: postwar expansion, international factors	A substantial boom in the early 1870s, fueled partially by the Franco-Prussian War, led to the establishment of a number of new banks. Several of these failed when the international crisis hit the Brussels stock exchange. A few smaller banks went into receivership, and the larger Banque de Belgique, Banque de Bruxelles, and Banque Centrale Anversoise had to be reorganized. Durviaux (1947: 75–76) calls this the third Belgian banking crisis; Chlepner (1943: 37) suggests that it may have been less serious.
Belgium	1900–1901	Boom-bust: Russian securities, end of expansion following the 1890s downturn	Many small new and stock-market-related institutions went out of business. The Caisse Commerciale de Bruxelles was absorbed by the Credit Liégeois. (Chlepner 1930: 96, 1943: 37, Durviaux 1947: 82)

APPENDIX TABLE 3.1 (*continued*)

Country	Year(s)	Category: causal factor	Description and sources
Belgium	1914	Confidence: war	The outbreak of World War I led to panic withdrawals and suspension of banknote convertibility.
Belgium	1920–21	Boom-bust: end of postwar expansion	The end of the postwar boom led to bank failures (Vanthemsche 1991). Chlepner (1943: 181) argues that this episode did not rise to the level of crisis.
Belgium	1926	Confidence: currency	Fears over currency depreciation led to panic deposit withdrawals. (Lemoine 1929: 278)
Canada	1837–39	Boom-bust: international factors; confidence: political instability	An international commercial crisis, originating in the United States and the United Kingdom, spread to Canada. There were also rebellion-related bank suspensions in Lower Canada. The Agricultural Bank in Upper Canada failed (November 1837). (Breckenridge 1910: 30–37, McIvor 1958: 42–43)
Canada	1879	Boom-bust: cyclical contraction	Toward the end of the severe cyclical downturn ushered in by the commercial crisis of 1873, several banks failed or were liquidated: one in 1873, one in 1876, and four in 1879 (one of these was voluntary). These accounted for about 7.5 per-cent of total bank capital at the time. According to McIvor (1958: 73), although the banks were criticized for reducing outstanding credit during this period, most banks survived by relying on their capital and reserves and by mergers. "In the strict sense of the word, Canada suffered no panic." (Breckenridge 1910: 114)

APPENDIX TABLE 3.1 (*continued*)

Country	Year(s)	Category: causal factor	Description and sources
			According to Jamieson (1953: 22), older, more established banks weathered the downturn well, while several smaller and newer banks that had been operating in smaller territories failed.
Canada	1908	Boom-bust: international factors	Seven banks were closed (one voluntarily) between 1905 and 1910, three in 1908. The crisis may have been related to the U.S. crisis of 1907. Breckenridge (1910: 170) argues that the failures were minor.
Canada	1923	No crisis	The Home Bank was a large (but relatively local) bank, accounting for approximately 1.5 percent of paid-up banking capital. Its failure, due to fraud, was notable but isolated.
Denmark	1857	Boom-bust: international factors	The international commercial crisis of November 1857 hit Hamburg particularly hard, which reverberated in Denmark. Danmarks Nationalbank intervened with funds borrowed from the Treasury. The banking system emerged without sustaining heavy losses, although the National Bank lost 1.8 million rigsdaler. (Glindemann 1929: 491)
Denmark	1877–78	Boom-bust: international factors	Downturn following widespread financial crises during the mid-1870s. (Hansen 1991: 20–21, 39)
Denmark	1908	Boom-bust: international factors	The 1907 crisis spread to Denmark in 1908. The state, Danmarks Nationalbank, and large commercial banks provided assistance to troubled banks that later had to be liquidated. (Hansen 1991: 20–21, 39)

APPENDIX TABLE 3.1 (*continued*)

Country	Year(s)	Category: causal factor	Description and sources
Denmark	1922	Boom-bust: end of postwar expansion	Landsmandsbanken, the largest bank in Scandinavia, failed. Assistance for this and other failures, beginning the previous year, came from Danmarks Nationalbank, other commercial banks, and the government. (Hansen 1991: 38, Frothingham 1924: 13–17)
England	1825	Boom-bust: Latin American investments, joint stock companies	Abundant harvests and the resulting gold imports they yielded led to booming macroeconomic conditions and an increase in funding for all manner of investment projects, especially those in Latin America. "Joint stock projects were formed with objects as indefinite and impracticable as in the time of the South Sea Bubble. One actually proposed to drain the Red Sea to recover the gold lost by the Egyptians when pursuing the Israelites"(Conant 1915: 620, citing Clément Juglar, *Les Crises Commerciales et de Leur Retour Periodique en France, en Angleterre, et aux États-Unis*. Paris 1889). (Thomas 1934: 50–53, McLeod 1896: 117–23, and Pressnell 1956: 477–500) According to Pressnell (1956: 443) at least sixty private banks failed during July 1825–June 1826, compared with 343 that had failed during 1750–1830.
England	1836–39	Boom-bust: cyclical expansion, international factors	Abundant harvests during 1832–37 led to increased gold inflows, which fed the boom. This was reversed by Jackson's specie circular in the U.S. (which required that govern-

APPENDIX TABLE 3.1 (*continued*)

Country	Year(s)	Category: causal factor	Description and sources
			ment land sales be settled in gold), the failure of the Agricultural and Commercial Bank in Ireland, and the difficulties of the North and Central Bank of Manchester. These events led to a drain on the Bank of England's gold reserves and forced it to extend assistance to at least one provincial bank. Poor harvests and the collapse of the Bank of Belgium, also in 1838, exacerbated the drain. Baring Brothers borrowed money from bankers in Paris and Hamburg to stem the crisis. (Andréadès 1966: 263–68, McLeod 1896: 134–38, and Thomas 1934: 313–17)
England	1847	Boom-bust: cyclical fluctuations, grain, and railroad securities	Poor harvests led to gold outflows and contributed to a collapse in railroad securities and the failure of a number of financial houses following a period of excessive speculation. The Chancellor of the Exchequer wrote to the bank and offered to introduce a bill in Parliament to indemnify the Bank of England if, in expanding loans and discounts to combat the crisis, it violated the terms of its charter. The publication of the letter had a "magical effect" in calming the panic. (Andréadès 1966: 336, Butson 1929: 1158–59)
England	1857	Boom-bust: end of Crimean war-related expansion, international factors	Overextension of credit at home, the accompanying increase in foreign trade, related in part to the Crimean War, combined with a financial crisis originating in the U.S., led to numerous bank failures.

APPENDIX TABLE 3.1 (*continued*)

Country	Year(s)	Category: causal factor	Description and sources
			The Prime Minister and Chancellor of the Exchequer secured passage of a bill of indemnity in Parliament, enabling the bank to extend its loans and discounts beyond that allowed by the bank's charter. (Butson 1929: 1159, Conant 1927: 636–42)
England	1866	Boom-bust: joint stock company formation	Overend, Gurney crisis. Speculation was fueled by an 1862 amendment to the Companies Act that made it easier to form limited liability companies. Numerous new companies were financed with the aid of "accommodation" bills, short-term IOUs that were issued against the security of shares in new, and possibly not-yet-started, projects. This violated the real bills doctrine, which held that bills of exchange should only be issued against the security of "real goods" such as inventories or goods in transit. (Andréadès 1966: 353–61, Grossman 1988, King 1936: 229–56)
England/ Scotland	1878	Confidence: fraud; structural: unlimited liability	The City of Glasgow Bank failure had its greatest impact in Scotland, but also had important effects on banking in England. Because of its unlimited liability and the heavy calls made upon its shares, a number of individuals and institutions that held the City Bank's shares were ruined. (Checkland 1975)
England	1890	Boom-bust: Latin American securities	Baring Brothers, the City of London's leading specialist in Latin American securities, faltered due to a variety of

APPENDIX TABLE 3.1 (*continued*)

Country	Year(s)	Category: causal factor	Description and sources
			setbacks (political, financial) in Argentina. Full-scale crisis was averted by the intervention of the Bank of England at the head of a coalition of London banks providing a guarantee fund. (Grossman 1988)
England	1914	Confidence: war; structure: war	The outbreak of World War I prevented many foreign debtors (particularly those in Germany) from remitting funds to London to meet their obligations. Such a large-scale default would have caused the credit market to collapse. The government instructed the Bank of England to discount these securities and hold them in "cold storage" until after the war, promising to guarantee the bank against any loss, thus avoiding a full-fledged financial crisis.
Finland	1878	Boom-slump: forest products	The Franco-Prussian War increased demand for forest products, which collapsed in the middle of the 1870s. A subsidiary of Pohjoismaiden Osakepankki suffered large stock market losses, which led to the parent bank's failure. (Herrala 1999)
Finland	1900	Boom-bust: end of expansion following the 1890s downturn	Failure of Suomen Maan-viljelys and Teollisuuspankki Osakeyhtiö, which had been founded in 1897 and expanded aggressively and recklessly (and engaged in fraudulent practices). (Herrala 1999)
Finland	1921	Boom-bust: post-independence inflation and exchange rate depreciation and end of post–civil war and post–World War I expansion	Helsingin Diskonttopankki failed and Suomen Teollisu-uspankki and Privatbanken were forced to merge. (Herrala 1999)

APPENDIX TABLE 3.1 (*continued*)

Country	Year(s)	Category: causal factor	Description and sources
France	1805	Confidence: war, politics	The Battle of Austerlitz, plus drains of specie to provinces (drawn by higher interest rates), plus government mismanagement, left the Bank of France unable to pay noteholders. It suspended business for several months from September 1805 to January 1806. (Des Essars 1896: 58–59, Cameron 1967: 102–3)
France	1814	Confidence: war, political instability	Fall of Paris and abdication of Napoleon. "In April 1814 the Bank (of France) went into virtual liquidation . . ." (Cameron 1967: 103).
France	1848	Confidence: political instability	Revolution of 1848. According to Cameron (1967: 107) almost all the 25-plus caisses (bank-like financial institutions) created in the previous few years failed.
France	1870–71	Confidence: war, political instability	Fallout from Franco-Prussian War and the Paris Commune. (Plessis 1994: 190)
France	1882	Boom-bust: railroad securities	Failure of the Union Générale. (Bouvier 1960, Plessis 1994: 190)
France	1889	Boom-bust: copper speculation	Failure and rescue of the Comptoir d'Escompte. (Des Essars 1896, Plessis 1994: 190)
Germany	1847–48	Boom-bust: crop failure, international factors	The failure of Schaaffhausen Bank of Cologne, the Rhineland's largest private bank, led to its reorganization as Germany's first incorporated commercial bank.
Germany	1857	Boom-bust: international factors	The fallout from the international commercial crisis of 1857 was particularly severe in Hamburg. (Ahrens 1986)

APPENDIX TABLE 3.1 (*continued*)

Country	Year(s)	Category: causal factor	Description and sources
Germany	1873	Boom-bust: railroads and other new corporations, international factors	Gründerkrach (Founders' Crash), shortly following the establishment of the German empire, was fuelled by French reparations payments and new corporate flotations. (Tilly 1994: 304)
Germany	1891–94	Boom-bust: cyclical downturn	Downturn in Europe and U.S., including fallout from the Baring crisis, led to "depression and the collapse of many Berlin banks" (Quittner 1929: 698, Mitchell 1913: 49ff.).
Germany	1900–1901	Boom-bust: end of post-1890s recovery	End of the post-1894 boom; this crisis was marked by the collapse of the Leipziger Bank. (Quittner 1929: 698–99, Mitchell 1913: 61)
Italy	1873	Boom-bust: international factors, corporate flotations	The crisis, which spread from Germany and Austria, was most severe in the stock market, particularly among banks and railroads.
Italy	1893	Boom-bust: real estate	Bank bailouts of real estate companies in late 1880s left banks illiquid and led to the failure of Banca Romana, Credito Mobiliare, and Banca Generale. Important motivating factor behind the subsequent establishment of Banca d'Italia. (LoFaro 1929: 769, 809, Des Essars 1896: 166–72, Fratianni and Spinelli 1997: 87–92)
Italy	1907	Boom-bust: international factors	Crisis in London and Paris cut off credit to overextended Italian market. (Kindleberger 1978: 133, Bonelli 1982)
Italy	1914	Confidence: war	Panic induced by outbreak of war led to moratorium on deposit withdrawals.

APPENDIX TABLE 3.1 *(continued)*

Country	Year(s)	Category: causal factor	Description and sources
Italy	1921–22	Boom-bust: end of postwar expansion	Failure of Banca Italiana di Sconto (1921), which had loaned heavily to war industries (Ansaldo Group). (LoFaro 1929: 814, Sraffa 1922)
Japan	1871	Structure: abolition of trade boards, limitations on note issues	Failure of nine of the ten exchange companies, precursors to banks that were established to provide banking services. (Soyeda 1896: 415–16, Tamaki 1995: 25–17)
Japan	1907	Boom-bust: end of postwar expansion	End of expansion following the conclusion of the Russo-Japanese war. (Fuji Bank 1967: 58)
Japan	1920	Boom-bust: end of postwar expansion	End of expansion following World War I. (Fuji Bank 1967: 78–80, Tamaki 1995: 140–46)
Japan	1927	Confidence: earthquake-related	Great Kanto earthquake of September 1923 destroyed 63 percent of Tokyo bank offices. Temporary moratorium on bills payable in stricken areas had been extended until 1927. Failure of Tokyo Watanabe Bank (March 15) amid discussion about how to deal with restructuring the financial system. (Tamaki 1995: 147–59)
Netherlands	1921–24	Boom-bust: end of postwar expansion	The war-related closure of money market led to rapid growth of the banking sector (1914–20) and its increasingly close connection with industry. The downturn in 1921 led to bankruptcies of many small local banks and the intervention of the Netherlands Bank in favor of the mid-sized Bank-Associatie and Marx & Co. (1922), and the extremely large Rotterdamsche Bankvereeniging (1924). The 1921–24 episode was ". . . perhaps

APPENDIX TABLE 3.1 (*continued*)

Country	Year(s)	Category: causal factor	Description and sources
			the only classic banking crisis experienced in the Netherlands in the entire period 1600–1990" ('t Hart, Jonker, and Van Zanden 1997: 143–44).
Norway	1899–1900	Boom-bust: building, banks	Boom in bank formation (1895–99), during which the number of banks "practically doubled" according to Nordvik (1993: 58), followed by collapse in 1899–1900. According to Swenson (1929: 880), the end of the Oslo building boom led to the failure of a number of small local banks, but did not affect "the bulk of Norwegian banking."
Norway	1886, 1889, 1908	No crisis	Minor, isolated banking failures. The 1886 failures were fraud-related.
Norway	1922–23	Boom-bust: agriculture, wood, mining, and shipping, end of postwar expansion	A substantial decrease in the number of banks during World War I (from 122 to 62), combined with a postwar price decline in many of Norway's major industries during 1920–21, led to a severe banking crisis. (Swenson 1929: 881, Frothingham 1924: 28, Knutsen 1991)
Sweden	1877–78	Boom-bust: railroad and industrial securities, cyclical downturn	An economic downturn of the later 1870s hit banks particularly hard, especially those with significant commitments to railroads and railroad-related industries. The public withdrew more than one-third of all deposits from Stockholms Enskilda Bank in December 1878, nearly resulting in suspension. (Olsson 1994: 964, 1997: 42–46)

APPENDIX TABLE 3.1 (*continued*)

Country	Year(s)	Category: causal factor	Description and sources
Sweden	1907	Boom-bust: international factors	Flux (1910: 121ff.) describes a mild banking disruption during 1908–11, in which the number of banks decreased slightly.
Sweden	1922–23	Boom-bust: end of postwar expansion	The end of the post–World War I boom caused prices to fall to less than 45 percent of their June 1920 level by the spring of 1922. A number of banks incurred heavy losses and had to be closed or reconstructed. The state, in cooperation with the commercial banks, established the Credit Bank of 1922 (A.B. Kreditkassen av 1922) to support banks that had suffered heavy losses. (Frothingham 1924: 52–54, Melin (1929: 1055–57)
Switzerland	1870	Structural: war, dependence on foreign financial system	Switzerland was highly dependent upon the French monetary and financial systems. The outbreak of the Franco-Prussian War and France's unilateral extension of maturity on commercial bills cut off Switzerland from its main sources of coins and credit. (Des Essars 1896: 288, Cassis 1994: 1016)
Switzerland	1914	Confidence: war	Several bank failures early in the year culminated in a generalized drain of deposits during the summer. The state-owned Federal Loan Institution was created in the autumn of 1914 to grant loans to banks, business, and agriculture that could not be made by the central bank. (Schwartzenbach 1929: 1116–19)
United States	1837	Boom-bust: cyclical downturn, cotton, land, international factors	This crisis followed a sustained period of economic growth—and speculation—fed by European investment and

APPENDIX TABLE 3.1 (*continued*)

Country	Year(s)	Category: *causal factor*	*Description and sources*
			was exacerbated by the winding up of the Second Bank of the United States (Sumner 1896: 266–85). For an opposing view on the importance of the Second Bank, see Temin (1968). On May 8, New York City banks suspended activity, followed by Philadelphia. Those of Natchez, Mobile, Montgomery, and New Orleans had failed several days before.
United States	1857	Boom-bust: end of postwar expansion, land, railroads	The crisis followed several years of increased speculation in land and railroads, fed by the end of the Mexican-American War and gold discoveries. Failure of the Ohio Life Insurance and Trust set off additional failures. (Calomiris and Schweikart 1991, Evans 1859 [1969])
United States	1873	Boom-bust: end of postwar expansion, railroads	The crisis occurred at the beginning of protracted cyclical downturn following the end of the post–Civil War boom. The number of bank failures in 1873 and 1874 was more than 2.5 times that in 1872 and more than six times that in 1871. (Sprague 1910, Friedman and Schwartz 1963, Bremer 1935)
United States	1884	Boom-bust: cyclical downturn; confidence: gold standard	New York banking panic in May after the failure of a brokerage firm (Grant and Ward, with assets of $700,000 and liabilities of $16 million), followed by the failure of Marine National Bank (capital of $400,000 and deposits of $5 million) and the defalcation of the Third National Bank (after $3 million in securities was stolen from its vault). Several banks, savings

APPENDIX TABLE 3.1 (*continued*)

Country	Year(s)	Category: causal factor	Description and sources
			banks, and brokerage firms in the New York area closed. Sprague (1910) and Friedman and Schwartz (1963) argue that the Bland-Allison Act of 1878, which required the U.S. Treasury to purchase substantial quantities of silver, led European investors to question the commitment of the U.S. to the gold standard. When the U.S. entered a cyclical downturn in 1882–84, these sales put pressure on the New York financial market.
United States	1890	Boom-bust: seasonal drain, international factors	Sprague (1910) refers to this as a "financial stringency." The pyramiding of reserves in the central reserve cities of New York, Chicago, and St. Louis, combined with seasonal demands for funds in the interior of the country to finance the movement of the harvest, drained funds from New York banks. The Baring crisis and the ensuing higher interest rates in the UK (after a period of falling rates) exacerbated withdrawals from New York. (Friedman and Schwartz 1963, Mitchell 1913)
United States	1893	Boom-bust: land, railroads; confidence: gold standard	Poor harvests in Europe and abundant harvests in the U.S. led to a recovery starting in the second half of 1891. This helped fundamentally weak banks survive the 1890 stringency; however, many remained in a precarious position and failed when a crisis erupted in 1893. A decline in agricultural prices worsened the situation for farmers and

APPENDIX TABLE 3.1 (*continued*)

Country	Year(s)	Category: causal factor	Description and sources
			increased their debt burden. Railroad overbuilding, combined with the depressed farm situation, contributed to the crisis. Bank failures erupted in the east, west, and south during the third week in July. Concern that the Sherman Silver Purchase Act of 1890 had undermined confidence in the gold basis of the currency, combined with a decline in Treasury gold holdings to a fifteen-year low, may have contributed to the crisis. (Sprague 1910, Mitchell 1913, Friedman and Schwartz 1963, Bremer 1935)
United States	1907	Boom-bust: copper, trust companies	The crisis followed a decade-long period of prosperity in the United States and a somewhat shorter revival in Europe. The boom lasted from about 1897 to 1907. The crisis was particularly strong among state banks, which had grown in number relative to national banks. (Sprague 1910: 224) Failures in 1908 were at their highest level in ten years. The failure of the Knickerbocker Trust Co. was a turning point. Bank holidays were declared in Oklahoma, Nevada, Washington, Oregon, and California. (Sprague 1910, Mitchell 1913, Friedman and Schwartz 1963)

Notes: Episodes are classified as being generated by one or more of the three crisis categories outlined in chapter 3: (1) boom-bust fluctuations; (2) shocks to confidence; (3) structural factors; or as not being a crisis (for episodes which are described as crises in some historical accounts but do not meet the criteria specified in chapter 3). The category is followed, for crisis episodes, by the principal causal factors—either the object of speculative excess or the source of the macroeconomic forces—in boom-bust crises, the specific shock to confidence, or the structural factor underlying the crisis. The catalogue includes several crises that predate the establishment of commercial banks.

APPENDIX TABLE 3.2
Banking Crises during the Great Depression

A. Crisis Countries

Country	Description
Austria	Failure of Boden Credit Anstalt (1929), Credit Anstalt, and Vienna Mercur-Bank (1931). Heavy losses to Wiener Bank-Verein and Escompte-Gesellschaft (1932).
Belgium	Rumors about imminent failure of Banque de Bruxelles (1931). Failure of Banque Belge de Travail (1934).
Estonia	Failure of Estonia Government Bank Tallin and Reval Credit Bank (1930). Run on banks following Britain's departure from the gold standard (1931). Temporary moratoria on banks declared by government (1931 and 1932). Government intervention through National Mortgage Bank and other state banks.
Finland	The number of banks declined during 1929–33; however, Kuusterä (1994: 141) claims that ". . . we cannot speak of a really extensive uncontrollable banking crisis in Finland during the depression." On the other hand, Herrala (1999) notes the merger of Atlas-pankki and Liittopankki with Helsingin Osakepankki, in which shareholders of the first two incurred losses. Suomen Vientipankki and Etelä-Pohjanmaan pankki went into bankruptcy, and Turunmaan pankki and Svenska Finlands Landtmannabank were closed. The Bank of Finland provided support to several troubled banks and the number of bank branches declined by nearly 25 percent between 1929 and 1936.
France	Failure of local banks, such as Banque Adam, Oustric Group, Banque Renauld, Charpenay, Veuve Guérin; a regional bank, Banque d'Alsace-Lorraine; and the national Banque Nationale de Crédit (1930–31). A major investment bank, Banque de l'Union Parisienne (1932), was rescued by the Bank of France working with Paris banks.
Germany	Failure of Berlin *Grossbank* ("major bank"), the Darmstäder und Nationalbank (Danat-Bank) and bank holiday (1931).
Hungary	Run on Budapest banks, bank holiday (1931).
Italy	Breakup of Banca Agricola Italiana. Panic and government reorganization of banks (1931).
Latvia	Run on banks following the collapse of Danat and Credit Anstalt. Government decree limiting depositors' rights to make withdrawals.
Norway	Suspension of two of the country's largest banks, Bergens Privatbank and Den norske Creditbank (1931). Temporary (three-month) moratorium on withdrawals

APPENDIX TABLE 3.2 (*continued*)

Country	Description
	and government guarantee of new deposits. Nordvik (1992) argues that Norwegian banks were stable.
Poland	Bank runs following Austrian and German banking crises. Severe external and internal drains.
Romania	Run on and/or collapse of Banca Generala a Tarii Românesti, Banca de Credit Roman, Banca Romaneasca, Banca Marmerosch, Blank & Co., Banque Générale du Pays Roumain. Many banks placed under government protection pending reorganization or final liquidation.
Switzerland	Rescue of Union Financière. Failure of Banque de Genève and three-week run on banks (1931). Restructuring of Banque Populaire Suisse (1933). Banque d'Escompte Suisse suspended.
United States	Three major waves of bank failures, beginning in October 1930, March 1931, and in January 1933, culminating in the declaration of a nationwide bank holiday of March 1933.
Yugoslavia	Bank runs following Credit Anstalt crisis and German and Hungarian suspensions.

B. Non-Crisis Countries

Country	Description
Bulgaria	Although several small banks failed, there was no generalized bank run. Bulgarian banks appear not to have been severely affected by the Austrian and German banking crises. In 1934, the government arranged mergers for of a number of banks, although this does not appear to have been the result of crisis.
Canada	Despite a severe economic downturn and a decline in bank profitability, there were no bank failures. Kryzanowski and Roberts (1993) argue that Canadian banks were, in fact, deeply troubled and that capital forbearance prevented a crisis.
Czechoslovakia	There were heavy domestic withdrawals, but no general panic. Commercial banks were less exposed than their neighbors to the Austrian and German crises. Despite exchange controls and substantial write-downs on the part of banks, there were no large failures and no bank holidays.
Denmark	Compared with other countries, commercial bank deposits fell only slightly during 1931. There was no general run on the banks and no suspension of payments by any commercial bank.

APPENDIX TABLE 3.2 *(continued)*

Country	Description
England	Despite a sterling crisis in 1931, not one bank failed during the period. As in 1914, the Bank of England discounted illiquid foreign bills, although they did not receive a guarantee.
Greece	Although there was a currency crisis and several banks did fail, according to Mazower (1991: 224–25) ". . . what is striking about Greek banks is their avoidance of the sort of crisis which occurred elsewhere in the Balkans."
Japan	Japan had suffered a banking crisis in 1927, leading to a substantial decline in the number of banks during the following decade (from 1,425 to 462). However, most of the post-1929 change appears to have been the result of mergers. (Tamaki 1995: 160–65)
Lithuania	Despite heavy withdrawals from the commercial banks, there were no moratoria or legal restrictions on withdrawals. Only one private banking firm was forced to suspend payments as a result of the crisis of 1931.
Netherlands	The German banking crisis and the suspension of sterling convertibility were severely felt and normal channels of payment with Germany were interrupted. Substantial write-downs of bank capital, but no major bank suspensions or bank holidays.
Portugal	The number of commercial banks increased slightly during the period 1929–32, and, according to Reis (1995), one of the distinctive features of the Portuguese economy was the absence of a banking crisis.
Spain	Although one large bank, Banca de Cataluña, was liquidated, according to Tortella and Palafox (1984: 105) ". . . nothing massive or drastic occurred, no really important banks suspended payments; no large scale 'salvaging operation' was required."
Sweden	The collapse of the Kreuger industrial and financial empire led to weakness of one large bank (Skandinaviska Kreditaktiebolaget), but ". . . the events of 1931 had no serious visible repercussions on the commercial banks" (League of Nations 1934: 193). Deposits and assets dropped only slightly during 1930–33 and, in fact, rose during 1929–33.

Source: Grossman (1994: appendix).

Appendix to Chapter 5

APPENDIX TABLE 5.1
Merger Movements before 1940

Country	Years	Description
Australia	1840–44	Crisis led to the elimination of small, local, branchless banks. London banks absorbed two such banks during the preceding expansion (1840–41) and a Tasmanian one (where the slump hit later) in 1843–44. Four more banks closed or failed during 1843–44.
Australia	1879–86	Six mergers in seven years (out of a total of less than thirty banks), mostly by banks beginning to build nationwide branch networks, although these mergers were primarily by banks that already had branches or main offices in the areas of the targets.
Australia	1891–92	Two large mergers: 1891 merger of two Australian-based banks and 1892 merger of two London-based banks.
Australia	1917–31	Twelve mergers in fourteen years: five in 1917–18, three in 1921–22, three in 1927, and one in 1931. About one-third involved large banks acquiring small local banks; about one-half involved banks with nationwide businesses as a party to the transaction; two involved the mergers of two regional banks based in the same geographic area (e.g., Bank of North Queensland and Royal Bank of Queensland).
Austria	1857	Crisis led to the downfall of many private banking houses and the absorption of others by new banks.
Austria	1873	Crisis led to substantial consolidation among banks.
Austria	1920s	The dismemberment of the Austro-Hungarian Empire led to consolidation among Austrian banks.
Belgium	Pre–World War I	Some consolidation, but (except for Société Générale) Belgium is dominated by unit (i.e., unbranched) banks. Houtman-De Smelt (1994) asserts that consolidations took place in the second half of the nineteenth century; Chlepner (1943) disagrees.

APPENDIX TABLE 5.1 (*continued*)

Country	Years	Description
Belgium	1920s, especially late 1920s	A law of July 23, 1927, made mergers easier to accomplish and a substantial number took place during 1928–29 and in the wake of the 1931 crisis. The Bank of Brussels increased its banking group throughout the 1920s (from four to twenty banks) and four major banking organizations emerged during the 1920s.
Canada	1900–1931	Approximately one bank merger took place per year, although no more than two in any year, during this period. According to Beckhart (1929), mergers occurred when banks that were doing poorly and were likely to become insolvent were acquired.
Denmark	none	The number of commercial banks rose throughout the 1870–1920 period, while concentration of the top three banks fell. Important acquisitions did take place, but mergers on a large scale did not occur until the 1960s.
England	1830s	Legislation of 1833 allowed the formation of non-note-issuing joint stock banks within a sixty-five-mile radius of London. A boom in the 1830s followed by a banking crisis (1836–39) contributed to the mergers wave. A large majority of mergers involved joint stock banks taking over private banks. (Sykes 1926)
England	1860s	The Companies Act (1862) introduced limited liability which made it easier for banks to raise capital with which to undertake mergers. The crisis of 1866 gave further impetus to mergers. The majority of mergers involved joint stock banks absorbing private banks. (Sykes 1926)
England	1880s–1925	Heavy merger activity, encouraged by the low interest rate environment of the late 1880s and as part of a retrenchment following the Baring crisis. There was an increase in regional consolidations, mergers to promote firm growth, and mergers to counter competition later in this period. By this time, most mergers involve joint stock banks as both bother acquirers and targets. Treasury Committee on Bank Amalgamations (Colwyn Committee), appointed in 1917, discourages further mergers. (Sykes 1926)

APPENDIX TABLE 5.1 (*continued*)

Country	Years	Description
Finland	1929–35	Decrease in number of banks from seventeen to nine, mostly as weaker banks, primarily among those established around the time of World War I, merged in order to avoid failure.
France	none	No indication of widespread amalgamation activity.
Germany	Post-1873	Banks that were liquidated during the crisis were taken over.
Germany	1890s	Formation of industrial cartels in 1890s encouraged greater concentration in banking, and "communities of interest" (i.e., banking groups) were formed. Stock market legislation starting in the 1880s encouraged concentration of stock market trading in centrally placed banks.
Germany	1900–1913	Distress-motivated mergers and an expansion of banking groups took place following the 1901 crisis.
Germany	1917–27	Concentration rose, mostly through outright acquisitions and mergers, including those leading to the creation of the Danat-Bank in 1920 and Commerz und Privatbank in 1922.
Italy	1879	Increased mergers among private banks occurred during the recovery following the downturn of 1873–78. (DeRosa 1997: 250)
Italy	1929–36	Increased mergers of savings banks and cooperative banks. (DeRosa 1997: 259)
Japan	1896–99	Increase in mergers (sixteen out of 153 total banks) as national banks converted to ordinary banks when their charters expired.
Japan	1901–32	With government encouragement, the number of banks decreased substantially: by 12 percent due to mergers in 1900–1910, and by 24 percent during 1911–23. The merger trend was especially vigorous during 1917–23 and following the Bank Act of 1927.
Netherlands	1911–25	There were nearly nine mergers per year during this period, culminating in the establishment of five dominant banks. Merger activity had picked up in the mid-1890s, averaging one per year during 1874–93 and seven per year during 1894–1913. Heightened merger activity resulted from increasing industrialization during 1890–1910 and greater demands for credit by industry. During World War I the stock exchange was closed,

APPENDIX TABLE 5.1 (*continued*)

Country	Years	Description
		which directed more business to the banks. The crisis of the early 1920s also encouraged mergers, as did the post-crisis increase in external trade.
Norway	Possibly 1919–22	Very little amalgamation activity. Some mergers took place in 1919 and during 1920–22 when the government tried to forced some mergers in response to the postwar crisis. More significant amalgamations came in the post–World War II period (1945–80; 1960–80 for savings banks).
Sweden	1903–25	There were few mergers prior to 1903. During 1903–10, a steady (two to three per year) stream of small mergers developed. Many of these resulted from the end of enskilda banknote-issuing privileges. In 1910, a merger between two large banks set off further rounds of mergers. New legislation in 1909 and 1911 that allowed banks to issue shares, limited bank liability, and raised capital requirements also contributed to this trend (Larsson 1991: 84). Mergers increased during the prosperous years of 1916–19 and during the post–World War I slump (1922–23). During the 1910s, the number of banks fell while the number of bank branches rose, suggesting that bankers were merging, at least in part, to develop nationwide networks. In the 1920s, the number of both banks and branches fell, indicating that mergers may have been the result of bank weakness. (Olsson 1994: 969)
Switzerland	Post-1906	After the establishment of and concentration of note issue within the Swiss National Bank in 1907, a sharp decrease in the number of smaller note-issuing banks occurred through increased merger activity. (Cassis 1994: 1018)
United States	1910–31	Between 113 and 146 mergers per year took place during 1910–18; between 178 and 172 during 1919–20; between 278 and 315 during 1921–24; and more than five hundred per year during 1927–30. Legislation in 1918 eased mergers of two national banks (previously liquidation and de novo incorporation had been necessary). The McFadden Act (1927) provided for merger of state and national banks. The rapid economic growth and stock market advances in the late 1920s were also conducive to merger activity. (White 1985)

Bibliography

——— (1877). "Banking in Babylon Some 2,500 Years Since." *The Bankers' Magazine*: 720–21.

Abiad, Abdul, and Ashoka Mody (2003). "Financial Reform: What Shakes It? What Shapes It?" IMF Working Paper no. 03/70. Washington: International Monetary Fund.

Abrams, Rickard K., and Michael W. Taylor (2000). "Issues in Financial Sector Supervision." IMF Working Paper no. 00/213. Washington: International Monetary Fund.

Acres, Wilfrid Marston (1931). *The Bank of England from Within, 1694–1900*. London: Oxford University Press.

Adams, Thomas Francis Morton (1964). *A Financial History of Modern Japan*. Tokyo: Research (Japan), Ltd.

Ahrens, Gerhard (1986). *Krisenmanagement 1857: Staat Und Kaufmannschaft in Hamburg Während Der Ersten Weltwirtschaftskrise*. Hamburg: Verlag Verein für Hamburgische Geschichte.

Akhavein, Jalal D., Allen N. Berger, and David B. Humphrey (1997). "The Effects of Megamergers on Efficiency and Prices: Evidence from a Bank Profit Function." *Review of Industrial Organization* 12(1): 95–139.

Alborn, Timothy L. (1998). *Conceiving Companies: Joint-Stock Politics in Victorian England*. London: Routledge.

Aliber, Robert Z. (1972). "The Commission on Money and Credit: Ten Years Later." *Journal of Money, Credit and Banking* 4(4): 915–29.

Allen, Arthur M., Sydney R. Cope, L.J.H. Dark, and H. J. Witheridge (1938). *Commercial Banking Legislation and Control*. London: Macmillan and Co.

Altman, Oscar L. (1961). "Foreign Markets for Dollars, Sterling, and Other Currencies." *Staff Papers of the International Monetary Fund* 8(3): 313–52.

——— (1963). "Recent Developments in Foreign Markets for Dollars and Other Currencies." *Staff Papers of the International Monetary Fund* 10(1): 48–93.

——— (1965). "Euro-Dollars: Some Further Comments." *Staff Papers of the International Monetary Fund* 12(1): 1–16.

Amel, Dean, Colleen Barnes, Fabio Panetta, and Carmelo Salleo (2004). "Consolidation and Efficiency in the Financial Sector: A Review of the International Evidence." *Journal of Banking and Finance* 28(10): 2493–2519.

American Bankers Association (1933). *The Guaranty of Bank Deposits*. New York: Economic Policy Commission of the American Bankers Association.

Amyx, Jennifer Ann (2004). *Japan's Financial Crisis: Institutional Rigidity and Reluctant Change*. Princeton: Princeton University Press.

Anderson, Christopher W., and Terry L. Campbell II (2000). "Restructuring the Japanese Banking System: Has Japan Gone Far Enough?" *International Review of Financial Analysis* 9(2): 197–218.

Andersson, Ingvar (1956). *A History of Sweden*. New York: Frederick A. Praeger.

Andréadès, Andreas Michael (1966). *History of the Bank of England, 1640–1903*. New York: August M. Kelley.

Andreau, Jean (1999). *Banking and Business in the Roman World*. Cambridge: Cambridge University Press.

Andrew, A. Piatt (1908). "Substitutes for Cash in the Panic of 1907." *Quarterly Journal of Economics* 22(4): 497–516.

Ang, James S., and Terry Richardson (1994). "The Underwriting Experience of Commercial Bank Affiliates Prior to the Glass-Steagall Act: A Reexamination of Evidence for Passage of the Act." *Journal of Banking and Finance* 18(2): 351–95.

Arndt, H. W., and W. J. Blackert (1977). *The Australian Trading Banks*. Carlton: Melbourne University Press.

Arrow, Kenneth J. (1971). *Essays in the Theory of Risk-Bearing*. Chicago: Markham Publishing Company.

Ashcraft, Adam B. (2004). "Are Bank Holding Companies a Source of Strength to Their Banking Subsidiaries?" Staff Report no. 189. New York: Federal Reserve Bank of New York.

Ashton, T. S. (1968). *The Industrial Revolution, 1760–1830*. London: Oxford University Press.

Australia. Commonwealth Bureau of Census and Statistics (various). *Finance Bulletin*. Melbourne: Commonwealth Bureau of Census and Statistics.

Australia. Parliament. House of Representatives. Standing Committee on Finance and Public Administration (1991). *A Pocket Full of Change: Banking and Deregulation*. Canberra: Australian Government Publishing Service.

Australia. Royal Commission on the Monetary and Banking Systems of Australia (1937). *Report*. Canberra: Commonwealth Printer.

Bagehot, Walter (1848). "The Currency Problem." *The Prospective Review* 4(15): 297–337.

——— (1924). *Lombard Street*. London: J. Murray.

Balke, Nathan S., and Robert J. Gordon (1986). "The American Business Cycle: Historical Data." In *The American Business Cycle: Continuity and Change*, ed. Robert J. Gordon, 781–850. Chicago: University of Chicago Press.

Baltensperger, Ernst (1990). "The Economic Theory of Banking Regulation." *Occasional Papers, Center for the Study of the New Institutional Economics, Universität des Saarlandes* 2: 1–21.

Baltensperger, Ernst, and Andrea Behrends (1994). "Financial Integration and Innovation in Europe: A Review Essay." *Open Economies Review* 5(3): 289–301.

Baltensperger, Ernst, and Jean Dermine (1987). "Banking Deregulation in Europe." *Economic Policy* 2(4): 63–109.

Baltzer, Markus (2006). "European Financial Market Integration in the Gründerboom and Gründerkrach: Evidence from European Cross-Listings." Working Paper no. 111. Vienna: Österreichische Nationalbank.

Bank for International Settlements (1996). *Sixty-Sixth Annual Report*. Basel: Bank for International Settlements.

——— (1999). *Sixty-Ninth Annual Report*. Basel: Bank for International Settlements.

Bank of Japan (1966a). *Hundred-Year Statistics of the Japanese Economy*. Tokyo: Bank of Japan.

———— (1966b). *Supplement to Hundred-Year Statistics of the Japanese Economy: English Translation of Explanatory Notes*. Tokyo: Bank of Japan.

———— (various). *Economic Statistics of Japan*. Tokyo: Bank of Japan.

Banque nationale de Belgique (1934). "La Situation Des Établissements De Crédit En Belgique En 1933." *Bulletin d'Information et Documentation* 11: 237–51.

Barendregt, Jaap, and Hans Visser (1997). "Towards a New Maturity, 1940–1990." In *A Financial History of the Netherlands*, ed. Marjolein C. 't Hart, Joost Jonker, and Jan Luiten van Zanden, 152–94. Cambridge: Cambridge University Press.

Baring, Francis (1797 [1993]). *Observations on the Establishment of the Bank of England, and on the Paper Circulation of the Country*. London: Minerva Press.

Barth, James R., Philip Bartholomew, and Carol Labich (1989). "Moral Hazard and the Thrift Crisis: An Analysis of 1988 Resolutions." FHLBB Research Paper no. 160. Washington: Office of Policy and Economic Research, Federal Home Loan Bank Board.

Barth, James R., Gerard Caprio, Jr., and Ross Levine (2001a). "Banking Systems around the Globe: Do Regulation and Ownership Affect Performance and Stability?" In *Prudential Supervision: What Works and What Doesn't*, ed. Frederic S. Mishkin, 31–88. Chicago and London: University of Chicago Press.

———— (2001b). "The Regulation and Supervision of Banks around the World: A New Database." World Bank Policy Research Working Paper no. 2588. Washington: World Bank.

———— (2004). "Bank Regulation and Supervision: What Works Best?" *Journal of Financial Intermediation* 13(2): 205–48.

———— (2006). *Rethinking Bank Regulation*. Cambridge: Cambridge University Press.

Basel Committee on Banking Regulation and Supervisory Practices (1975). "Report to the Governors on the Supervision of Banks' Foreign Establishments." Basel: Bank for International Settlements.

Basel Committee on Banking Supervision (1988). "International Convergence of Capital Measurement and Capital Standards." Basel: Bank for International Settlements.

———— (1997). "Core Principles for Effective Banking Supervision." Basel: Bank for International Settlements.

———— (1999). "A New Capital Adequacy Framework." Basel: Bank for International Settlements.

———— (2004). "Basel II: International Convergence of Capital Measurement and Capital Standards: A Revised Framework." Basel: Bank for International Settlements.

———— (2005). "International Convergence of Capital Measurement and Capital Standards: A Revised Framework." Basel: Bank for International Settlements.

———— (2009). "History of the Basel Committee and Its Membership." Basel: Bank for International Settlements.

Batchelor, Roy A. (1986). "The Avoidance of Catastrophe: Two Nineteenth-Century Banking Crises." In *Financial Crises and the World Banking System*, ed. Forrest Capie and Geoffrey Wood, 41–73. New York: St. Martin's Press.

Batenburg, A., S. Brouwer, and D. W. Louman (1954). "The Netherlands." In *Banking Systems*, ed. Benjamin H. Beckhart, 609–56. New York: Columbia University Press.

Battilossi, Stefano (2000). "Financial Innovation and the Golden Ages of International Banking: 1890–1931 and 1958–81." *Financial History Review* 7(2): 141–75.

Beck, Thorsten, Asli Demirgüç-Kunt, Luc Laeven, and Ross Levine (2008). *Finance, Firm Size, and Growth*. Journal of Money, Credit and Banking 40(7): 1379–1405.

Beck, Thorsten, Asli Demirgüç-Kunt, and Ross Levine (2000). "A New Database on Financial Development and Structure." *World Bank Economic Review* 14(3): 597–605.

——— (2001). "Law, Politics, and Finance." World Bank Policy Research Working Paper no. 2585. Washington: World Bank.

Becker, Gary (1983). "A Theory of Competition among Pressure Groups for Political Influence." *Quarterly Journal of Economics* 98(3): 371–400.

Beckhart, Benjamin H. (1929). "The Banking System of Canada." In *Foreign Banking Systems*, ed. H. Parker Willis and Benjamin H. Beckhart, 289–488. New York: Henry Holt and Company.

——— (1937). "The German Bank Inquiry." *Political Science Quarterly* 52(1): 86–116.

———, ed. (1956). *Banking Systems*. New York: Columbia University Press.

Belgium. Institut National de Statistique (various). *Annuaire Statistique de la Belgique*. Brussels: Institut National de Statistique, Ministère de l'intérieur.

Benink, Harald A. (2000). "Europe's Single Banking Market." *Journal of Financial Services Research* 17(1): 319–22.

Benink, Harald A., and David T. Llewellyn (1994). "Fragile Banking in Norway, Sweden and Finland: An Empirical Analysis." *Journal of International Financial Markets, Institutions and Money* 4(3–4): 5–19.

Benston, George J. (1990). *The Separation of Commercial and Investment Banking: The Glass-Steagall Act Revisited and Reconsidered*. New York and Oxford: Oxford University Press.

Berger, Allen N. (1995). "The Relationship between Capital and Earnings in Banking." *Journal of Money, Credit and Banking* 27(2): 432–56.

——— (2003). "The Efficiency Effects of a Single Market for Financial Services in Europe." *European Journal of Operational Research* 150(3): 466–81.

Berger, Allen N., Asli Demirgüç-Kunt, Ross Levine, and Joseph G. Haubrich (2004). "Bank Concentration and Competition: An Evolution in the Making." *Journal of Money, Credit and Banking* 36(3: part 2): 433–53.

Berger, Allen N., Rebecca S. Demsetz, and Philip E. Strahan (1999). "The Consolidation of the Financial Services Industry: Causes, Consequences, and Implications for the Future." *Journal of Banking and Finance* 23(2–4): 135–94.

Berger, Allen N., Richard J. Herring, and Giorgio Szegő (1995). "The Role of

Capital in Financial Institutions." *Journal of Banking and Finance* 19(3–4): 393–430.

Berger, Allen N., Anil K. Kashyap, and Joseph M. Scalise (1995). "The Transformation of the U.S. Banking Industry: What a Long, Strange Trip It's Been." *Brookings Papers on Economic Activity* 1995(2): 55–218.

Berger, Helge, and Jakob de Haan (1999). "A State within the State? An Event Study on the Bundesbank (1948–1973)." *Scottish Journal of Political Economy* 46(1): 17–39.

Bergman, U. Michael, Michael D. Bordo, and Lars Jonung (1998). "Historical Evidence on Business Cycles: The International Experience." In *Beyond Shocks: What Causes Business Cycles*, ed. Jeffrey C. Fuhrer and Scott Schuh, 65–113. Boston: Federal Reserve Bank of Boston.

Bergo, Jarle (2003). "Crisis Resolution and Financial Stability in Norway." Speech at the 50th Anniversary of Bank Indonesia, 10 December, 2003 (http://www.norges-bank.no/templates/article____18098.aspx#footnote2).

Bernanke, Ben S. (1983). "Nonmonetary Effects of the Financial Crisis in Propagation of the Great Depression." *American Economic Review* 73(3): 257–76.

———— (2001). "Comment On: Synergies between Bank Supervision and Monetary Policy: Implications for the Design of Bank Regulatory Structure." In *Prudential Supervision: What Works and What Doesn't,* ed. Frederic S. Mishkin, 293–97. Chicago and London: University of Chicago Press.

Bernanke, Ben S., and Harold James (1991). "The Gold Standard, Deflation, and Financial Crisis in the Great Depression: An International Comparison." In *Financial Markets and Financial Crises*, ed. R. Glenn Hubbard, 33–68. Chicago and London: University of Chicago Press.

Bernard, Jacques (1976). "Trade and Finance in the Middle Ages, 900–1500." In *The Fontana Economic History of Europe*. Vol. 1, *The Middle Ages*, ed. Carlo Cipolla, 274–338. New York: Harper and Row.

Biucchi, B. M. (1975). "Switzerland, 1830–1914." In *The Fontana Economic History of Europe*. Vol. 4, Part. 2, *The Emergence of Industrial Societies*, ed. Carlo Cipolla, 627–55. Glasgow: William Collins Sons and Co., Ltd.

Black, Harold A., M. Cary Collins, Breck L. Robinson, and Robert L. Schweitzer (1997). "Changes in Market Perception of Riskiness: The Case of Too-Big-to-Fail." *Journal of Financial Research* 20(3): 389–406.

Blanchard, Olivier, and John Simon (2001). "The Long and Large Decline in U.S. Output Volatility." *Brookings Papers on Economic Activity* 2001(1): 135–64.

Blass, Asher A., and Richard S. Grossman (1998). "Who Needs Glass-Steagall? Evidence from Israel's Bank Shares Crisis and the Great Depression." *Contemporary Economic Policy* 16(2): 185–96.

———— (2001). "Assessing Damages: The 1983 Israeli Bank Shares Crisis." *Contemporary Economic Policy* 19(1): 49–58.

Blocker, John Gary (1929). *The Guaranty of State Bank Deposits*. Lawrence: University of Kansas, School of Business.

Board of Governors of the Federal Reserve System (1976). *Banking and Monetary Statistics, 1941–1970*. Washington: Board of Governors of the Federal Reserve System.

———— (various). *Annual Statistical Digest*. Washington: Board of Governors of the Federal Reserve System.

Bodenhorn, Howard (1992). "Capital Mobility and Financial Integration in Antebellum America." *Journal of Economic History* 52(3): 585–610.

———— (2003). *State Banking in Early America: A New Economic History*. New York: Oxford University Press.

———— (2006). "Bank Chartering and Political Corruption in Antebellum New York: Free Banking as Reform." In *Corruption and Reform: Lessons from America's History*, ed. Edward Glaeser and Claudia Goldin, 231–57. Chicago: University of Chicago Press.

Bodfish, H. Morton (1931). *History of Building and Loan in the United States*. Chicago: United States Savings and Loan League.

Bogaert, Raymond (1966). *Les Origines de la Banque de Dépôt*. Leyden, The Netherlands: A.W. Sijthoff.

———— (1968). *Banques et Banquiers dans les Cités Grecques*. Leyden, The Netherlands: A. W. Sijthoff.

———— (1994). *Trapezitica Aegyptiaca : Recueil de Recherches sur la Banque en Egypte Gréco-Romaine*. Florence: Edizioni Gonnelli.

Bonelli, Franco (1982). "The 1907 Financial Crisis in Italy: A Peculiar Case of the Lender of Last Resort in Action." In *Financial Crises: Theory, History, and Policy*, ed. Charles P. Kindleberger and Jean-Pierre Laffargue, 51–65. Cambridge and New York: Cambridge University Press.

Bonin, Hubert (1992). *La Banque et les Banquiers en France: Du Moyen Age à Nos Jours*. Paris: Larousse.

———— (2005). "The Challenged Competitiveness of the Paris Banking and Finance Markets, 1914–1958." In *London and Paris as International Financial Centres in the Twentieth Century*, ed. Éric Bussière and Youssef Cassis, 183–204. New York: Oxford University Press.

Boot, Arnoud W. A. (1999). "European Lessons on Consolidation in Banking." *Journal of Banking and Finance* 23(2–4): 609–13.

Borchardt, Knut (1975). "Germany, 1700–1914." In *The Fontana Economic History of Europe*. Vol. 4, Part. 1, *The Emergence of Industrial Societies*. ed. Carlo Cipolla, 76–160. Glasgow: William Collins Sons and Co., Ltd.

Bordo, Michael D. (1985). "Some Historical Evidence (1870–1933) on the Impact and International Transmission of Financial Crises." *Revista di Storia Economica* 2(3): 41–78.

———— (1990). "The Lender of Last Resort: Alternative Views and Historical Experience." *Federal Reserve Bank of Richmond Economic Review* 76(1): 18–29.

Bordo, Michael D., and Barry Eichengreen, eds. (1993). *A Retrospective on the Bretton Woods System*. Chicago: University of Chicago Press.

———— (1999). "Is Our Current International Economic Environment Unusually Crisis Prone?" In *Capital Flows and the International Financial System*, ed. David Gruen and Luke Gower, 18–74. Sydney: Reserve Bank of Australia.

Bordo, Michael D., Barry Eichengreen, Daniela Klingebiel, and Maria Soledad Martinez-Peria (2001a). "Is the Crisis Problem Growing More Severe?" *Economic Policy* 32: 53–82.

———— (2001b). "Is the Crisis Problem Growing More Severe?" *Economic Policy* 32: Web appendices. www.economic-policy.org/pdfs/WebAppendices/bordo.pdf.

Bordo, Michael D., and Angela Redish (1987). "Why Did the Bank of Canada Emerge in 1935?" *Journal of Economic History* 47(2): 405–17.

Bordo, Michael D., and Hugh Rockoff (1996). "The Gold Standard as a 'Good Housekeeping Seal of Approval.'" *Journal of Economic History* 56(2): 389–428.

Bordo, Michael D., Hugh Rockoff, and Angela Redish (1994). "The U.S. Banking System from a Northern Exposure: Stability versus Efficiency." *Journal of Economic History* 54: 325–41.

———— (1996). "A Comparison of the United States and Canadian Banking Systems in the Twentieth Century: Stability versus Efficiency?" *Financial History Review* 3(1): 49–68.

Born, Karl Erich (1977). *Geld Und Banken Im 19. Und 20. Jahrhundert*. Stuttgart: Kröner.

Bosman, Hans W. J. (1986). *The Netherlands Banking System*. Amsterdam: Netherlands Institute for the Banking and Stockbroking Industry.

Bouvier, Jean (1960). *Le krach de l'Union Générale, 1878–1885*. Paris: Presses Universitaires de France.

Boyd, John (1999). "Expansion of Commercial Banking Powers . . . or, Universal Banking Is the Cart, Not the Horse." *Journal of Banking and Finance* 23: 655–62.

Boyd, John, and Mark Gertler (1994). "Are Banks Dead? Or Are the Reports Greatly Exaggerated?" *Federal Reserve Bank of Minneapolis Quarterly Review* 18(3): 2–23.

Braudel, Fernand (1972). *The Mediterranean and the Mediterranean World in the Age of Philip II*. New York: Harper and Row.

Breckenridge, Roeliff Morton (1895). "The Canadian Banking System 1817–1890." *Publications of the American Economic Association* 10(1–3): 13–476.

———— (1898). "Discount Rates in the United States." *Political Science Quarterly* 13(1): 119–42.

———— (1910). *The History of Banking in Canada*. National Monetary Commission. 61st Cong., 2d sess., 1910, S. Doc. 332. Washington: Government Printing Office.

Bremer, Cornelius Daniel (1935). *American Bank Failures*. New York: Columbia University Press.

Briault, Clive (1999). "The Rationale for a Single Financial Services Regulator." FSA Occasional Paper no. 2. London: Financial Services Authority.

Broaddus, J. Alfred, Jr. (1998). "The Bank Merger Wave: Causes and Consequences." *Federal Reserve Bank of Richmond Economic Quarterly* 84(3): 1–11.

Bröker, G. (1989). *Competition in Banking: Trends in Banking Structure and Regulation in OECD Countries*. Paris: Organization for Economic Cooperation and Development.

Bromberg, Benjamin (1942). "The Origin of Banking: Religious Finance in Babylonia." *Journal of Economic History* 2(1): 77–88.

Brown, Rayna, and Kevin Davis (1997). "The Wallis Report: Functionality and the Nature of Banking." *Australian Economic Review* 30(3): 310–15.

Browne, Lynn E., and Eric S. Rosengren (1988). "The Merger Boom: An Overview."

In *The Merger Boom: Proceedings of a Conference Held in October 1987*, ed. Lynn E. Browne and Eric S. Rosengren, 1–16. Boston: Federal Reserve Bank of Boston.

Broz, J. Lawrence (1997). *The International Origins of the Federal Reserve System*. Ithaca, NY: Cornell University Press.

Broz, J. Lawrence, and Richard S. Grossman (2004). "Paying for Privilege: The Political Economy of Bank of England Charters, 1694–1844." *Explorations in Economic History* 41(1): 48–72.

Burger, Albert E. (1969). "A Historical Analysis of the Credit Crunch of 1966." *Federal Reserve Bank of St. Louis Review* 51(9): 13–30.

Burns, Arthur F. (1988). *The Ongoing Revolution in American Banking*. Washington: American Enterprise Institute.

Butkiewicz, James L. (1995). "The Impact of a Lender of Last Resort During the Great Depression: The Case of the Reconstruction Finance Corporation." *Explorations in Economic History* 32(2): 197–216.

Butlin, S. J. (1953). *Foundations of the Australian Monetary System, 1788–1851*. Carlton: Melbourne University Press.

––––––– (1986). *The Australian Monetary System, 1851 to 1914*. J.F. Butlin.

Butlin, S. J., A. R. Hall, and R. C. White (1971). *Australian Banking and Monetary Statistics, 1817–1945*. Sydney: Reserve Bank of Australia.

Butson, H. E. (1929). "The Banking System of the United Kingdom." In *Foreign Banking Systems*, ed. H. Parker Willis and Benjamin H. Beckhart, 1144–1241. New York: Henry Holt and Company.

Caballero, Ricardo J., Takeo Hoshi, and Anil K. Kashyap (2008). "Zombie Lending and Depressed Restructuring in Japan," *American Economic Review* 98(5): 1943–77.

Cafagna, Luciano (1975). "Italy, 1830–1914." In *The Fontana Economic History of Europe*. Vol. 4, Part 1, *The Emergence of Industrial Societies*. ed. Carlo Cipolla, 279–328. Glasgow: William Collins Sons and Co., Ltd.

Cagan, Phillip (1963). "The First Fifty Years of the National Banking System—An Historical Appraisal." In *Banking and Monetary Studies*, ed. Deane Carson, 15–42. Homewood, IL: Richard D. Irwin.

––––––– (1965). *Determinants and Effects of Changes in the Stock of Money, 1875–1960*. New York: National Bureau of Economic Research.

Calhoun, George M. (1930). "Risk in Sea Loans in Ancient Athens." *Journal of Economic and Business History* 2: 561–84.

Calomiris, Charles W. (1989). "Deposit Insurance: Lessons from the Record." *Federal Reserve Bank of Chicago Economic Perspectives* 13(3): 10–30.

––––––– (1990). "Is Deposit Insurance Necessary? A Historical Perspective." *Journal of Economic History* 50(2): 283–95.

––––––– (1995). "The Costs of Rejecting Universal Banking: American Finance in the German Mirror, 1870–1914." In *Coordination and Information: Historical Perspectives on the Organization of Enterprise*, ed. Naomi R. Lamoreaux and Daniel Raff, 257–322. Chicago: University of Chicago Press.

––––––– (1999). "Gauging the Efficiency of Bank Consolidation During a Merger Wave." *Journal of Banking and Finance* 23(2–4): 615–21.

Calomiris, Charles W., and Gary Gorton (1991). "The Origins of Banking Panics: Models, Facts, and Bank Regulation." In *Financial Markets and Financial Crises*, ed. R. Glenn Hubbard, 109–73. Chicago: University of Chicago Press.

Calomiris, Charles W., and Jason Karceski (2000). "Is the Bank Merger Wave of the 1990s Efficient? Lessons from Nine Case Studies." In *Mergers and Productivity*, ed. Steven N. Kaplan, 93–161. Chicago: University of Chicago Press.

Calomiris, Charles W., and Joseph R. Mason (1997). "Contagion and Bank Failures During the Great Depression: The June 1932 Chicago Banking Panic." *American Economic Review* 87(5): 863–83.

Calomiris, Charles W., and Larry Schweikart (1991). *The Panic of 1857: Origins, Transmission, and Containment.* Journal of Economic History 61(4): 807–34.

Calomiris, Charles W., and Berry Wilson (2004). "Bank Capital and Portfolio Management: The 1930s 'Capital Crunch' and the Scramble to Shed Risk." *Journal of Business* 77(3): 421–55.

Cameron, Rondo (1953). "The Credit Mobilier and the Economic Development of Europe." *Journal of Political Economy* 61(6): 461–88.

———, ed. (1967). *Banking in the Early Stages of Industrialization: a Study in Comparative Economic History.* New York: Oxford University Press.

———, ed. (1972). *Banking and Economic Development: Some Lessons of History.* New York: Oxford University Press.

Canada (various). *Canada Gazette.* Ottawa: Queen's Printer.

——— (various). Census and Statistics Office. *Canada Year Book.* Ottawa. Statistics Canada.

Canada. Royal Commission on Banking and Finance. (1964). *Report of the Royal Commission on Banking and Finance (Porter Commission).* Ottawa: Queen's Printer.

Canals, Jordi (1997). *Universal Banking: International Comparisons and Theoretical Perspectives.* Oxford: Clarendon Press.

Cannon, James Graham (1900). *Clearing-Houses: Their History, Methods and Administration.* New York: D. Appleton and Company.

——— (1910). *Clearing Houses.* National Monetary Commission. 61st Cong., 2d sess., 1910, S. Doc. 491. Washington: Government Printing Office.

Capie, Forrest (2002). "The Bank of England as a Mature Central Bank." In *The Political Economy of British Historical Experience, 1688–1914*, ed. Donald Winch and Patrick O'Brien, 295–318. Oxford: Oxford University Press.

——— (2004). "Money and Economic Development in Eighteenth-Century England." In *Exceptionalism and Industrialization: Britain and Its European Rivals, 1688–1815*, ed. Leandro Prados de la Escosura, 216–32. Cambridge: Cambridge University Press.

Capie, Forrest, and Michael Collins (1999). "Banks, Industry and Finance, 1880–1914." *Business History* 41(1): 37–62.

Capie, Forrest, Charles Goodhart, Stanley Fischer, and Norbert Schnadt, eds. (1994). *The Future of Central Banking: The Tercentenary Symposium of the Bank of England.* Cambridge: Cambridge University Press.

Capie, Forrest, and Ghila Rodrik-Bali (1982). "Concentration in British Banking, 1870–1920." *Business History* 24(3): 280–92.

Caprio, Gerard, Jr., and Daniela Klingebiel (1996). "Bank Insolvencies: Cross-Country Experience." World Bank Research Working Paper no. 1620. Washington: World Bank.

——— (1997). "Bank Insolvency: Bad Luck, Bad Policy, or Bad Banking." In *Annual World Bank Conference on Economic Development 1996*, ed. Michael Bruno and Boris Pleskovic, 79–104. Washington: World Bank.

——— (1999, revised 2003). "Episodes of Systemic and Borderline Financial Crises." Data set. Washington: World Bank. Permanent link is http://go.worldbank .org/5DYGICS7B0.

Cargill, Thomas F. (2000). "What Caused Japan's Banking Crisis?" In *Crisis and Change in the Japanese Financial System*, ed. Takeo Hoshi and Hugh Patrick, 37–58. Boston, Dordrecht and London: Kluwer Academic.

Cargill, Thomas F., Michael M. Hutchison, and Takatoshi Ito (2000). *Financial Policy and Central Banking in Japan*. Cambridge, MA: MIT Press.

Carlson, Mark (2004). "Are Branch Banks Better Survivors? Evidence from the Depression Era." *Economic Inquiry* 42(1): 111–26.

Carlson, Mark, and Kris James Mitchener (2006). "Branch Banking, Bank Competition, and Financial Stability." *Journal of Money, Credit and Banking* 38(5): 1293–1328.

Carosso, Vincent P. (1970). *Investment Banking in America: A History*. Cambridge, MA: Harvard University Press.

Carr, Jack L., and G. Frank Mathewson (1988). "Unlimited Liability as a Barrier to Entry." *Journal of Political Economy* 96(4): 766–84.

Carr, Jack L., G. Frank Mathewson, and Neil Quigley (1995). "Stability in the Absence of Deposit Insurance: The Canadian Banking System, 1890–1966." *Journal of Money, Credit and Banking* 27(4): 1137–58.

Carruthers, Bruce G. (1996). *City of Capital: Politics and Markets in the English Financial Revolution*. Princeton: Princeton University Press.

Cassese, Sabino (1983). "The 'Division of Labour in Banking': the Functional and Geographical Distribution of Credit from 1936 to Today." *Review of Economic Conditions in Italy* 1983(3): 381–411.

Cassis, Youssef (1994). "Banks and Banking in Switzerland in the Nineteenth and Twentieth Centuries." In *Handbook on the History of European Banks*, ed. Manfred Pohl, 1015–1133. Brookfield, VT: Elgar.

——— (1995). "Commercial Banks in Twentieth-Century Switzerland." In *The Evolution of Financial Institutions and Markets in Twentieth-Century Europe*, ed. Youssef Cassis, Gerald D. Feldman, and Ulf Olsson, 64–77. Aldershot, Hampshire: Scolar Press.

——— (2006). *Capitals of Capital: A History of International Financial Centres*, 1780–2005. New York: Cambridge University Press.

Catterall, Ralph C. H. (1902 [1968]). *The Second Bank of the United States*. Chicago: University of Chicago Press.

Cetorelli, Nicola, and Michele Gambera (2001). "Banking Market Structure, Financial Dependence and Growth: International Evidence from Industry Data." *Journal of Finance* 56(2): 617–48.

Chami, Ralph, Mohsin S. Khan, and Sunil Sharma (2003). "Emerging Issues in Banking Regulation." IMF Working Paper no. 03/101. Washington: International Monetary Fund.

Checkland, S. G. (1975). *Scottish Banking: A History, 1695–1973*. Glasgow: Collins.

Chisholm, G. D. (1910). "Is Centralisation in Banking Conducive to the Best Interests of the Community?" *Bankers' Magazine* 90: 332–45.

Chlepner, B. S. (1926). *La Banque en Belgique*. Brussels: Maurice Lamertin.

——— (1930). *Le Marche Financier Belge Depuis Cent Ans*. Brussels: Falk Fils.

——— (1943). *Belgian Banking and Banking Theory*. Washington: Brookings Institution.

Ciocca, Pierluigi, and Gianni Toniolo (1984). "Industry and Finance in Italy, 1918–1940." *Journal of European Economic History* 13(2): 113–36.

Clair, Robert T., and Gerald P. O'Driscoll, Jr. (1993). "Learning from One Another: The U.S. and European Banking Experience." *Journal of Multinational Financial Management* 2(3–4): 33–52.

Clapham, John H. (1930). *An Economic History of Modern Britain: The Early Railway Age (1820–1850)*. Cambridge: Cambridge University Press.

——— (1932). *An Economic History of Modern Britain: Free Trade and Steel (1850–1886)*. Cambridge: Cambridge University Press.

——— (1938). *An Economic History of Modern Britain: Machines and National Rivalries (1887–1914) with an Epilogue (1914–1929)*. New York: Macmillan.

——— (1945). *The Bank of England: A History*. 2 vols. Cambridge: Cambridge University Press.

Clarke, M. St. Clair, and D. A. Hall (1832 [1967]). *Legislative and Documentary History of the Bank of the United States, Including the Original Bank of North America*. New York: A.M. Kelly.

Clements, Mary Ann (1966). "Deposit Interest Rate Regulation and Competition for Personal Funds." *Federal Reserve Bank of St. Louis Review* 51(11): 17–20.

Cohen, Jon S. (1972). "Italy, 1861–1914." In *Banking and Economic Development*, ed. Rondo Cameron, 58–90. New York: Oxford University Press.

——— (1988). "Was Italian Fascism a Developmental Dictatorship? Some Evidence to the Contrary." *Economic History Review* 41(1): 95–113.

Collins, Michael (1972). "The Langton Papers: Banking and Bank of England Policy in the 1830s." *Economica* 39(153): 47–59.

——— (1988). *Money and Banking in the United Kingdom: A History*. London and New York: Croom Helm.

——— (1989). "The Banking Crisis of 1878." *Economic History Review* 42(4): 504–27.

——— (1991). *Banks and Industrial Finance in Britain: 1800–1939*. Houndmills, Basingstoke, Hampshire: Macmillan.

——— (1992). "The Bank of England as Lender of Last Resort, 1857–1878." *Economic History Review* 45(1): 145–53.

——— (1998). "English Bank Development within a European Context, 1870–1939." *Economic History Review* 51(1): 1–24.

Collins, Michael, and Mae Baker (2003). *Commercial Banks and Industrial Finance in England and Wales, 1860–1913*. Oxford and New York: Oxford University Press.

Columbia University School of Business (1926). *Scandinavian Banking Laws: A Translation of the Acts and Regulations Governing the Central Banks*. New York: Columbia University Press.

Colvin, Christopher Louis (2007). "Universal Banking Failure? An Analysis of the Contrasting Responses of the Amsterdamsche Bank and the Rotterdamsche Bankvereeniging to the Dutch Financial Crisis of the 1920s." Economic History Working Paper no. 98/07. London: London School of Economics.

Conant, Charles A. (1915). *A History of Modern Banks of Issue.* New York: G.P. Putnam's Sons.

Cooper, Richard N., and Jane Sneddon Little (2001). "U.S. Monetary Policy in an Integrating World: 1960–2000." *New England Economic Review* 2001(3): 33–56.

Copland, D. B. (1929). "The Banking System of Australia." In *Foreign Banking Systems*, ed. H. Parker Willis and Benjamin H. Beckhart, 45–98. New York: Henry Holt and Company.

Cottrell, Philip L. (1979). *Industrial Finance, 1830–1914: The Finance and Organization of English Manufacturing Industry.* London and New York: Methuen.

—— (1994). "The Historical Development of Modern Banking within the United Kingdom." In *Handbook on the History of European Banks*, ed. Manfred Pohl, 1137–1273. Brookfield, VT: Ashgate.

Cotula, Franco, Tullio Raganelli, Valeria Sannucci, Stefania Alieri, and Elio Cerrito, eds. (1996). *I Bilanci delle Aziende di Credito, 1890–1936.* Rome: Editori Laterza.

Crafts, N.F.R. (1983). "British Economic Growth, 1700–1831: A Review of the Evidence." *Economic History Review* 36(2): 177–99.

—— (1998). "Forging Ahead and Falling Behind: The Rise and Relative Decline of the First Industrial Nation." *Journal of Economic Perspectives* 12(2): 193–210.

Craig, Valentine V. (1998). "Japanese Banking: A Time of Crisis." *FDIC Banking Review* 11(2): 9–17.

Crick, W. F., and J. E. Wadsworth (1936). *A Hundred Years of Joint Stock Banking.* London: Hodder and Stoughton.

Critchfield, Tim, Tyler Davis, Lee Davison, Heather Gratton, George Hanc, and Katherine Samolyk (2004). "Community Banks: Their Recent Past, Current Performance, and Future Prospects." *FDIC Banking Review* 16(3 and 4): 1–56.

Crockett, Andrew, Trevor Harris, Frederic S. Mishkin, and Eugene N. White (2003). *Conflicts of Interest in the Financial Services Industry: What Should We Do About Them?* Geneva and London: International Center for Monetary and Banking Studies and Centre for Economic Policy Research.

Curry, Timothy, and Lynn Shibut (2000). "The Cost of the Savings and Loan Crisis: Truth and Consequences." *FDIC Banking Review* 13(2): 26–35.

Curtis, Clifford Austin, Kenneth W. Taylor, and H. Michell (1931). *Statistical Contributions to Canadian Economic History.* Vol. 1, *Statistics of Banking.* Toronto: The Macmillan Company of Canada, Limited.

Cybo-Ottone, Alberto, and Maurizio Murgia (2000). "Mergers and Shareholder Wealth in European Banking." *Journal of Banking and Finance* 24(6): 831–59.

Danmarks Statistik (1969). *Kreditmarkedsstatistik: Statistiske Undersøgelser Nr. 24.* Copenhagen: Danmarks Statistik.

—— (various). *Statistisk Aarbog.* Copenhagen: Danmarks Statistik.

Davies, Glyn (1994). *A History of Money: From Ancient Times to the Present Day.* Cardiff: University of Wales Press.

Davis, Lance (1965). "The Investment Market, 1870–1914: The Evolution of a National Market." *Journal of Economic History* 25(3): 355–99.

de Bondt, Gabe J., and Henriette M. Prast (2000). "Bank Capital Ratios in the 1990s: Cross-Country Evidence." *Banca Nazionale del Lavoro Quarterly Review* 53(212): 71–97.

De Gregorio, José, and Pablo E. Guidotti (1995). "Financial Development and Economic Growth." *World Development* 23(3): 433–48.

De Jong, A. M. (1929). "The Banking System of Holland." In *Foreign Banking Systems*, ed. H. Parker Willis and Benjamin H. Beckhart, 723–64. New York: Henry Holt and Company.

De Jonge, J. A. (1971). "Industrial Growth in the Netherlands, 1850–1914." *Acta Historiae Neerlandicae* 5: 159–212.

De Long, J. Bradford (1991). "Did J. P. Morgan's Men Add Value?: An Economist's Perspective on Financial Capitalism." In *Inside the Business Enterprise: Historical Perspectives on the Use of Information*, ed. Peter Temin, 205–36. Chicago: University of Chicago Press and National Bureau of Economic Research.

de Luna Martinez, José, and Thomas A. Rose (2003). "International Survey of Integrated Financial Sector Supervision." World Bank Policy Research Working Paper no. 3096. Washington: World Bank.

De Roover, Raymond Adrien (1942). "Money, Banking, and Credit in Medieval Bruges." *Journal of Economic History* 2: 52–65.

——— (1946a). "The Medici Bank: Organization and Management." *Journal of Economic History* 6(1): 24–52.

——— (1946b). "The Medici Bank: Financial and Commercial Operations." *Journal of Economic History* 6(2): 153–72.

——— (1947). "The Decline of the Medici Bank." *Journal of Economic History* 7(1): 69–82.

——— (1948a). *Money, Banking and Credit in Mediaeval Bruges; Italian Merchant Bankers, Lombards and Money-Changers.* Cambridge, MA: Mediaeval Academy of America.

——— (1948b). *The Medici Bank: Its Organization, Management, Operations, and Decline.* New York: New York University Press.

——— (1953). *L'evolution de la Lettre de Change, XIVe–XVIIIe Siecles.* Paris: A. Colin.

——— (1954). "New Interpretations of the History of Banking." *Journal of World History* 2:38–76.

——— (1963). "The Organization of Trade." In *The Cambridge Economic History of Europe*, ed. M. M. Postan, E. E. Rich, and Edward Miller, 42–118. Cambridge: Cambridge University Press.

——— (1968). *The Rise and Decline of the Medici Bank, 1397–1494.* Cambridge, MA: Harvard University Press.

——— (1974). *Business, Banking, and Economic Thought in Late Medieval and Early Modern Europe.* Chicago: University of Chicago Press.

De Rosa, Luigi (1997). "The Role of Banking in Italy's Industrialization, Nineteenth to Twentieth Century." *Banking, Trade, and Industry: Europe, America and Asia from the Thirteenth to the Twentieth Century,* ed. Alice Teichova, Ginette Kurgan-Van Henenryk, and Dieter Ziegler, 245–62. Cambridge: Cambridge University Press.

De Vries, Johan (1994). "The Netherlands Financial Empire." In *Handbook on the History of European Banks,* ed. Manfred Pohl, 719–87. Brookfield, VT: Ashgate.

Deane, Phyllis (1979). *The First Industrial Revolution.* Cambridge: Cambridge University Press.

Dehejia, Rajeev, and Adriana Lleras-Muney (2003). "Why Does Financial Development Matter? The United States from 1900 to 1940." NBER Working Paper no. 9551. Cambridge, MA: National Bureau of Economic Research.

Dekle, Robert, and Kenneth Kletzer (2002). "Domestic Bank Regulation and Financial Crises: Theory and Empirical Evidence from East Asia." In *Preventing Currency Crises in Emerging Markets,* ed. Sebastian Edwards and Jeffrey A. Frankel, 507–58. Chicago: University of Chicago Press.

Della Volta, Richard (1893). "The Italian Banking Crisis." *Journal of Political Economy* 2(1): 1–25.

Demirgüç-Kunt, Asli, and Edward J. Kane (2001). "Deposit Insurance around the World: Where Does It Work?" NBER Working Paper no. 8493. Cambridge, MA: National Bureau of Economic Research.

Demirgüç-Kunt, Asli, and Ross Levine, eds. (2001). *Financial Structure and Economic Growth: A Cross-Country Comparison of Banks, Markets, and Development.* Cambridge, MA: MIT Press.

Demirgüç-Kunt, Asli, and Tolga Sobaci (2000). "Deposit Insurance around the World: A Data Base." World Bank Policy Research Working Paper no. 3628. Washington: World Bank.

Demsetz, Rebecca S., and Philip E. Strahan (1997). "Diversification, Size, and Risk at Bank Holding Companies." *Journal of Money, Credit and Banking* 29(3): 300–13.

Dermine, Jean (1996). "European Banking Integration, Ten Years After." *European Financial Management* 2(3): 331–53.

——— (2000). "Bank Mergers in Europe: The Public Policy Issues." *Journal of Common Market Studies* 38(3): 409–25.

——— (2002). "European Banking: Past, Present and Future." *Paper presented to the Second ECB Central Banking Conference: The Transformation of the European Financial System,* Frankfurt am Main, Germany, October 24 and 25, 2002.

Des Essars, Pierre (1896). "A History of Banking in the Latin Nations." In *A History of Banking in All the Leading Nations,* Vol. 3, 1–412. New York: Journal of Commerce and Commercial Bulletin.

Dessauer, Marie (1935). "The German Bank Act of 1934." *Review of Economic Studies* 2(3): 214–24.

Deutsche Bundesbank (1976). *Deutsches Geld- und Bankwesen in Zahlen, 1876–1975.* Frankfurt: Knapp.

Dewald, William G. (1972). "The National Monetary Commission: A Look Back." Journal of Money, Credit and Banking 4(4): 930–56.

Dewey, Davis Rich (1934). *Financial History of the United States*. New York: Longmans, Green and Co.

Dewey, Davis Rich, and Robert Emmet Chaddock (1910). *State Banking before the Civil War and the Safety Fund Banking System in New York, 1828–1866*. National Monetary Commission. 61st Cong., 2d sess., 1910, S. Doc. 581. Washington: Government Printing Office.

Dhondt, Jan, and Marinette Bruwier (1975). "The Low Countries." In *The Fontana Economic History of Europe*, Vol. 4, Part 1: *The Emergence of Industrial Societies*, ed. Carlo Cipolla, 329–66. Glasgow: William Collins Sons and Co., Ltd.

Diamond, Douglas W., and Philip H. Dybvig (1983). "Bank Runs, Deposit Insurance, and Liquidity." *Journal of Political Economy* 91(3): 401–19.

Diamond, Douglas W., and Raghuram G. Rajan (2000). "A Theory of Bank Capital." *Journal of Finance* 55(6): 2431–65.

Dickson, P.G.M. (1967). *The Financial Revolution in England*. London: Macmillan.

Dixon, Rob (1993). *Banking in Europe: The Single Market*. London: Routledge.

Dodd, Donald B. (1993). *Historical Statistics of the States of the United States: Two Centuries of the Census, 1790–1990*. Westport, CT: Greenwood Press.

Domett, Henry Williams (1902). *A History of the Bank of New York, 1784–1884*. Cambridge, MA: The Riverside Press.

Drees, Burkhard, and Ceyla Pazarbaştioğlu (1995). "The Nordic Banking Crises: Pitfalls in Financial Liberalization?" IMF Working Paper no. 95/61. Washington: International Monetary Fund.

Dunbar, Charles F. (1892). "The Bank of Venice." *Quarterly Journal of Economics* 6(3): 308–35.

——— (1893). "The Bank of Venice." *Quarterly Journal of Economics* 7(2): 210–16.

Durviaux, Roland (1947). *La Banque Mixte*. Brussels: Établissements Émile Bruylant.

Dymski, Gary (1999). *The Bank Merger Wave: The Economic Causes and Social Consequences of Financial Consolidation*. Armonk, NY: M.E. Sharpe.

Eagly, Robert V. (1969). "Monetary Policy and Politics in Mid-Eighteenth-Century Sweden." *Journal of Economic History* 29(4): 739–57.

——— (1970). "Monetary Policy and Politics in Mid-Eighteenth-Century Sweden: A Reply." *Journal of Economic History* 30(3): 655–56.

Easterbrook, Frank H., and Daniel R. Fischel (1985). "Limited Liability and the Corporation." *University of Chicago Law Review* 52(1): 89–117.

——— (1991). *The Economic Structure of Corporate Law*. Cambridge, MA: Harvard University Press.

Economides, Nicholas, R. Glenn Hubbard, and Darius Palia (1996). "The Political Economy of Branching Restrictions and Deposit Insurance: A Model of Monopolistic Competition among Small and Large Banks." *Journal of Law and Economics* 39(2): 667–704.

Edelstein, Michael (1982). *Overseas Investment in the Age of High Imperialism*. New York: Columbia University Press.

Edey, Malcolm, and Brian Gray (1996). "The Evolving Structure of the Australian Financial System." Research Discussion Paper no. 9605. Sydney: Reserve Bank of Australia.

Edirisuriya, Piyadasa, and G. C. O'Brien (2001). "Financial Deregulation and Economies of Scale and Scope: Evidence from the Major Australian Banks." *Asia-Pacific Financial Markets* 8(3): 197–214.

Edwards, Jeremy, and Klaus Fischer (1994). *Banks, Finance and Investment in Germany*. Cambridge: Cambridge University Press.

Edwards, Jeremy, and Sheilagh Ogilvie (1996). "Universal Banks and German Industrialization: A Reappraisal." *Economic History Review* 49(3): 427–46.

Edwards, J. R. (1980). *British Company Legislation and Company Accounts, 1844–1976*. New York: Arno Press.

——— (1986). *Legal Regulation of British Company Accounts, 1836–1900*. New York: Garland.

Egge, Åsmund (1983). "The Transformation of Bank Structures in the Industrial Period: The Case of Norway." *Journal of European Economic History* 12(2): 271–94.

Ehrenberg, Richard (1928). *Capital and Finance in the Age of the Renaissance: A Study of the Fuggers and Their Connections*. New York: Harcourt, Brace and Company.

Ehrlich, Edna E., and Frank M. Tamagna (1954). "Japan." In *Banking Systems*, ed. Benjamin H. Beckhart, 517–72. New York: Columbia University Press.

Eichengreen, Barry (1984). "Mortgage Interest Rates in the Populist Era." *American Economic Review* 74(5): 995–1015.

——— (1987). "Agricultural Mortgages in the Populist Era: Reply to Snowden." *Journal of Economic History* 47(3): 757–60.

——— (1992). *Golden Fetters: The Gold Standard and the Great Depression, 1919–1939*. New York: Oxford University Press.

——— (1996). *Globalizing Capital*. Princeton: Princeton University Press.

——— (2008). "Thirteen Questions About the Subprime Crisis." Prepared for a conference of the Tobin Project, "Toward a New Theory of Financial Regulation," White Oak Conference and Residency Center, Yulee, Florida, 1–3 February 2008.

Eichengreen, Barry, and Michael D. Bordo (2002). "Crises Now and Then: What Lessons from the Last Era of Financial Globalization?" NBER Working Paper no. 8716. Cambridge, MA: National Bureau of Economic Research.

Eichengreen, Barry, and T. J. Hatton (1988). *Interwar Unemployment in International Perspective*. Dordrecht, The Netherlands and Boston: Kluwer Academic Publishers.

Eichengreen, Barry, and Kevin O'Rourke (2009). "A Tale of Two Depressions." Working Paper in progress. http://www.voxeu.org/index.php?q=node/3421.

Eichengreen, Barry, and Richard Portes (1987). "The Anatomy of Financial Crises." In *Threats to International Financial Stability*. ed. Richard Portes and Alexander K. Swoboda, 10–58. Cambridge: Cambridge University Press.

Eichengreen, Barry, Andrew K. Rose, and Charles Wyplosz (1995). "Exchange Market Mayhem: The Antecedents and Aftermath of Speculative Attacks." *Economic Policy* (21): 249–96.

Eichengreen, Barry, and Christof Ruehl (2000). "The Bail-in Problem: Systematic Goals, Ad Hoc Means." NBER Working Paper no. 7653. Cambridge, MA: National Bureau of Economic Research.

Eis, Carl (1969). "The 1919–1930 Merger Movement in American Industry." *Journal of Law and Economics* 12(2): 267–96.

Eitrheim, Øyvind, Jan T. Klovland, and Jan F. Qvigstad (2004). "Historical Monetary Statistics for Norway from 1819." Norges Bank Occasional Papers no. 35. Oslo: Norges Bank.

Elfakhani, Said, Rita F. Ghantous, and Imad Baalbaki (2003). "Mega-Mergers in the US Banking Industry." *Applied Financial Economics* 13(8): 609–22.

Enderle-Burcel, Gertrude (1994). "The Failure of Crisis Management: Banking Laws in Inter-War Austria." In *Universal Banking in the Twentieth Century: Finance, Industry and the State in North and Central Europe*, ed. Alice Teichova, Terry Gourvish, and Agnes Pogány, 116–128. London: Elgar.

Englund, Peter (1999). "The Swedish Banking Crisis: Roots and Consequences." *Oxford Review of Economic Policy* 15(3): 80–97.

Englund, Peter, and Vesa Vihriälä (2003). "Financial Crises in Developed Countries: The Cases of Sweden and Finland." Pellervo Economic Research Institute Working Paper no. 63. Helsinki: Pellervo Economic Research Institute.

Esty, Benjamin C. (1998). "The Impact of Contingent Liability on Commercial Bank Risk Taking." *Journal of Financial Economics* 47(2): 189–218.

European Commission (2005). "Cross-Border Consolidation in the EU Financial Sector." Commission Staff Working Document. Brussels: Commission of the European Communities. http://ec.europa.eu/internal_market/finances/docs/cross-sector/mergers/cross-border-consolidation_en.pdf.

European Commission and DRI Europe Ltd. (1997). *The Single Market Review.* Luxembourg: Office for Official Publications of the European Communities.

Evans, D. Morier (1849 [1969]). *The Commercial Crisis 1847–1848.* New York: Augustus M. Kelly.

——— (1859 [1969]). *The History of the Commercial Crisis, 1857–58, and the Stock Exchange Panic of 1859.* New York: Augustus M. Kelly.

Evans, Frank (1908). "The Evolution of the English Joint-Stock Limited Trading Company: VII. Trading Companies Incorporated under General Act of Parliament." *Columbia Law Review* 8(6): 461–80.

Evans, Lewis T., and Neil C. Quigley (1995). "Shareholder Liability Regimes, Principal-Agent Relationships, and Banking Industry Performance." *Journal of Law and Economics* 38(2): 497–520.

Fabozzi, Frank J., ed. (1981). *A Case History of Bank Failures: 1971–1975.* Hempstead, NY: Hofstra University.

Feavearyear, Albert (1963). *The Pound Sterling.* Oxford: Clarendon Press.

Federal Deposit Insurance Corporation. *Historical Statistics of Banking (HSOB)* Washington: Federal Deposit Insurance Corporation. http://www4.fdic.gov/hsob/index.asp.

——— (1997). *History of the Eighties—Lessons for the Future.* Vol. 1: *An Examination of the Banking Crises of the 1980s and Early 1990s.* Washington: Federal Deposit Insurance Corporation.

——— (1998a). *A Brief History of Deposit Insurance in the United States.* Washington: Federal Deposit Insurance Corporation.

——— (1998b). *Managing the Crisis: The FDIC and RTC Experience, 1980–1994.* Washington: Federal Deposit Insurance Corporation.

——— (various). *Statistics on Banking: A Statistical History of the United States Banking Industry*. Washington: Federal Deposit Insurance Corporation.

Feinstein, Charles H. (1972). *National Income, Expenditure and Output of the United Kingdom, 1855–1965*. Cambridge: Cambridge University Press.

Feis, Herbert (1930). *Europe, the World's Banker, 1870–1914*. New Haven: Yale University Press.

Fenstermaker, J. Van (1965a). *The Development of American Commercial Banking: 1782–1837*. Kent, OH: Kent State University Press.

——— (1965b). "The Statistics of American Commercial Banking, 1782–1818." *Journal of Economic History* 25(3): 400–13.

Ferguson, Roger W. (2003). "Capital Standards for Banks: The Evolving Basel Accord." *Federal Reserve Bulletin* 89(9): 395–405.

Ferrarini, Guido (2002). "Origins of Limited Liability Companies and Company Law Modernisation in Italy: A Historical Outline." Centro di Diritto e Finanza Working Paper no. 5-2002. Genoa: Center for Law and Finance.

Fetter, Frank W. (1965). *Development of British Monetary Orthodoxy, 1797–1875*. Cambridge, MA: Harvard University Press.

Findlay, Ronald, and Kevin H. O'Rourke (2003). "Commodity Market Integration, 1500–2000." In *Globalization in Historical Perspective*, ed. Michael D. Bordo, Alan M. Taylor, and Jeffrey G. Williamson, 13–62. Chicago: University of Chicago Press.

Fisher, Douglas, and Walter N. Thurman (1989). "Sweden's Financial Sophistication in the Nineteenth Century: An Appraisal." *Journal of Economic History* 49(3): 621–34.

Fisher, Irving (1932). *Booms and Depressions: Some First Principles*. New York: Adelphi.

——— (1933). "The Debt-Deflation Theory of Great Depressions." *Econometrica* 1(4): 337–57.

——— (1935). *100% money: designed to keep checking banks 100% liquid; to prevent inflation and deflation; largely to cure or prevent depressions; and to wipe out much of the national debt*. New York: Adelphi.

Fishlow, Albert (2003). "Review of Alexander Gerschenkron. *Economic Backwardness in Historical Perspective: A Book of Essays*." EH.Net Economic History Services, Feb. 14, 2003. http://eh.net/bookreviews/library/fishlow.

Fitz-Gibbon, Bryan, and Marianne Gizycki (2001). "A History of Last-Resort Lending and Support for Other Troubled Financial Institutions in Australia." System Stability Department Working Paper no. 2001–07. Sydney: Reserve Bank of Australia.

Flandreau, Marc (1997). "Central Bank Cooperation in Historical Perspective: A Sceptical View." *Economic History Review* 50(4): 735–63.

Flannery, Mark J., and Kasturi P. Rangan (2008). "What Caused the Bank Capital Build-up of the 1990s?" *Review of Finance* 12(2): 391–429.

Flood, Mark D. (1992). "The Great Deposit Insurance Debate." *Federal Reserve Bank of St. Louis Review* 74(4): 51–77.

Flux, Alfred William (1910). *The Swedish Banking System*. National Monetary Commission. 61st Cong., 2d sess., 1910, S. Doc. 576. Washington: Government Printing Office.

Fohlen, Claude (1975). "France, 1700–1914." In *The Fontana Economic History of Europe*. Vol. 4, Part 1: *The Emergence of Industrial Societies,* ed. Carlo Cipolla, 7–75. Glasgow: William Collins Sons and Co., Ltd.

Fohlin, Caroline (1999). "Universal Banking in Pre-World War I Germany: Model or Myth?" *Explorations in Economic History* 36(4): 305–43.

Forbes, Kevin F. (1986). "Limited Liability and the Development of the Business Corporation." *Journal of Law, Economics, and Organization* 2(1): 163–77.

Formoy, Ronald Ralph (1923). *The Historical Foundations of Modern Company Law.* London: Sweet and Maxwell.

Frame, W. Scott, and Lawrence J. White (2004). "Empirical Studies of Financial Innovation: Lots of Talk, Little Action?" *Journal of Economic Literature* 42(1): 116–44.

Fratianni, Michele (2006). "Government Debt, Reputation and Creditors' Protections: The Tale of San Giorgio." *Review of Finance* 10(4): 487–506.

Fratianni, Michele, and Franco Spinelli (1997). *A Monetary History of Italy.* Cambridge: Cambridge University Press.

Freedeman, Charles E. (1979). *Joint-Stock Enterprise in France, 1807–1867.* Chapel Hill: University of North Carolina Press.

———— (1993). *The Triumph of Corporate Capitalism in France, 1867–1914.* Rochester: University of Rochester Press.

Freixas, Xavier (1999). "Optimal Bailout Policy, Conditional and Constructive Ambiguity." Working Paper no. 400. Barcelona: Universita Pompeu Fabra.

Fremdling, Rainer, and Richard Tilly (1976). "German Banks, German Growth, and Econometric History." *Journal of Economic History* 36(2): 416–24.

Frennberg, P., and B. Hansson (1992). "Computation of a Monthly Index for Swedish Stock Returns, 1919–1989." *Scandinavian Economic History Review* 40(1): 3–27.

Friedman, Milton (1959). *A Program for Monetary Stability.* New York: Fordham University Press.

———— (1970). "Controls on Interest Rates Paid by Banks." *Journal of Money, Credit and Banking* 2(1): 15–32.

———— (1971). "The Euro-Dollar Market: Some First Principles." *Federal Reserve Bank of St. Louis Review* 53(7): 16–24.

Friedman, Milton, and Anna Jacobson Schwartz (1963). *A Monetary History of the United States, 1867–1960.* Princeton: Princeton University Press.

———— (1982). *Monetary Trends in the United States and the United Kingdom.* Chicago and London: University of Chicago Press.

Frisell, Lars, and Martin Noréus (2002). "Consolidation in the Swedish Banking Sector." *Riksbank Economic Review* 2002(3): 20–38.

Frothingham, Donald (1924). "Scandinavian Banking Situation." *U.S. Department of Commerce Trade Information Bulletin* 293: 1–59.

Fryde, E. B., and M. M. Fryde (1963). "Public Credit, with Special Reference to North-Western Europe." In *The Cambridge Economic History of Europe,* ed. M. M. Postan, E. E. Rich, and Edward Miller, 430–553. Cambridge: Cambridge University Press.

Fuji Bank. Research Division (1967). *Banking in Modern Japan.* Tokyo: Fuji Bank.

Galati, Gabriele (2002). "Settlement Risk in Foreign Exchange Markets and CLS Bank." *Bank for International Settlements Quarterly Review* (December 2002): 55–65.

Gale, Douglas, and Xavier Vives (2002). "Dollarization, Bailouts, and the Stability of the Banking System." *The Quarterly Journal of Economics* 117(2): 467–502.

Gallatin, Albert (1879). *The Writings of Albert Gallatin.* 3 vols. Philadelphia: J.B. Lippincott and Co.

Gardener, Edward P. M., and Philip Molyneux (1990). *Changes in Western European Banking.* London: Unwin Hyman.

Garrett, Thomas A., Gary A. Wagner, and David C. Wheelock (2003). "A Spatial Probit Analysis of State Banking Regulation." Working Paper no. 2003–044C. St. Louis: Federal Reserve Bank of St. Louis.

Gasslander, Olle (1962). *History of Stockholms Enskilda Bank to 1914.* Stockholm: Esselte AB.

Gatell, Frank Otto (1964). "Spoils of the Bank War: Political Bias in the Selection of Pet Banks." *American Historical Review* 70(1): 35–58.

——— (1965). "Secretary Taney and the Baltimore Pets: A Study in Banking and Politics." *Business History Review* 39(2): 205–27.

——— (1966). "Sober Second Thoughts on Van Buren, the Albany Regency, and the Wall Street Conspiracy." *Journal of American History* 53(1): 19–40.

Gerbi, Antonello (1954). "Italy." In *Banking Systems*, ed. Benjamin H. Beckhart, 421–516. New York: Columbia University Press.

Gerdrup, Karsten R. (2003). "Three Episodes of Financial Fragility in Norway since the 1890s." BIS Working Paper no. 142. Basel: Bank for International Settlements.

Gerlach, Stefan (1997). "Monetary Policy in the Nordic Countries after 1992." BIS Policy Paper no. 2. Basel: Bank for International Settlements.

Germain-Martin, Henry (1954). "France." In *Banking Systems*, ed. Benjamin H. Beckhart, 225–310. New York: Columbia University Press.

Gerschenkron, Alexander (1962). *Economic Backwardness in Historical Perspective.* Cambridge, MA: Harvard University Press.

Gertler, Mark (2001). "Comment On: Banking Systems around the Globe: Do Regulation and Ownership Affect Performance and Stability?" In *Prudential Supervision: What Works and What Doesn't*, ed. Frederic S. Mishkin, 88–94. Chicago: University of Chicago Press.

Gilbert, R. Alton (1986). "Requiem for Regulation Q: What It Did and Why It Passed Away." *Federal Reserve Bank of St. Louis Review* 68(2): 22–37.

Gillard, Lucien (2004). *La Banque d'Amsterdam et le Florin européen: Au Temps de la République néérlandaise (1610–1820).* Paris: Ecole des Hautes-Etudes en Sciences Sociales.

Gilman, Theodore (1904). "The Clearing-House System." *Journal of Political Economy* 12(2): 208–24.

Glassman, Cynthia A., and Stephen A. Rhoades (1980). "Owner vs. Manager Control Effects on Bank Performance." *Review of Economics and Statistics* 62(2): 263–70.

Glindemann, Paul (1929). "The Banking System of Denmark." In *Foreign Banking Systems*, ed. H. Parker Willis and Benjamin H. Beckhart, 489–521. New York: Henry Holt and Company.

Goldsmith, Raymond W. (1958). *Financial Intermediaries in the American Economy since 1900*. Princeton: Princeton University Press.

—— (1969). *Financial Structure and Development*. New Haven: Yale University Press.

—— (1982). "Comment on Minsky." In *Financial Crises: Theory, History, and Policy*, ed. Charles P. Kindleberger and Jean-Pierre Laffargue, 41–43. Cambridge: Cambridge University Press.

—— (1985). *Comparative National Balance Sheets: A Study of Twenty Countries, 1688–1978*. Chicago: University of Chicago Press.

Golembe, Carter H. (1960). "The Deposit Insurance Legislation of 1933: An Examination of Its Antecedents and Its Purposes." *Political Science Quarterly* 75(2): 181–200.

Good, David F. (1974). "Stagnation and 'Take-Off' in Austria, 1873–1913." *Economic History Review* 27(1): 72–87.

—— (1977). "Financial Integration in Late Nineteenth-Century Austria." *Journal of Economic History* 37(4): 890–910.

—— (1991). "Austria-Hungary." In *Patterns of European Industrialization*, ed. Richard Sylla and Gianni Toniolo, 218–47. New York: Routledge.

Goodhart, Charles (1969). *The New York Money Market and the Finance of Trade, 1900–1913*. Cambridge, MA: Harvard University Press.

Goodhart, Charles, Philipp Hartmann, David Llewellyn, Liliana Rojas-Suárez, and Steven Weisbrod (1998). *Financial Regulation: Why, How, and Where Now?* London: Routledge.

Goodhart, Charles, and Dirk Schoenmaker (1995). "Institutional Separation between Supervisory and Monetary Agencies." In *The Central Bank and the Financial System*, ed. C.A.E. Goodhart, 333–413. Cambridge, MA: MIT Press.

Goodhart, Charles, Dirk Schoenmaker, and Paolo Dasgupta (2002). "The Skill Profile of Central Bankers and Supervisors." *European Finance Review* 6(3): 397–427.

Gort, Michael, and Steven Klepper (1982). "Time Paths in the Diffusion of Product Innovations." *Economic Journal* 92(367): 630–53.

Gorton, Gary (1985). "Clearinghouses and the Origin of Central Banking in the United States." *Journal of Economic History* 45(2): 277–83.

Gorton, Gary, and Donald J. Mullineaux (1987). "The Joint Production of Confidence: Endogenous Regulation and Nineteenth Century Commercial-Bank Clearinghouses." *Journal of Money, Credit and Banking* 19(4): 457–68.

Gras, N.S.B. (1937). *The Massachusetts First National Bank of Boston, 1784–1934*. Cambridge, MA: Harvard University Press.

Greenspan, Alan (2004). "Banking." Remarks at the American Bankers Association Annual Convention, New York, October 5, 2004.

Gregory, T. E. (1929). *Select Statutes, Documents and Reports Relating to British Banking: 1832–1928*. 2 vols. London: Oxford University Press.

Gregory, T. E., and Annette Henderson (1936). *The Westminster Bank through a Century*. London: Westminster Bank.

Gross, Nahum T. (1975). "The Hapsburg Monarchy, 1750–1914." In *The Fontana Economic History of Europe*. Vol. 4, Part 1: *The Emergence of Industrial Societies*, ed. Carlo Cipolla, 228–78. Glasgow: William Collins Sons and Co., Ltd.

Grossman, Eugene (1954). "Switzerland." In *Banking Systems*, ed. Benjamin H. Beckhart, 693–732. New York: Columbia University Press.

Grossman, Peter Z. (1995). "The Market for Shares of Companies with Unlimited Liability: The Case of American Express." *Journal of Legal Studies* 24(1): 63–85.

Grossman, Richard S. (1988). *The Role of Bank Failures in Financial Crisis: Three Historical Perspectives*. Unpublished Ph.D. thesis, Cambridge, MA: Harvard University.

——— (1992). "Deposit Insurance, Regulation, and Moral Hazard in the Thrift Industry: Evidence from the 1930s." *American Economic Review* 82(4): 800–21.

——— (1993). "The Macroeconomic Consequences of Bank Failures under the National Banking System." *Explorations in Economic History* 30(3): 294–320.

——— (1994). "The Shoe That Didn't Drop: Explaining Banking Stability During the Great Depression." *Journal of Economic History* 54(3): 654–82.

——— (1999). "Rearranging Deck Chairs on the Titanic: English Banking Concentration and Efficiency, 1870–1914." *European Review of Economic History* 3(3): 323–49.

——— (2001a). "Double Liability and Bank Risk Taking." *Journal of Money, Credit and Banking* 33(2): 143–59.

——— (2001b). "Charters, Corporations, and Codes: Entry Restriction in Modern Banking Law." *Financial History Review* 8(2): 107–121.

——— (2002). "New Indices of British Equity Prices, 1870–1913." *Journal of Economic History* 62(1): 121–46.

——— (2007a). "Fear and Greed: The Evolution of Double Liability in American Banking, 1865–1930." *Explorations in Economic History* 44(1): 59–80.

——— (2007b). "Other People's Money: The Evolution of Bank Capital in the Industrialized World." In *The New Comparative Economic History: Essays in Honor of Jeffrey G. Williamson*, ed. Tim Hatton, Kevin O'Rourke, and Alan Taylor, 141–63. Cambridge, MA: MIT Press.

——— (2010). "The Emergence of Central Banks and Banking Regulation in Comparative Perspective." In *The State and Financial Systems in Europe and the USA: Historical Perspectives on Regulation and Supervision in the Nineteenth and Twentieth Centuries*, ed. Stefano Battilosi and Jaime Reis. Farnham, Surrey, UK: Ashgate.

Grossman, Richard S., and Masami Imai (2008). "The Evolution of a National Banking Market in Pre-War Japan." *Explorations in Economic History* 45(1): 17–29.

Group of Ten (2001). *Report on Consolidation in the Financial Sector*. Basel: Bank for International Settlements.

Grubel, Herbert G. (1971). "Risk, Uncertainty and Moral Hazard." *Journal of Risk and Insurance* 38(1): 99–106.

Grundfest, Joseph A. (1992). "The Limited Future of Unlimited Liability." *Yale Law Journal* 102(2): 387–426.

Gual, Jordi (1999). "Deregulation, Integration and Market Structure in European Banking." *EIB Papers* 4(2): 34–48. Luxembourg: European Investment Bank.

Guex, Sebastien (2000). "The Origins of the Swiss Banking Secrecy Law and its Repercussions for Swiss Federal Policy." *Business History Review* 74(2): 237–66.

Guinnane, Timothy W. (2002). "Delegated Monitors, Large and Small: Germany's Banking System, 1800–1914." *Journal of Economic Literature* 40(1): 73–124.

Guinnane, Timothy W., Ron Harris, Naomi Lamoreaux, and Jean-Laurent Rosenthal (2007). "Putting the Corporation in its Place." *Enterprise and Society* 8(3): 687–729.

Guiso, Luigi, Paola Sapienza, and Luigi Zingales (2007). "The Cost of Banking Regulation." European University Institute Working Paper ECO 2007/43. Florence: European University Institute.

Gurley, John G. (1967). "Review of *Banking in the Early Stages of Industrialization: A Study in Comparative Economic History* by Rondo Cameron, Olga Crisp, Hugh T. Patrick, and Richard Tilly." *American Economic Review* 57(4): 950–53.

Gurley, John G., and E. S. Shaw (1955). "Financial Aspects of Economic Development." *American Economic Review* 45(4): 515–38.

Hagberg, Thomas, and Lars Jonung (2002). "Financial and Economic Crises in the North: The Case of Denmark, Finland, Norway, and Sweden, 1870–2000." Working Paper: Seminar om Finanskrisen i Oslo 11–12 September, 2002. Oslo: Kredittilsynet.

Halpern, Paul, Michael J. Trebilcock, and Stuart Turnbull (1980). "An Economic Analysis of Limited Liability in Corporation Law." *University of Toronto Law Journal* 30: 119–50.

Hamao, Yasushi, Takeo Hoshi, and Tetsuji Okazaki (2005). "The Genesis and the Development of the Pre-War Japanese Stock Market." CIRJE no. F-320. Tokyo: University of Tokyo, Center for International Research on the Japanese Economy.

Hammes, David (2001). "Locating Federal Reserve Districts and Headquarters Cities." *The Region*, September 2001. Minneapolis: Federal Reserve Bank of Minneapolis.

Hammond, Bray (1947). "Jackson, Biddle, and the Bank of the United States." *Journal of Economic History* 7(1): 1–23.

——— (1957). *Banks and Politics in America: From the Revolution to the Civil War*. Princeton: Princeton University Press.

——— (1963). "Banking before the Civil War." In *Banking and Monetary Studies*. ed. Deane Carson, 1–14. Homewood, IL: Richard D. Irwin.

Hanc, George (2004). "The Future of Banking in America." *FDIC Banking Review* 17(4): 1–28.

Hanisch, Tore (1978). "The Economic Crisis in Norway in the 1930s: A Tentative Analysis of its Causes." *Scandinavian Economic History Review* 26(2): 145–55.

Hannan, Timothy H., and Stephen A. Rhoades (1992). "Future U.S. Banking Structure: 1990 to 2010." *Antitrust Bulletin* 37(3): 737–98.

Hansen, Per H. (1991). "From Growth to Crisis: The Danish Banking System from 1850 to the Interwar Years." *Scandinavian Economic History Review* 39(3): 20–40.

—— (1994). "Banking Crises and Bank Regulation: Denmark in the Interwar Period." Research on Banking, Capital and Society. Report no. 60. Oslo: The Research Council of Norway.

—— (1995). "Banking Crises and Lenders of Last Resort: Denmark in the 1920s and the 1990s." In *The Evolution of Financial Institutions and Markets in Twentieth-Century Europe*, ed. Youssef Cassis, Gerald D. Feldman, and Ulf Olsson, 20–46. London: Scolar Press.

—— (2000). "The Danish Savings Banks Association and the Deregulation of the Savings Banks, 1965–1975." In *Business and Society. Entrepreneurs, Politics and Networks in a Historical Perspective*, ed. A. M. Kuijlaars, K. Prudon and J. Visser, 219–36. Rotterdam: Center for Business History.

—— (2001). "Bank Regulation in Denmark from 1880 to World War Two: Public Interests and Private Interests." *Business History* 43(1): 43–68.

Hansen, Svend Aage (1982). "The Transformation of Bank Structures in the Industrial Period: The Case of Denmark." *Journal of European Economic History* 11(3): 575–603.

Hansmann, Henry, and Reinier Kraakman (1991). "Toward Unlimited Shareholder Liability for Corporate Torts." *Yale Law Journal* 100(7): 1879–1934.

—— (1992a). "Do the Capital Markets Compel Limited Liability? A Response to Professor Grundfest." *Yale Law Journal* 102(2): 427–36.

—— (1992b). "A Procedural Focus on Unlimited Shareholder Liability." *Harvard Law Review* 106(2): 446–60.

Hansson, Pontus, and Lars Jonung (1997). "Finance and Economic Growth: The Case of Sweden 1834–1991." *Research in Economics* 51(3): 275–301.

Hardach, Gerd (1995). "Banking in Germany, 1918–1939." In *Banking, Currency, and Finance in Europe between the Wars*, ed. Charles Feinstein, 269–95. New York: Oxford University Press.

Harley, C. Knick (1982). "British Industrialization before 1841: Evidence of Slower Growth During the Industrial Revolution." *Journal of Economic History* 42(2): 267–89.

Harper, Ian R. (1997). "The Wallis Report: An Overview." *Australian Economic Review* 30(3): 288–300.

Harris, Ron (2000). *Industrializing English Law: Entrepreneurship and Business Organization, 1720–1844*. Cambridge: Cambridge University Press.

Hart, Marjolein C. 't, Joost Jonker, and J. L. van Zanden (1997). *A Financial History of the Netherlands*. Cambridge: Cambridge University Press.

Hartcher, Peter (1998). *The Ministry: How Japan's Most Powerful Institution Endangers World Markets*. Boston: Harvard Business School Press.

Hawtry, R. G. (1918). "The Bank Restriction of 1797." *Economic Journal* 28 (109): 52–65.

—— (1938). *A Century of Bank Rate*. London: Longmans Green and Co.

Hay, John (1906). *Addresses of John Hay*. New York: Century Company.

Heckscher, Eli F. (1934). "The Bank of Sweden in its Connection with the Bank of Amsterdam." In *History of Principal Public Banks,* ed. J. G. Van Dillen, 161–200. The Hague: Martins Nijhoff.

——— (1954). *An Economic History of Sweden.* Cambridge, MA: Harvard University Press.

Heichelheim, Fritz M. (1958, 1964, 1970). *An Ancient Economic History, from the Palaeolithic Age to the Migrations of the Germanic, Slavic and Arabic Nations.* 3 vols. Leiden, The Netherlands: A.W. Sijthoff.

Herrala, Risto (1999). "Banking Crises vs. Depositor Crises: The Era of the Finnish Markka, 1865–1998." *Scandinavian Economic History Review* 47(2): 5–22.

Herrick, Myron T. (1908). "The Panic of 1907 and Some of Its Lessons." *Annals of the American Academy of Political and Social Science* 31(2): 8–25.

Hertner, Peter (1994). "Modern Banking in Italy." In *Handbook on the History of European Banks*, ed. Manfred Pohl, 561–671. Brookfield, VT: Elgar.

Hicks, John R. (1969). *A Theory of Economic History.* Oxford: Clarendon Press.

Hickson, Charles R., and John D. Turner (2003). "The Trading of Unlimited Liability Bank Shares in Nineteenth-Century Ireland: The Bagehot Hypothesis." *Journal of Economic History* 63(4): 931–58.

Hickson, Charles R., John D. Turner, and Claire McCann (2005). "Much Ado About Nothing: The Limitation of Liability and the Market for 19th Century Irish Bank Stock." *Explorations in Economic History* 42(3): 459–76.

Hidy, Ralph Willard (1949). *The House of Baring in American Trade and Finance; English Merchant Bankers at Work, 1763–1861.* Cambridge, MA: Harvard University Press.

Hildebrand, Karl-Gustaf (1971). *Banking in a Growing Economy: Svenska Handelsbanken since 1871.* Stockholm: Esselte Tryck.

Hildreth, Richard (1840). *Banks, Banking, and Paper Currencies.* Boston: Whipple and Damrell.

Hjerppe, Riitta (1989). *The Finnish Economy 1860–1985: Growth and Structural Change.* Helsinki: Government Printing Centre.

Hoffman, Philip T., Gilles Postel-Vinay, and Jean-Laurent Rosenthal (2000). *Priceless Markets: The Political Economy of Credit in Paris, 1660–1870.* Chicago: University of Chicago Press.

Holdsworth, John Thom, and Davis R. Dewey (1910). *The First and Second Banks of the United States.* National Monetary Commission. 61st Cong., 2d sess., 1910, S. Doc. 571. Washington: Government Printing Office.

Hollander, Jacob H. (1911). "The Development of the Theory of Money from Adam Smith to David Ricardo." *Quarterly Journal of Economics* 25(3): 429–70.

Holtfrerich, Carl-Ludwig (1988). "Relations between Monetary Authorities and Government Institutions: The Case of Germany from the 19th Century to the Present." In *Central Banks' Independence in Historical Perspective*, ed. Gianni Toniolo, 105–59. Berlin and New York: W. de Gruyter.

——— (1989). "The Monetary Unification Process in 19th-century Germany: Relevance and Lessons for Europe Today." In *A European Central Bank? Perspectives on Monetary Unification after Ten Years of the EMS,* ed. Marcello De Cecco and Alberto Giovannini, 216–41. Cambridge: Cambridge University Press.

Homer, Sidney, and Richard Sylla (1996). *A History of Interest Rates.* New Brunswick, NJ: Rutgers University Press.

Honohan, Patrick, and Daniela Klingebiel (2003). "The Fiscal Cost Implications of an Accommodating Approach to Banking Crises." *Journal of Banking and Finance* 27(8): 1539–60.

Honold, Eduard (1956). *Die Bankenaufsicht.* Mannheim: Wirtschafts-Hochschule Mannheim.

Horsefield, Keith J. (1960). *British Monetary Experiments, 1650–1710.* Cambridge, MA: Harvard University Press.

Hoshi, Takeo (2001). "What Happened to Japanese Banks?" *Bank of Japan Monetary and Economic Studies* 19(1): 1–29.

——— (2002). "The Convoy System for Insolvent Banks: How it Originally Worked and Why it Failed in the 1990s." *Japan and the World Economy* 14(2): 155–80.

——— (2006). "Economics of the Living Dead." *Japanese Economic Review* 57(1): 30–49.

Hoshi, Takeo, and Anil Kashyap (2000). "The Japanese Banking Crisis: Where Did it Come from and How Will it End?" In *NBER Macroeconomics Annual 1999,* ed. Ben S. Bernanke and Julio J. Rotemberg, 129–201. Cambridge, MA: MIT Press.

——— (2001). *Corporate Financing and Governance in Japan: The Road to the Future.* Cambridge, MA: MIT Press.

——— (2009). "Will the U.S. Bank Recapitalization Succeed? Eight Lessons from Japan." Chicago Booth Working Paper no. 09–28. Chicago: University of Chicago Booth School of Business.

Hoshi, Takeo, and Hugh T. Patrick (2000). "The Japanese Financial System: An Introductory Overview." In *Crisis and Change in the Japanese Financial System,* ed. Takeo Hoshi and Hugh Patrick, 1–33. Boston: Kluwer Academic.

Hosono, Kaoru, Koji Sakai, and Kotaro Tsuru (2007). "Consolidation of Banks in Japan: Causes and Consequences." NBER Working Paper no. 13399. Cambridge, MA: National Bureau of Economic Research.

Hotchkiss, Philo Pratt (1888). *Banks and Banking, 1171–1888.* New York: The Knickerbocker Press.

Houston, Joel F., Christopher M. James, and Michael D. Ryngaert (2001). "Where Do Merger Gains Come From? Bank Mergers from the Perspective of Insiders and Outsiders." *Journal of Financial Economics* 60(2-3): 285–331.

Houtman-De Smedt, Helma (1994). "The Banking System in Belgium through the Centuries." In *Handbook on the History of European Banks,* ed. Manfred Pohl, 47–94. Brookfield, VT: Ashgate.

Hughes, Joseph P., William W. Lang, Loretta J. Mester, Choon-Geol Moon, and Michael S. Pagano (2003). "Do Bankers Sacrifice Value to Build Empires? Managerial Incentives, Industry Consolidation, and Financial Performance." *Journal of Banking and Finance* 27(3): 417–47.

Hughes, J.R.T. (1956). "The Commercial Crisis of 1857." *Oxford Economic Papers* 8(2): 194–222.

Humphrey, Thomas M. (1975). "The Classical Concept of the Lender of Last Resort." *Federal Reserve Bank of Richmond Economic Review* 61(1): 2–9.

Humphrey, Thomas M., and Robert E. Keleher (1984). "The Lender of Last Resort: A Historical Perspective." *Cato Journal* 4(1): 275–318.

Hunt, Bishop Carleton (1936). *The Development of the Business Corporation in England, 1800–1867.* Cambridge, MA: Harvard University Press.

Hunt, Edwin S. (1990). "A New Look at the Dealings of the Bardi and Peruzzi with Edward III." *Journal of Economic History* 50(1): 149–62.

Hutchison, Michael, and Kathleen McDill (1999). "Are All Banking Crises Alike? The Japanese Experience in International Comparison." *Journal of the Japanese and International Economies* 13(3): 155–80.

Hyndman, H. M. (1932 [1967]). *Commercial Crises of the Nineteenth Century.* New York: Augustus M. Kelly Publishers.

Inter-Bank Research Organization (1978). *Banking Systems Abroad.* London: IBRO.

Irmler, H. (1954). "Western Germany." In *Banking Systems,* ed. Benjamin H. Beckhart, 311–72. New York: Columbia University Press.

Jackson, Howell E. (1993). "Losses from National Bank Failures During the Great Depression: A Response to Professors Macey and Miller." *Wake Forest Law Review* 28: 919–32.

James, Christopher (2000). "Is the Bank Merger Wave of the 1990s Efficient? Lessons from Nine Case Studies: Comment." In *Mergers and Productivity,* ed. Steven N. Kaplan, 162–71. Chicago: University of Chicago Press.

James, Harold (2001). *The End of Globalization: Lessons from the Great Depression.* Cambridge, MA: Harvard University Press.

James, John A. (1976a). "Banking Market Structure, Risk, and the Pattern of Local Interest Rates in the United States, 1893–1911." *Review of Economics and Statistics* 58(4): 453–62.

———(1976b). "The Development of the National Money Market, 1893–1911." *Journal of Economic History* 36(4): 878–97.

——— (1978). *Money and Capital Markets in Postbellum America.* Princeton: Princeton University Press.

Jamieson, Archibald Black (1953). *Chartered Banking in Canada.* Toronto: Ryerson Press.

Japan. Naikaku Tokeikyoku (Statistics Division of Cabinet) (various). *Nippon Teikoku Tokei Nenkan (Statistical Yearbook of Japanese Empire).* Tokyo: Naikaku Tokeikyoku.

Japan. Kaijo Gijutsu Anzenkyoku (1926). *Japanese Banking Regulations (Ordinary Banks).* Translated by J. E. De Becker.

Jayaratne, Jith, and Philip Strahan (1996). "The Finance-Growth Nexus: Evidence from Bank Branch Deregulation." *Quarterly Journal of Economics* 111(3): 639–71.

Jefferys, J. B. (1946). "The Denomination and Character of Shares, 1855–1885." *Economic History Review* 16(1): 45–55.

Jensen, Adolph (1896). "Banking in the Scandinavian Nations." In *A History of Banking in All the Leading Nations,* Vol. 4, 373–406. New York: Journal of Commerce and Commercial Bulletin.

Johansen, Hans Christian (1985). *Dansk Historisk Statistik 1814–1980.* Copenhagen: Gyldendal.

————— (1994). "Danish Banking History." In *Handbook on the History of European Banks*, ed. Manfred Pohl, 97–131. Brookfield, VT: Ashgate.

Johnes, Trevor (1928). "The Recent Banking Crisis and Industrial Conditions in Japan." *Economic Journal* 38(149): 76–80.

Johnson, Joseph French (1910). *The Canadian Banking System*. National Monetary Commission. 61st Cong., 2d sess., 1910, S. Doc. 583. Washington: Government Printing Office.

Johnston, Louis D., and Samuel H. Williamson (2008). "What Was the U.S. GDP Then?" *MeasuringWorth*, http://www.measuringworth.org/usgdp/.

Jones, Kenneth D., and Tim Critchfield (2004). "Consolidation in the U.S. Banking Industry: Is the 'Long, Strange Trip' About to End?" *FDIC Banking Review* 17(4): 31–61.

Jonker, Joost (1995). "Spoilt for Choice? Banking Concentration and the Structure of the Dutch Capital Market, 1900–40." In *The Evolution of Financial Institutions and Markets in Twentieth-Century Europe*, ed. Youssef Cassis, Gerald D. Feldman, and Ulf Olsson, 187–208. London: Scolar Press.

————— (1996a). *Merchants, Bankers, Middlemen: The Amsterdam Money Market During the First Half of the 19th Century*. Amsterdam: NEHA.

————— (1996b). "Between Private Responsibility and Public Duty. The Origins of Bank Monitoring in the Netherlands." *Financial History Review* 3(2): 139–52.

————— (1997). "The Alternative Road to Modernity: Banking and Currency, 1814–1914." In *A Financial History of the Netherlands*, ed. Marjolein C. 't Hart, Joost Jonker, and Jan Luiten van Zanden, 94–123. Cambridge: Cambridge University Press.

————— (2003). "Competing in Tandem: Securities Markets and Commercial Banking Patterns in Europe During the Nineteenth Century." In *The Origins of National Financial Systems*, ed. Douglas J. Forsyth and Daniel Verdier, 64–86. London: Routledge.

Jonker, Joost, and Jan Luiten Van Zanden (1995). "Method in the Madness? Banking Crises between the Wars, an International Comparison." In *Banking, Currency, and Finance in Europe between the Wars*, ed. Charles H. Feinstein, 77–93. New York: Oxford University Press.

Jonung, Lars (1993). "The Rise and Fall of Credit Controls: The Case of Sweden, 1939–1989." In *Monetary Regimes in Transition*, ed. Michael Bordo and Forrest Capie, 346–70. Cambridge: Cambridge University Press.

————— (2008). "Lessons from Financial Liberalization in Scandinavia." *Comparative Economics Studies* 50(4): 564–98.

Jonung, Lars, Jaakko Kiander, and Pentti Vartia (2008). "The Great Financial Crisis in Finland and Sweden: The Dynamics of Boom, Bust and Recovery, 1985–2000." Economic Papers no. 350. Brussels: Directorate-General for Economic and Financial Affairs of the European Commission.

—————, eds. (2009). *The Great Financial Crisis in Finland and Sweden: The Nordic Experience of Financial Liberalization*. Cheltenham, UK, and Northampton, MA: Edward Elgar.

Jörberg, Lennart (1975). "The Nordic Countries, 1850–1914." In *The Fontana Economic History of Europe*. Vol. 4, Part 2, *The Emergence of Industrial So-*

cieties, ed. Carlo Cipolla, 375–485. Glasgow: William Collins Sons and Co., Ltd.

Joslin, D. M. (1954). "London Private Bankers, 1720–1785." *Economic History Review* 7(2): 167–86.

Journal of Commerce and Commercial Bulletin (1896). *A History of Banking in all the Leading Nations*. 4 vols. New York: Journal of Commerce and Commercial Bulletin.

Jovanovic, Boyan, and Glenn M. MacDonald (1994). "The Life Cycle of a Competitive Industry." *Journal of Political Economy* 102(2): 322–47.

Kanaya, Akihiro, and David Woo (2000). "The Japanese Banking Crisis of the 1990s: Sources and Lessons." IMF Working Paper no. 00/7. Washington: International Monetary Fund.

Kane, Edward J. (1970). "Short-Changing the Small Saver: Federal Government Discrimination against the Small Saver During the Vietnam War." *Journal of Money, Credit and Banking* 2(4): 513–22.

——— (1977). "Good Intentions and Unintended Evil: The Case against Selective Credit Allocation." *Journal of Money, Credit and Banking* 9(1, part 1): 55–69.

——— (1988). "Interaction of Financial and Regulatory Innovation." *American Economic Review* 78(2): 328–34.

——— (1996). "De Jure Interstate Banking: Why Only Now?" *Journal of Money, Credit and Banking* 28(2): 141–61.

Kane, Edward J., and Berry K. Wilson (1998). "A Contracting-Theory Interpretation of the Origins of Federal Deposit Insurance." *Journal of Money, Credit and Banking* 30(3, part 2): 573–95.

Kaplan, Edward S. (1999). *The Bank of the United States and the American Economy*. Westport, CT: Greenwood Press.

Kapopoulos, Panayotis, and Fotios Siokis (2005). "Market Structure, Efficiency and Rising Consolidation of the Banking Industry in the Euro Area." *Bulletin of Economic Research* 57(1): 67–91.

Kapstein, Ethan B. (1989). "Resolving the Regulator's Dilemma: International Coordination of Banking Regulations." *International Organization* 43(2): 323–47.

Kashyap, Anil K. (1999). "What Should Regulators Do About Merger Policy?" *Journal of Banking and Finance* 23(2–4): 623–27.

——— (2000). "Is the Bank Merger Wave of the 1990s Efficient? Lessons from Nine Case Studies: Comment." In *Mergers and Productivity*, ed. Steven N. Kaplan, 171–77. Chicago: University of Chicago Press.

——— (2002). "Sorting out Japan's Financial Crisis." NBER Working Paper no. 9384. Cambridge, MA: National Bureau of Economic Research.

Kawai, Masahiro (2003). "Japan's Banking System: From Bubble and Crisis to Reconstruction." PRI Discussion Paper no. 03A–28. Tokyo: Policy Research Institute, Ministry of Finance.

Keehn, Richard H. (1974). "Federal Bank Policy, Bank Market Structure, and Bank Performance: Wisconsin, 1863–1914." *Business History Review* 48(1): 1–27.

Keeley, Michael (1990). "Deposit Insurance, Risk, and Market Power in Banking." *American Economic Review* 80(5): 1183–1200.

Kemmerer, E. W. (1914). "Issue of Emergency Currency in the United States." *Economic Journal* 24(96): 604–5.

Kemp, Tom (1993). *Historical Patterns of Industrialization*. London: Longman.

Kennedy, William P. (1987). *Industrial Structure, Capital Markets, and the Origins of British Economic Decline*. Cambridge: Cambridge University Press.

Kent, Raymond (1963). "Dual Banking between the Two Wars." In *Banking and Monetary Studies*, ed. Deane Carson, 43–63. Homewood, IL: Richard D. Irwin.

Kerr, Andrew William (1918). *History of Banking in Scotland*. London: A. and C. Black.

Kindleberger, Charles P. (1973). *The World in Depression, 1929–1939*. Berkeley: University of California Press.

―――― (1978). *Manias, Panics, and Crashes: A History of Financial Crises*. New York: Basic Books.

―――― (1982). "Sweden in 1850 as an 'Impoverished Sophisticate': Comment." *Journal of Economic History* 42(4): 918–20.

―――― (1984). *A Financial History of Western Europe*. London: Allen and Unwin.

―――― (1996). *Manias, Panics and Crashes: A History of Financial Crises*. Basingstoke: Macmillan.

King, Robert G., and Ross Levine (1993). "Finance and Growth: Schumpeter Might Be Right." *Quarterly Journal of Economics* 108(3): 681–737.

King, W.T.C. (1936). *History of the London Discount Market*. London: George Routledge and Sons.

Kishi, Masumi (1996). "Regulation Issues in the Era of Financial Liberalization: Japan, Korea and Taiwan." *Journal of Asian Economics* 7(3): 487–502.

Kleinert, Jörn, and Henning Klodt (2002). "Causes and Consequences of Merger Waves." Kiel Working Paper no. 1092. Kiel, Germany: Kiel Institute for the World Economy.

Klepper, Steven (1996). "Entry, Exit, Growth, and Innovation over the Product Life Cycle." *American Economic Review* 86(3): 562–83.

―――― (2002). "Firm Survival and the Evolution of Oligopoly." *RAND Journal of Economics* 33(1): 37–61.

Klepper, Steven, and Elizabeth Graddy (1990). "The Evolution of New Industries and the Determinants of Market Structure." *RAND Journal of Economics* 21(1): 27–44.

Klepper, Steven, and Kenneth L. Simons (2005). "Industry Shakeouts and Technological Change." *International Journal of Industrial Organization* 23(1–2): 23–43.

Kling, Gerhard (2006). "The Long-Term Impact of Mergers and the Emergence of a Merger Wave in Pre-World-War I Germany." *Explorations in Economic History* 43(4): 667–88.

Klingebiel, Daniela (2000). "The Use of Asset Management Companies in the Resolution of Banking Crises." World Bank Policy Research Working Paper no. 2284. Washington: World Bank.

Knutsen, Sverre (1991). "From Expansion to Panic and Crash: The Norwegian Banking System and Its Customers, 1913–1924." *Scandinavian Economic History Review* 39(3): 41–71.

——— (1995). "Phases in the Development of Norwegian Banking, 1880–1980." In *The Evolution of Financial Institutions and Markets in Twentieth-Century Europe*, ed. Youssef Cassis, Gerald D. Feldman, and Ulf Olsson, 78–121. London: Scolar Press.

Knutsen, Sverre, and Einar Lie (2002). "Financial Fragility, Growth Strategies and Banking Failures: The Major Norwegian Banks and the Banking Crisis, 1987–92." *Business History* 44(2): 88–111.

Koch, Richard (1910). *German Imperial Banking Laws*. National Monetary Commission. 61st Cong., 2d sess., 1910, S. Doc. 574. Washington: Government Printing Office.

Kohn, Meir (2003). "Business Organization in Pre-Industrial Europe." Working Paper 03-09. Hanover, NH: Dartmouth College.

Komlos, John (1983). "The Diffusion of Financial Technology into the Austro-Hungarian Monarchy toward the End of the Nineteenth Century." In *Economic Development in the Hapsburg Monarchy in the Nineteenth Century*, ed. John Komlos, 137–63. New York: Columbia University Press.

Koskenkylä, Heikki (1994). "The Nordic Banking Crisis." *Bank of Finland Bulletin* 68(8): 15–22.

Kotsopoulos, John (1981). "Franklin National Bank." In *A Case History of Bank Failures: 1971–1975*, ed. Frank J. Fabozzi, 322–47. Hempstead, NY: Hofstra University.

Krasa, Stefan, and Anne P. Villamil (1992). "A Theory of Optimal Bank Size." *Oxford Economic Papers* 44(4): 725–49.

Krooss, Herman Edward (1969). *Documentary History of Banking and Currency in the United States*. 4 vols. New York: Chelsea House Publishers.

Kroszner, Randall S. (1999a). "The Impact of Consolidation and Safety-Net Support on Canadian, US and UK Banks: 1893–1992: Comment." *Journal of Banking and Finance* 23(2–4): 572–77.

——— (1999b). "Is the Financial System Independent? Perspectives on the Political Economy of Banking and Financial Regulation." Unpublished working paper prepared for Swedish Government Inquiry on the Competitiveness of the Swedish Financial Sector. Chicago: University of Chicago.

Kroszner, Randall S., and Raghuram G. Rajan (1994). "Is the Glass-Steagall Act Justified? A Study of the U.S. Experience with Universal Banking before 1933." *American Economic Review* 84(4): 810–32.

Kroszner, Randall S., and Philip Strahan (1999). "What Drives Deregulation? The Economics and Politics of the Relaxation of Bank Branching Restrictions." *Quarterly Journal of Economics* 114(4): 1437–67.

——— (2001). "Obstacles to Optimal Policy: The Interplay of Politics and Economics in Shaping Bank Supervision and Regulation Reforms." In *Prudential Supervision: What Works and What Doesn't*, ed. Frederic S. Mishkin, 233–66. Chicago and London: University of Chicago Press.

Kryzanowski, Lawrence, and Gordon S. Roberts (1993). "Canadian Banking Solvency, 1922–1940." *Journal of Money, Credit and Banking* 25(3): 361–76.

——— (1999). "Perspectives on Canadian Bank Insolvency During the 1930s." *Journal of Money, Credit and Banking* 31(1): 130–36.

Kurgan-van Hentenryk, Ginette (1995). "Commercial Banking in Belgium, 1935–90." In *The Evolution of Financial Institutions and Markets in Twentieth-Century Europe*, ed. Youssef Cassis, Gerald D. Feldman, and Ulf Olsson, 47–63. London: Scolar Press.

Kuusterä, Antti (1994). "The Finnish Banking System in Broad Outline from the 1860s to the mid-1980s." *Handbook on the History of European Banks*, ed. Manfred Pohl, 135–81. Brookfield, VT: Elgar.

La Croix, Sumner J., and Christopher Grandy (1993). "Financial Integration in Antebellum America: Strengthening Bodenhorn's Results." *Journal of Economic History* 53(3): 653–58.

Laderman, Elizabeth, Ronald Schmidt, and Gary Zimmerman (1991). "Location, Branching, and Bank Portfolio Diversification: The Case of Agricultural Lending." *Federal Reserve Bank of San Francisco Economic Review* 1991(1): 24–38.

Laeven, Luc, and Fabian Valencia (2008). "The Use of Blanket Guarantees in Banking Crises." IMF Working Paper no. 08/250. Washington: International Monetary Fund.

Lamoreaux, Naomi R. (1985). *The Great Merger Movement in American Business, 1895–1904*. Cambridge: Cambridge University Press.

——— (1991). "Bank Mergers in Late Nineteenth-Century New England: The Contingent Nature of Structural Change." *Journal of Economic History* 51(3): 537–57.

——— (1994). *Insider Lending: Banks, Personal Connections, and Economic Development in Industrial New England*. Cambridge: Cambridge University Press.

Landes, David (1963). "A Chapter in the Financial Revolution of the Nineteenth Century: The Rise of French Deposit Banking." *Journal of Economic History* 23(2): 224–31.

Landmann, Julius (1906). "The Swiss National Bank." *Quarterly Journal of Economics* 20(3): 468–82.

Lane, Frederic C. (1937). "Venetian Bankers, 1496–1533: A Study in the Early Stages of Deposit Banking." *Journal of Political Economy* 45(2): 187–206.

——— (1944). "Family Partnerships and Joint Ventures in the Venetian Republic." *Journal of Economic History* 4(2): 178–96.

Lange, Even (1994). "The Norwegian System of Banking Institutions." *Handbook on the History of European Banks*, ed. Manfred Pohl, 791–818. Brookfield, VT: Elgar.

Lapeyre, H. (1956). "La Banque, les Changes et le Crédit au XVIe Siècle." *Revue d'Histoire Moderne et Contemporaine* 3: 284–97.

LaPorta, Rafael, Florencio Lopez-de-Silanes, Andrei Shleifer, and Robert W. Vishny. (1997). "Legal Determinants of External Finance." *Journal of Finance* 52(3): 1131–50.

——— (1998). "Law and Finance." *Journal of Political Economy.* 106(6): 1113–55.

Larsson, Mats (1989). "Public Control of Commercial Banks and Their Activities: The Swedish Example 1910–1970." Uppsala Papers in Economic History no. 2. Uppsala: University of Uppsala.

——— (1991). "State, Banks and Industry in Sweden, with Some Reference to the Scandinavian Countries." In *The Role of Banks in the Interwar Economy*, ed. Harold James, Håkan Lindgren, and Alice Teichova, 80–103. Cambridge: Cambridge University Press.

—— (1992). "Government Subsidy or Internal Restructuring? Swedish Commercial Banks During the Crisis Years of the 1920s." In *European Industry and Banking between the Wars*, ed. Philip L. Cottrell, Håkan Lindgren, and Alice Teichova, 126–46. Leicester, UK: Leicester University Press.

—— (1995). "Overcoming Institutional Barriers: Financial Networks in Sweden." In *The Evolution of Financial Institutions and Markets in Twentieth-Century Europe*, ed. Youssef Cassis, Gerald D. Feldman, and Ulf Olsson, 122–42. London: Scolar Press.

Larsson, Mats, and Håkan Lindgren (1992). "The Political Economy of Banking: Retail Banking and Corporate Finance in Sweden, 1850–1939." *Finance and Financiers in European History, 1880–1960*, ed. Youssef Cassis, 337–55. Cambridge: Cambridge University Press.

Laughlin, J. Laurence (1903). *The Principles of Money*. New York: C. Scribner's Sons.

Lavington, Frederick (1921). *The English Capital Market*. London: Methuen and Co.

Layton, Walter, and Charles Rist (1925). *The Economic Situation of Austria*. Geneva: League of Nations.

Le Goff, Jacques (1979). "The Usurer and Purgatory." In *The Dawn of Modern Banking*, ed. Robert S. Lopez, 25–52. New Haven: Yale University Press.

Leacy, F. H., ed. (1983). *Historical Statistics of Canada*. 2nd ed. Ottawa: Statistics Canada.

League of Nations (1934). *Commercial Banks, 1925–1933*. Geneva: League of Nations.

—— (1938). *Commercial and Central Banks*. Geneva: League of Nations.

—— (various). *Statistical Year-Book*. Geneva: League of Nations.

Lebergott, Stanley (1964). *Manpower in Economic Growth: The American Record since 1800*. New York: McGraw-Hill.

—— (1970). "Migration within the U.S., 1800–1960: Some New Estimates." *Journal of Economic History* 30(4): 839–47.

Lemoine, R. J. (1929a). "The Banking System of Belgium." In *Foreign Banking Systems*, ed. H. Parker Willis and Benjamin H. Beckhart, 175–288. New York: Henry Holt and Company.

—— (1929b). "The Banking System of France." In *Foreign Banking Systems*, ed. H. Parker Willis and Benjamin H. Beckhart, 522–626. New York: Henry Holt and Company.

Levi, Leone (1870). "On Joint Stock Companies." *Journal of the Statistical Society of London* 33(1): 1–41.

Levine, Ross (1997). "Financial Development and Economic Growth: Views and Agenda." *Journal of Economic Literature* 35(2): 688–726.

Levine, Ross, Norman Loayza, and Thorsten Beck (2000). "Financial Intermediation and Growth: Causality and Causes." *Journal of Monetary Economics* 46(1): 31–77.

Levine, Ross, and Sara Zervos (1998). "Stock Markets, Banks, and Economic Growth." *American Economic Review* 88(3): 537–58.

Lewis, Kenneth A., and Kozo Yamamura (1971). "Industrialization and Interregional Interest Rate Structure, the Japanese Case: 1889–1925." *Explorations in Economic History* 8(4): 473–99.

Lewis, W. Arthur (1978). *Growth and Fluctuations*. London: Allen and Unwin.

Lexis, W. (1910). "The German Bank Commission, 1908–9." *Economic Journal* 20(78): 211–21.

Liesse, Andre (1910). *Evolution of Credit and Banks in France from the Founding of the Bank of France to the Present Time*. National Monetary Commission. 61st Cong., 2d sess., 1910, S. Doc. 522. Washington: Government Printing Office.

Lim, G. C. (1984). "The Martin Report." *Australian Economic Review* 17(1): 26–34.

——— (1997). "The Wallis Report: An Agenda for Financial Reform?" *Australian Economic Review* 30(3): 301–03.

Lincoln, Edward J. (1998). "Japan's Financial Mess." *Foreign Affairs* 77(3): 57–66.

Lindgren, Carl-Johan, G. G. Garcia, and Matthew I. Saal (1996). *Bank Soundness and Macroeconomic Policy*. Washington: International Monetary Fund.

Lindgren, Håkan (1991). "Swedish Historical Research on Banking During the 1980's: Tradition and Renewal." *Scandinavian Economic History Review* 39(3): 5–19.

——— (1997). "The Influence of Banking on the Development of Capitalism in the Scandinavian Countries." In *Banking, Trade and Industry: Europe, America and Asia from the Thirteenth to the Twentieth Century*, ed. Alice Teichova, Ginette Kurgan-van Hentenryk, and Dieter Ziegler, 191–213. Cambridge: Cambridge University Press.

——— (2002). "The Modernization of Swedish Credit Markets, 1840–1905: Evidence from Probate Records." *Journal of Economic History* 62(3): 810–32.

Lindgren, Håkan, and Hans Sjögren (2003). "Banking Systems as 'Ideal Types' and Political Economy: The Swedish Case, 1820–1914." In *The Origin of National Financial Systems*, ed. Douglas J. Forsyth and Daniel Verdier, 126–43. London: Routledge.

Lindsey, David E., Athanasios Orphanides, and Robert H. Rasche (2005). "The Reform of October 1979: How it Happened and Why." *Federal Reserve Bank of St. Louis Review* 87(2, part 2): 187–235.

Lisle-Williams, Michael (1984). "Merchant Banking Dynasties in the English Class Structure: Ownership, Solidarity and Kinship in the City of London, 1850–1960." *British Journal of Sociology* 35(3): 333–62.

Llewellyn, David T. (2003). "Institutional Structure of Financial Regulation: The Basic Issues." Paper presented at World Bank seminar "Aligning Supervisory Structures with Country Needs." Washington, DC, June 6–7, 2006.

Lo Faro, Francesco (1929). "The Banking System of Italy." In *Foreign Banking Systems*, ed. H. Parker Willis and Benjamin H. Beckhart, 765–815. New York: Henry Holt and Company.

London and Cambridge Economic Service (1973). *The British Economy, Key Statistics*. London: London and Cambridge Economic Service.

Lopez, Robert S. (1956). "Back to Gold, 1252." *Economic History Review* 9(2): 219–40.

—— (1971). *The Commercial Revolution of the Middle Ages, 950–1350*. Englewood Cliffs, NJ: Prentice-Hall.

—— (1979). "The Dawn of Medieval Banking." In *The Dawn of Modern Banking*, ed. Robert S. Lopez, 1–23. New Haven: Yale University Press.

Lovell, Michael C. (1957). "The Role of the Bank of England as Lender of Last Resort in the Crises of the Eighteenth Century." *Explorations in Entrepreneurial History* 10(1): 8–20.

Lucas, Robert E., Jr. (1988). "On the Mechanics of Economic Development." *Journal of Monetary Economics* 22(1): 3–42.

Lumpkin, Stephen (2002). "Supervision of Financial Services in the OECD Area." Paper presented at the OECD Third Conference on Insurance Regulation and Supervision in Latin America. San Pedro Sula, Honduras, July 15–16, 2002.

Luzzatto, Gino (1934). "Les Banques Publiques de Venise (Siècles XVI–XVIII)." In *History of Principal Public Banks*, ed. J. G. Van Dillen, 39–78. The Hague: Martins Nijhoff.

Macey, Jonathan R., and Geoffrey P. Miller (1992). "Double Liability of Bank Shareholders: History and Implications." *Wake Forest Law Review* 27: 31–62.

—— (1993). "Double Liability of Bank Shareholders: A Look at the New Data." *Wake Forest Law Review* 28: 933–41.

MacIntosh, R. M. (1967). "The 1967 Revision of the Canadian Banking Acts. Part II: A Banker's View." *Canadian Journal of Economics* 1(1): 91–96.

Madden, John T., and Marcus Nadler (1935). *The International Money Markets*. New York: Prentice-Hall.

Maddison, Angus (1995). *Monitoring the World Economy, 1820–1992*. Paris: Organization for Economic Cooperation and Development.

—— (2001). *The World Economy: A Millennial Perspective*. Paris: Organization for Economic Cooperation and Development (data downloaded from http://www.ggdc.net/maddison/Historical_Statistics/vertical-file_03-2009.xls).

Maltby, Josephine (1998). "UK Joint Stock Companies Legislation 1844–1900: Accounting Publicity and 'Mercantile Caution'." *Accounting History* 3(1): 9–32.

Martin, J. B. (1891). "The Evolution of our Banking System." *Economic Journal* 1(3): 539–44.

März, Eduard (1983). "The Austrian Credit Mobilier in a Time of Transition." In *Economic Development in the Hapsburg Monarchy in the Nineteenth Century*, ed. John Komlos, 117–35. New York: Columbia University Press.

—— (1984). *Austrian Banking and Financial Policy: Creditanstalt at a Turning Point, 1913–1923*. London: Weidenfeld and Nicolson.

Mayer, Thomas (1982). "A Case Study of Federal Reserve Policymaking: Regulation Q in 1966." *Journal of Monetary Economics* 10(2): 259–71.

Mazower, Mark (1991). "Banking and Economic Development in Interwar Greece." In *The Role of Banks in the Interwar Economy*, ed. Harold James,

Håkan Lindgren and Alice Teichova, 206–31. Cambridge: Cambridge University Press.

McCartney, E. Ray (1935). *Crisis of 1873*. Minneapolis: Burgess.

McIvor, R. Craig (1958). *Canadian Monetary, Banking, and Fiscal Development.* Toronto: Macmillan Company of Canada.

McKenzie, Michael D. (1999). "Risk in the Japanese Banking Sector: Implications of the Financial System Reform Act (1992)." *Asia Pacific Journal of Economics and Business* 3(1): 4–20.

McLeod, Henry Dunning (1896). "A History of Banking in Great Britain." In *A History of Banking in All the Leading Nations*, Vol. 2, 1–337. New York: Journal of Commerce and Commercial Bulletin.

Meissner, Christopher (2005). "A New World Order: Explaining the Emergence of the Classical Gold Standard." *Journal of International Economics* 66(2): 385–406.

Melin, Hilding (1929). "The Banking System of Sweden." In *Foreign Banking Systems*, ed. H. Parker Willis and Benjamin H. Beckhart, 1011–74. New York: Henry Holt and Company.

Meltzer, Allan (1967). "Major Issues in the Regulation of Financial Institutions." *Journal of Political Economy* 75(4): 482–501.

Merrett, D. T. (1989). "Australian Banking Practice and the Crisis of 1893." *Australian Economic History Review* 29(1): 60–85.

——— (1990). "Paradise Lost? British Banks in Australia." In *Banks as Multinationals*, ed. Geoffrey Jones, 62–84. New York: Routledge.

——— (2002). "The State and the Finance Sector: The Evolution of Regulatory Apparatus." *Australian Economic History Review* 42(3): 267–83.

Michie, R. C. (1987). *The New York and London Stock Exchanges, 1850–1914.* London: Allen and Unwin.

——— (1999). *The London Stock Exchange: A History.* Oxford: Oxford University Press.

Minsky, Hyman P. (1975). *John Maynard Keynes.* New York: Columbia University Press.

——— (1982a). *Can 'It' Happen Again?* New York: M. E. Sharp.

——— (1982b). "The Financial Instability Hypothesis: Capitalist Processes and the Behavior of the Economy." In *Financial Crises: Theory, History, and Policy*, ed. Charles P. Kindleberger and Jean-Pierre Laffargue, 13–39. Cambridge: Cambridge University Press.

Miron, Jeffrey A. (1986). "Financial Panics, the Seasonality of the Nominal Interest Rate, and the Founding of the Fed." *American Economic Review* 76(1): 125–40.

Mishkin, Frederic (1991). "Asymmetric Information and Financial Crises: A Historical Perspective." In *Financial Markets and Financial Crises*, ed. R. Glenn Hubbard, 69–108. Chicago: University of Chicago Press.

——— (1992). "Anatomy of a Financial Crisis." *Journal of Evolutionary Economics* 2(2): 115–30.

——— (1996a). "Channels of Monetary Transmission: Lessons for Monetary Policy." NBER Working Paper no. 5464. Cambridge, MA: National Bureau of Economic Research.

——— (1996b). "Understanding Financial Crises: A Developing Country Perspective." NBER Working Paper no. 5600. Cambridge, MA: National Bureau of Economic Research.

——— (2001). "Prudential Supervision: Why Is It Important and What Are the Issues?" In *Prudential Supervision: What Works and What Doesn't*, ed. Frederic S. Mishkin, 1–29. Chicago and London: University of Chicago Press.

——— (2007). "Is Financial Globalization Beneficial?" *Journal of Money, Credit and Banking* 39(2–3): 259–94.

Mitchell, B. R. (1978). *European Historical Statistics, 1750–1970*. New York: Columbia University Press.

——— (1995). *International Historical Statistics: Africa, Asia and Oceania, 1750–1988*. 2nd ed. New York: Stockton Press.

Mitchell, Wesley Clair (1913). *Business Cycles*. Berkeley: University of California Press.

Miyajima, Shigeki, and Warren E. Weber (2001). "A Comparison of National Banks in Japan and the United States between 1872 and 1885." *Bank of Japan Monetary and Economic Studies* 19(1): 31–48.

Modigliani, Franco, and Merton Miller (1958). "The Cost of Capital, Corporation Finance, and the Theory of Investment." *American Economic Review* 48(3): 261–97.

Moe, Thorvald G., Jon A. Solheim, and Bent Vale, eds. (2004). *The Norwegian Banking Crisis*. Oslo: Norges Bank.

Moen, Jon R., and Ellis W. Tallman (2000). "Clearinghouse Membership and Deposit Contraction During the Panic of 1907." *Journal of Economic History* 60(1): 145–63.

Mokyr, Joel (1976). *Industrialization in the Low Countries, 1795–1850*. New Haven: Yale University Press.

——— (1981). "Industrialization in Two Languages." *Economic History Review* 34(1): 143–49.

Mørck, Randall, Andrei Shleifer, and Robert W. Vishny (1988). "The Characteristics of Targets of Hostile and Friendly Takeovers." In *Corporate Takeovers: Causes and Consequences*, ed. Alan J. Auerbach, 101–36. Chicago: University of Chicago Press.

——— (1989). "Alternative Mechanisms for Corporate Control." *American Economic Review* 79(4): 842–52.

Morgan, E. Victor (1943). *The Theory and Practice of Central Banking*. Cambridge: Cambridge University Press.

Morgan, E. Victor, and W. A. Thomas (1962). *The Stock Exchange: Its History and Functions*. London: Elek Books.

Morrison, Rodney J. (1967). "Financial Intermediaries and Economic Development: The Belgian Case." *Scandinavian Economic History Review* 15(1): 56–70.

Möschel, Wernhard (1991). "Public Law of Banking." In *International Encyclopedia of Public Law*, ed. Jacob S. Ziegel, Chapter 3. Boston: Martinus Nijhoff.

Mueller, Reinhold C. (1997). *The Venetian Money Market: Banks, Panics, and the Public Debt, 1200–1500*. Baltimore: Johns Hopkins University Press.

Murphy, Neil B. (2000). "European Union Financial Developments: The Single

Market, the Single Currency, and Banking." *FDIC Banking Review* 13(1): 1–18.

Myers, Margaret G. (1936). *Paris as a Financial Centre.* New York: Columbia University Press.

—— (1949). "The Nationalization of Banks in France." *Political Science Quarterly* 64 (2): 189–210.

—— (1970). *A Financial History of the United States.* New York: Columbia University Press.

Nakaso, Hiroshi (2001). "The Financial Crisis in Japan During the 1990s: How the Bank of Japan Responded and the Lessons Learnt." BIS Papers no. 6. Basel: Bank for International Settlements.

National Industrial Conference Board (1932). *The Banking Situation in the United States.* New York: National Industrial Conference Board, Inc.

Neal, Larry (1990). *The Rise of Financial Capitalism: International Capital Markets in the Age of Reason.* Cambridge: Cambridge University Press.

Nederlandsche Bank (1986). *Financiële Instellingen in Nederland 1900–1985: Balansreeksen En Naamlijst Van Handelsbanken.* Amsterdam: De Nederlandsche Bank.

—— (2003). *Financiële Instellingen in de twinigste eeuw: balansreeksen en naamlijst van handelsbanken.* DNB Statistische Cahiers nr. 3. Amsterdam: De Nederlandsche Bank.

Nelson, Ralph L. (1959). *Merger Movements in American Industry, 1895–1956.* Princeton: Princeton University Press.

Neuberger, Hugh, and Houston Stokes (1974). "German Banks and German Growth, 1883–1913: An Empirical View." *Journal of Economic History* 34(3): 710–31.

Neufeld, Edward Peter, ed. (1964). *Money and Banking in Canada: Historical Documents and Commentary.* Toronto: McClelland and Stewart.

Nordvik, Helge W. (1993). "The Banking System, Industrialization and Economic Growth in Norway, 1850–1914." *Scandinavian Economic History Review* 41(1): 51–72.

—— (1995). "Norwegian Banking in the Inter-War Period: A Scandinavian Perspective." In *Banking, Currency, and Finance in Europe between the Wars,* ed. Charles Feinstein, 434–57. New York: Oxford University Press.

Norges Offisielle Statistikk (1948). *Statistiske Oversikter, 1948.* Oslo: I kommisjon hos Aschehoug.

North, Douglass C. (1966). *Growth and Welfare in the American Past: A New Economic History.* Englewood Cliffs, NJ: Prentice-Hall.

North, Douglass C., and Barry R. Weingast (1989). "Constitutions and Commitment: The Evolution of Institutions Governing Public Choice in Seventeenth-Century England." *Journal of Economic History* 49(4): 803–32.

Noyes, Alexander D. (1909a). *Forty Years of American Finance.* New York: Putnam.

—— (1909b). "A Year after the Panic of 1907." *Quarterly Journal of Economics* 23(2): 185–212.

Nyberg, Peter (1995). "The Banking Crisis in Finland." *Ekonomiska Samfundets Tidskrift* 48(3): 115–20.

Nyberg, Peter, and Vesa Vihriälä (1994). "The Finnish Banking Crisis and its Handling (an Update of Developments Through 1993)." Discussion Paper no. 7/94. Helsinki: Bank of Finland.

Nygren, Ingemar (1983). "The Transformation of Bank Structures in the Industrial Period. The Case of Sweden 1820–1913." *Journal of European Economic History* 12(1): 29–68.

––––––– (1985). *Från Stockholms banco till Citibank: svensk kreditmarknad under 325 år*. Stockholm: Liber Förlag.

Oppers, Stefan (1996). "Was the Worldwide Shift to Gold Inevitable? An Analysis of the End of Bimetallism." *Journal of Monetary Economics* 37(1): 143–62.

Oda, Nobuyuki, and Tokiko Shimizu (2000). "Prospects for Prudential Policy: Toward Achieving an Efficient and Stable Banking System." *Bank of Japan Monetary and Economic Studies* 18(1): 119–36.

Ögren, Anders (2003). "Commercial Note Issuing Banks and Capital Market Development: An Empirical Test of the Enskilda Banks' Assets, Liabilities and Reserves in Relation to Evolving Capital Market Liquidity in Sweden, 1834–1913." SSE/EFI Working Paper Series in Economics and Finance no. 540. Stockholm: Stockholm School of Economics, Economic Research Institute.

––––––– (2006). "Free or Central Banking? Liquidity and Financial Deepening in Sweden, 1834–1913." *Explorations in Economic History* 43(1): 64–93.

O'Hara, Maureen, and Wayne Shaw (1990). "Deposit Insurance and Wealth Effects: The Value of Being 'Too Big to Fail.'" *Journal of Finance* 45(5): 1587–1600.

Okazaki, Tetsuji, and Michiru Sawada (2007). "Effects of a Bank Consolidation Promotion Policy: Evaluating the 1927 Bank Law in Japan." *Financial History Review* 14(1): 29–61.

Okazaki, Tetsuji, Michiru Sawada, and Kazuki Yokoyama (2005). "Measuring the Extent and Implications of Director Interlocking in the Prewar Japanese Banking Industry." *Journal of Economic History* 65(4): 1082–1115.

Olmstead, A. T. (1930). "Materials for an Economic History of the Ancient Near East." *Journal of Economic and Business History* 2: 219–40.

Olsson, Ulf (1994). "Swedish Commercial Banking Over 150 Years." *Handbook on the History of European Banks*, ed. Manfred Pohl, 963–1012. Brookfield, VT: Ashgate.

––––––– (1997). *At the Centre of Development: Skandinaviska Enskilda Banken and Its Predecessors, 1856–1996*. Stockholm: Skandinaviska Enskilda Banken.

Olsson, Ulf, and Jan Jörnmark (2007). "The Political Economy of Commercial Banking in Sweden: A Bird's-Eye View on the Relations Between Industry and Banking During 150 Years." In *Centres and Peripheries in Banking*, ed. Philip L. Cottrell, Even Lange, and Ulf Olsson, 197-210. Burlington, VT: Ashgate.

Ongena, Steven, David C. Smith, and Dag Michalsen (2000). "Firms and Their Distressed Banks: Lessons from the Norwegian Banking Crisis (1988–1991)." International Finance Discussion Paper no. 686. Washington: Board of Governors of the Federal Reserve System.

Organization for Economic Cooperation and Development (1992). *Banks under Stress*. Paris: Organization for Economic Cooperation and Development.

––––––– (2000). *OECD Economic Outlook No. 68*. Washington: Organization for Economic Cooperation and Development.

——— (various). *Bank Profitability*. Paris: Organization for Economic Cooperation and Development.

Organization for Economic Cooperation and Development. Expert Group on Banking. (1985). *Trends in Banking in OECD Countries*. Paris: Organization for Economic Cooperation and Development.

O'Rourke, Kevin H., and Jeffrey G. Williamson (1999). *Globalization and History: The Evolution of a Nineteenth-Century Atlantic Economy*. Cambridge, MA: MIT Press.

Orsingher, Roger (1967). *Banks of the World*. New York: Walker and Company.

Packer, Frank (2000). "The Disposal of Bad Loans in Japan: The Case of the CCPC." In *Crisis and Change in the Japanese Financial System*, ed. Takeo Hoshi and Hugh Patrick, 137–57. Boston: Kluwer Academic.

Palgrave, Robert Harry Inglis (1873). *Notes on Banking in Great Britain and Ireland, Sweden, Denmark and Hamburg; with Some Remarks on the Amount of Bills in Circulation*. London: John Murray.

Parker, Geoffrey (1974). "The Emergence of Modern Finance in Europe, 1500–1730." In *The Fontana Economic History of Europe*. Vol. 2, *The Sixteenth and Seventeenth Centuries*, ed. Carlo Cipolla, 527–89. London: Collins/ Fontana.

Patrick, Hugh T. (1967). "Japan, 1868–1914." In *Banking in the Early Stages of Industrialization*, ed. Rondo E. Cameron, 239–89. New York: Oxford University Press.

——— (1999). "The Causes of Japan's Financial Crisis." Pacific Economic Papers no. 288. Canberra: Australia-Japan Research Centre.

Peach, W. Nelson (1941). *The Security Affiliates of National Banks*. Baltimore: The Johns Hopkins University Press.

Pecora, Ferdinand (1939). *Wall Street under Oath*. New York: Simon and Schuster.

Peek, Joe, Eric S. Rosengren, and Geoffrey M. B. Tootell (2001). "Synergies between Bank Supervision and Monetary Policy: Implications for the Design of Bank Regulatory Structure." In *Prudential Supervision: What Works and What Doesn't*, ed. Frederic S. Mishkin, 273–93. Chicago and London: University of Chicago Press.

Peltzman, Sam (1965). "Entry in Commercial Banking." *Journal of Law and Economics* 8: 11–50.

——— (1976). "Towards a More General Theory of Regulation." *Journal of Law and Economics* 19(2): 211–40.

——— (1989). "The Economic Theory of Regulation after a Decade of Deregulation." *Brookings Papers: Microeconomics* 1989: 1–41. Washington: Brookings Institution.

Perkins, Edwin J. (1983). "Langdon Cheves and the Panic of 1819: A Reassessment." *Journal of Economic History* 44(2): 455–61.

Perkins, J.O.N. (1990). *The Deregulation of the Australian Financial System*. Melbourne: Melbourne University Press.

Philippovich, Eugen Von (1911). *History of the Bank of England and its Financial Services to the State*. National Monetary Commission. 61st Cong., 2d sess., 1911, S. Doc. 591. Washington: Government Printing Office.

Pilloff, Steven J. (2004). "Bank Merger Activity in the United States, 1994–2003." Federal Reserve Board Staff Studies no. 176. Washington: Board of Governors of the Federal Reserve System.

Plessis, Alain (1994). "The History of Banks in France." *Handbook on the History of European Banks*, ed. Manfred Pohl, 185–296. Brookfield, VT: Elgar.

—— (2003). "The History of Banks in France." Working Paper.

Pollard, Sidney (1990). *Typology of Industrialization Processes in the Nineteenth Century*. Chur, Switzerland: Harwood Academic Publishers.

Postan, M. M. (1928). "Credit in Medieval Trade." *Economic History Review* 1(2): 234–61.

—— (1935). "Recent Trends in the Accumulation of Capital." *Economic History Review* 6(1): 1–12.

—— (1973). *Medieval Trade and Finance*. Cambridge: Cambridge University Press.

Powell, Ellis T. (1915 [1966]). *The Evolution of the Money Market, 1385–1915*. New York: Augustus Kelley.

Pozdena, Randall J. (1992). "Danish Banking: Lessons for Deposit Insurance Reform." *Journal of Financial Services Research* 5(2): 289–98.

Pressnell, L. S. (1956). *Country Banking in the Industrial Revolution*. Oxford: Clarendon Press.

Pryor, Frederic L. (2001). "New Trends in U.S. Industrial Concentration." *Review of Industrial Organization* 18(3): 301–26.

Quigley, Neil C. (1997). "The Wallis Report: Balancing Regulation and the Evolution of the Market." *Australian Economic Review* 30(3): 316–22.

Quinn, Stephen, and William Roberds (2006). "An Economic Explanation of the Early Bank of Amsterdam, Debasement, Bills of Exchange, and the Emergence of the First Central Bank." Working Paper no. 2006-13. Atlanta: Federal Reserve Bank of Atlanta.

Quittner, Paul (1929). "The Banking System of Germany." In *Foreign Banking Systems*, ed. H. Parker Willis and Benjamin H. Beckhart, 627–722. New York: Henry Holt and Company.

Rajan, Raghuram, and Luigi Zingales (1998). "Financial Dependence and Growth." *American Economic Review* 88(3): 559–86.

—— (2001). "Financial Systems, Industrial Structure, and Growth." *Oxford Review of Economic Policy* 17 (4): 467–82.

—— (2003a). "Banks and Markets: The Changing Character of European Finance." In *The Transformation of the European Financial System,* ed. Vítor Gaspar, Philipp Hartmann, Olaf Sleijpen, 123–68. Frankfurt: European Central Bank.

—— (2003b). "The Great Reversals: The Politics of Financial Development in the 20th Century." *Journal of Financial Economics* 69(1): 5–50.

—— (2003c). *Saving Capitalism from the Capitalists: Unleashing the Power of Financial Markets to Create Wealth and Spread Opportunity*. New York: Crown Business.

Ramseyer, J. Mark (1994). "Explicit Reasons for Implicit Contracts: The Legal Logic to the Japanese Main Bank System." In *The Japanese Main Bank System,* ed. Masahiko Aoki and Hugh Patrick, 231–57. Oxford: Oxford University Press.

——— (1996). *Odd Markets in Japanese History: Law and Economic Growth.* Cambridge: Cambridge University Press.

Ramseyer, J. Mark, and Frances M. Rosenbluth (1995). *The Politics of Oligarchy: Institutional Choice in Imperial Japan.* Cambridge: Cambridge University Press.

Ravenscraft, David J. (1987). "The 1980s Merger Wave: An Industrial Organization Perspective." In *The Merger Boom: Proceedings of a Conference Held in October 1987*, ed. Lynne E. Browne and Eric Rosengren, 17–37. Boston: Federal Reserve Bank of Boston.

Redish, Angela (2001). "Lender of Last Resort Policies: From Bagehot to Bailout." Working Paper. Vancouver: University of British Columbia.

Redlich, Fritz (1947). *The Molding of American Banking: Men and Ideas.* 2 vols. New York: Hafner.

Reid, Margaret (1982). *The Secondary Banking Crisis, 1973–75.* London: Macmillan.

Reis, Jaime (1995). "Portuguese Banking in the Inter War Period." In *Banking, Currency, and Finance in Europe between the Wars*, ed. Charles Feinstein, 472–502. New York: Oxford University Press.

Revell, Jack (1980). *Costs and Margins in Banking, an International Survey.* Paris: Organization for Economic Cooperation and Development.

——— (1985a). *Costs and Margins in Banking, Statistical Supplement.* Paris: Organization for Economic Cooperation and Development.

———(1985b). *Costs and Margins in Banking, Statistical Supplement 1978–1982.* Paris: Organization for Economic Cooperation and Development.

——— (1987). *Mergers and the Role of Large Banks.* Bangor: University College of North Wales.

Reynolds, Robert L. (1931). "Genoese Trade in the Late Twelfth Century, Particularly in Cloth from the Fairs of Champagne." *Journal of Economic and Business History* 3: 362–81.

——— (1952). "Origins of Modern Business Enterprise: Medieval Italy." *Journal of Economic History* 12(4): 350–65.

Rhoades, Stephen A. (1996). "Bank Mergers and Industrywide Structure, 1980–94." Working Paper no. 169. Washington: Board of Governors of the Federal Reserve System.

Rich, George (1972). "A Theoretical and Empirical Analysis of the Eurodollar Market." *Journal of Money, Credit and Banking* 4(3): 616–35.

Richards, Richard David (1929). *The Early History of Banking in England.* London: P. S. King and Son.

Riesser, Jacob (1911). *The German Great Banks and Their Concentration in Connection with the Economic Development of Germany.* National Monetary Commission. 61st Cong., 2d sess., 1911, S. Doc. 593. Washington: Government Printing Office.

Robb, Thomas Bruce (1921). *The Guaranty of Bank Deposits.* Boston: Houghton Mifflin Company.

Roberts, Michael (1967). *Essays in Swedish History*. London: Weidenfeld and Nicolson.

—— (1986). *The Age of Liberty: Sweden, 1719–1772*. Cambridge: Cambridge University Press.

Robins, Philip K. (1974). "The Effects of State Usury Ceilings on Single Family Homebuilding." *Journal of Finance* 29(1): 227–35.

Robinson, Joan (1952). *The Rate of Interest and Other Essays*. London: Macmillan.

Robinson, Roland I. (1941). "The Capital-Deposit Ratio in Banking Supervision." *Journal of Political Economy* 49(1): 41–57.

Rockoff, Hugh (1975). *The Free Banking Era: A Re-examination*. New York: Arno Press.

Rodrik, Dani (1996). "Understanding Economic Policy Reform." *Journal of Economic Literature* 34(1): 9–41.

Romer, Christina, and David Romer (1989). "Does Monetary Policy Matter? A New Test in the Spirit of Friedman and Schwartz." *NBER Macroeconomics Annual* 4: 121–70.

Root, Hilton. L. (1994). *The Fountain of Privilege: Political Foundations of Markets in Old Regime France and England*. Berkeley: University of California Press.

Rosovsky, Henry (1966). "Japan's Transition to Modern Economic Growth, 1868–1885." In *Industrialization in Two Systems: Essays in Honor of Alexander Gerschenkron*, ed. Henry Rosovsky, 91–139. New York: Wiley and Sons.

Rostow, W. W. (1956). "The Take-Off into Self-Sustained Growth." *Economic Journal* 66(261): 25–48.

Rousseau, Peter L., and Richard Sylla (2003). "Financial Systems, Economic Growth, and Globalization." In *Globalization in Historical Perspective*, ed. Michael D. Bordo, Alan M. Taylor, and Jeffrey G. Williamson, 373–413. Chicago: University of Chicago Press.

—— (2005). "Emerging Financial Markets and Early U.S. Growth." *Explorations in Economic History* 42(1): 1–26.

Rousseau, Peter L., and Paul Wachtel (1998). "Financial Intermediation and Economic Performance: Historical Evidence from Five Industrialized Countries." *Journal of Money, Credit and Banking* 30(4): 657–78.

Rudolph, Richard L. (1972). "Austria, 1800–1914." In *Banking and Economic Development*, ed. Rondo Cameron, 26–57. New York: Oxford University Press.

—— (1976). *Banking and Industrialization in Austria-Hungary: The Role of Banks in the Industrialization of the Czech Crownlands, 1873–1914*. Cambridge: Cambridge University Press.

Saint Marc, Michèle (1983). *Histoire monétaire de la France, 1800–1980*. Paris: Presses Universitaires de France.

Sakurai, Kinichiro (1964). *Financial Aspects of Economic Development of Japan, 1868–1958*. Tokyo: Science Council of Japan. Division of Economics, Commerce, and Business Administration.

Salt, Thomas (1891). "Inaugural Address of the President." *Journal of the Institute of Bankers* 12(9): 607–21.

Samuelsson, Kurt (1958). "The Bank and the Financing of Industry in Sweden, c. 1900–1927." *Scandinavian Economic History Review* 6(2): 176–90.

Sandal, Knut (2004). "The Nordic Banking Crisis in the Early 1990s—Resolution Methods and Fiscal Costs." In *The Norwegian Banking Crisis*, ed. Thorvald G. Moe, Jon A. Solheim, and Bent Vale, 77–115. Oslo: Norges Bank.

Sandberg, Lars G. (1970). "Monetary Policy and Politics in Mid-Eighteenth-Century Sweden: A Comment." *Journal of Economic History* 30(3): 653–54.

——— (1978). "Banking and Economic Growth in Sweden Before World War I." *Journal of Economic History* 38(3): 650–80.

——— (1979). "The Case of the Impoverished Sophisticate: Human Capital and Swedish Economic Growth Before World War I." *Journal of Economic History* 39(1): 225–41.

——— (1982). "Sweden as an 'Impoverished Sophisticate': A Reply." *Journal of Economic History* 42(4): 921–22.

Sandoz, M. (1898). "The Bank-Note System of Switzerland." *Quarterly Journal of Economics* 12(3): 280–306.

Sannucci, Valeria (1989). "The Establishment of a Central Bank: Italy in the 19th Century." In *A European Central Bank? Perspectives on Monetary Unification after Ten Years of the EMS*, ed. Marcello De Cecco and Alberto Giovannini, 244–80. Cambridge: Cambridge University Press.

Saunders, Anthony, and Ingo Walter (1996). *Universal Banking: Financial System Design Reconsidered*. Chicago: Irwin Professional.

Saunders, Anthony, and Berry Wilson (1999). "The Impact of Consolidation and Safety-Net Support on Canadian, US and UK Banks: 1893–1992." *Journal of Banking and Finance* 23(2–4): 537–71.

Sawada, Michiru, and Tetsuji Okazaki (2004). "Effects of Bank Consolidation Promotion Policy: Evaluating the Bank Law in 1927 Japan." RIETI Discussion Paper Series no. 04-E-004. Tokyo: Ministry of Economy, Trade and Industry.

Sayers, Richard S. (1976). *The Bank of England, 1891–1944*. Cambridge and New York: Cambridge University Press.

Schaeck, Klaus and Martin Cihák (2007). "Banking Competition and Capital Ratios." IMF Working Paper no. 07/216. Washington: International Monetary Fund.

Schedvin, C. B. (1989). "The Growth of Bank Regulation in Australia." Joint Universities Conference on Regulating Commercial Banks. Unpublished Working Paper. Canberra: Australian National University.

——— (1992). *In Reserve: Central Banking in Australia, 1945–75*. St. Leonards, NSW, Australia: Allen and Unwin.

Schenk, Catherine R. (1998). "The Origins of the Eurodollar Market in London: 1955–1963." *Explorations in Economic History* 35(2): 221–38.

Scherer, Frederic M. (1980). *Industrial Market Structure and Economic Performance*. Chicago: Rand McNally College Publishing Company.

Schumpeter, Joseph Alois (1934). *The Theory of Economic Development: An Inquiry into Profits, Capital, Credit, Interest, and the Business Cycle*. Cambridge, MA: Harvard University Press.

——— (1939). *Business Cycles: A Theoretical, Historical, and Statistical Analysis of the Capitalist Process*. New York: McGraw-Hill Book Company.

——— (1942). *Capitalism, Socialism, and Democracy*. New York: Harper and Brothers.

Schwartz, Anna Jacobson (1947). "The Beginning of Competitive Banking in Philadelphia, 1782–1809." *Journal of Political Economy* 55(5): 417–31.

——— (1986). "Real and Pseudo-Financial Crises." In *Financial Crises and the World Banking System*, ed. Forrest Capie and Geoffrey E. Wood, 11–40. New York: St. Martin's Press.

Schwarzenback, Ernest (1929). "The Banking System of Switzerland." In *Foreign Banking Systems*, ed. H. Parker Willis and Benjamin H. Beckhart, 1075–1143. New York: Henry Holt and Company.

Scott, Franklin D. (1977). *Sweden: The Nation's History*. Minneapolis: University of Minnesota Press.

Shearer, Ronald A. (1977). "The Porter Commission Report in the Context of Earlier Canadian Monetary Documents." *Canadian Journal of Economics* 10(1): 34–49.

——— (1978). "Proposals for the Revision of Banking Legislation." *Canadian Journal of Economics* 11(1): 121–36.

Shepherd, Henry L. (1936). *The Monetary Experience of Belgium, 1914–1936*. Princeton: Princeton University Press.

Sheppard, David K. (1971). *The Growth and Role of U.K. Financial Institutions, 1880–1962*. London: Methuen and Co., Ltd.

Shortt, Adam (1897a). "The Early History of Canadian Banks (IV): The First Banks in Lower Canada." *Journal of the Canadian Bankers' Association* 4(4): 341–60.

——— (1897b). "The Early History of Canadian Banks (V): The First Banks in Upper Canada." *Journal of the Canadian Bankers' Association* 5(1): 1–21.

Shull, Bernard (1999). "The Separation of Banking and Commerce in the United States: An Examination of Principal Issues." *Financial Markets, Institutions and Instruments* 8(3): 1–55.

Sieveking, Heinrich (1934). "Die Hamburger Bank." In *History of the Principal Public Banks*, ed. J. G. Van Dillen, 125–60. The Hague: Martinus Nijhoff.

Simmons, Beth (2001). "The International Politics of Harmonization: The Case of Capital Market Regulation." *International Organization* 55(3): 589–620.

Simon, Miguel Cantillo (1998). "The Rise and Fall of Bank Control in the United States: 1890–1939." *American Economic Review* 88(5): 1077–93.

Slater, David W. (1968). "The 1967 Revision of the Canadian Banking Acts Part I: An Economist's View." *Canadian Journal of Economics* 1(1): 79–91.

Smiley, Gene (1975). "Interest Rate Movement in the United States, 1888–1913." *Journal of Economic History* 35(3): 591–620.

——— (1985). "Banking Structure and the National Capital Market, 1869–1914: A Comment." *Journal of Economic History* 45(3): 653–59.

Smith, Adam (1776 [1994]). *An Inquiry into the Nature and Causes of the Wealth of Nations*. New York: Modern Library.

Smith, K. C., and G. F. Horne (1934). *An Index Number of Securities, 1867–1914*. London: Royal Economic Society and London and Cambridge Economic Service.

Smith, Walter Buckingham (1953 [1969]). *Economic Aspects of the Second Bank of the United States*. New York: Greenwood Press.

Snowden, Kenneth A. (1987). "Mortgage Rates and American Capital Market

Development in the Late Nineteenth Century." *Journal of Economic History* 47(3): 671–91.

Soetbeer, A (1866). "Die Hamburger Bank, 1619–1866. Einer Geschichtliche Skizze. (Erste Hälfte)." *Vierteljahrschrift für Volkswirthschaft und Kulturgeschichte* 15(3): 21–54.

Soyeda, Juichi (1896). "Banking and Money in Japan." In *A History of Banking in All the Leading Nations,* Vol. 4, 409–544. New York: Journal of Commerce and Commercial Bulletin.

Spero, Joan Edelman (1980). *The Failure of the Franklin National Bank.* New York: Columbia University Press.

Spong, Kenneth (2000). *Banking Regulation.* Kansas City: Federal Reserve Bank of Kansas City.

Sprague, Irvine H. (1986). *Bailout: An Insider's Account of Bank Failures and Rescues.* New York: Basic Books.

Sprague, O.M.W. (1908). "The American Crisis of 1907." *Economic Journal* 18(71): 353–72.

—— (1910). *History of Crises under the National Banking System.* National Monetary Commission. 61st Cong., 2d sess., 1910, S. Doc. 538. Washington: Government Printing Office.

Spufford, Peter (1988). *Money and its Use in Medieval Europe.* Cambridge: Cambridge University Press.

Sraffa, Piero (1922). "The Bank Crisis in Italy." *Economic Journal* 32(126): 178–97.

Starbuck, William H., and P. Narayan Pant (1997). "Trying to Help S&Ls: How Organizations with Good Intentions Jointly Enacted Disaster." In *Organizational Decision Making,* ed. Z. Shapira, 35–60. Cambridge and New York: Cambridge University Press.

Statistiska Centralbyrån (various). *Statistiske Årsbok för Sverige.* Stockholm: Statistiska Centralbyrån.

Steele, F. E. (1896). "Bank Amalgamations." *Economic Journal* 6(24): 535–41.

—— (1897). "Bank Amalgamations." *Journal of the Institute of Bankers* 18: 111–39.

Steigum, Erling (2004). "Financial Deregulation with a Fixed Exchange Rate: Lessons from Norway's Boom-Bust Cycle and Banking Crisis." In *The Norwegian Banking Crisis,* ed. Thorvald G. Moe, Jon A. Solheim, and Bent Vale, 23–76. Oslo: Norges Bank.

Stein, Jeremy C. (2001). "Comment: Obstacles to Optimal Policy: The Interplay of Politics and Economics in Shaping Bank Supervision and Regulation Reforms." In *Prudential Supervision: What Works and What Doesn't,* ed. Frederic S. Mishkin, 267–70. Chicago: University of Chicago Press.

Steinherr, Alfred (1992). "Introduction and Overview." In *The New European Financial Marketplace,* ed. Alfred Steinherr, 1–28. London: Longman.

Stigler, George (1971). "The Economic Theory of Regulation." *Bell Journal of Economics and Management Science* 2: 3–21.

Stiglitz, Joseph, and Andrew Weiss (1981). "Credit Rationing in Markets with Imperfect Information." *American Economic Review* 71(3): 393–410.

Stiroh, Kevin, and Adrienne Rumble (2005). "The Dark Side of Diversification: The Case of US Financial Holding Companies." *Journal of Banking and Finance* 30(8): 2131–61.

Summers, Bruce J. (1980). "Negotiable Certificates of Deposit." *Federal Reserve Bank of Richmond Economic Review* 66(4): 8–19.

Summers, Lawrence H. (1991). "Panel Discussion: Price Stability: How Should Long-Term Monetary Policy Be Determined?" *Journal of Money, Credit and Banking* 23(3, part 2): 625–31.

Sumner, William Graham (1896). "A History of Banking in the United States." In *A History of Banking in All the Leading Nations*, Vol. 1. New York: Journal of Commerce and Commercial Bulletin.

Suomen Tilastokekus (various). *Suomen Tilastollinen Vuosikirja*. Helsinki: Suomen Tilastokekus.

Sushka, Marie Elizabeth, and W. Brian Barrett (1984). "Banking Structure and the National Capital Market, 1869–1914." *Journal of Economic History* 44(2): 463–77.

——— (1985). "Banking Structure and the National Capital Market, 1869–1914: A Reply." *Journal of Economic History* 45(3): 661–65.

Sussman, Nathan (1993). "Debasements, Royal Revenues, and Inflation in France During the Hundred Years' War, 1415–1422." *Journal of Economic History* 53(1): 44–70.

Sussman, Nathan, and Yishay Yafeh (2004). "Constitutions and Commitment: Evidence on the Relation between Institutions and the Cost of Capital." CEPR Discussion Paper no. 4404. London: Centre for Economic Policy Research.

Sveriges Riksbank (1931). *Statistiska Tabeller, 1668–1924*. Stockholm: P. A. Norstedt. In *Sveriges Riksbank, 1668–1918[–1924]*. Part 5. 1–221. Stockholm: Riksbankens Statistiska Avdelning.

Swenson, Harold (1929). "The Banking System of Norway." In *Foreign Banking Systems*, ed. H. Parker Willis and Benjamin H. Beckhart, 869–92. New York: Henry Holt and Company.

Sykes, Joseph (1925). "The Effect of English Bank Amalgamations on Working Expenses and Profits." *Economic Journal* 35(140): 583–89.

——— (1926). *The Amalgamation Movement in English Banking, 1825–1924*. London: P. S. King and Son, Ltd.

Sylla, Richard (1969). "Federal Policy, Banking Market Structure, and Capital Mobilization in the United States, 1863–1913." *Journal of Economic History* 29(4): 657–86.

——— (1985). "Early American Banking: The Significance of the Corporate Form." In *Business and Economic History*, ed. Jeremy Atack, 105–23. Champaign: University of Illinois.

——— (1991). "The Role of Banks." In *Patterns of European Industrialization*, ed. Richard Sylla and Gianni Toniolo, 45–63. New York: Routledge.

——— (1998). "U.S. Securities Markets and the Banking System, 1790–1840." *Federal Reserve Bank of St. Louis Review* 80(3): 83–98.

——— (1999). "Shaping the U.S. Financial System, 1690–1913: The Dominant Role of Public Finance." In *The State, the Financial System and Economic*

Modernization, ed. Richard Sylla, Richard Tilly, and Gabriel Tortella, 249–70. Cambridge: Cambridge University Press.

—— (2002). "Financial Systems and Economic Modernization." *Journal of Economic History* 62(2): 277–92.

—— (2006). "Schumpeter Redux: A Review of Raghuram G. Rajan and Luigi Zingales's Saving Capitalism from the Capitalists." *Journal of Economic Literature* 44(2): 391–404.

Sylla, Richard, John B. Legler, and John Joseph Wallis (1987). "Banks and State Public Finance in the New Republic: The United States, 1790–1860." *Journal of Economic History* 47(2): 391–403.

Sylla, Richard, Robert E. Wright, and David J. Cowan (2009). "Alexander Hamilton, Central Banker: Crisis Management during the U.S. Financial Panic of 1792." *Business History Review* 83(1): 61–86.

Tamaki, Norio (1995). *Japanese Banking: A History, 1859–1959*. Cambridge: Cambridge University Press.

Taus, Esther Rogoff (1943). *Central Banking Functions of the United States Treasury, 1789–1941*. New York: Columbia University Press.

Taylor, Michael, and Alex Fleming (1999). "Integrated Financial Supervision: Lessons from Northern European Experience." World Bank Policy Research Working Paper no. 2223. Washington: World Bank.

Teichova, Alice (1994). "Banking in Austria." In *Handbook on the History of European Banks*, ed. Manfred Pohl, 3–44. Brookfield, VT: Ashgate.

—— (1997). "Banking and Industry in Central Europe, nineteenth to twentieth century." In *Banking, Trade, and Industry: Europe, America and Asia from the Thirteenth to the Twentieth Century*, ed. Alice Teichova, Ginette Kurgan-Van Henenryk, and Dieter Ziegler, 214–28. Cambridge: Cambridge University Press.

Teichova, Alice, Ginette Kurgan-van Hentenryk, and Dieter Ziegler (1997). "Editor's Introduction." In *Banking, Trade, and Industry: Europe, America, and Asia from the Thirteenth to the Twentieth Century*, ed. Alice Teichova, Ginette Kurgan-van Hentenryk, and Dieter Ziegler, 1–16. Cambridge: Cambridge University Press.

Temin, Peter (1968). "The Economic Consequences of the Bank War." *Journal of Political Economy* 76(2): 257–74.

—— (1976). *Did Monetary Forces Cause the Great Depression?* New York: Norton.

—— (1989). *Lessons from the Great Depression*. Cambridge, MA: MIT Press.

—— (1997). "The Golden Age of European Growth: A Review Essay." *European Review of Economic History* 1(1): 127–49.

—— (2002). "The Golden Age of European Growth Reconsidered." *European Review of Economic History* 6(1): 3–22.

Temin, Peter, and Hans-Joachim Voth (2008). "Private Borrowing During the Financial Revolution: Hoare's Bank and its Customers, 1702–24." *Economic History Review* 61(3): 541–64.

Teranishi, Juro (1994). "Japan: Development and Structural Change of the Financial System." In *The Financial Development of Japan, Korea, and Taiwan*, ed. Hugh T. Patrick and Yung Chul Park, 27–80. New York and Oxford: Oxford University Press.

Thomas, Samuel Evelyn (1934). *The Rise and Growth of Joint Stock Banking.* London: Sir I. Pitman and Sons, Ltd.

Thomson, Di, and Malcolm Abbott (2001). "Banking Regulation and Market Forces in Australia." *International Review of Financial Analysis* 10(1): 69–86.

Thornton, Henry (1802 [1939]). *An Enquiry into the Nature and Effects of the Paper Credit of Great Britain (1802).* London: Allen and Unwin Ltd.

Thunholm, Lars-Erik (1954). "Sweden." In *Banking Systems,* ed. Benjamin H. Beckhart, 657–92. New York: Columbia University Press.

Tilly, Richard H. (1966). *Financial Institutions and Industrialization in the Rhineland, 1815–1870.* Madison: University of Wisconsin Press.

——— (1967). "Germany, 1815–1870." In *Banking in the Early Stages of Industrialization,* ed. Rondo E. Cameron, 151–82. New York: Oxford University Press.

——— (1994). "A Short History of the German Banking System." In *Handbook on the History of European Banks,* ed. Manfred Pohl, 299–487. Brookfield, VT: Elgar.

——— (2003). "German Banking and Its Historiography: A Review of Recent Literature." Unpublished Working Paper.

Timberlake, Richard H. (1978). *The Origins of Central Banking in the United States.* Cambridge, MA: Harvard University Press.

——— (1984). "The Central Banking Role of Clearinghouse Associations." *Journal of Money, Credit and Banking* 16(1): 1–15.

Todd, Geoffrey (1932). "Some Aspects of Joint Stock Companies, 1844–1900." *Economic History Review* 4(1): 46–71.

Toniolo, Gianni (1990). *An Economic History of Liberal Italy, 1850–1918.* New York: Routledge.

——— (1995). "Italian Banking, 1919–1936." In *Banking, Currency, and Finance in Europe Between the Wars,* ed. Charles Feinstein, 296–314. New York: Oxford University Press.

Tortella, Gabriel, and Jordi Palafox (1984). "Banking and Industry in Spain, 1918–1936." *Journal of European Economic History* 13(2): 81–111.

Troy, Leo (2004). *Almanac of Business and Industrial Financial Ratios.* Englewood Cliffs, NJ: Prentice-Hall.

Tussing, A. D. (1967). "The Case for Bank Failures." *Journal of Law and Economics* 10: 129–47.

Ueda, Kazuo (2000). "Causes of Japan's Banking Problems in the 1990s." In *Crisis and Change in the Japanese Financial System,* ed. Takeo Hoshi and Hugh Patrick, 59–81. Boston, Dordrecht, and London: Kluwer.

Urquhart, M. C., and K.A.H. Buckley (1965). *Historical Statistics of Canada.* Cambridge: Cambridge University Press.

U.S. Bureau of the Census (various). *Census of the United States.* Washington: Bureau of the Census.

U.S. Comptroller of the Currency (various). *Annual Report of the Comptroller of the Currency.* Washington: Government Printing Office.

U.S. Congress. House. Committee on Banking and Currency (1924). *Consolidation of National Banking Associations, etc. Hearings before the Committee on Banking and Currency.* 68th Cong., 1st sess. *April 9–18, 1924.* Washington: Government Printing Office.

U.S. Congress. Senate. Banking and Currency Committee (1934). *Report on Stock Exchange Practices. Hearings before the Committee on Banking and Currency Pursuant to S.Res. 84 and S.Res. 56 and S.Res. 97 June 6, 1934.* Multiple volumes. Washington: Government Printing Office.

U.S. Congress. Senate. Committee on Finance (1893). *Wholesale Prices, Wages, and Transportation [Aldrich Report].* 52nd Congress, 2nd session, report 1394, Part III, March 3, 1893. Washington: Government Printing Office.

U.S. Department of Commerce (1989). *Historical Statistics of the United States.* White Plains, NY: Kraus International Publications.

U.S. National Monetary Commission (1910). *Miscellaneous Articles on German Banking.* National Monetary Commission. 61st Cong., 2d sess., 1910, S. Doc. 508. Washington: Government Printing Office.

——— (1911). *Interviews on the Banking and Currency Systems of Canada.* National Monetary Commission. 61st Cong., 2d sess., 1911, S. Doc. 584. Washington: Government Printing Office.

U.S. President (1975). *Economic Report of the President Transmitted to the Congress.* Washington: Government Printing Office.

U.S. President's Commission on Financial Structure and Regulation (1973). *The Report of the President's Commission on Financial Structure and Regulation (Hunt Commission).* Washington: Government Printing Office.

Usher, Abbot Payson (1934). "The Origins of Banking: The Primitive Bank of Deposit, 1200–1600." *Economic History Review* 4(4): 399–428.

——— (1943). *The Early History of Deposit Banking in Mediterranean Europe.* Cambridge, MA: Harvard University Press.

Utton, M. A. (1991). "Some Features of the Early Merger Movements in British Manufacturing Industry." In *Mergers and Acquisitions,* ed. Gregory P. Marchildon, 152–61. Brookfield, VT: Elgar.

Vale, Bent (2004). "The Norwegian Banking Crisis." In *The Norwegian Banking Crisis,* Thorvald G. Moe, Jon A. Solheim, and Bent Vale, 1–22. Oslo: Norges Bank.

Valentine, Tom (1997). "Wallis on Prudential Regulation." *Australian Economic Review* 30(3): 304–9.

Vamplew, Wray (1987). *Australians, Historical Statistics.* Broadway, N.S.W., Australia: Fairfax.

Van der Borght, Richard (1896). "A History of Banking in the Netherlands." In *A History of Banking in All the Leading Nations,* Vol. 4, 189–371. New York: Journal of Commerce and Commercial Bulletin.

Van der Wee, Herman (1963). *The Growth of the Antwerp Market and the European Economy.* Louvain, Belgium: Bureaux du Recueil, Bibliotheque de l'Université.

Van der Wee, Herman, and Monique Verbreyt (1997). *The Generale Bank 1822–1997: A Continuing Challenge.* Tielt, Belgium: Lannoo.

Van der Werf, Douwe C. J. (1999). "The Two Dutch Bank Mergers of 1964: The Creations of Algemene Bank Nederland and Amsterdam-Rotterdam Bank." *Financial History Review* 6(1): 67–84.

Van Dillen, J. G. (1934). "The Bank of Amsterdam." In *History of Principal Public Banks*, ed. J. G. Van Dillen, 79–124. The Hague: Martins Nijhoff.

Van Driel, G. (1985–86). "The Rise of the House of Egibi." *Jaarbericht van het Vooraziatisch-Egyptisch Genootschap Ex Oriente Lux* 29: 50–67.

Van Nierop, H. A. (1937). "Banking in the Netherlands: Main Features of Control." *Financial Times* May 10, 1937.

van Zanden, Jan Luiten (1997). "Old Rules, New Conditions, 1914–1940." In *A Financial History of the Netherlands*, ed. Marjolein C. 't Hart, Joost Jonker, and Jan Luiten van Zanden, 124–51. Cambridge: Cambridge University Press.

van Zanden, Jan Luiten, and Arthur van Riel (2004). *The Strictures of Inheritance: The Dutch Economy in the Nineteenth Century*. Princeton: Princeton University Press.

Vanderlip, Frank A. (1908). "The Panic as a World Phenomenon." *Annals of the American Academy of Political and Social Science* 31: 2–7.

Vanthemsche, Guy (1991). "State, Banks and Industry in Belgium and the Netherlands, 1919–1939." In *The Role of Banks in the Interwar Economy*, ed. Harold James, Håkan Lindgren, and Alice Teichova, 104–21. Cambridge: Cambridge University Press.

Vanthoor, Wim (2005). *The King's Eldest Daughter: A History of the Nederlandsche Bank 1814–1998*. Amsterdam: Uitgeverij Boom.

Vastrup, Claus (2009). "How did Denmark Avoid a Banking Crisis?" In *The Great Financial Crisis In Finland And Sweden The Nordic Experience of Financial Liberalization*, ed. Lars Jonung, Jaakko Kiander, and Pentti Vartia, 245–64. Cheltenham, UK; Northampton, MA: Edward Elgar.

Vaudagna, Maurizio (1978). "Structural Change in Fascist Italy." *Journal of Economic History* 38(1): 181–201.

Verlinden, O. (1963). "Markets and Fairs." In *The Cambridge Economic History of Europe*, ed. M. M. Postan, E. E. Rich, and Edward Miller, 119–56. Cambridge: Cambridge University Press.

Vihriälä, Vesa (1997). "Banks and the Finnish Credit Cycle, 1986–1995." Study no. E:7. Helsinki: Bank of Finland.

Vives, Xavier (2001). "Competition in the Changing World of Banking." *Oxford Review of Economic Policy* 17(4): 535–47.

Vogel, Steven K. (1996). *Freer Markets, More Rules: Regulatory Reform in Advanced Industrial Countries*. Ithaca: Cornell University Press.

Volpi, Giuseppe, Bonaldo Stringher, and Mario Pennachio (1927). *The Financial Reconstruction of Italy*. New York: Italian Historical Society.

von Hagen, Jürgen (1994). "Herstatt Crisis." In *The Palgrave Dictionary of Money and Finance*, ed. Peter Newman, Murray Milgate, and John Eatwell, 303–4. New York: The Stockton Press.

Wadsworth, John Edwin (1954). "United Kingdom of Great Britain and Northern Ireland." In *Banking Systems*, ed. Benjamin H. Beckhart, 769–838. New York: Columbia University Press.

Wallace, William (1905). *Trial of the City of Glasgow Bank Directors*. Glasgow: William Hodge and Company.

Wallich, Henry (1977). "Central Banks as Regulators and Lenders of Last Resort in an International Context: A View from the United States." In *Key Issues in International Banking*, 91–98, Conference series no. 18. Boston: Federal Reserve Bank of Boston.

Warburg, Paul M. (1930). *The Federal Reserve System: Its Origin and Growth: Reflections and Recollections*. New York: Macmillan.

Webb, Steven B. (1980). "Tariffs, Cartels, Technology, and Growth in the German Steel Industry, 1879 to 1914." *Journal of Economic History* 40(2): 309–29.

Weber, Warren E. (2005). "Early State Banks in the United States: How Many Were There and When Did They Exist?" Working Paper no. 634. Minneapolis: Federal Reserve Bank of Minneapolis.

Weil, David N. (2005). *Economic Growth*. Boston: Addison-Wesley.

Welch, Jane, ed. (1981). *The Regulation of Banks in the Member States of the EEC*. The Hague: Martinus Nijhoff Publishers.

Welldon, Samuel A. (1910). National Monetary Commission. 61st Cong., 2d sess., 1910, S. Doc. 353. Washington: Government Printing Office.

Westermann, William Linn (1930). "Warehousing and Trapezite Banking in Antiquity." *Journal of Economic and Business History* 3: 30–54.

Whale, Philip Barrett (1930). *Joint Stock Banking in Germany: A Study of the German Creditbanks Before and After the War*. London: Macmillan.

Wheelock, David C., and Paul Wilson (2004). "Consolidation in US Banking: Which Banks Engage in Mergers?" *Review of Financial Economics* 13(1–2): 7–39.

White, Eugene N. (1981). "State-Sponsored Insurance of Bank Deposits in the United States, 1907–1929." *Journal of Economic History* 41(3): 537–57.

——— (1982). "The Political Economy of Banking Regulation, 1864–1933." *Journal of Economic History* 42(1): 33–40.

——— (1983). *The Regulation and Reform of American Banking, 1900–1929*. Princeton: Princeton University Press.

——— (1985). "The Merger Movement in Banking, 1919–1933." *Journal of Economic History* 45(2): 285–91.

——— (1986). "Before the Glass-Steagall Act: An Analysis of the Investment Banking Activities of National Banks." *Explorations in Economic History* 23(1): 33–55.

——— (2001). "Making the French Pay: The Costs and Consequences of the Napoleonic Reparations." *European Review of Economic History* 5(3): 337–65.

——— (2007). "The Crash of 1882 and the Bailout of the Paris Bourse." *Cliometrica* 1(2): 115–44.

White, Lawrence H. (1989). *Competition and Currency*. New York: New York University Press.

White, Lawrence J. (1992). "What Should Banks Really Do?" *Contemporary Policy Issues* 10(3): 104–12.

——— (2002). "Trends in Aggregate Concentration in the United States." *Journal of Economic Perspectives* 16(4): 137–60.

White, R. C. (1972). *Australian Banking and Monetary Statistics, 1945–1970*. Sydney: Reserve Bank of Australia.

Wicker, Elmus (1980). "A Reconsideration of the Causes of the Banking Panic of 1930." *Journal of Economic History* 40(3): 571–83.

———— (1996). *The Banking Panics of the Great Depression*. Cambridge and New York: Cambridge University Press.

———— (2000). *Banking Panics of the Gilded Age*. Cambridge and New York: Cambridge University Press.

Wikawa, Tadao (1929). "The Banking System of Japan." In *Foreign Banking Systems*, ed. H. Parker Willis and Benjamin H. Beckhart, 816–68. New York: Henry Holt and Company.

Williams, Robert (1898) "The Inaugural Address of the President, Robert Williams, Esq. MP [Delivered before the Institute on Wednesday, December 1st, 1897]." *Journal of the Institute of Bankers* 19(1):1–12.

Williamson, John, and Molly Mahar (1998). *A Survey of Financial Liberalization*. Princeton: Princeton University, International Finance Section.

Willis, H. Parker, and Benjamin H. Beckhart, eds. (1929). *Foreign Banking Systems*. New York: Henry Holt and Company.

Willis, H. Parker, and John Chapman (1934). *The Banking Situation*. New York: Columbia University Press.

Willis, J. Brooke (1954). "United States." In *Banking Systems*, ed. Benjamin H. Beckhart, 839–918. New York: Columbia University Press.

Wilson, Berry K., and Edward J. Kane (1996). "The Demise of Double Liability as an Optimal Contract for Large-Bank Shareholders." NBER Working Paper no. 5848. Cambridge, MA: National Bureau of Economic Research.

Wilson, John Stuart Gladstone (1947). "Australia's Central Bank." *Journal of Political Economy* 55(1): 28–38.

———— (1957). *French Banking Structure and Credit Policy*. Cambridge, MA: Harvard University Press.

———— (1986). *Banking Policy and Structure: A Comparative Analysis*. New York: New York University Press.

Wilson, Stuart J. (2001). "Financial Intermediation, Capital Accumulation and Growth: Evidence from Canada." Discussion Paper no. 87. Regina: University of Regina, Department of Economics.

Winningham, Scott, and Donald G. Hagan (1980). "Regulation Q: An Historical Perspective." *Federal Reserve Bank of Kansas City Economic Review*: 3–17.

Winton, Andrew (1993). "Limitation of Liability and the Ownership Structure of the Firm." *Journal of Finance* 48(2): 487–512.

Wirth, Max (1874). *Geschichte Der Handelskrisen*. Frankfurt: J. D. Sauerländers Verlag.

———— (1896). "Banking in Germany and Austria-Hungary." In *A History of Banking in All the Leading Nations*, Vol. 4. 1–187. New York: Journal of Commerce and Commercial Bulletin.

Withers, Hartley, R. H. Inglis Palgrave, et al. (1910). *The English Banking System*. National Monetary Commission. 61st Cong., 2d sess., 1910, S. Doc. 492. Washington: Government Printing Office.

Wojnilower, Albert M. (1980). "The Central Role of Credit Crunches in Recent Financial History." *Brookings Papers on Economic Activity* (2): 277–339.

Wood, Geoffrey (2000). "The Lender of Last Resort Reconsidered." *Journal of Financial Services Research* 18(2/3): 203–27.

Wunsch, Cornelia (1999). "The Egibi Family's Real Estate in Babylon (6th Century BC)." In *Urbanization and Land Ownership in the Ancient Near East*, ed. Michael Hudson and Baruch A. Levine, 391–419. Cambridge, MA: Peabody Museum of Archaeology and Ethnology.

Yamamura, Kozo (1972). "Japan, 1868–1930: A Revised View." In *Banking and Economic Development*, ed. Rondo Cameron, 168–98. New York: Oxford University Press.

Zahn, Johannes Carl Detloff, and Deutschen Instituts für Bankwissenschaft und Bankwesens (1937). *Die Bankaufsichtsgesetze Der Welt in Deutscher Sprache*. Berlin: de Gruyter.

Zamagni, Vera (1993). *The Economic History of Italy, 1860–1990*. Oxford: Clarendon Press.

Ziegler, Philip (1988). *The Sixth Great Power: A History of the House of Barings 1762–1929*. New York: Knopf.

Zimmerman, Gary C. (1995). "Implementing the Single Banking Market in Europe." *Federal Reserve Bank of San Francisco Economic Review* (3): 35–51.

Index

The letters *t*, *f*, or *n* following a page number indicate a table, figure, or note on that page. The number following the *n* indicates the number of the note cited when there is more than one note on the page.